THE

SCIENCE OF EDUCATION;

AND

ART OF TEACHING.

IN TWO PARTS.

BY JOHN OGDEN, A. M.

CINCINNATI:
MOORE, WILSTACH, KEYS & CO.,
25 West Fourth Street.
1859.

PREFACE.

THE only apology we make, in offering the public a text-book on Education and Teaching, is, that necessity has driven us to it. A combination of unforeseen events and circumstances, over which we could have but little control, and from whose pressure it was almost impossible to escape, has, as it were, forced the production of this work. On the one hand, the entire absence of a text-book of the kind this professes to be, and the universal conviction of the necessity and practicability of such a work ; and on the other, the importunities and encouragements of Teachers, and of friends of Education, have led us to undertake a work which, under other circumstances, would have been regarded as the hight of presumption. Under these circumstances, we have written ; but it has been with a conscious sense of insufficiency. What has been written, must, therefore, be *very* imperfect; but we have simply done our duty, as we best could.

But we beg leave to say here, that we have not written for those who know a great deal more than we do on these subjects ; nor for those who may feel they have no need of help ; but for those who are struggling into the light, and for those who may never, as yet, have felt the responsibilities of their labors. There are thousands of such teachers; and for these, and also for parents (for without their coöperation no adequate reform can be effected), we, with the dangers and difficulties, to which they are exposed, constantly before our eyes, have prepared the following pages. To wake up a proper sense of responsibility and duty in such, and to give them a knowledge of those technical details so necessary to their success and usefulness, are the specific objects of this book.

We have not the vanity to suppose, however, that we are an oracle to the profession; nor have we the ambition to become one; neither have we the presumption to dictate special modes, or to offer our plans to the exclusion of all others. This would be traveling out of the line of policy as well as of good sense. It would be downright empiricism. But we have endeavored so to present the whole subject of HUMAN CULTURE, and so to lay open and enforce the principles of right Education and Teaching, that the humblest may understand; so that by a careful study of these principles, every teacher and parent may be able rather to build up his own system, and exercise his own judgment in the special application of them, than to adopt, entirely, the measures of another; for any one can see that to attempt to develop the *Teaching Talent* by cumbering it with the real or supposed excellencies of special methods exclusively, would be like prescribing special modes of treatment for the cure of all diseases, irrespective of their character, or the constitutional peculiarities of the patient. This would be empiricism indeed; since it would deny the privilege of individual judgment, investigation and discovery. So, to palm off upon teachers, as qualifications, the plans and specialities (and too frequently the errors and whims) that *may* have been successful in the hands of others, without developing native ability, would tend only to circumscribe the limits of improvement, and to cripple individual talent and enterprise. And, on the other hand, to discuss general theories, and to enlarge upon the importance and advantages of Education, without reducing the theories to practice, would be equally objectionable.*

We have tried, therefore, to guard carefully against these two extremes; for, while PART FIRST treats principally of Theory, or the Philosophy of Education, PART SECOND takes up the principles as developed in the *Science*, or *Part First*, and explains and enforces their application in the *Art*, or *Part Second*, which treats of modes of teaching and learning. For this reason the latter will be more interesting and instructive to those who may be well versed in general principles, but not so familiar with their special application. We entertain the hope, however, that both parts may be examined before judgment is passed upon either; and that the merits of the subjects presented, aside from the manner in which they are treated, will be a sufficient passport to public attention. With this hope, and claiming only that indulgence which is the common right of *mortals*, and which we know a courteous public will grant, we present this book to the candid consideration of Teachers and friends of Education.

CINCINNATI, July, 1859.

---

* See Introduction on this point.

CONTENTS.

PART FIRST.

PART SECOND.

SYNOPSIS I.

EDUCATION OR HUMAN CULTURE.
DISCURSIVE. THEORETICAL. A SCIENCE.
CAPACITY AND SUSCEPTIBILITY.
Objective. Physical. Intellectual. Moral.
Transition. Physical. Intellectual. Moral.
Subjective. Physical. Intellectual. Moral.
FORCES AND INSTRUMENTALITIES
Objective. Physical. Intellectual. Moral.
Transition. Physical. Intellectual. Moral.
Subjective. Physical. Intellectual, Moral
PROCESSES AND MODES.
Objective. Physical. Intellectual. Moral.
Transition. Physical. Intellectual. Moral
Subjective. Physical. Intellectual. Moral.
DIDACTIC. PRACTICAL. AN ART.
HOME DUTIES. Labor. Recreation. Rest.
SCHOOL-ROOM DUTIES. Preliminaries. Study. Recitation. Business. Recreation. Government.
MISCELLANEOUS DUTIES.

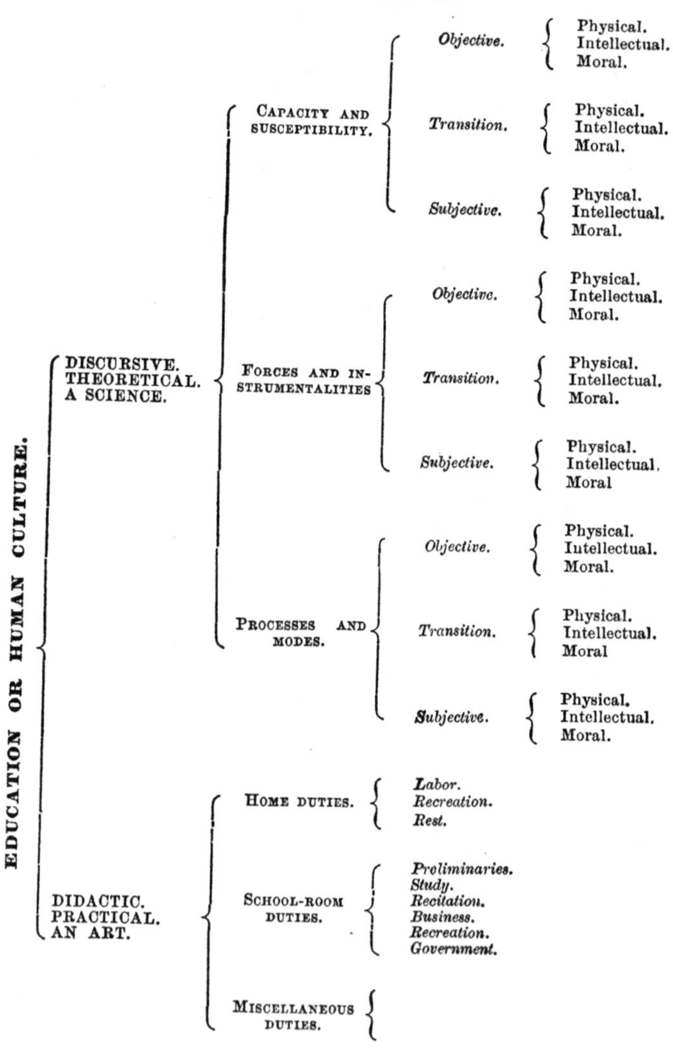

PART FIRST.

CHAPTER I.

INTRODUCTION.

THE SCIENCE OF EDUCATION is based upon immutable principles; and, so far as these principles relate to human beings, they are no less established than when they relate to other beings. They exist in the very nature of things, and are coextensive with man's existence.

The Philosophy of Education is therefore the philosophy of man. *The Science of Human Culture* is that which relates to his nature, laws of growth, and modes of treatment.

Man is created with *Educational Susceptibility*, with the undeveloped or latent *capacity to know* and *to do*. His powers of feeling and motion, at birth, though in a feeble state, are, nevertheless, more perfect than those of *knowing*, *willing* and *doing*. His sentient organism constitutes the medium through which, in their nascent state, these faculties of the mind are addressed.

Now, these knowing and doing capacities—for they can scarcely be called powers at this stage of their growth—would for ever remain in an undeveloped state, were either the avenues leading to them closed, or were there no instrumentalities employed to reach down to them, to excite them to activity, and to bring them out.

This presupposes *Educational Instrumentalities* or Forces, as well as educational capacity, which, in their nature and constitution, must be adapted to the educational susceptibility, or want. These, again, must be brought in contact with the faculties, in order to excite them to activity and develop them. For, if man possess, originally, educational capacity undeveloped, it would be unwise, if not wicked, to suppose there are no instrumentalities or forces suited to these wants. But on the contrary, for every educational want there is an educational supply precisely suited to that want. To argue the opposite of this proposition, would not only lead to infidelity, but would charge God with folly in bringing human beings into the world with educational wants to torment them, and a capacity to mock them.

The bringing out, the developing and cultivation, of these faculties, presuppose *Modes* or *Processes*: for it would be equally unwise to suppose—there being latent *capacity* and *forces* suited to its development—that there were no right and certain modes or processes by which these educational instrumentalities could be applied to the educational susceptibilities. It would be just as unwise as to suppose that God had created seeds for growth, and a soil every way suited to nourish them, and yet had made it impossible that the two should be brought in contact.

There are, therefore, educational susceptibilities or *capacities;* and suited to the exact nature of these, there are educational instrumentalities or *forces;* and superadded to these, there are certain and right modes or *processes* of applying these forces to the capacities: and these plain truths shall constitute the basis of the theoretical part of this work.

To render this matter plain, we assume the following propositions: 1. That *there is no necessary antagonism existing between the educational capacities and their appropriate forces or supplies judiciously administered—except that induced by disease or disordered growth.* 2. That *all true modes of education proceed in exact harmony with the nature, design and growth of man's faculties, intellectual, physical and moral.* 3. That *God has not only made it possible for us to understand the true modes of education, but that he has made it necessary, and absolutely imperative. He requires this at our hands.*

In reference to the first we remark, that this is true in an intellectual and moral sense no less than in a physical. The hungry body does not loathe the food that nourishes it: neither does the hungry mind loathe knowledge, or the food that nourishes it: nor yet does the soul abhor the love, the sympathy, the sweet affections that cherish the moral and religious nature, unless one or all of those departments of our being are laboring under the influence of disease. And here we wish to be understood that diseases exist every where within the dominion of sin; and that it is the duty and peculiar province of education to alleviate and remove them. There are, therefore, intellectual and moral diseases, as well as those of a purely physical character. The disordered state of one department of our being often induces disorder in the others. And, on the other hand, the healthy condition of the one promotes the health and growth of all the others. These diseases may be considered either constitutional, chronic or acute, or recent in their origin and formation. Indeed, we may conclude that they are all, to a great extent, of the first class; since sin has so corrupted our entire race, that the whole being, physical, intellectual and moral, is tainted, to a greater or less extent, with the corruptions peculiar to each; and so deep-seated have become these complaints, that nothing short of Divine agencies, co-operating, it may be, with the human, can avail for their removal. What we mean, therefore, is that this depravity—for by this name it is best known—or this disease is either aggravated or abated according as the causes or influences operating have been bad or good,—whether we consider these as having operated in the past, or as still operating in the present, generations of men. And now it becomes a matter of the gravest importance, a question of most startling significance: can these diseases be removed or alleviated by any means, human or Divine, or by both of these agencies combined? We infer, as before intimated, that they can, since they admit of increase and decrease. The causes of difficulty removed, and a class of opposite influences at work, would surely produce opposite results. The steps by which we have descended to our present depth, retraced, would surely bring us back to the point whence we started, *provided* the nature of our offense did not render it impossible. This, we apprehend, is the case, so far, at least, as absolute perfection is concerned. But we have unbounded faith in the efficacy of the remedial agents, provided by the merciful Being who first gave us our powers, and commanded us to keep and perpetuate them. But since man failed to do this, through a greater than creative kindness, the same Being has provided a ransom in the atonement, so ample as to reach to the lowest depths of his depravity, renovating his moral nature, healing his moral disease, and thereby rendering it possible, at least, by a course of education and discipline, by obedience to the laws of his being, and a strict observance of the laws of God, to retrace those steps and regain, if not a primitive and absolute state of perfection, at least to attain to the sublimest hights of human excellence.

Education, therefore, in its largest sense, proposes the alleviation and removal of those diseases, so far at least as human instrumentality can be efficient in so difficult a case. And while we claim for it, only that it is human, and therefore subject to error, nevertheless, it should always so co-operate with Divine agencies as to produce the results anticipated. To inquire earnestly after this way, to learn the real nature and importance of a *true* education, and to enforce its claims to the highest possible place in human consideration, shall be our present object.

Our second proposition is, *that all true modes of education proceed in exact harmony with the nature, design and growth of man's faculties*, etc. The correctness of this position will at once be admitted; for, to admit its opposite, would be to admit the establishment of discord instead of harmony in the works of the Creator. At no stage of growth should the educational forces and processes interfere with the natural order of development. This would be no less disastrous here, than would any interference with the natural conditions, supplies, and laws of growth, in the vegetable world. All *true* methods of educating man, therefore, must be based upon sound philosophy; for if education, as such, has any claims to the dignified title of *Science*, its operations must proceed in harmony with the nature, design and laws of growth pertaining to the subject of such education, and in accordance with the principles involved in such science. And then it follows, as a matter of necessity, that those principles and processes are susceptible of classification and arrangement, or else education is no science: for without these conditions no science can exist. And then again, if these principles and processes can be thus classified and arranged, they can be studied and mastered; and if they can be classified, arranged, studied and mastered, they can be applied in the education of every human being—not beyond the reach of education—just as definitely, though perhaps not with as certain results, as the principles and processes of chemistry and mathematics are studied and applied in agriculture and the arts. And surely the claims of this science upon our consideration are as urgent as any other, if we consider the character, the value of the materials and agents with which it proposes to operate.

The agriculturist, for instance, can afford to make a mistake in raising a crop: so can the mechanic, in building a ship or a house; for these appertain only to the grosser interests, and perishable substances. The painter can afford to make a mistake in mingling his colors, or in giving form and expression to the features of his picture; or he can afford to see it blurred and marred, and even rent asunder by unskilled or wicked hands; for in such case, the only loss is the waste of material and labor, and perchance his hopes of gain. The sculptor can afford to see his beautiful figure, upon which he has spent years of anxious toil, shattered to atoms in his presence, or sunk to the bottom of the ocean. The loss might be more than compensated by reproduction. But who will undertake to compensate for the loss of a human being, freighted with a deathless cargo of eternal interests? Who will undertake to repair the damages done to an immortal spirit? Who will undertake to remove the blurs and stains from the face of human character, or to stop the influences involved in error? The agriculturist, the artist, and all material workers can well afford to make mistakes; but in educating boys and girls, in forming habits and molding character, in giving direction to the energies of immortal minds, in rearing and training human beings for their duties and responsibilities here, and their destiny hereafter, we can not afford to make mistakes. These are more costly and enduring than the senseless stone, or the inanimate clod. The influences evolved, too, are of a more enduring nature; for the mistakes or the master-strokes here, unlike those upon the canvas or the marble, perpetuate themselves, and operate on other beings to all eternity. If then it becomes necessary that the agriculturist and the artist have knowledge of the character of their substances, and skill to manage them; if it becomes necessary that they have rules and definite methods by which to make application of the principles of their peculiar sciences; much more does this necessity increase, when we come to apply the same principle to that most difficult and enduring, that most artistic of all arts, the art of educating human beings.

The question seems to be settled therefore, as to the importance and necessity both of accurate and extensive knowledge upon these subjects, and of rules by which to be guided in the applications. The possibility of such rules seems the only point now.

Our third proposition reads as follows: *That God has not only made it possible for us to understand the true modes of education, but that he has made it necessary, absolutely imperative.*

We are at liberty here, to draw the following conclusions: 1. That God requires us to do nothing but what is right. Wrong is opposed to right, is the offshoot of evil, and therefore can not be included. He has commanded us further, or at least given us as a sacred precept, "To train up a child in the way he should go." This is right, and because it is thus given, it is obligatory. It, of course, presupposes knowledge of that way, and skill to direct others in it. 2. He does not require of us any impossibilities; or, in general, what is necessary for the accomplishment of any good purpose is possible. Right modes of education are necessary, and therefore possible. This is conclusive. God has not created a single necessity, in all his dominions, without, at least, indicating the mode of supply; and we go still further and say that there is not a single evil existing under the sun, but what has its appropriate remedy, though it may possibly be beyond the reach of man. To suppose the contrary would be to admit that God has been defeated in establishing the order of creation and providence. So that we shall be safe in concluding that whatever is right or necessary is possible; and further, that there is both a necessity here and a possibility of supplying it.

The investigation now turns upon the nature and extent of our knowledge, and the characteristics of those principles, rules and modes of application best adapted to produce the required results.

It will be readily granted, we think, that this knowledge must be peculiar; that it must reach beyond the mere range of scholastic attainments; that no knowledge, however perfect, relating to mere common subjects, will be of any further utility here, than as a mere instrument by which the education of the individual may be promoted. Hence, the popular idea of education appears to be erroneous, so far, at least, as it makes education consist in the mere acquisition of knowledge, without any reference to its uses as a means of accomplishing the end; for a man is not thoroughly educated until he knows how to educate other men.

Man's education, therefore, consists in the ability he acquires to use his powers of thinking, willing and doing; and the chief uses of knowledge, aside from the enlarged scope it gives to these powers, is so to discipline, subdue and strengthen them, as that they may be able, both to control their own energies, and to operate with due force upon surrounding objects. No mere amount of knowledge, therefore, can compensate for the want of discipline and vigor which constitute the soul, object and the end of education. But the mere acquisition is best accomplished at the same time, and in connection with the best discipline; so that in true education, the two processes mutually aid each other.

"The proper study of mankind is man." To the educator, no knowledge is so important as self-knowledge, or that which relates to man and his education. It ranks highest, both as it relates to discipline, and to its utility in the education of others. Indeed it is the "*Scientia Scientiarum*," since it relates to all sciences, and teaches their proper uses. In this sense, it is to him, though more general in its character, and intrinsic in its merits, what diagnostics and therapeutics are to the physician. Without this knowledge, the teacher would be fitly represented by an individual having a large collection of drugs and medicines, yet ignorant of their effect upon the human system. He would be unable to wield his instrumentalities skillfully in the accomplishment of the purposes for which they were intended.

But the educator should, above all other artists, know

the nature and capacity of the powers, intellectual, physical, and moral, with which he proposes to operate. He should acquaint himself with this wonder-working machine whose secret springs of thought and motion lie hidden from the eye of the casual observer; and whose products outvie the costliest fabrics of human art. He should not only familiarize himself with their nature, capacity, and laws of growth, but, as far as possible, with their antecedent influences; that he may judge with greater clearness and accuracy in the selection of means and modes to be employed in their subsequent treatment. But here, as in every other case where great interests are involved, however certain and reliable the means in themselves may be, such is the imperfection of human knowledge and experience, that there is a constant demand for Divine aid to give potency to the means employed. The educator is, at best, but the weak instrument in the hands of the wise Disposer of events; and his strength for good or for evil is usually measured by the presence or absence of this Divine guidance; and it is safe to say further, that his moral force is regulated by his ideas of God, and the estimate he places upon the observance of his precepts.

Again: so intricate and multiform are the shades of distinctions in the intellectual, moral, and physical fabric; and such a diversity obtains in the capacities, both with respect to the natural endowment of children, and to the influences that have been brought to bear upon them, that no two results, precisely similar, can safely be predicated of the same forces operating. The forces, therefore, must be varied to suit every individual case. And here it is proper to remark that the forces themselves are as various as the individual wants for whose supply they were evidently intended; and it is because educators do not seek out and observe this harmony and adaptation, that so many errors are committed in the education of the young.

To adopt a particular course of treatment, and to insist upon its observance in all cases, irrespective of constitutional and acquired differences, argue a dogmatism and dullness almost unpardonable. It would surely be regarded in this light, in every other profession. It would be substantially to adopt the theory, that all minds and bodies are of the same type, have the same constitutional peculiarities and educational capacities, and have been exposed to the same antecedent causes.

No human being, therefore, possesses the wisdom, foresight or authority to legislate for the particular cases that arise in a course of education or teaching. Neither was it designed that such should be the case, even to a limited extent. Its effects would be to deprive both teacher and pupil of their appropriate individuality, and to circumscribe the limits of thought and human development.

Hence, many of the improved (?) methods which have become the particular hobbies of some particular teachers, amount to but little more than an exposition of this error; save so far as these particular methods can be generalized and referred to a philosophic system of education.

Hence, likewise, those particular plans for teaching the particular branches of science, however excellent in themselves, become useless when put into the hands of one unskilled in the sciences themselves, or ignorant of the nature and capacity of the mind, and of the uses of knowledge. It is like placing a sharp sword in the hands of a child, who is liable, not only to injure others, but to destroy his own life.

Precisely similar effects are produced by attempting to educate teachers by filling their heads (more frequently, however, their hats) with diagrams and plans for giving instruction, while they are profoundly ignorant, both of the nature and treatment of mind and body, and of the branches to be taught, as well as the objects to be attained in teaching them. What can be expected from such a course but failure and disgrace? And the results show that the law of cause and effect has not yet been abolished.

But all sound Theory and Practice are based upon the immutable laws of Truth. They must arise out of the fundamental principles lying at the foundation of this science of human culture, and be regulated by the laws adopted for their government. These principles and these laws, in their essential nature, are logically and chronologically antecedent to all experience and all theory and all practice. Experience may develop them, but it does not constitute any essential part of them, any more than the experiments in chemistry and natural philosophy constitute parts of these sciences. The experience is all well so far as it goes to establish any general principle, or so far as it conforms to any; and it may be useful in the discovery of new principles. In this last case, it should be placed to the credit of the discoverer: but who would think of incorporating the mere experiment or the experience of the author, as a fundamental principle in the science, instead of the fact or principle discovered?

Hence the inadequacy, so far as the purposes of a text-book are concerned, of any treatise on modes, that deals thus exclusively with experience, or with methods which have been successful perchance, in the hands of particular teachers. When, therefore, these things are put forth in the shape of a science, to be learned and practiced by others as such, the unwarrantable assumption is made that all children require the same treatment; and that all teachers will be equally successful with the same methods, regardless of constitutional and acquired differences.

This would be as unreasonable as to suppose that all plants would grow equally well in the same soil; that all animals could subsist on the same food; that all men would succeed equally well in the same employment; or that all kinds of labor could be carried on with the same tools.

Therefore, we find that when mere experience is exhausted, the light of the so-called science expires, and leaves us too often to grope our way in darkness, or to lean upon a broken reed. No text-book, therefore, is worthy of confidence, that embodies nothing more than mere experience. The science of education is as different from all this, as the sun himself is different from his own rays; and the attempt to embody these things into a science is not unlike an attempt would be to collect the sun's rays and retain them in his absence. The nature and capacity of the subject to be operated upon, must be studied and understood, no less than the character of the forces employed and the modes of application.

Hence again we infer, that *all true Theory and Practice must be, to a very great extent, the product of the teacher's own originality.*

No teacher can be eminently successful by adopting the entire plans of another. He should not—nay, he *can not* wholly divest himself of his individuality. To whatever extent he does, he becomes a parasite. David could not fight in Saul's armor, for very cogent reasons. The teacher must, therefore, with the same originality, and the same kind of dependence that characterized this great warrior, choose his own instruments; and in most cases, the simpler the better. He must fight in his own armor, if he expect to win. The thoughts and feelings he brings forth must be coined in his own mint, though the ore may be brought from a foreign mine. His own native energies must stamp them, and set the seal upon them, and give the impress of originality to them; must breathe into them the breath of life, and inspire them with the living, acting, energizing *spirit*, if he would plant these thoughts deep in the sanctuary of the soul. He must shine with his *own*, and not with a reflected light. He must warm and invigorate with his *own*, not with a borrowed heat; or he becomes the mere reflector of the rays of some superior orb. Unless he thus vitalizes his teachings, all his borrowed excellence will become useless in his hands; and instead of hiding, will only serve to expose, his deficiencies.

Hence all the modern improvements and plans for the education of children, however excellent in themselves, will be of little service unless they are warmed into life by the invigorating influence of intelligence. The teacher should therefore know the hidden springs of thought, of feeling and of will. He should understand the structure and organism of the machinery through which these act. He should acquaint himself intimately with the nature and value of the educational forces, their influence upon the subject educated; and with the modes or processes of controling and applying these forces. He thus becomes master of them, and consequently of his profession. He wields them in his own peculiar way, as this to him is the *only right way.*

The whole *Science* of *Human Culture*, or of man and his education, therefore, admits of the following classification and assumes the following characteristics.

First: it is both *Discursive* and *Didactic* in its nature and its application. Discursive, in that it discusses the general principles which lie at the foundation of all human growth and development. Didactic, in that it teaches the proper application of these principles in the actual education of man.

Second: it is both *Theoretical* and *Practical.* Theoretical, in that it treats of theories in reference to capacity, forces and modes of culture. Practical, in that it puts these theories into actual operation.

Third: it is both a *Science* and an *Art.* A Science, in that it deals in scientific principles, classifying and arranging them in systematic order. It investigates the elements and principles of education, as well as the modes of treatment involved in it. An Art, in that it applies these to the actual production of the results anticipated.

Viewed in this light, as a Discursive Science, it treats, *first*, of the *Educational Capacities*, or susceptibilities of man: Secondly, of the nature and characteristics of the *Educational forces*, or instrumentalities employed in his education: and thirdly, of the *processes* or modes of applying these forces to produce the required results.

As a Didactic Art, it treats of the duties and employments, as well as the modes of treatment and methods of teaching, concerned in the education of man.

These again are classified under the following heads; viz., HOME DUTIES, or employment; SCHOOL-ROOM DUTIES; and MISCELLANEOUS DUTIES. The first have reference to the early treatment and training of children, while under the parental roof; the influence this treatment has upon the education of the child at school; and indeed of all the Home influences and employments, under the following heads, viz.: *Labor*, in its numerous departments, physical, intellectual, and moral: *Recreation*, in its various forms; and *Rest*, in its conditions and uses.

The second, or SCHOOL-ROOM DUTIES and exercises, are those in which every thing relating to school-keeping as a profession will be examined under the following heads:

1. *Preliminaries*, including the *organization* of *Schools*, *The opening exercises*, and *the assigning of lessons*, with the various subdivisions which arise from the consideration of those topics.

2. *Study*, its *objects* and *uses*, its *requisites* and *modes*, and the *means* of securing study.

3. *Recitation*, its *objects* and *motives*, its *conditions* and *requisites*, and the *methods* of conducting recitations.

4. *Business*, its *objects* and *designs*, its *necessity* and *requisites*, and the *manner* of conducting it.

5. *Recreation*, its objects and ends, its requisites as to time, place and manner, and the methods or kinds best suited to the purposes.

6. *Government*, as it relates to the family, the school and the community; its objects and aims, its qualifications and requisites, and the means and methods of securing good government.

SYNOPSIS II.

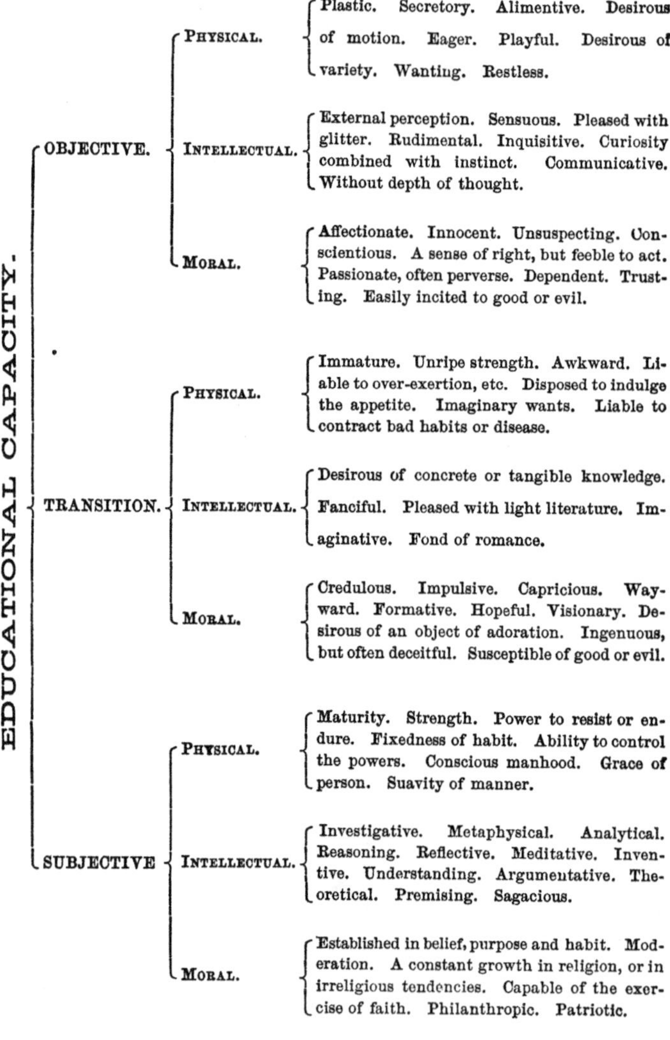

EDUCATIONAL CAPACITY.

- OBJECTIVE.
  - PHYSICAL. — Plastic. Secretory. Alimentive. Desirous of motion. Eager. Playful. Desirous of variety. Wanting. Restless.
  - INTELLECTUAL. — External perception. Sensuous. Pleased with glitter. Rudimental. Inquisitive. Curiosity combined with instinct. Communicative. Without depth of thought.
  - MORAL. — Affectionate. Innocent. Unsuspecting. Conscientious. A sense of right, but feeble to act. Passionate, often perverse. Dependent. Trusting. Easily incited to good or evil.
- TRANSITION.
  - PHYSICAL. — Immature. Unripe strength. Awkward. Liable to over-exertion, etc. Disposed to indulge the appetite. Imaginary wants. Liable to contract bad habits or disease.
  - INTELLECTUAL. — Desirous of concrete or tangible knowledge. Fanciful. Pleased with light literature. Imaginative. Fond of romance.
  - MORAL. — Credulous. Impulsive. Capricious. Wayward. Formative. Hopeful. Visionary. Desirous of an object of adoration. Ingenuous, but often deceitful. Susceptible of good or evil.
- SUBJECTIVE
  - PHYSICAL. — Maturity. Strength. Power to resist or endure. Fixedness of habit. Ability to control the powers. Conscious manhood. Grace of person. Suavity of manner.
  - INTELLECTUAL. — Investigative. Metaphysical. Analytical. Reasoning. Reflective. Meditative. Inventive. Understanding. Argumentative. Theoretical. Premising. Sagacious.
  - MORAL. — Established in belief, purpose and habit. Moderation. A constant growth in religion, or in irreligious tendencies. Capable of the exercise of faith. Philanthropic. Patriotic.

CHAPTER II.

EDUCATIONAL CAPACITY.

We now return to the more general characteristics of our subject, viz., "*Education as a Science;*" and shall, in the following chapter, briefly speak of the character and design of man's educational wants, physical, intellectual and moral.

Section 1—Objective Period.

The whole cycle of human life, so far as the educational susceptibility of the individual is concerned, may be reckoned under three distinct periods. The first, or *Objective*, is that period in which the body is in its earlier stages of growth, and is consequently, delicate and tender, and possesses peculiaries never afterward realized; and in which the mind also partakes of similar peculiarities, being most impressible, and for the most part, indebted to the outer world, the objects of nature and art, for its sources of development.

The knowledge itself is characterized as objective, since it is chiefly of an external nature, and is acquired mainly through the avenues of the senses. True, there is some knowledge peculiar to this age and advancement, which would not appropriately belong to this list—such as knowledge of personal identity, cause and effect, right and wrong, etc.; but the knowledge which relates to the physical world, that which is of daily contact, and whose acquisition depends upon the researches into nature and art, is the kind of which we speak.

The moral powers, too, are in an objective state, clinging, like the vine, to some earthly support, and twining themselves about some tangible objects, as parents, brothers, sisters, friends, and sensible objects of early association, whose office it is to nourish them and lift them up from the tangible to the intangible, from the earthly to the heavenly.

It will be seen, from a close examination of this subject, that a moral and religious education is contemplated, not merely in a theoretical sense, or as a thing desirable under certain circumstances, but as absolute, certain and practical; for God has not planted these longing desires after some object of worship, after the pure, the exalted, the true, and the good, in his creatures, to mock and torment them. But he has made their gratification not only possible, but practical, and the source of the highest enjoyment: *practical* and even necessary, since the very wants of man's nature demand it. The soul cries out after God, the living, loving God, not God in the dead letter of doctrines and creeds, but God in nature, God in Revelation, God in the soul, as an object of love and exaltation, These wants become sometimes almost insatiable; and if they are not gratified in a manner calculated to exalt the intellectual and moral powers, the affections will go out and attach themselves to improper objects; and the rending of them loose, sometimes even rends the soul.

The religious tendencies usually commence at a much earlier period than many suppose. These desires are among the very first manifestations of intelligence, and they are never strengthened by delay. As soon, therefore, as the child is old enough to sin, it is old enough to pray. The very first lispings of infant intelligence should be of God, home and heaven. The very first sentences should be framed in love and tender affection—not in curses, blasphemy and deceit. Some parents and teachers say, "O there is time enough for religious teaching after other things are learned." "The minds of children should not be biased by doctrines and creeds." It is not necessary at all that they should. This would defeat true religious teaching. But would the same policy in reference to reading, geography and arithmetic be a wise one, or one likely to be adopted by any parent or teacher? Is there not truth in religion as well as in mathematics? And will that truth not produce as healthy results? Will it not expand the mind? Who would dare say, "There is time enough for intellectual culture." "Do not bias the child's mind with grammar and arithmetic." "Wait till he comes to maturity." "Wait till he can judge for himself." How soon would his judgment mature sufficiently to decide upon a course of study suitable for his wants, without previous training? Do not parents and teachers direct him in these things? It should be so in religious training. When is there a better time to commence this teaching than in youth? It is not necessary that wickedness should be the first product of the human heart, to the extent that some would have us believe. It is not necessary that a child should lie before he becomes truthful; that he should kill or steal before he learns to respect the rights of person or property; that he should cheat and defraud before he becomes honest; that he should profane the name of God and his holy day, before he becomes reverent and conscientious; or that he should be disobedient and reckless, before he learns obedience and circumspection. But rather the reverse of this is true.

The period of youth is fraught with immense interests. If good seed is not sown in the human heart, bad will be; and in its natural and unguarded condition, these seeds will grow with a strange luxuriance. If the tender and good affections of the heart are not cultivated, their opposites will be. If these affections are not garnered by the righteous, they will be perverted; and Satan and his emissaries will have them. The seeds of morality and religion will not grow more vigorously in a soil that has been poisoned and hardened by sin. The tender plants of virtue will not bear more precious fruit, by being reared side by side with the weeds of vice, nor will their luxuriance be increased by any preoccupancy. The young affections of the human heart, offered upon the altar of religion and sanctified by Divine grace, become a sweet-smelling savor unto the Lord. The offerings that smoked upon Jewish altars, "the firstlings of the flock, the field, and of all the increase," were not more acceptable. This is the period, therefore, when direction should be given to man's moral and religious nature. It is the one most favorable for making impressions, and consequently good impressions. This constitutes the chief reason for commencing this kind of education at the very outset in life.

Again: a moral and religious education is insisted upon, on the principle, that *that* education which does not affect a man's faith, or weakens rather than strengthens it; which leaves his heart untouched, or in a worse state than it found it; which sharpens the intellect, but blunts the moral powers; which enlightens the understanding, but darkens the soul; which awakens thought, but warps the judgment; which warms the imagination, but freezes the affections; which strengthens the reason, but enfeebles the will; which quickens perception, but deadens conscience, *is simply monstrous;* that all true education makes man better, wiser, happier, stronger intellectually, physically and morally just in the same ratio; that every step in knowledge should mark a corresponding advance in goodness; that the sublimest hights of human acquisition and excellence are never scaled, unless the heart soar with the head. These and sundry other reasons are surely sufficient to induce any one to give due importance to moral and religious training in early life.

ARTICLE 1—PHYSICAL CAPACITY.—But to particularize in reference to the objective capacity. The condition of the physical powers and their characteristic wants may be briefly described thus: The body itself is in a plastic or formative state. The bones are comparatively soft and flexible. The flesh is tender and delicate. The brain is spongy, rare, and thin in consistency, and the digestive and vital apparatuses are weak, and, for the most part, partake of the same general characteristics that other organs possess. The secretion of fluids in the body largely predominates over the more solid deposits. The whole structure may be fitly compared to a young and tender plant, before its vital functions have changed its juices into the more solid substances of the stock or leaves, etc. Changes, of course, take place in the character and structure of the body every day and every hour. These are carried on chiefly by the vital functions, so that while in health, the deposits exceeding the removals, the body is constantly increasing and maturing. Some of the chief wants or desires are those of food or nourishment and sleep. Hence the being may be described as alimentive and somnolent. But these wants are only periodical. They give way, or rather make way for the desires for motion and activity, which are in themselves, about as strong and imperative and necessary as the desires for food and rest. Hence the continual restlessness of children during their waking hours, and their multiplied and multiform motions and gestures. These are all necessary for their health and growth; at least they all originate primarily in those natural desires wisely planted in children, without which they would not move a hand or foot; nor would they scarcely eat or breathe. But with them, they become eager and grasping — literal absorbents. They resemble the hungry polyp grasping in a hundred directions for some object of gratification. It is not only amusing but instructive to watch the motions of a young child in one of those hungry, playful moods, as it lies and kicks and strikes in all its possible directions, without any apparent design: yet the teacher or parent that can not see both order and design in all this, has yet to learn his first lessons in the science of education. At a little more advanced period, the grasping commences, and every thing within reach of those little hands is appropriated to gratify those wants. This eagerness, so common to children, to lay hold upon every object, whether harmless or hurtful,—and what seems strange, the more injurious the more eager they seem to grasp it and generally to convey it to the mouth, is only an additional evidence of an educational capacity, and of the necessity of furnishing that capacity with suitable educational instruments. These are but the first lessons, prompted by natural desires, to become acquainted with the properties of matter. Other animals are provided with certain instincts that prompt them either to select or to reject, and thus to guard themselves from danger. Hence they do not stand in so great need of education. But children learn by experience. They appropriate indiscriminately, and acquire knowledge by experimenting. Again: the young of all animals are playful. Children possess this propensity in a remarkable degree. This desire should not be checked too early or too severely, and surely never repressed entirely, but rather encouraged and made a means of physical culture. A rational gratification of this desire also keeps the mind in a healthy state.

The desire for novelty and change is another strong characteristic of this period. Nature has kindly furnished a vast supply of pleasing variety, and endless change of objects and scenery; and has as wisely, and munificently planted in the child's nature, a desire to be brought in contact with these things. The gratification of this desire also furnishes the requisite amount of healthy exercise. This wanting and restless longing for variety, change and novelty, is a kind of semi-intellectual want, inasmuch as the mind is about an equal sharer with the body in the benefits of its gratification.

ARTICLE 2—INTELLECTUAL CAPACITY.—Intellectually considered, the human being at this age, presents a strange variety — a world of mystery: and the world into which he is introduced, is not less wonderful and mysterious to him. No wonder then that strange inconsistencies and seeming paradoxes, present themselves in the path of the educator! The intellectual powers have so many different ways of manifesting themselves, in early youth, as almost to baffle description. But this inability on our part is evidently owing to the great want of extensive and accurate knowledge of the human powers, especially those of the mind, at this early period. What seems to our imperfect understanding of the entire scope of intellectual power, to be incomprehensible and sometimes antagonistic to what we have come to regard as truth, when submitted to the severest scrutiny, often reveals new truths and new wonders; and astonishes us with the striking analogy of truth in all the departments of nature: so that we shall be safe in assuming that these powers are guided, universally, in their development, by fixed laws, whose boundary and scope can be sufficiently defined, and whose operations can be sufficiently limited and controlled by human agencies, to render them subservient to the purposes of education. But to give to these intellectual powers, as a whole, a characteristic description at their several periods of growth, seems to be a matter of the greatest difficulty. We shall be safe in saying, however, that, in the objective state, their early manifestations are exhibited chiefly through external perception. The eye and the ear are the chief avenues to the mind and soul. Through them impressions are first made. These are prompted to act and to acquire by a certain desire for activity they have in themselves, and an inquisitiveness or curiosity combined with instinct, planted in the mind as a kind of stimulator, or mental appetite. And while these prompt to action, from within, the world of form, color, sound and beauty invite from without; so that the young powers are thus, by degrees, led forth to revel in new delights. And though it may be anticipating a little, it is proper to remark here, that this mode of educating should not be interrupted throughout all the subsequent course of the pupil. No artificial stimulants can be substituted without deranging the order and harmony of the growth. The child is first led to observe, and then to think. He is first sensuous and slightly imaginative in his essential characteristics, before he is rational and argumentative. He is pleased with form and color, and the glitter and show of external beauty, before his thoughts take a subjective turn. His appropriate knowledge, as a basis of thought, and consequently, his capacity and thoughts themselves, may be characterized as rudimental, partaking in a slight degree of whatever peculiarities they shall afterward inherit. They are just receiving shape and definite proportions. They are striking out in all directions, and seeking ever for new objects of investigation and discovery. Hence, in addition to the child's inquisitive nature, he is communicative, but without depth of thought. There is an energy, a sprightliness, about his powers at this period, which is very remarkable. This urges him on with a restless longing, ever to new fields of inquiry, until the mind gathers stores sufficient to set up a stock of thoughts and a process of thinking at home, or on its own individual responsibility.

This, it is true, is but a rude and imperfect sketch of the intellectual capacity, as we generally find it throughout this period; but it is hoped it may serve as a guide in that most interesting and profitable department of study.

Article 3—Moral Capacity.—It has already been remarked, that the moral nature of the child at this period, is peculiarly susceptible. It is sufficient to add, perhaps, by way of particularizing, that the affections of the child bear about the same relation to his moral nature, that perception does to his intellectual. The one is the avenue to the mind, the other is the avenue to the soul; and as perceptions are antecedent to thinking and reason, so affections are to conscience and will. If we say therefore, that he is *affectional*, we shall describe him in this particular. But these affections and faculties, as to their susceptibility, are both good and bad. As the eye and the ear may drink in sights and sounds erroneous and false in themselves, and thus leave erroneous impressions upon the intellectual faculties; so may the affections, even from the same and other sources, become corrupted, and thus carry mildew and moral death into the very soul.

The child is comparatively innocent—entirely so, antecedent to any actual transgression—and his subsequent guilt is usually measured both by his natural disposition or capacity for sin, and by the advantages (if they may be termed such) he has enjoyed for cultivating it. His actual transgression is therefore, to a great extent, the product of mismanagement.

He is also unsuspecting. Not having been trained in the hypocritical practices of maturer guilt, he is therefore, at first, easily imposed upon. But he soon learns, and usually becomes an apt scholar in deception. He is likewise conscientious, having a sense of right and wrong, but feeble to act. This sense is easily shocked at this period, and it too often becomes somewhat paralyzed, which is generally the first step in the hardening process which follows. It can not be denied also that the child is passionate and often perverse. This is usually more observable in children of a sensitive nature, than those of a dull and morose disposition; hence due allowances should be made. There is a natural dependence however in children, which renders these proclivities more or less subject to wholesome restraints. The child is not only dependent by virtue of his natural helplessness, but he is likewise, by nature, a trusting and confiding creature. This renders him easily incited either to good or to evil. Thus, it will be seen, his moral capacity may be estimated.

Section 2—Transition Period.

The second period may, from its nature and peculiarities, be denominated the transition period, since the mind and body, during this period, are both supposed to be undergoing a radical change; and in all right education and growth, this change is effected simultaneously in each; for the body should grow with the mind, since the healthiest development of the one depends upon a corresponding state of the other.

This period, however, is subject to great abuse. An unhealthy ripeness of both mind and body, is frequently provoked here by the fashionable follies of the age, and our modern modes of education.

Children become miniature men and women before they become respectable boys and girls. The reason is, vice stimulates the mind, or at least, some departments of it, to a precocious maturity, so that its native energies are soon exhausted, and then it ceases to expand, but assumes a kind of conceit and low cunning, which will, in a measure, account for the characteristic smartness of some of our boys and girls, who are exposed to the vices of a city life.

But the mind is not the only sufferer. The body becomes dwarfed and enfeebled under these unnatural drains upon its resources; and thus insulted and thwarted in its natural endeavors, it ceases to grow at an early age, and assumes some of the semblances of manhood; while a healthy, full and large size is seldom attained.

This period is marked in the body by the earliest indications of change from boyhood to manhood, or from girlhood to womanhood; and in the mind, by a corresponding change in the tastes and mental habits; by a desire for a higher class of literature, or other and higher kinds of knowledge; by an ability to pursue metaphysical studies, though the physical constitute the chief media through which the transition is made.

It is that period in life when the mind is neither fully objective in its manifestations, nor yet fully subjective, but changing, as it were, from the one state to the other. It holds fast by one hand to the tangible forms upon which, in early life, it depended almost exclusively for the stimulus to action; and with the other, it reaches forward with a strange fascination to the intangible or the unknown world of thought and pure intellection, with increasing and enlarged desires, and feasts upon the newly discovered dainties of reason, abstraction, and the higher forms of thought and investigation.

It by no means follows, however, that it loses any of its objective characteristics. Its power to observe and enjoy outward forms, and to appropriate objective knowledge and beauty, is only increased by the waking up of a new world of inner life, as is evidenced by the increased interest a highly cultivated mind takes in all the operations of nature and of art. It is, in fact, not only the point at which the two worlds are joined together, but it is the link itself that unites them; the objective being instrumental chiefly in waking up the subjective, while it, in turn, is more than compensated by the additional loveliness and beauty with which the latter invests the former.

Article 1—Physical Capacity.—The physical powers in this period may be briefly described thus. The body is generally in a state of rapid growth. There is a certain immaturity or greenness about it, which renders it susceptible of the slightest impressions. It may have the semblance of strength, but it is a flashy, unripe kind of strength, which renders the body liable to over-exertion. It lacks durability and stability. It is, for the most part, incapable of severe and protracted efforts. The movements are generally awkward; because there are continually new spheres of action imposed upon the powers, and they must become habituated to these, before they can act in them with grace, ease and precision. The voice is usually broken, half inclined to the manly and to the boyish tones. There is also a strong tendency to excess or over-indulgence, since the appetite, and indeed nearly all the desires are necessarily strong, while the judgment and will are apt, through neglect or otherwise, to be weak. There is a class of imaginary wants, liable to spring up here, and to plead lustily for redress; but they are the mere perversions of the natural and legitimate desires. Indulgence, therefore, only aggravates them; and they beget another brood of similar character, until the unfortunate victim is haunted, as it were, by a hoard of hungry passions. Bad habits, diseases, and distempers of various kinds grow up from this state of things, to the no small annoyance of the youth who indulges too freely.

Other characteristics similar to these might be described; but they will readily be inferred from what has already been said.

Article 2—Intellectual Capacity.—The intellectual condition has been partially described. It is in an objecto-subjective state in relation to its characteristic wants. It seeks concrete and tangible knowledge as a means of inducing the discrete and intangible. The literary taste is rather inaccurate and fanciful, than true and well defined. There is a special fondness for light literature, extravagant theories, and "windy" eloquence. The judgment is not entirely settled, and the understanding is immature. Even the memory is in a transition state, passing from the notice of facts to principles and theories. It grasps both classes, but it usually finds difficulty in assuming and discharging both functions entire. Hence it is not an uncommon thing for the memory, under bad treatment, to become treacherous in this period, and to remain so for life. But this is by no means a necessary result. Under proper treatment, it may all the time improve, notwithstanding it may exhibit these peculiarities as above stated.

The individual is also imaginative, and apt to become somewhat sentimental; though, this is more a moral affection than an intellectual. Hence a fondness for romance is peculiar to this period. This taste in itself, is a useful one, but liable to great abuse. It should not therefore be crushed out, but directed. By crushing it, all taste for literature is sometimes obliterated: but of this under the head of Processes.

ARTICLE 3 — MORAL CAPACITY. — The moral condition at this period will scarcely need additional description. It has already been treated, in a general way, in the preceding remarks. One of its marked characteristics, however, is hopefulness. The individual is supposed to be just entering upon a new sphere. Every thing seems to wear an inviting aspect. Hence the real value of men and things is often misjudged and over-estimated. This, while it is chiefly an intellectual operation, has, like most others of a similar import, a most decided moral effect. The heart generally becomes more or less impressible, as the truthfulness or falsity of these mental impressions become more or less apparent. The individual is apt to be visionary and chimerical, yet equally susceptible of truthful impressions. The heart is comparatively tender, and the sensibilities quick and lively. The religious tendencies are strong; but the world and sensual pleasures usually invite, and the conscience and will are frequently too feeble, unless strengthened by subsequent treatment, to interpose a successful barrier. Many, therefore, fall into bad habits here. There is, however, most unmistakably a strong desire, on the part of most youth of the age of which we are speaking, for some object of religious worship or adoration. Hence in this respect, they may be said to be of a religious turn. But they are usually credulous and impulsive, ready to believe almost any thing congenial to taste or inclination. They eagerly grasp at whatever dogmas or doctrines promise the largest liberty to belief, and sometimes to sensual pleasure. Hence the great importance of instilling correct religious sentiments and practices early in life; so as to anticipate these difficulties. Children are usually generous and benevolent in their impulses at this period; and these qualities are not unfrequently associated with a capricious and wayward disposition, often whimsical and inconsistent, full of conceit and levity sometimes, at others, proud and ambitious. But these peculiarities are seldom permanently established at this age, and hence subject to removal. The moral character is in a formative state, which will account in no small degree for these oscillations, seeming inconsistencies, and the preponderance of evil. Hence the boy, in this period, may, as it were, be both ingenuous and frank, and treacherous and deceitful: not however, that either of these traits has become settled in all cases, but in this unsettled state, both dispositions may be manifested. Girls are generally more humane and tenderhearted; while boys, whose dispositions may result not less fortunately, will manifest a degree of cruelty and barbarism absolutely astonishing. Boys usually possess the greater frankness; and girls, the greater sensibility. The first possess more will; and the latter, more affection. Both are, however, subject to great change; but more with the boys than with the girls. Girls usually mature sooner than boys, which may in some measure account for the difference. Both may be said, however, to vary with circumstances, and to be very susceptible at this period, either to good or to evil impressions, and hence to good or evil tendencies and habits.

Section 3—Subjective Period.

The third, or subjective period will scarcely need description, since its chief characteristics will be inferred from the account given of the other two. It is, however, that period in life when both the mind and body begin to assume their greatest strength and activity. It is the fully developed state of both; or rather that period when the various processes of manly and womanly development are most marked.

Article 1—Physical Capacity.—This period is distinguished in the bodily and physical powers, by certain and well known characteristics—such for instance, as a general maturity; a fullness and plumpness or roundness of form; sonorousness of voice; vigorous development of bodily strength; the power to resist and endure; fixedness of habit;—for a person at twenty-five or thirty years of age, seldom, if ever, entirely changes his habits and desires, unless some "stronger than the strong man armed" with habit, attacks, binds and casts out the former inhabitant; and even in this case, there is a constant tendency to revert to former practices.

It is further marked by ability to control the desires and appetites as well as the motions of the body. Conscious manhood or womanhood, grace and beauty of person, suavity of manner and a general appearance of maturity of bodily power, give full indications of the entire preponderance of subjective influences and wants.

Of course due allowance must be made in this estimate, for those who, either from natural deficiencies or acquired peculiarities, never fill these conditions. All such require additional care in order to regulate the conflicting forces.

ARTICLE 2—INTELLECTUAL CAPACITY.—Intellectually considered, this period exhibits some marked peculiarities. As it has been intimated, the intellectual faculties are distinguished by a state of development corresponding with the growth and maturity of the body.

The reasoning and reflective powers assume their highest forms of action. Metaphysical investigations —which seemed to the preceding periods as dry abstractions—become matters of peculiar pleasure now. The imagination, quickened into new life by these subjective beauties, walks abroad into the hitherto unknown fields of the ideal world, and gathers the materials and combinations for the richest creations of art. The understanding, ripened into perfect conceptions, takes comprehensive views of plans, theories, and general principles; and dwells with increasing interest upon the useful, the true and the good. The judgment, matured in its discriminations, weighs, compares, classifies and adjusts the points and principles of argumentation. The memory, having received a bountiful supply of facts and principles, gathers them up, associates them, retains them and reproduces them at pleasure. The taste, corrected and refined by the combined action and aid of the other powers, discriminates truly in the æsthetic world, and the whole intellectual machinery moves in harmony.

ARTICLE 3—MORAL CAPACITY.—In a moral, religious and social capacity, the characteristics are not less apparent. There is a strength, power and stability of will, and fixedness of purpose and habit, seldom, if ever, attained in either of the other periods. The affections assume a loftier sphere, and the conscience, under proper culture, becomes a fixed principle. A moderation characterizes the desires and wishes, and controls the decisions; a toleration and forbearance for the mistakes and weaknesses of others prevail here,—all of which are almost the direct antipodes of the rabid opinions and hasty and ill-digested decisions, peculiar to the period preceding this.

The religious tendencies and principles, under certain circumstances, are apt to be strong in this period, and they will increase with advancing years and subsequent development of the mind, provided, in both cases, the influences have been, and are still, favorable to such growth. But on the other hand, if the influences have been adverse, whether constitutional or otherwise; and if there is no yielding up of the powers, to be controlled by the Divine agency, irreligious tendencies increase in about the same ratio; moral and religious feelings become hardened, and the tendencies are altogether toward infidelity. The man is capable, therefore, of the exercise of the largest faith in the promises of Divine revelation, or he may be the subject of the most distressing doubts, and of the blindest unbelief. He is capable of the exercise of the widest and the loftiest philanthrophy, or his sympathies may be dried and withered by the rankest selfishness. His patriotism may be of the purest and loftiest character, and flow on in the widest stream; or it may be narrowed down to the meanest and most crooked channel of corrupt party spirit. His expanding powers may be taught to grasp the world, and his love to embrace the whole brotherhood of the race, and his affections all to center in God, the great source of every lofty aspiration; or by simple neglect or positive effort, he may turn these living streams, these springs and fountains of the soul into the filthiest cesspools, or streams of the dirtiest gall, or stagnant marshes whose dreadful malaria shall poison and corrupt every living thing in the heart.

This gives us, at least, a partial view of the educational susceptibility or capacity of the human being at the respective periods of development, as well as the changes to which these capacities are subject.

It is proper to remark in the conclusion of this part of the subject, that these changes, in different individuals, are not always accompanied with the same phenomena, nor do they occur at the same age; nor yet, in all cases, do the mind and body keep pace with each other, owing to constitutional differences. For to suppose this to be the case, would be in effect, to revive the unwarrantable assumption that individual capacity is universally the same. But it should be the object of education, so to equalize and distribute the forces, as to counteract, so far as possible, any abnormal growth or precocious development of the faculties on the one hand, and disease or imbecility on the other.

As a general review of this part of the subject, viz., man's Educational Capacity, the reader is referred to the scheme or general view placed at the beginning of this chapter.

The matter is placed in this shape for the convenience of the student.

SYNOPSIS III.

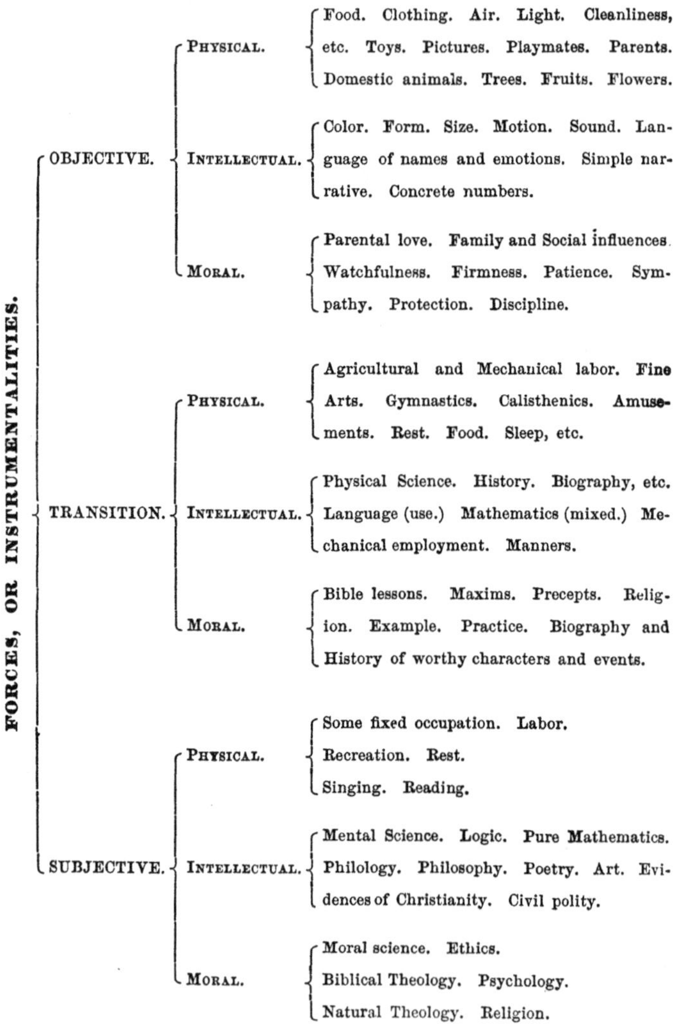

FORCES, OR INSTRUMENTALITIES.

- OBJECTIVE.
  - PHYSICAL. — Food. Clothing. Air. Light. Cleanliness, etc. Toys. Pictures. Playmates. Parents. Domestic animals. Trees. Fruits. Flowers.
  - INTELLECTUAL. — Color. Form. Size. Motion. Sound. Language of names and emotions. Simple narrative. Concrete numbers.
  - MORAL. — Parental love. Family and Social influences. Watchfulness. Firmness. Patience. Sympathy. Protection. Discipline.
- TRANSITION.
  - PHYSICAL. — Agricultural and Mechanical labor. Fine Arts. Gymnastics. Calisthenics. Amusements. Rest. Food. Sleep, etc.
  - INTELLECTUAL. — Physical Science. History. Biography, etc. Language (use.) Mathematics (mixed.) Mechanical employment. Manners.
  - MORAL. — Bible lessons. Maxims. Precepts. Religion. Example. Practice. Biography and History of worthy characters and events.
- SUBJECTIVE.
  - PHYSICAL. — Some fixed occupation. Labor. Recreation. Rest. Singing. Reading.
  - INTELLECTUAL. — Mental Science. Logic. Pure Mathematics. Philology. Philosophy. Poetry. Art. Evidences of Christianity. Civil polity.
  - MORAL. — Moral science. Ethics. Biblical Theology. Psychology. Natural Theology. Religion.

CHAPTER III.

EDUCATIONAL FORCES.

We now invite the reader's attention to the examination of the educational forces or instrumentalities, as they exist in the world of matter and of mind. These forces are as numerous as the wants they were intended to supply. And here we reaffirm, that there exists no want, of an educational character, which the Creator has not wisely considered and provided for. The eye, for instance, was made for the light—with a most wonderful adaptation too, with educational wants which light alone can supply—and light was furnished that the eye might find ample scope for exercise. The ear was made for sounds, and sounds for the ear; the lungs for the air, and air for the lungs; food for the body, and the body for food; labor for the hands, and the hands for labor. Just examine their wonderful mechanism, and then say, if you can, that they were made to be idle! The mind, too, was made for labor, for thought, for science; and the world of investigation and science was made for mind. The soul was made to love, to sympathize, to worship and adore; and God is, and man was created, that its every power might find room for expansion and perfect development. It starves too, without these supplies, just as surely as the body starves

without its supplies. How vain, and worse than foolish, therefore, the argument of atheists, or that which would rob man of an essential part of his being, and deprive him of his appropriate exercise!

Thus every sense and every faculty of body, mind and soul, finds appropriate stimulants in the world of matter, or in the more occult mysteries of metaphysics. In no department of the works of the Creator, do we observe happier adaptations of means to ends, or stronger evidences of wisdom and design; and the whole creation abounds and rejoices in this marvelous harmony.

But to return. These Educational Forces, as they are termed, embrace all the means and influences of an educational character, that are or can be brought to bear upon mind, body and soul, throughout the whole period of life. Indeed, they begin with man's very existence, and are doubtless co-extensive with that existence. Those, however, that relate more immediately to his present education, will claim attention here. They may be classified according to their nature and the influence they exert, in the following general groups, viz.: *Objects of nature and art; Books of science, religion and literature; Living teachers*, and whatever other influences may be addressed to man's faculties, either from an external or from an internal source. All these, again, admit of the same classification, that we find in the educational capacity or susceptibility, viz.: Objective, or primary; Transition or intermediate; and Subjective or advanced: not, however, that these forces are necessarily or inherently so; but that they so accommodate themselves to the educational capacity of man; and so arrange themselves that every educational want, physical, in-

tellectual and moral, is provided for, at these several periods. But to particularize.

Section 1—Objective Period.

It will be seen, by a brief reference to Chapter Second, Section 1, Art. 1, that appetite, motion and kindred desires are among the earlier wants of infant man or woman. Therefore, the appropriate supplies would be food, light, air, temperature, clothing, exercise, sleep, cleanliness, etc., as administering more directly to the physical wants; and toys, pictures, playmates, parents, domestic animals—both bird and beast—trees, fruits, flowers, etc, etc., as instruments, not only of the best physical culture, at this early age, but aiding much in the intellectual and moral; since the surest and safest means of reaching these infant powers, is through the physical man. This fact must be borne in mind constantly; that whatever merit these things possess in a physical sense, they are no less valuable as a means of waking up mind and calling out the affections. Indeed, they seem to be the Divinely appointed instruments of infant education; and no attempts to abandon them, or to barter them for their artificial substitutes, should be tolerated. They need not, and indeed, they will not, displace others of a judicious character. They only fill the hiatus that too often offers an easy ingress to idleness and vice.

Of course, these supplies are constant throughout all the periods of life, the quantity and quality varied, only to suit the character of the wants. No one, for instance, would maintain, that the food and exercises best suited for the infant, or even the youth, would be best for the adult. And the same is true mainly of the other forces. The character of the want will indicate the quantity and quality of the supply.

A mere allusion to some of the chief characteristics of these forces must suffice for the present, while their peculiar fitness will be inferred from their mode of application, discussed in another place.

ARTICLE 1—PHYSICAL FORCES.—The *food* should be plain, simple and nutritious. Nature has kindly indicated its quality, as well as, in part, its quantity, in the supply she has furnished for the tender age of infancy. Whatever changes are necessary, should be made after consulting the wants of childhood—real wants, not imaginary ones. It is often the case that a false demand is created by injudicious supplies, which becomes imperious in after life.

The *light* should be the natural light, and as equally diffused as possible, throughout childrens' apartments. This seems to be indicated by the general diffusion of light throughout all the departments of nature, where plants and animals exist. The sunlight is God's light, and one of his best gifts to man. Its quality has never yet been equaled or improved by any artificial compound. It is an essential element in the healthy growth and development of plants and animals, as has been abundantly proved by experiment. Why then should we attempt to shun it, or to change its essential ingredients by any artificial means? This light may change the color of the skin slightly; but then this change should be coveted, rather than dreaded. It is the change from the pale, sickly hues of disease, or the shaded life, to that of health, vigor and hardihood.

Children should be allowed the free use of sunlight;

for nothing seems so unreasonable as to deprive them of it, or to put them on a stinted allowance, since it is nature's own bounty. What looks more healthy, and consequently beautiful, than sun-embrowned boys and girls, if they have observed the laws of health in other respects? But we pass this to notice the

Air.—This, of course, should be pure, and used freely. It, like the light, is a free gift; and no one therefore should be allowed to speculate upon it, or to deprive any one of the free use of it. It is well known also, that after being once used, for the purposes of breathing, etc., it is utterly unfit for use again, until it is purified by natural processes. It becomes poisonous. No one therefore should be compelled to use it in this condition; much less to breathe it a third or fourth time, without its being first submitted to the purifying processes. What, for instance, would be thought of a man who would poison a fountain of water, at which the whole neighborhood drank? He would not only be publicly execrated, but publicly executed. But we do a deed similar to this, when we compel our children to breathe fetid atmosphere. But much has been said on this subject, in other works.

The *Temperature* of the body has an important bearing upon the health. All parts should maintain nearly the same temperature; i. e., the heat should be uniformly distributed, in order to keep up healthy circulation. This brings us to notice the *clothing.* This, of course, should be adapted to age, employment, climate, constitutional peculiarities, etc. For information on this subject, the reader is referred to works on physiology and hygiene. It is a remarkable fact, however, that no parts of the human body, especially in childhood and youth, need protection more than the upper and lower extremities; and it is equally remarkable, and more strange than remarkable, that no parts are more exposed, especially at that age, when the danger from exposure is greatest. The physical and moral evils arising from this whim of fashion, are too apparent and too appalling to need exposition here. They can not, however, be too distinctly pointed out, and carefully guarded against.

Sleep is a necessity, and has a remarkable effect upon childhood. Without it, some, and indeed all the important functions of the living being, would cease. Its necessity and effects are scarcely less apparent in the moral and intellectual man. To become useful, however, it must be taken periodically, and, except in cases of infancy and early childhood, or in disease, should be taken in the absence of the sun's rays from the earth. Night is the time appointed to man for sleep, and the day for labor, activity and enterprise; and no attempt to change this beautiful order, should be tolerated. The individual, therefore, who, without good and sufficient reasons, such as named above, lies abed while the sun is shining upon *his* part of the world, violates a clearly implied law of God; and so does he who wantonly spends that portion of the night, designed for sleep, in labor, pleasure or dissipation. No animal except man, willingly violates this law; and none suffer its penalties so fearfully.

Cleanliness is so nearly allied to Godliness, that its importance can scarcely be over-estimated. It is so essential to the health and happiness of the human race, that its claims, as an educational force, will scarcely be disputed by any one; and so intimately allied is it to man's true education, that we find it keeping steady and even pace with him, throughout all his various stages of advancement. This is true no less of nations than of individuals, as will at once appear, upon a comparison of the manners and customs of some of the more enlightened nations, with those of the Chinese, or the still less fastidious Arabs. What enlightened nation, for instance, would be willing to adopt the beastly habits of the filthy Esquimau, or the South-Sea Islander? It is safe to say, therefore, that a nation's true advancement, may be measured by its cleanliness: and the same is true, no less of individuals than of masses.

We have no charity, and but little patience, for that kind of education which does not improve a man's habits and general appearance; which does not refine and elevate him in his social capacity, and indeed in every other respect. But if filthiness is unpardonable any where, it is certainly so, in the family and in the school-room, where children are forming opinions and habits for life.

Toys and Apparatus are of great service in the education of children. They are the tools with which they conduct the various operations and experiments in their miniature world, the nursery, the school room and their surroundings. They are also safe and cheap investments; for they not only afford the means of innocent amusement and healthy development, but they often save doctor-bills, and not unfrequently *bills* of a more exceptionable character. The school apparatus is too generally confined to the high-school, and the home apparatus to the parlor, or locked up safe from mischievous hands, whose annoyance sometimes becomes almost insufferable, in consequence of this privation. The apparatus in many of our best high-schools and colleges, costs thousands of dollars; while the primary and secondary schools, if furnished with any, can usually sum up theirs in the brief catalogue,—"a disordered globe, a broken numeral frame, and a few antiquated maps and charts;" and in many instances, indeed, the walls of these departments are as bare as those of a prison. Now *this is wrong.* The primary and secondary schools, by virtue of the objective nature of their inmates, need the most apparatus, though it should differ in quality from that of the high-school. The advanced scholars, for a similar reason, are capable, for the most part, of carrying forward their investigations without such helps, however great the advantages of having them may be. It would by no means be wise, therefore, to diminish the apparatus in the higher departments; but it would be, to increase it in the lower; being careful, of course, to select such a variety as would suit the wants of children — such, for instance, with which they can experiment.

Pictures are no less useful than toys, since they are the representatives of objects, and thereby aid the mind in making its transfer of knowledge from the tangible to the intangible. Their chief utility, however, as instruments of physical culture, is in training the eye to trace the outlines of beauty, and the hand in imitating it. They might be classed with toys, etc., only that they are one step higher in the scale. Their use will be explained more fully under the head of "*physical culture,*" in chapter fifth.

Playmates are almost as essential to the healthy and natural development of children, as light is to the plant. A child reared alone is deprived of a large share of those youthful sports which constitute so essential an element in his physical culture; and if exclusively with old people, he not only assumes their habits, but the shape of the body is often modified by the unnatural influences; so that he becomes gradually, in habits and decrepitude, the aged invalid. Any attempt, therefore, to thwart nature, by furnishing old heads for young shoulders, or bringing children to maturity before they have passed through the child period, will only be accompanied with disastrous consequences. But

Parents and Teachers are indispensable to the accomplishment of all that is desirable in the physical education of the child. They are so necessary that it does not seem important that their particular functions should be pointed out here. They, however, become objects of love and veneration, as well as the instruments of instruction, protection, direction, and restraint. But, as necessary as they are in these respects, it would seem that many children would fare better without them than with them; for when they scold them, and beat them, and look upon them continually with suspicion, they poison not only their minds, but interfere, in no small degree, with their physical growth. And when they pamper and indulge them, especially their appetites, they breed conceit, laziness and physical diseases. But of this, more particularly under Modes of Culture.

Domestic Animals, both birds and beasts, are the delight of children, and usually afford them their first lessons in natural history, as well as the means for their physical exercises. No one who has ever witnessed the gambols of rosy-cheeked boys and girls, with a noble Newfoundland dog, or their playful excursions with a Shetland pony, or perhaps, what is just as useful, and a good deal more common, the healthy care and labor with domestic animals on the farm, can doubt for one moment, the utility of these educational forces.

Trees, *Fruits* and *Flowers*, are usually linked with the early associations of childhood; especially when these are in a natural state; but when cultivated, their influence is scarcely less potent. They afford ample amusement for them, while their cultivation begets a love for the beautiful, at the same time that it gives physical employment and forms habits of industry. He who plants a tree is said to be a benefactor to his race; but children, if only allowed to indulge their tastes, thus early, not only become public benefactors, but they form habits and attachments that time will never efface.

The above comprehends a brief description of some of the more important physical educational forces, peculiar to the objective period. But it will be remembered that whatever of excellence they possess in early life, they lose no essential force in subsequent periods. Their potency usually increases as the inner life becomes developed in man.

Article 2 — Intellectual Forces. — *Intellectually* considered, the nature and characteristics of these supplies are not less varied and striking. For the objective or dawning intellect, they are thoroughly objective, and suited to its capacity: for the transition, they are not less appropriate; and for the subjective, the same mutual adaptation is very distinct. Not to admit this, would be in effect to call in question the wisdom and goodness of the Creator. To admit a part of it, and not the whole, would be to compromise a great and fundamental principle. To doubt the practicability of the application of this principle in the education of man, involves an absurdity.

The first class of these objective forces includes all the objects and influences of nature and art that appeal to the new-born powers of the mind, more directly through the senses. All the external world, with its strange and delightful changes, is brought into requisition here. Those alluded to under physical forces are, for the most part, equally well adapted to the intellectual wants. Their intellectual force will here be shown in connection with others.

Among the first of these may be classed *Color*, with its endless variety of shadings, from the gorgeous hues of the rainbow to the pale blue sky and colorless vapor. The blushing morn, the subdued and mellow eve, the delicate penciling in flowers and the varied tints in the plumage of birds, the pleasant shades of forest green, the meadow, the lawn, the distant mountains dressed in their somber hues,—these all speak in silent but soft beseeching language, that stirs the feeble pulses of mind, and gives the first motions to thought and investigation. They operate with a charm upon these newly awakened powers, far excelling any of the boasted plans and brain-racking theories, too frequently adopted by modern educators.

But not only color, but *Form* or outline, as it appears in forest trees, the sloping woodlands, the winding rivers, the dancing waterfall, the glassy lake and overhanging margin, the graceful foliage, the exquisite shape of animals and plants and flowers, the graceful curves and arches that abound in works of nature and art, the abrupt outline of the precipice or the mountain, the ever changing, yet ever pleasing circling and eddying in clouds, and bodies of water,—all these convey impressions to the mind, silent, though they may be, yet so powerful that they become the most pleasing themes of contemplation in subsequent life.

And then the endless variety of *Sounds*, from the sighing zephyr to the rushing tornado; from the rippling of the brook to the deafening roar of the cataract; from the murmur of the half quiet lake to the thundering crash of waves, when the storm-rent Ocean lifts up his voice; from the chirping of the cricket at the hearth-stone to the deep-toned thunder, the lowing herds, the animated voice of pleasure and the hum of business; the singing of birds and the sweet strains of music, all move the mind's dormant energies, and wake its powers to life and activity.

And then again, *Motion*, with its thousand tropes as exhibited in the animated world, its curves and angles, its grace and ease, and beauty, and poetry—these and all the external manifestations of nature we have named, and ten thousand more, stand as so many sentinels on the outposts of science, to awaken and delight the incipient mind, and to beckon it on to drink of these pure, healthy streams. They invite the young body forth to activity, enterprise and manly development. They are nature's means for educating man. Why then should we interfere with them, when they are so obviously in accordance, not only with sound philosophy, but with our unbiased inclinations? Why should children be kept confined and shut out from all those nobler forms of loveliness, in order that they may be educated? Even supposing the schoolhouse or the dwelling to be passable or even elegant, does this afford any excuse for the rejection of these natural educational forces? Instead of interfering in any degree with the discipline of children, or the acquisition of knowledge, even from books and teachers, they only prepare the way by opening up every avenue of the mind, to the most wholesome discipline and the most vigorous development.

From the above it will be inferred that the natural sciences, language, and we might add, concrete mathematics are best adapted to the wants of both body and mind at this period. Natural sciences, in their simpler form open up the way to the mind, and afford abundant activity for the body. They give knowledge of the physical universe, and acquaintance with the beauties and attractions of nature and art.

Language affords an opportunity to give expression to feeling. Its study also cultivates close observation, whereby a higher order of thought is awakened. It should, however, relate only to the simple and exact modes of expression, the beauty, richness and accuracy in description, etc.

Mathematics, or arithmetical and geometrical exercises as they relate to simple, external form and proportion, cultivate quickness of apprehension, clearness and closeness of reasoning and investigation. They strengthen and prepare the mind for abstract and metaphysical research.

It must not be inferred from the above that the exercises, as they will be described in another place, are intended to usurp the place of those in common use, so far as the latter conform to sound philosophy.

So far from any usurpation, or even an interruption, they only excite a laudable interest in them. A child who has been taught to observe closely, and whose faculties have been trained in this natural process, will not only possess keener perception, stronger memory, a better understanding and judgment, and a livelier imagination, but every emotion of the soul will be quickened into healthy activity. Thus an early taste for study and habits of accuracy will be formed, which will be a basis for subsequent pursuits. It is the natural order; and any methods that conflict with nature, will check the real progress of the child.

In every department of the works of the Creator, there is the most rigid economy combined with the most benevolent designs, and the happiest harmony. Man should therefore be very careful how he interferes with these.

ARTICLE 3 — MORAL FORCES. — The instruments of man's moral and religious culture next claim attention. This department of his education, no less than all others, is dependent upon antecedent causes, subject, for the most part, to his own control. Among the first and foremost of these forces, for the objective period, may be placed Parental Love, and the family and social influences.

The family seems to be not only the first compact or association ordained by heaven, but the one into which every human being is, or ought to be, first introduced. It is the proper nursery of infant thought and infant action. It is the natural home of the child. No artificial association should be allowed to usurp its place. The parent stands by nature and by Divine appointment, at the head of this social compact; and holds in his hands, to a greater extent than any other, the fundamental Educational Forces of the child. Especially is this true in a moral and religious sense; for whatever may be the intellectual training of the child, and to whomever committed, its moral and religious tendencies are generally controlled and guided by the home and parental influences.

Now, whatever of influence was attributed to the intellectual forces, will justly apply to the moral; for it is impossible, according to the well known laws of mind, to educate one department of man's nature truly, without appealing to all other departments. The proper education of the head will always affect the heart, and vice versa.

This truth can not be too often repeated and too carefully inculcated. It is one of the fundamental principles, associated with right education. By overlooking or disregarding it, the ancient world groped in darkness; and the modern educational world has run into the wildest vagaries and the strangest extremes.

But the truth is plain and simple like all of God's truths. *Every intellectual force is virtually a moral force.* So intimately allied are they, that were it not for the distinctions which exist in man, as to his moral and intellectual qualities, and also, as to the moral and intellectual qualities of actions, the two forces would mutually blend.

To illustrate: the child first learns to love and obey its parents. This is but a simple act, and yet it implies an intellectual act, a moral act, and may include a physical act; but not one of them singly can be performed, in the true sense, without the other.

We might as well talk of nourishing one arm at a time, or one leg, or the body without the limbs, by simply taking food into the stomach, as to talk of educating a man, and not affecting for good or ill, all the departments of his nature.

The affectional nature of the child is the first to show signs of development. It goes out, and naturally entwines itself about the parent. The manifestations may be feeble at first, like all its powers, but under proper management it soon acquires strength. The mother's soothing voice is the first sound that addresses its ear intelligently. The tender, gentle embrace, stirs the fountains of love in its soul; the latent affections are moved, and they rise up to meet and mingle with her own. How swift and how sweet the response thus given! Here then is the educational want. Where are the supplies? Ay: are they not at hand? Do they not exist in a mother's love, a father's care, and all the endearing ties of home and friends? Now if those supplies are not cut off or poisoned—as is too frequently the case—if they are constant, and are judiciously administered, it is easy to see how the little heart might be led on, step by step, to love, to trust and to obey.

But Watchfulness, Patience and Firmness are necessary ingredients in a parent's stock of forces to control and direct the growing energies of the child; watchfulness to detect the first buddings of sinful desires; for such is their deceptive nature, that they grow up sometimes under the immediate eye of the parent, and are not unfrequently fostered by fond and doting friends as indications of smartness. At other times they manifest themselves in outbreaking vices, not less to be deplored, and seem to summon every demon to their aid. In all these forms, patience must have her perfect work. She teaches us to bear the ills of life. Much more should she teach us to bear with the waywardness of children. If their sins *are* many, the occasions and weaknesses that draw them aside, and cause them to fall, are not less numerous.

It often becomes necessary, therefore, to interpose authority; and in such cases, firmness and unyielding integrity are in great demand, in order to check the irrational desires, and to turn them into their proper channels. The child soon loses confidence in one not possessed of these qualifications, and, whatever other excellencies he may possess will be taken for less than half their real value, in consequence of the absence of these qualities. A decision once rendered, should not be changed for light causes.

Children are no less the objects of sympathy than they are themselves sympathetic. In all their weaknesses and follies, they not only need the mantle of charity to hide their seeming depravity, but they need the sympathy of their seniors; not, by any means, to encourage them in crime, but to lift them up from weakness and irresolution to strength and determination in the various ways of duty. They need that protection from the uncharitable assaults of the world, which the home circle alone can afford. They need an asylum into which they may retreat from the storm and the tempest with which the sky of youth is frequently overcast.

These trials may all be necessary as discipline; but, at this tender age, unless assistance or protection is at hand, the little sufferer bends too often, and sinks beneath the load, and the moral powers are bruised and broken instead of being strengthened.

Mother or teacher, stand by your little one, in those fearful hours of temptation and strife, and see that the world and the passions do not overcome him. A moral conquest here is better than the conquest of a kingdom; but a defeat may carry disaster into all the chambers of the soul.

The family and social influences, as educational forces to give direction to the moral and religious powers of the child, can not be over-estimated. The child not only learns to love his brothers and sisters, and to revere and obey his father and mother, as well as love them, but numberless occasions arise when it becomes necessary in the little community, that the personal preferences and individual liberty of the few must be sacrificed to the general good. Here the child learns to respect the rights of his fellows, to submit to wholesome restraints, and to render cheerful obedience to the properly constituted authorities. He thus acquires the feelings and habits of a good citizen. And what is true of the family, in this respect, is also true of the school, for *it* should be modeled as nearly as possible on the plan of a well regulated family. The only essential difference in the government is, that in the latter it is generalized, and on a larger scale.

But what a dark picture that family or that school presents, where all these moral forces are perverted and made to act as so many influences against the right development of the moral powers! What a repulsive sight where love is turned to hate, trust to jealousy and suspicion, watchfulness to careless indifference, firmness to vacillation and irresolution, patience to petulance, sympathy to malevolence, protection to neglect, discipline to disorder, and all the social endearments to so many sources of discontent and bitterness!

Man's happiness would thus be turned to misery, his social ties would be only so many clanking chains, to fret and chafe his humor, and to strew his pathway with thorns. His cup of connubial bliss would be a cup of gall; and the happiest spot on earth for man —*his own dear home*—would be a hell.

But we turn from this dark picture to consider the educational forces at another and an important period in life.

Section 2—Transition Period.

It was a remark of a distinguished educator, while describing a course of study for high-schools, that "a hiatus occurs in the history of every human being between the ages of 11 and 15, and that this is exceedingly difficult to fill up." In this he refers doubtless to the period of which we are about to speak.

While we agree, that such a period does occur, and that its characteristics are distinctly marked; yet we can not agree with the learned Dr. when he tells us, that this period is *necessarily* more difficult to supply than any other. We admit that it is more liable to neglect and abuse than any other; and that many who have made shipwreck of their powers, may date their ruin back to the incidents occurring in this period; but it no more follows that this is a necessary result, than that people should die of hunger, while the land abounds in plenty: or that they should fail to become educated in any case, when the means for such education are within their reach. Because men starve is no proof that there is no food, though this would be a sequence, were there none.

It only proves that there is none for them; or that they have not availed themselves of its advantages. So in the case before us. Many suffer for want of proper supplies, at this period, not because there *are* no such supplies, for this would be charging God with neglect; but because these supplies are not brought within their reach. They exist in great abundance, but because of their simplicity and universality, men are apt to overlook them. They are like those common blessings whose visits are so silent, so frequent, and yet so necessary, that we forget to credit them.

ARTICLE 1—PHYSICAL FORCES.—In casting about for supplies for the physical wants and powers, we are apt to look beyond the real ones, and to select something artificial or foreign to their nature. Nature offers an abundant supply, and on the most reasonable terms.

We see by reference to chapter second, section 1st, that the capacity is very marked; and that these powers, in their semi-educated state, are constantly seeking employment. Activity is their essential characteristic, and in it they find their chief enjoyment. But there is great danger of excess. Hence the greater need of special direction and control. The question then recurs, what are the natural and legitimate supplies for these wants?

In addition to those enumerated in the Objective Period, it will be found necessary to introduce others, differing, not so much, perhaps, in kind, as in quantity and quality. Hence, many of those there enumerated, will be readily exchanged for others, similar in kind, but of a higher order. Thus, the toys will be exchanged for farming, mechanical and household utensils and implements. Playmates will become companions and friends in a truer sense; co-laborers in a higher calling.

Among the many avocations of life, no one perhaps, is more congenial to man than Agricultural Pursuits. They are probably the first that ever engaged the attention of the race, and afforded exercise to the physical powers: and like all other institutions of Divine appointment, they are the most necessary to man's existence, and conducive to his happiness.

They offer better opportunities for full and free exercise of all his physical powers, than any others. If they have their hardships, they have likewise their rewards. If they have their exposures to inclement seasons, they have likewise their pure and free atmosphere, freighted with the odors of a thousand flowers. It is a matter of astonishment, since this employment is at once so congenial and necessary to the human race, that so many are inventing ways and means to escape from it.

The earth uncovers her broad bosom, and displays her matchless beauty of valley, plain, mountain and woodland, and says to her children, "Come, cultivate my fields, and I will pour you out a blessing, such that your garners shall not be able to contain it." "Come, eat of my pleasant fruits, my honey and butter, and drink of my wine and milk, and let your hearts be glad and rejoice all your days." And yet men will huddle together in crowded cities, and even tread one upon another, that they may get gain.

It would seem that the inculcation of right views upon this subject, would in time correct this abuse. Where, then, is there a better place to begin this inculcation, than in the family and in the school-room?

Next in importance to agricultural pursuits may be ranked the Mechanic arts and employments. These likewise seem necessary for man's subsistence: for, without them, he would be unable to protect himself against the wrath of the elements, or control the forces of nature, so as to accomplish the purposes of life. Inventions and machinery, the products of genius and labor, stand among the proudest achievements of the present age; and the mechanical employments are the nurseries where this kind of genius is fostered. Labor is the means by which these achievements are wrought out.

The mechanic arts afford scope for all that is ingenious in man, while they cultivate his taste and his physical nature. This is more apparent in the subjective period than in the transition; nevertheless, it has its origin here, since the man is the boy first, and the woman is the girl, before she is the matron. The same is true of the Fine Arts. They do not attain any degree of perfection here; yet they exist in an incipient state. Their uses and modes of culture will be pointed out in another place.

But "All work and no play would make Jack a dull boy." Thus philosophized "Poor Richard;" and every one will allow that his philosophy is sound. It is a well established fact that our physical organism needs the health-giving influences of Amusement; and children in particular, who have the greatest need of it, have an instinctive desire for it. It may be said, however, by some cross-grained devotee of asceticism, that "So they have for many other vices." But before any thing can be made out of this argument, it must be shown that play is a vice, which position is untenable. The fact is, the love of rational amusement is a virtue, no less to be cultivated, than the love of innocence and truth, with which it stands intimately related: and the desires for vicious indulgence are all perverted desires, often so too, from neglect. These legitimate desires exist every where in the animal world, especially with the young; and their rational gratification is always accompanied with pleasure. It is only when they are not properly regulated, that they become sources of mischief. Hence Gymnastic and Calisthenic exercises,* since these are regulated plays, are best suited to the accomplishment of one of the most obvious designs of amusement, viz.: the healthy and symmetrical development of the physical powers.

And then amusement serves another important purpose. It rests the body from the fatigue of labor, and clears away the cobwebs and clouds from the mind, and lets in a bright ray of the real, living sunshine of enjoyment.

Article 2—Intellectual Forces.—We come now to notice the intellectual forces, appropriate for this period.

The supposed "hiatus," alluded to in another place, has more of an existence in an intellectual sense, than in a physical. But a proper study of man, and of his educational forces, will soon discover to the inquirer

* It should be remembered however, that unless these last named exercises are conducted with strict reference to the objects to be attained, they are of but little service. Indeed, they are frequently very injurious, owing to excesses and wrong applications. They should, therefore, be conducted under the eye and special direction of an accomplished master.

the vast supplies that have been laid up in store for this period. So that the hiatus is more the result of our mistakes than otherwise.

The proper adjustment of the physical forces, will not only suggest the proper disposition of the intellectual ones, but will lead to a juster appreciation of such culture, and assist materially in carrying it forward.

As in the objective state, the physical world afforded the greatest amount of influence, calculated to awaken and develop the thinking powers; so in the transition, the forces are chiefly of a material character. The intellectual eyes of the learner, at this period, however, are just opening upon the immaterial world, and he stands bewildered while he gazes upon its wonders. The physical sciences, properly pursued, lead directly to the metaphysical, just as the study of language leads to the development of thought. Indeed the physical sciences are but the initials or elements of the metaphysical. Hence they are first in order of time. All things material have antecedents, either material or immaterial; and all actions and effects produced have causes. These causes again have their antecedents, until all causes are traced back to the great *First Cause* of all things.

The mind passes by steps from the tangible to the intangible, from the material to the immaterial, from the simple to the more abstruse. From the well-known, it at once sets out in pursuit of the unknown. From the effect, it travels back to the cause, and soon becomes merged in metaphysical research. At least, this is one of its routes of travel, and the one usually selected by the learner, in this period.

The physical sciences, therefore, since they abound

in facts, offer the safest medium, through which the transition may be made. They are pleasing and attractive, and abound in the strange and beautiful. But their chief excellence lies in the fact that they are so intimately related to all the operations of daily life. We can scarcely breathe or move without bringing into requisition some of the strangest phenomena, and awakening in the mind the profoundest curiosity. The natural sciences, therefore, seem to be the Divinely appointed stepping-stones which lead from the physical universe, to that universe of mind and spirit, into which the learner is introduced in his more advanced stages. A list of these sciences might here be given, were not the circumstances, under which it would be necessary to pursue them, so various, as to render such a list nothing more than an approximation.

History and Biography, likewise, hold an important place among the educational forces of this period. Their descriptive as well as their objective nature renders them peculiarly appropriate. There is a novelty and an interest connected with a well prepared history or biography, which perhaps do not exist in works of mere fiction. They are strangely attractive for that class of mind of which we are now speaking. Their chief excellence, however, consists in the narrative style, their simplicity and the power they possess in awakening mind, and provoking a desire to excel.

Great care should be exercised, however, in the selection of authors. An unholy ambition may be fostered here, which will lead to untold disaster. But a proper taste for the above named studies, formed in early life, would offer a strong barrier to the formation of a morbid love of fiction and light reading. It is not because the mind is more averse to the truth than to a lie, that this taste for morbid trash is formed. Neither is it because truth lacks any of the essential elements of attractiveness; for it is even stranger than fiction; but it results from overlooking this most obvious truth, that our education should begin with the heart, and for intellectual advancement it should make use of natural objects first.

Language is a medium for the communication of thoughts, feelings and desires. Its manifestations commence with the commencement of being, and they can cease only when existence ceases. Viewed in this light, it becomes a science which admits of culture, and is also an educational force. To none of the sources of culture is man more indebted than to this. Its elements exist within him, and its capacity increases with the increase of knowledge.

Language has been regarded too much as merely an objective thing, an outward adorning instead of a living, acting principle, whose elements are interwoven with the very fibers of thought. There is therefore a language of thought, as well as of word and action. No other science holds precisely the same relations to man, that this one holds. It is not only his medium, means and object of culture, but it is used in the investigation of every other science, and its study should be prosecuted in connection with every other.

Serious blunders, however, are frequently committed in the use of language as an educational force. It might, with respect to its meaning, uses, and philosophy, adopt the classification selected for education in general; viz., objective, transition, and subjective. Its first office is—aside from merely making known our wants — to give names to objects, actions and qualities. The second is to arrange and combine these so as to represent the relations existing among them, and to express the ideas suggested and developed under modes of culture. The third is to investigate the properties of language itself as an abstract or metaphysical study.

This latter department is usually presented first, so far at least as any scientific use is made of it; and this is one of the blunders to which allusion is made. The child should be allowed to pass through the other periods first, and to acquire the meaning and use of words and language, before the technicalities are arrayed before him.

Mathematics is an early and constant necessity. It is the great staple of the common school. As a disciplinary study, it perhaps has few, if any equals. It is similar in some respects to language, in that it has several departments which are exactly suited to the several wants of the child. Simple numbers and counting stand among the first, and correspond to names and the meaning of words. The concrete or mixed mathematics come next, and are best adapted to the capacity of the child in the transition state. There is just enough of the objective nature about this science, here, to enable the learner, without too great an effort of abstract reasoning, to cling to it; and yet enough of the subjective nature to lift the powers up into more exalted spheres of thought. It should be borne in mind here, that elementary geometry is one of the principal and most important and appropriate branches of mathematics for this period, and even for the one preceding it.

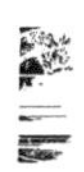

There is another department of science which has a peculiar fitness for this period. It is, perhaps, as much a moral force as an intellectual, and as much the result of the combined action of all the sciences, as a distinct science. We speak of *good manners.*

This period offers peculiar advantages for teaching this science; but, in too many instances, it is neglected. There is a spurious article, sometimes used as a substitute; but this only aggravates the evil. Good manners consist in pure thinking, pure speaking, and pure acting. It is, therefore, to a great extent, under the control of the teacher and parent, and serves as a most potent instrument, in his hand, for the accomplishment of good.

Article 3—Moral and Religious Forces.—At no period in life are the moral powers in a more critical condition than in this. This, perhaps, is not so much because their impressibility is any greater, but because of the many counteracting influences. The period is described briefly in chapter second, section 2, article 3.

The wants here are most palpable, and the condition would be most lamentable, were there no means of supplying them. But we are not at liberty, for a moment, to believe that so gross a blunder could be committed even by a wise man, much less by a Supreme Being.

It is our business now to inquire after the moral and religious forces, as means of culture.

Whatever excellence the moral forces described in Sec. 1, Art. 3, of this chapter possess, they are all thrown into the shade, when compared with one that can now be rendered available. We mean the Bible. It is not without its force in the objective period; but its sublimer truths, as a general thing, are of such a character, that their full force is not felt, until the mind acquires more maturity. If any one should inquire, why the Bible possesses such a power, as an educational instrument, we would reply that God made it, and he made man, having a full knowledge of his capacity, and of the best educational forces. He therefore made the Bible for the very purposes for which we propose to use it,—for the moral and religious culture of youth; and he, knowing all things from the beginning, is supposed to have a better understanding, as to what is best calculated for this purpose, than any merely human tribunal. No creeds, or confessions, or human devises, therefore, should be allowed to usurp its place. God made mind and matter. The one administers to the other. He also gave man his Revelation. The design is very obvious. Nature and revelation are designed to make man wiser, better, happier. This they do, when we allow them to act in harmony as they were designed; and when they are properly studied and their precepts practiced.

The Bible has stood the shock of error and falsehood, the combined opposition of infidelity leagued with darkness, for four thousand years; and yet its truths shine brighter to-day than ever before. Like the oak that is buffeted by the storm, these truths have taken deeper root in the soil of the human heart, and they lift their boughs higher and higher to scatter their fruits among the nations of the earth.

It is not our purpose to enter into a discussion upon the authenticity or inspiration of the Bible. We take for granted that it is Divine in its origin, and therefore true. We admit also, that there are some truths which, from their nature and origin, must be taken—

especially at this period—on trust or faith; for the powers of comprehension are too feeble, at their most exalted stage of development, to grasp the wisdom and foresight of God.

The Bible abounds in these truths. It often finds man struggling with the most difficult problems of existence and destiny. It finds him perplexed and confounded at the very threshold of science. But science and human philosophy are forever impotent to the great task of solving man's future destiny and happiness. He must needs have, therefore, a higher authority, a brighter light, and a surer pilot, an *infallible* guide. The Bible comes to him in these periods of doubt and uncertainty, and offers him those great moral truths, of a primal and universal nature, upon which he may rest his faith and belief with entire certainty. These become, to him, not only the basis of moral character, but a standard by which all moral truths are tested. Without such a basis, he is liable to fall a prey to every false doctrine that floats in the moral atmosphere.

The grounds for belief in such truths may at first appear weak, the light dim; but they soon grow strong, and the dim nebula is soon resolved by the telescope of faith, and reveals, to the astonished soul, stars of the first magnitude. These will light his path to more exalted conceptions and discoveries in the moral universe, until the whole firmament shall glow with a radiance before unknown.

In this period likewise, he is about making a transfer of his affections, from the objective world, to the subjective or spiritual. A thousand phantoms dance before him to lure him to doubt, and to win those affections from their legitimate sphere. The truths of the Bible step in and ask for belief, and to become a guide to the soul in this hour of solicitude. It is just as though God looked down upon the wanderer, groping his way in darkness, clinging to this thing awhile, and then to that, and said to him, "Here, child, is my hand. I know the way through this darkness." "It is light further on." "Hold to my hand, and you are safe." "My power is omnipotent, and there is no contingency for which I have not provided." Would it be wise to ask for evidence here, or to question his power and goodness? Because people *will* not believe, is the very reason they are always in the dark. *Bible Lessons*, therefore, are among the first and strongest educational forces; and they may be rendered available in uprooting a false belief, and of awakening, correcting and strengthening the moral powers of man.

Maxims and *Precepts* take a strong hold upon the mind at this period. They may be classed with the "facts," in the intellectual forces. Hence, moral truth may be readily conveyed through them. And nearly allied to these are *Biographical* and *Historical sketches*, especially when they relate to worthy characters and events. They not only gratify a thirst for the grand and heroic in action, but, when proper selections are made, they hold up worthy examples for imitation, and establish the heart in virtue.

But example alone will never make a child heroic or virtuous, any more than citing him to an example of extraordinary mathematical powers, would make him a mathematician. This may be useful as an incentive, but to make a man mathematical, he must practice mathematics. So to make a child benevolent, it is not enough to cite an example of this virtue; but to make him heroic, virtuous, or good in any sense, he must be practiced in these virtues.

Religion is a necessity growing out of the relation man sustains to his fellow man and to his God. He is therefore by nature religious, though his religion may be a curse to him. He *must* worship something; and the more exalted the object of his worship, the more exalted his moral powers, and indeed, all his powers. Hence it is wisdom to worship the highest possible object; and since God himself is the highest, the devotion naturally belongs to him. This is looking at the subject merely in the light of philosophy. Were we to examine it from the common standpoint, we should find the obligations vastly increased.

It is a matter of the profoundest wonder and regret, that a man should harbor in his heart any repugnance to religion. Religion joins the link severed by sin, and unites man again to his God. Who could, rationally object to this, especially after considering man's wretched condition without it, his apostasy from God, his father? Religion therefore proposes to reinstate man, and to furnish all rational supplies to his moral and religious nature.

Section 3—Subjective Period.

We come now to notice a new and higher class of instrumentalities for the education of man. But since these are of a more general character; and since the individual for whom they are intended is supposed here to have passed the most critical period in life, and, for the most part, from under the immediate influence of the teacher or parent,—it does not seem necessary that any thing more than a mere allusion to them be made.

Man is described in Chap. II, Sec. 3, as having arrived at that period when his powers are assuming their greatest strength and greatest activity. Of course their capacity and wants are changed, and they demand an additional and somewhat different class of forces or supplies.

Art. 1—Physical Forces.—Man's physical powers are more or less subject to habit; and are affected by antecedent influences. Too much importance can not, therefore, be attached to regular and *periodic labor.* Man needs some fixed occupation, in which his physical powers may find exercise. Unless this is provided, his energies, which were made for activity and enterprise, will be continually annoying him, and urging him into difficulty. Did parents realize this truth, they would not bring up their children in habits of idleness; neither would they fail to provide for them some fixed and regular physical employment, as well as mental, to be pursued in after life, as a means of securing a livelihood. The young man who is thus provided for, is comparatively safe; while the practice, on the part of parents or others, of hoarding up money for children, and anticipating all their wants and whims, thus depriving them of the exertion necessary to secure their happiness, is only providing for them the means of self-destruction.

What was said in Sec. 2, Art. 1, on the various kinds of labor, will apply with equal force here. Too much importance can not be attached to a proper division of time:—though this subject would come more particularly under modes of culture. Man is such a creature of habit, that, having once thoroughly adopted a course of conduct, it is quite easy to adhere to it through life. If he would, therefore, merely consider the physical good, he would set aside a certain portion of his time for labor, a certain portion for recreation, and another for rest. The recreation and rest are just as necessary in a physical sense, as the labor. In addition to these, there are certain other exercises which seem necessary. They might not at first seem to be physical forces yet such is their influence upon health, and upon physical culture generally, that we can not help regarding them as such. We refer to audible reading and singing. These, in connection with suitable devotional exercises, as preparatory to taking rest in sleep, will be found to exert a magic influence upon the health and happiness of man, to say nothing of their moral effects.

ARTICLE 2—INTELLECTUAL FORCES.—The intellectual powers of man at this period are supposed to have acquired sufficient strength and vigor, to grapple with the sterner truths and more occult mysteries of science. A proper pursuit of the physical sciences will have led to this result. They are the steps which lead from Nature up to her Author; and while they reveal wonders which seem too vast for the comprehension of finite minds, they are nevertheless not wanting in suggestions and results of a metaphysical character, which at once enlist the reasoning powers, and lead them to the higher walks of science. Hence *Mental Sciences*, in which these powers are permitted to turn their energies in upon themselves, and to trace the interesting relation between mind and matter, possess strong attractions, to one well inducted into this period.

As the field of thought and investigation grows

wider and more productive, a demand for increased facilities of communication arises. *Language*, in its higher departments, therefore, as Philology, Logic and Rhetoric, is intimately associated with mental science, and affords ample supply for this demand.

The higher *Mathematics* reveal to us some of the sublimest truths in nature; while at the same time they afford the discipline most needed.

Philosophy reveals its hidden treasures, and pours light in upon the astonished and delighted sense.

Poetry and the Fine Arts correct, elevate and refine the taste, and afford ample scope for the imagination.

The reasoning powers, not content with bare assumption, seek for demonstrative evidence of the great truths of Revelation; and are delighted to find that in *Evidences* of *Christianity*, they are all corroborated by the most conclusive testimony.

His country and his fellow men have claims upon the man. *Law* and *Civil Polity* expound the nature of these claims, and lead to a proper appreciation of his civil and political rights and obligations. Thus it will be observed that every want is provided for in this, the most exalted sphere of man's intellectual powers.

ARTICLE 3—MORAL FORCES.—*Moral Science* spreads out her truths and propositions, and invites to investigation. *Ethics* explains the principles that should regulate human conduct, defines man's social position, and lays down a code of rules to govern him in his actions. But whatever may be said of the value of these sciences, as educational forces, the Bible is the grand text book, both in morals and in religion. From it the excellencies of all forms of government, and of every system of true religion, have been derived. At this stage of man's growth, it either becomes a stone of stumbling, a rock of offense, or a beacon light to pilot him to the skies.

Biblical and Natural Theology, Psychology, and all that relates to God or the soul, are studies in which the mind finds special pleasure, and the moral powers gather additional strength.

True, most and indeed all the last named studies afford food for the intellectual powers. This is not only true of every other science, but it is in accordance with the doctrine heretofore taught, that those sciences best calculated for the culture of the moral and religious nature are either the best in themselves, or lead to the best ones for the cultivation of the intellectual powers; and that the very best for the culture of man's moral and intellectual nature, always point with unerring certainty to those exercises best suited for the culture of the body. So that we are safe in drawing the inference that our minds, souls and bodies were made to dwell together in this state of existence without conflict, and to be united in the happiest harmony hereafter.

What a glorious truth! What a sublime view it gives of the true science of education! Into what utter insignificance all the trifling plans and halfway modes of culture sink, when compared with the *true* mode. They fade as the light of the moon or stars before the beams of the rising sun. Let us be thankful, therefore, to the gracious giver of every good and perfect gift, that he has thus created us and all our surroundings in the most wonderful harmony, and with the most evident design of making us happy here and hereafter.

SYNOPSIS IV.

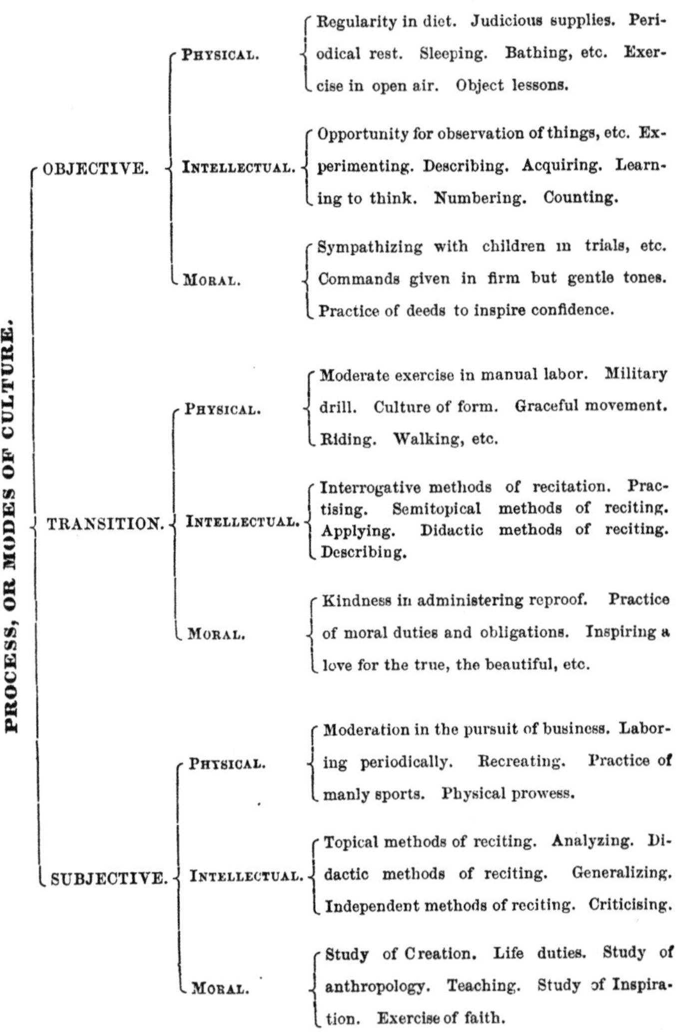

PROCESS, OR MODES OF CULTURE.

- OBJECTIVE.
  - PHYSICAL. — Regularity in diet. Judicious supplies. Periodical rest. Sleeping. Bathing, etc. Exercise in open air. Object lessons.
  - INTELLECTUAL. — Opportunity for observation of things, etc. Experimenting. Describing. Acquiring. Learning to think. Numbering. Counting.
  - MORAL. — Sympathizing with children in trials, etc. Commands given in firm but gentle tones. Practice of deeds to inspire confidence.
- TRANSITION.
  - PHYSICAL. — Moderate exercise in manual labor. Military drill. Culture of form. Graceful movement. Riding. Walking, etc.
  - INTELLECTUAL. — Interrogative methods of recitation. Practising. Semitopical methods of reciting. Applying. Didactic methods of reciting. Describing.
  - MORAL. — Kindness in administering reproof. Practice of moral duties and obligations. Inspiring a love for the true, the beautiful, etc.
- SUBJECTIVE.
  - PHYSICAL. — Moderation in the pursuit of business. Laboring periodically. Recreating. Practice of manly sports. Physical prowess.
  - INTELLECTUAL. — Topical methods of reciting. Analyzing. Didactic methods of reciting. Generalizing. Independent methods of reciting. Criticising.
  - MORAL. — Study of Creation. Life duties. Study of anthropology. Teaching. Study of Inspiration. Exercise of faith.

CHAPTER IV.

EDUCATIONAL PROCESSES.

A GENERAL description of the educational processes is all that will be attempted in this chapter, since the special modes will be brought under careful consideration in *Part Second*, under the head of *School-room Duties.*

It is thought, however, that a brief explanation of the accompanying diagram of Processes and Modes might be of service in the following manner:

1. It would show the adaptation of means to the ends to be accomplished, throughout every department of education.

2. It would show the possibility and practicability of classification in this as well as in any other science.

3. It would lead to a more careful examination of the subject, by the teacher, and a more rigid application of these principles, in the education of the young.

With this hope, we proceed at once to remark that the teacher, thus far, is supposed to have acquainted himself with the educational capacity and wants of the pupil; also with the nature and design of the educational forces and supplies; and now he is to investigate the modes of application.

While much that relates to these modes of application has, doubtless, been inferred from the discussions of the two preceding topics; nevertheless, they constitute, independently, no small share of the teacher's professional qualifications. They would fall under special didactics, were it not that they have, specifically, a theoretical character which we proceed to notice.

Section 1—Objective Period.

By reference to chapters second and third, and by a brief comparison of Capacity and Force, it will be seen that for every rational desire or want, whether physical, intellectual or moral, there is supposed to exist an appropriate supply. This truth is so palpable and so general, that it needs no argument or illustration. But the fact we now wish to impress upon the minds of parents and teachers is, that these supplies are often misdirected, and rendered not only useless, but injurious, simply from a want of knowledge and skill in managing them. The benevolent designs of the Creator are often thus thwarted by our stupidity; and his wisdom and goodness will seem to have been expended in vain; for of what service, for instance, would food, and the materials for clothing be, if man knew not how to use them, or knowing, if he abused them? Or of what service would be any of the countless blessings God has bestowed upon his children, if he had left them without the means of discovering their design and application? They would become curses to them, while their wants would mock and tantalize them. And scarcely less ruinous do they become when, through neglect or obstinacy, they refuse to appropriate them to their proper uses.

Is it not true, that men do actually starve in the midst of abundance, either from the want of knowledge, inclination or the means to procure supplies? But those isolated cases are by no means the ones most to be deplored. It is the improper use of these supplies and educational forces, that has filled the land with groans and suffering. These irregularities and abuses most frequently take their rise in causes least suspected by the young and inexperienced. Here again would appear the necessity for parents and teachers; and that these possess the requisite knowledge and skill, to direct the education of those committed to their care.

The education of the human being begins with the beginning of his existence; and it may not be inappropriate to say, that it will end only with his existence; or in other words, will never end.

Article 1—Physical Processes.—The child's education is first physical, so far at least as it falls under our observation and control. The first object therefore, would be to regulate the physical forces. These, in the brute creation, are regulated, for the most part, by instinct. Not so with the human animal. His first hours are spent with those supposed to have reason and experience. Where these are wanting or defective, he always suffers. His education being first physical, or mainly so, his physical habits should first receive attention. One of the first of these, and perhaps the first, after due attention to clothing, is to regulate the child's diet. How many unreasonable desires are engendered here, and how many whims begotten, by unwisely and inconsiderately yielding to and gratifying the imaginary wants of childhood! Reason and judgment should be eyes to the passions or affections, for these latter are stone-

8

blind. They are born blind. Were their impulses blindly followed, they would, in many cases lead to the destruction of the child. These wants of childhood, real or imaginary, thus injudiciously gratified, breed new desires; and these again multiply, until the brood overruns the bounds of all reason, and the whole being becomes a mass of misery and suffering.

Mothers, and those having charge of young children, should therefore regulate their diet with regard to *frequency*, as well as to quantity and quality. The too common practice of keeping their stomachs distended to their utmost capacity, either through excessive kindness or to gratify their whims, is a fruitful source of mischief, both to body and mind. And the evils are greatly aggravated when children are allowed to indulge their appetites, upon highly seasoned dishes or confectionaries. Is it any wonder that children, under this regime, become fretful, passionate, stupid, filthy and diseased? The stomach and digestive apparatus stand in as great need of occasional, and we might add, periodical relaxation, as do any other physical powers.

But this subject, in detail, is one of too great length to admit of a full discussion here. It covers, in fact, a great part of the subject of hygiene. We must therefore beg the reader to consult this science for the detail upon diet, as well as upon *sleeping*, *bathing* and kindred exercises.

Exercise in the nursery and in the open air, is of so much importance, however, as to demand a mere passing notice. A large share of the peevishness and irritability of children, might be prevented by attending to their wants—not their whims—in this respect.

Instead of feeding them on cakes and candies to keep them quiet, a better way would be, most generally, to give them healthy and appropriate exercise in the open air, which would bring into play those little muscles, bones and nerves, whose inactivity is the chief cause of the uneasiness.

Again: children are anxious to learn the names, qualities and uses of things. They must, therefore, as far as possible, be brought in contact with them; and this seems to be the chief employment and delight of young children. It affords an agreeable exercise, when properly directed, and an excellent substitute for that mischief which becomes so annoying to mothers.

This exercise might be arranged in the form of Object Lessons, in which names of objects, their qualities and uses, might be connected with the sports and amusements of the young; and this need not occupy as much of the mother's time as is usually spent in watching them, scolding them, and repairing damages committed by them.

But it must be borne in mind that in order to render any and all of these exercises and processes highly beneficial, they must be periodical, and their practice regulated and continued until the habits are formed and fixed. They thus become a kind of second nature, and proceed without any special effort. But with these hasty suggestions we leave this part of the subject, to notice briefly.

Article 2—Intellectual Processes.—With a bare mention of a few general principles and directions illustrative of the "chart," the reader is referred to chapter sixth, "Intellectual Culture," for a more extended view of this subject; and to *Part Second* for the particular mode of study, recitation, etc.

As we have already remarked, childrens' first lessons are taken from their surroundings. These have been described. Their opportunities for observation, therefore, should not be circumscribed. The practice of confining the young to one apartment, not only proves very irksome to them, but deprives them of one of the chief sources of intellectual culture.

Their powers of observation are usually very active, if not accurate, and constitute the chief means of acquiring knowledge. Therefore, let their eyes feast upon the beautiful in nature and art, and their ears be saluted with their harmonies.

The next step, and the one usually associated with observation, is that of experimenting with objects for the purpose of testing their qualities and ascertaining their uses. While the objects and exercises, to which young children are exposed, should not be so numerous and diversified as to distract their minds, or weary their feeble energies, yet they should be sufficiently numerous to afford that pleasing variety which their desires for novelty rationally demand.

At this period one of the greatest necessities belonging to childhood, arises; to wit: a want of suitable terms to express the ingathered stores of observation and experiment. Language is the demand.

One of the best means of cultivating the expressive powers, is to give frequent opportunities to children to relate their little experiences, and to describe the objects and actions which have fallen under their notice, observing to correct any inaccuracies and exaggerations that may arise. The imagination, or rather the fancy, may get the advance of judgment and discretion;

and unless watched carefully, children will form the habit of falsifying, or omitting important points in narrative, without realizing the enormity of the offense.

The practice of describing frequently and accurately, is useful, not only in the manner indicated above, but also as being one of the surest and most rapid methods of acquiring. In teaching, it is always best to encourage the child to tell all it knows, as a means not only of ascertaining its capacity and advancement, but as the best mode of inducing thought. It gives comparative accuracy, point and direction to the thinking powers, and renders the acquisitions much more easy and certain.

One of the first things to be done in intellectual training, is to accelerate and facilitate the early processes of thinking. Children, in the majority of cases, have not the ability to confine their thinking powers, and therefore need this aid in their early efforts, just as the child beginning to walk, needs aid in that exercise.

Among the many obstacles to successful thinking, weakness or want of mental force is one. This weakness sometimes arises from want of development, and at other times it is constitutional inaptitude. Another obstacle is mental aberration or want of concentration, which, by the way, is a species of weakness. Another is the formation of superficial and inattentive habits.

Most of these hindrances may be regarded as a species of disease, subject, however, to the control of the master; and they must all be removed before any successful study or thinking can be done. The best method of removing them, however, is the formation of right habits. The exercises used for the cure of these weaknesses, serve to establish their opposites.

Special methods for overcoming these difficulties and of establishing correct mental habits, will be described in Part Second, Chapter Second—STUDY.

ARTICLE 3—MORAL PROCESSES. — The moral treatment of children is a matter of extreme delicacy and care. A little mistake committed here often leads to great mischief. Their natures, susceptible of the slightest impression, can be molded into almost any shape the hand of the parent or teacher may chance to direct. Warm, ardent and unsuspecting, their belief and practices are subject to the almost unbounded control of their superiors. They are not, however, without their little griefs and sorrows, trials and temptations. These are not always appreciated by their elders. They are apt to be treated as trifles, and as unworthy of attention, simply because they happen to be viewed from a different, and it may be, a higher, stand-point. They, however, exist, and have upon the child the same effect that trials of a greater magnitude have upon children of a larger growth; and so with their labors and sports and other employments. These, to them, are what the genuine life-duties are to the adult, and are evidently sent before to prepare them for the sterner realities which must follow. They should therefore be treated with some consideration.

Nothing, perhaps, gives the teacher greater power over the child, either for good or for evil, than the exercise of sympathy with him in his joys or sorrows, in his labors and enterprises. We do not mean that he should descend to the same level with the child, or that he should indulge him in all or any of his whims. These he should correct. But we mean simply, that

he should not disregard this educational want, but make use of it for the moral elevation of the child. The very existence of it, and the activity of these feebler moral powers, constitute the occasion for such treatment, while their neglect may lead to ruin.

Again: children are to be controled; but how sad the abuse of this power! They are too frequently scolded and beaten in such a manner that they lose their self-respect and self-control; and come, by-and-by, to believe that they are the veriest vipers that ever crawled; and, to be consistent, they strive *to be* all they are *taken* to be. If there is one thing, in the treatment of children, that is of no possible benefit, or has not one redeeming quality; if there is one sin that is without excuse, and, for wickedness, almost without a parallel; one that is more offensive than all others,—that sin is passionate scolding. It is out of place every where. We venture the assertion that there never was an occasion, in all the education of a child, that rendered a resort to this practice necessary. It is purely gratuitous, and purely demoniac. Its effects upon the moral nature of the child are sad beyond comparison. It poisons every stream of happiness; it deadens every generous impulse; it destroys moral confidence, and discourages every high and noble aspiration. In fact, it is not only without its uses, but, for fruitful sources of evil, it is almost without any equal. Hence all commands should be given in firm but gentle tones. There are frequent occasions, however, in which it becomes necessary for the teacher to point out the shortcomings and vices of children in a very decided, and it may be, earnest manner; but can not this be done without resort to that tirade of abuse and faultfinding, which make up the sum total of scolding? Can not all the vices, to which children are addicted, be pointed out in a calm, dispassionate, yet earnest and loving manner? If there ever was a call for calmness, it is certainly here; and if they can not thus be pointed out, it will surely aggravate them to resort to abuse.

There is yet another mode of appealing to the moral nature of children, that claims a brief notice here. We mean the practice of those deeds of truthfulness and strict honesty in their presence, that will inspire their confidence and their love for the truth. Children should never be deceived, either by word or deed. They never should hear or practice a lie. They would then learn to fear and abhor it and kindred evils. But the practice of deceit and hypocrisy in their presence, has not only a tendency to destroy their confidence in the integrity of others, but leads them to practice the same vices themselves. The occasions on which this temptation arises, are very numerous. The child, for example, is often induced to comply with the wishes of the parent or teacher, without knowing the motives and means made use of, to secure such compliance. But the probability is, that he will find out some time; and then what a low estimate will he set on moral honesty! And some, again, have come to think that deceit may be practiced with impunity, provided a desirable object may be accomplished by it. Hence they govern on the principle of craft. They deceive their children into unwilling submission, esteeming it sufficient if the thing desired is done, without taking into account the means employed. Now the *manner* of obedience is often of greater moment than the obedience itself, or the object accomplished by it. "Behold to obey is better than sacrifice, and to hearken than the fat of rams," was Samuel's righteous sentence to a faltering and disobedient king; and the sequel shows the enormity of the sin of disobedience, as well as in what it consists. It is a safe rule, therefore, to practice nothing, in the presence of children, which would have a tendency to impair their confidence in you, or which you would not be willing should appear in them, as a part of their moral character.

Section 2—Transition Period.

We come now to notice the educational processes, appropriate to that period in life when the faculties are in a condition of change, or when the change is going on most rapidly.

The peculiarities and susceptibilities of these faculties have been briefly described under the head of "Educational Capacity," Chapter Second, Section 2; and their supplies under the head of "Educational Forces," Chapter Third, Section 2. It now remains to discuss briefly the modes of treatment, reserving the special applications for *Part Second*.

ARTICLE 1—PHYSICAL PROCESSES.—Many of the modes and exercises, prescribed for the objective period, will have their full force here, varied slightly however, to suit the nature of the wants.

Moderate exercise in manual labor, though an old-fashioned, and by some, almost forgotten practice, is nevertheless one of the surest and safest modes of securing healthy physical development, that ever was invented. Indeed, it can scarcely be said to be invented, since it always existed as a necessity. It can not therefore be laid aside without injury. We venture the assertion, that if this one simple practice were persistently followed, in the education of children, they would be delivered from untold woes, miseries, vices, bad habits and bad health. Idleness is the parent of vice ; and vice strikes at the very root of social order and happiness. The faculties at this age—and indeed at every other—seek, yea, *demand* activity and employment. If this demand is not heeded, supplies will be sought from such quarters, and in such a manner, as to bring with them habits and diseases that will poison the very fountains of health and happiness.

The importance of labor of various kinds, as the means of securing the healthiest development of all the physical powers, has been alluded to in several places. Its objects, as an educational force, are often defeated, however, by injudicious management. To be effective, either as a profitable or as a healthy exercise, it must, for this period especially, be periodical, and not too severe or too long continued. Its purposes as an educational instrumentality, are not answered by working hard for a few days, weeks, or even months, and then refraining for as long, or even a longer time, any more than the purposes of eating and sleeping are answered by adopting a similar course with them. All the exercises should be periodical, and all the habits regulated, if we would render them useful.

The effects of too severe and long-continued labor at an early age, are most strikingly exhibited in the miserable sickly condition of children in the mines and factories of Great Britain; and many in the United States and other countries suffer from similar causes. Their powers, too heavily taxed, fail to attain their

full development, but hasten into an unhealthy maturity, and as rapidly decay.

But labor alone, let it be ever so wisely arranged, does not accomplish, for the child of this age, all that is desirable. Unless the exercises are varied, there is constant danger of imposing too much on some of the powers, while others may be suffering for want of a due supply. Hence the many instances of crooked and deformed persons among the laboring classes.

For a school exercise, the Military Drill, or something similar to it, as practiced in some of our best schools, is an excellent means of correcting many of these abuses. It gives the child command over his physical powers, and promotes promptness and precision in his movements. It cultivates the erect posture and manly form, and prevents, in a measure, the formation of those slovenly and disagreeable habits, so liable to be contracted at this age.

The practice in graceful movement of the body, such as is usually secured in a calisthenium, or, where this advantage is not enjoyed, such as may be adopted in any school or family, will be found useful in furnishing to girls the advantages which the boys enjoy in the drill or gymnasium. The bodies of girls need as much active exercise as those of the boys, though differing somewhat in kind. Indeed there seems to be a greater necessity, in their case, for special arrangements, since their modes of life, and kinds of employment, do not afford them the advantages which boys have.

The practice of making the physical training of youth—as far, at least, as it relates to their bodily movements—a part of their family and school education, would not only prevent the contraction of dis-

eases and physical suffering, but it would supersede the supposed necessity of employing a dancing-master, and the evils and miseries arising from committing this part of the education of children to the hands of those who are too frequently destitute of the first principles of sound morality.

Riding, either on horseback or otherwise, walking, rowing, etc., etc., are healthy exercises; but to be rendered most serviceable, they should be conducted under the direction of a master; since many of these physical exercises are rendered useless, and in some instances positively hurtful, for the want of proper skill in managing them. But more particular directions will be given under the head of Recreation, Part II., Chap. v.

Art. 2.—Intellectual Processes.—The modes of intellectual culture are so numerous and well known, that we shall only allude to a few of the more general and important principles involved in them.

They should differ from those of the objective period in the following particulars:

1. They should cover a wider field; and should address the faculties of the understanding and judgment more directly.

2. They should cultivate the habits and powers of independent thinking and acting.

3. They should cultivate the expressive powers, and originality, as they relate to descriptions and the uses of knowledge.

Hence the Interrogative, Semitopical, and Analytic methods of recitation may be used here, as well as corresponding modes of study, etc.

The first is the one most appropriate in the objective period, but should not be entirely abandoned here.

The topical method is the one most appropriate for the subjective period, since it throws all the labor of recitation, etc., upon the pupil, he being at an age when helps are unnecessary. But in the transition period, the pupil is supposed to be in a state in which he requires both the assistance of the questions in recitation, etc., and also of the topics,—the one to enable him to stand, the other to induct him into the more independent modes of investigation.

It will be remembered, however, that these principles and directions are general; and that, while they will be found true in the main, many seeming exceptions will arise.

Article 3—Moral Processes. — It is a well established fact that discipline is a necessary ingredient in the education of man; that without it, he would be an untamed animal, a fit associate for wild beasts and savages. His powers would be of little service to himself, or any of the race.

The period in which we are now considering man, in a moral and religious point of view, is one of decided interest. If there is one period in the education of the child, in which he needs the special guidance of mother, father or teacher, it is this. His moral powers are just now assuming that shape and direction which are to give character to the man; at the same time, they are beset on all sides by temptation, and are struggling against a host of evil influences, that break in upon them from every quarter. These unassisted powers, for the most part, are unequal to bear the severity of this rude shock, and they often fall an easy prey to vice.

There is no period, either, in which the desire to

throw off parental restraint is so strong. The boy of eleven or sixteen thinks it unmanly to obey his mother; and the little miss puts on airs that would do credit (?) to the maid of forty. But wholesome discipline will, in the majority of cases, ward off these evils, and will make use of these temptations to strengthen the moral powers. This discipline may be derived from various sources, and may apply alike to the moral, intellectual or physical powers. We propose to speak of but two sources, together with modes of administering and receiving it.

1. Parental discipline and influence.
2. That which is derived from other sources.

Obedience is an obligation due from the child to the parent, no less in this period than in the preceding one. This will be admitted by all except those who run wild upon new theories and new doctrines.

We shall not stop, therefore, to discuss either the grounds or the nature and extent of this obligation. It is enough for our purpose to know that it exists, and that it is one of the first and most important lessons to be learned by the child. There are, in a popular sense, two kinds of obedience, the voluntary and the involuntary. The voluntary is the genuine; but it often happens that we are compelled to resort to the latter as an expedient to secure the former. But it never should be relied upon. It is only a substitute, to be thrown aside whenever the genuine can be made to take its place. Hence when requests are made, orders issued or commands given (all these forms are admissible, but not all under the same circumstances), it may be necessary to resort to the latter first, in order to maintain authority; but the whole transaction, request and all, should, if possible, be repeated for the purpose of securing the willing obedience; for that is not really obedience which is performed unwillingly. It is forced submission rather. Many mistake the means for the end, however, and satisfy themselves with mere submission, while the heart may be in a state of absolute rebellion. To leave it in that condition, is to cultivate a cowardly, morose and treacherous disposition.

What wonder then that so few obey from proper motives; or that deceit, treachery and falsehood everywhere abound, when so little genuine obedience is secured in childhood!

Kindness in administering reproof or correction is indispensable in right moral training. Like produces its like, no less in the moral world, than in the physical. The parent or teacher is apt to arouse the same spirit in the child, he manifests himself. Perhaps no greater abuse obtains any where in dealing with children than at this very place. The vindictive spirit is so apt to manifest itself, that many are incapable of administering reproof or punishment, without yielding themselves to its control. And then again, some think it not worth while to act, so long as their wrath is not kindled; and therefore, always wait until it reaches the exploding point, before they open the battery; and then, woe to the luckless wight that happens to be the object of vengeance!

Now, it is needless to say this is all wrong. It would be wrong in the management of dumb animals; much more then, in the management of children.

2. That discipline which is derived from other sources, will now claim attention. The willing and cheerful obedience, rendered in early life, the lessons of submission and privation there learned fit man for

the life-struggle which awaits him in the world. They give him power to conquer his enemies, having first subdued the worst one he will be likely to meet, viz., himself, a foe too, with whom few, if any, can grapple single handed. But if discipline be administered in kindness, though it be severe, and if we are taught that it comes from the hand of our best friend, and that it is inflicted for our good, it will not arouse those vindictive and rebellious feelings, but rather their opposites; and we can look up in meek submission and bless the hand that afflicts us.

This spirit will ease the hand of affliction, and will mitigate much of the rigors of punishment, making it even for the present, joyous and not grievous. This is the kind of discipline that should be exercised in our families and schools, to prepare their inmates to meet these trials; for meet them they must, since they are but the common lot of humanity. Why not then prepare for them at a time when the severity of the strokes may be lightened by parent or teacher. It will be too late in most cases to begin when these days and advantages are past. "In time of peace, prepare for war," was a wise maxim given by a distinguished statesman, and which is not without its bearing upon this subject. In time of youth prepare for life; in time of life prepare for death; for it is only after this period that life's harvest is gathered, and we begin to live in earnest.

Again: the practice of moral and religious duties and obligations, as the surest means of developing moral power, is a subject of such importance, as to compel a passing notice here, though its practical bearings will be reserved for another place. We pass it therefore, with this single remark, that all the

moral precepts and examples combined, and enforced with the most scrupulous care, can never equal the actual practice of these duties by the children themselves. There is a tangibility, a force, a meaning and a power about them, when practiced by the children themselves, which take right hold of the heart and habits, and make them feel what moral elevation there is in doing good. They learn from their own experience, from their own feelings, that "it *is* more blessed to give than to receive;" and that it is better to do a good deed, than to theorize on goodness.

Another mode of moral culture claims a word of explanation; i. e., the process of inspiring a love for the Beautiful, the True and the Good. This love of the beautiful etc., is an innate affection. It usually commences with objective beauty, and advances through all the stages, until the full development of the subjective. There is usually an exact correspondence between the outer and the inner world, between the objective and the subjective. The objective, if properly directed, leads into the subjective. The cultivation of objective beauty not only indicates the degree of subjective development, but will, when the powers are well regulated, constitute the very best and most direct means of cultivation. Thus: if a boy has been taught to love a rose, for instance, and really to appreciate the outer forms of beauty and purity, his inner nature seeks their counterparts; he will therefore more easily be taught to love the truth, and the morally beautiful, since these are counterparts of the former. Ugliness and deformity are begotten of depravity, and are fit accompaniments of vice and vulgarity. Hideousness and a lie are both born of

the same parents, and are both monsters. They are inseparable companions, notwithstanding falsehood and deceit may dress themselves in angel garbs, as they most frequently do; but this only renders "their deformity more deform." They are unlovely and unloved, save by corresponding natures. But on the other hand, goodness, mercy, peace, purity, humility, honesty, integrity and every christian virtue, are the legitimate offspring of all that is morally beautiful and sublime, and the inseparable associates of all that is really beautiful in nature and art. It is the province of education to develop these forms of beauty, and to regulate the outer and inner world, so that these elements of living, loving beauty and truth, shall assimilate and form one grand and harmonious system of loveliness.

Section 3—Subjective Period.

The Subjective Processes next claim attention. Here, as in the case of the instrumentalities, there seems to be but little necessity for special directions. The individual is supposed to be passing beyond the more immediate influence of the family and school. He is now coming forth to take his stand beside his fellows, in the battle of life; and the great problem, whether he shall lose or win, is about to be solved. He becomes a man of business; for if he is educated, there will be no margin left for inglorious ease, or vile and sensual pleasure.

He is still, however, a mortal man, a physical, intellectual and moral being: and these qualities are now assuming a decided and positive character. They are not therefore, without special interest; and in order to preserve them in as perfect a state as possible, and to transmit them unimpaired to posterity, they demand special treatment.

ARTICLE 1—PHYSICAL PROCESSES.—In addition to what has been suggested in another place, as appropriate to physical processes, others of a higher order might now be introduced, in view of the new relationship sustained. Business, therefore, becomes a pursuit. The physical powers are supposed to have been trained to some avocation, in which they will be called upon to act in one capacity or another. The danger is, therefore, where the business is of such a character as to demand physical labor, that, in the outset, since the desire for success is usually so great, the demand made upon these powers will be greater than they can satisfy, without sustaining an injury. Moderation, therefore, in the pursuit of business, becomes necessary to success. Indeed, moderation is necessary every where, but chiefly here. Labor becomes a drudgery if this precaution is not observed; and that which was intended as a blessing for man, becomes a curse. Of course, this precaution would be uncalled for in the case of those drones in society, whose excessive moderation excels their wisdom. But these cases are exceptions, involving the condition of those who may be laboring under the disease of laziness, the removal of which will depend much upon its character and the remedies employed.

Again: Moderation in the pursuit of business will be most likely to cultivate the same virtue in the desires and modes of life. Extravagance is the bane of social happiness. It has filled the world with misery. It is an irregularity that strikes at the very root of the tree of domestic peace. It entails wretchedness upon what might otherwise be happy families. It is a fruitful source of intemperance, bankruptcy, and villainy. It can only be corrected by adopting its opposite.

But the physical powers yield willingly, nay, gladly to whatever reasonable demands are made upon them, provided they are informed in due time, so as to make preparation; or, in other words, provided the habit is formed. Hence, here, as in other periods, labor should be periodical. This will not only render it more pleasant, but more profitable. When this habit is once thoroughly established, these powers will not ask to be released, but will always manifest uneasiness until they are permitted to return to their accustomed employment. This is proved by the experience of thousands.

But how miserable is that poor wretch who has nothing to do! His own physical energies tormenting him, his conscience goading him, and a world of labor upbraiding him, no wonder that he seeks, in dissipation, to drown these unwelcome visitations. Out upon all such vagabonds, wherever found; whether they crawl amid the slime and filth of poverty, or cling like leeches to the living body of industry, or wallow in luxurious ease! Let us have a world of workers, and then we shall have a happy world.

These powers also demand recreation, which may consist either of a change of physical exercise, or of diversions of a lighter sort. In either case, it should be taken after the physical energies have become somewhat exhausted from the labors of the day. It should also be taken amid pleasant associations, so that the mind may lend its aid to invigorate the body. Hence the practice of manly sports for those whose

sedentary or mental habits deprive them of the requisite amount of physical exercises; and those lighter diversions, more of a mental and moral character, for those whose physical powers have been taxed during the day, seem most appropriate.

These diversions, however, should be guarded against excesses into which they are liable to run. They should be regulated, therefore, as to time, place, and manner, and never allowed to infringe upon other duties.

ART. 2—INTELLECTUAL PROCESSES.—Our next topic is the general discussion of modes of intellectual culture best suited for the subjective period.

As the individual advances in true education, he requires less and less teaching. His powers, once awakened and properly directed, go forward per force of their own native energies, until, by and by, all the helps being removed, the man stands up a living, acting, positive being, fitted alike for the joys and sorrows, the reverses and successes, the conflicts and triumphs of this life.

His intellectual powers demand continued activity; and, like the physical powers, unless this is afforded them, they fall into decay. The world of science and art, into which they are about to be introduced, furnishes ample scope and the necessary materials for such activity.

The idea that an education, i. e., the full development of these powers, can be acquired in a few years, by attending college, is absurd. The preparation, indeed, may be made there, though this itself is not always done; the tools may be sharpened there, but their edge must be tried and their temper tested in subsequent contest with actual duties. And not only so, but the tempering and developing of these powers are effected in this life struggle. The efforts must be continuous, and the acquisitions constant.

The false notion alluded to above, needs correcting. It is a mischievous one. The young man comes to believe that when he graduates he is educated, and hence entitled to some consideration. And so he is; but he gets the idea that he is then ready to commence in the world, and that it has some special opening for him. He thinks that said world is under an obligation to receive him *fresh* from the arms of his "Alma mater," and to compensate him for his long years of toil. He thus makes up his bill of items, and presents his claims; but the heartless world tells him "to tarry at Jericho until his beard be grown," or to prove his claim, and to make good his title, and then to come, and it will listen to him. If he obey this admonition, he may succeed. If he disregard it, he will be apt to meet with disappointment, and to fall back among that numerous class of splendid failures who graduate for a name.

But what are the modes of continuing this education, which we have supposed to be commenced and carried forward successfully thus far? One of the best methods of promoting healthy thought, so far as it relates to the school, and of introducing the learner to the higher modes of investigation, is the method of study and recitation by Topics. It cultivates that manly independence and self-reliance which constitute so large a share of the necessary elements of success. But a fuller description of this mode will be given in another place.

The practice of Analysis also, now becomes inviting;

and the dry abstractions of science yield before this powerful battery of thought, as the snow and the ice yield under the influence of the sun's rays.

The Generalization processes follow; and every thing learned assumes its proper place in the superstructure of knowledge, until the whole stands out in fair proportions and beautiful outline, a symmetrical temple of truth.

Criticism also forms a part of the modes of learning and teaching; and texts and authors are examined with care. Every thing is submitted to the severest scrutiny before it is admitted into the mind as a part of the intellectual fabric.

Independent modes of teaching, and the inductive and deductive processes of investigating, form a part of those mental processes by which the individual is carried forward into the higher department of science and literature.

Art. 3—Moral Processes.—At no period in man's education do his moral powers claim more attention than when they are assuming that fixedness which gives the various shadings to moral character. A *man*, in the true sense of that word, standing out in all his manliness, and exhibiting these moral qualities, presents one of the finest objects for contemplation of which the mind can conceive. It would seem that those powers were given man, that in him might shine the noblest perfections of creation.

But what a fearful and melancholy picture is presented, when we behold these powers dragged down from their lofty position, and made the slaves and sport of man's sensual desires! It would seem that no sadder phase of human wretchedness could be exhibited; that no darker shade could be thrown over the scene; for these powers, having been created to occupy the highest seat in the human mind, are subject, when once dethroned, to the saddest reverses, and generally descend to the lowest depths. Abundant provision, however, has been made, both in the physical and in the metaphysical world, for reclaiming and perpetuating these powers.

The study of the works of Creation, as exhibited in the universe of matter, has claims to a high position among educational processes. Man here has an excellent opportunity of viewing and comparing his own insignificance with the stupendous works of God, which overpower his mind. Under the influence of these feelings, he cries out with the Psalmist, "When I consider thy heavens, the work of thy fingers, the moon and the stars which thou hast ordained; what is man that thou art mindful of him, or the son of man that thou visitest him?" He traces the finger of God in the works of creation, as exhibited in the most delicate pencilings of the smallest flower, and in the blushing hues of the rainbow: in the minutest atoms of matter up through all the forms and grades of creation, until he arrives at the very presence-chamber of Omnipotence, where he bows with meek reverence before Jehovah. He worships, he adores. This gives him a more exalted view of life duties and obligations; and he studies the relations he sustains to his fellow men and to his God.

But the study of man himself is a most wonderful subject; and if rightly pursued, will lead to the most exalted conclusions in reference to the wisdom and goodness of the Creator.

We find man compounded of the strangest extremes: "mortality and immortality; life and death; soaring loftiness and humbling littleness,—an ally at once of earth and heaven." And yet this is man, distinct from all other beings, and destined to an endless existence. These truths can not fail to produce the profoundest humility in a mind properly imbued with the principles of early piety.

Again: teaching offers a fine opportunity for the pursuit of this subject. The study of man, his physical and metaphysical nature, their wonderful union, the adaptation of means to ends, the modes of culture, the harmony in the laws of mind and matter, and all that pertains to human culture, can not fail to impress the learner with awe and reverence.

But the study of Inspiration, as a moral process, possesses merits to which no other can lay claims. If man's reason, assisted thus by the light of science, can approach so near to God, in the universe of matter, and if it can trace his handiwork in the metaphysical world, with what clearness can it apprehend these truths, when inspiration pours in its floods of light upon them! And if the study of the universe of matter and of mind, and all that pertains to them, from the minutest atom or spark of intelligence up through all the grades of creation, until we lose sight of the created, in the effulgence of the Creator, fills the mind with such astonishment, and calls forth such profound reverence and adoration, what must be its overwhelming sensations, when it approaches that strange and mysterious sacrifice, upon which angels gazed with astonishment, the sacrifice that redeemed

the world? Here the feeble powers droop their wings. They can soar no higher; and the trembling soul, overcome with this exhibition of vengeance and mercy joined, falls prostrate before its Maker. With unutterable fullness, it looks up through this wilderness of mystery, and with feelings of mingled awe and love, it adores and worships that God who planned and executed the scheme of creation and of redemption. The living faith now takes hold upon this scheme, and strengthens itself in the promises left on record for it, and lives and grows in the beatitudes of Spirit life.

It is thus, that, through all these periods and processes, the child, the youth, the man, passes until he ripens,into that noble being of power and excellence; or, by an opposite course, he renders all these blessings so many curses, and flings defiance in his Maker's face.

CONCLUSION.

Thus, it will be observed, that the whole subject of Education, or Human Culture, resolves itself into a certain science. The whole curriculum of duties, as well as the sciences to which they relate, may be so arranged as to meet the exact wants of the human being at every stage of his progress.

The periods, to which allusion is made, are distinctly marked in the history of every educated man and woman, not so much, however, by the sole activity of any faculty or sets of faculties, or by the exclusive condition of the mind or body, as by the preponderance of objective or subjective manifestations and influences.

The transition is not so much a distinct period as it is a mere condition of mind and body, when the change from one period to the other is most marked and rapid. Indeed, there is no distinction in the essential characteristics of the essence of mind, at any particular age, only that produced by its manifestations through a material organism.

The ultimate principle of intelligence is strictly a unit; the difference in kind, both as to quantity and quality, being more the result of physical causes, and different degrees of maturity, than of any original distinction in the character of the thinking principle itself, at its several stages of growth. It is the same intelligent agent, whether we regard it while looking out through the senses, upon the diversified forms and groups of physical phenomena, or turning its energies inward, and contemplating those more wonderful groupings of thought, affection and will, and threading the more intricate mazes of reasoning, imagination and abstraction.

SYNOPSIS V.

PHYSICAL EDUCATION.

- **HAND CULTURE.**
  - BLACKBOARD EXERCISES.
    - Copying lines. Angles. Geometrical figures. Drawing pictures. Familiar objects. Drawing maps. Familiar places.
  - SLATE EXERCISES.
    - Copying letters. Numerical figures. Copying and forming words representing things. Copying and forming sentences. Composition.
  - CARD EXERCISES.
    - Painting and coloring pictures and maps. Perspective and landscape drawing. Architectural drawing. Painting.
- EXCURSION AND LABOR.
  - FIELD EXERCISES.
    - Botanical, Geological, Mineralogical expeditions. Zoological and Entomological expeditions. Topographical and Historical expeditions.
  - MANUAL EXERCISES.
    - Agricultural and Horticultural pursuits. Mechanical and Architectural pursuits. Commercial and general business pursuits.
  - EXPERIMENT & MANIPULATION.
    - Chemical and Philosophical experiments. Classification of specimens. Arrangement of cabinets.
- GYMNASTICS.
  - ATHLETIC EXERCISES.
    - Walking. Running. Skating. Drilling. Climbing. Leaping. Vaulting. Balancing. Fencing. Swimming, etc.
  - VOCAL EXERCISES.
    - Breathing. Exploding Sounds. Reading. Declaiming in Concert. Singing. Chanting.
  - CALISTHENIC EXERCISES.
    - Arm movements.
    - Body movements.
    - Feet movements.

CHAPTER V.

PHYSICAL CULTURE.

REMARKS.

WE propose in the three following chapters to give a more condensed and connected view of the three departments of education, viz.: Physical, Intellectual, and Moral and Religious, without special reference to any particular periods, but chiefly in those in which the child is under parental and school training.

This might seem, at first view, like a repetition of the topics heretofore discussed; but upon careful examination, it will be found that while the same principles are brought forward in hasty review, the object is to show their practical utility and more immediate bearing upon the exercises of the school-room and the family. The former chapters have dealt chiefly with the theoretical part of education; because it is more in harmony with the subject, and better suited to the purposes of a text-book, to dispose of the theory first.

The following three chapters will discuss the more general modes of teaching, as applicable both to the school and the private circle. And so far as they relate to the theory, they may be regarded discursive; and so far as they relate to practice, they may be regarded didactic. They will sustain the same relation

to the theory, that the particular recitations in Reading, Arithmetic or English Grammar would sustain to school-room duties; and hence they may be regarded as supplementary.

Argument.

We begin with man's physical nature first, because he is, in an educational sense, a physical being before he is a moral or intellectual being; and secondly, because it is through the physical organism that we approach the mental and moral faculties, especially in childhood.

The following inquiries might arise in the minds of some, viz.:

1. Is there any special need of physical culture?

2. If so, will not this necessity provide for itself in the ordinary duties of life?

3. Is there any special necessity of connecting it with, and making it a part of, an educational system?

We shall endeavor to answer these questions in the order in which they occur, and then proceed to show the modes of application.

The answer to the first, perhaps, could best be given by a reference to the maladies, imbecility and physical suffering of the human race. If it be objected that these are the necessary results arising out of man's peculiar relations, we answer, that this is true no farther than it relates to violated law at some period; that suffering is not necessary to man's happiness (and he was not made for misery), any further than it goes to correct his irregularities, and to call him back to the path of duty; that its mission is accomplished when this is effected; and that it would finally disappear, if the causes which produce it were removed.

It might, therefore, be pertinent to the point in hand, to inquire how far a correct physical education would go to reduce physical suffering.

Educating in this, as in any other sense, means developing, strengthening, fortifying, and preparing for the fullest and freest activity; and, consequently, for the largest, the most perfect and prolonged enjoyment. This, therefore, would cut off just as much physical suffering; since suffering and disease diminish and disappear in the same proportion in which physical development takes place, the one being incompatible with the other. This point then is settled; and it goes far to settle the main issue,—the necessity of physical education.

It might be further added, however, by way of a conclusion, that, since deformity, disease, and suffering do exist; and that—as it has been demonstrated, not only theoretically, but practically—they disappear proportionally as correct physical development takes place, other things being favorable; and that this last result is secured just in proportion to the right application of physical exercises and correct treatment,—therefore physical exercises, and all that appertains to correct physical treatment, are not only the best antidotes for physical suffering as it now exists, but the best possible means for developing the powers, and fortifying them against the encroachment of disease, and preparing them for the largest and fullest enjoyment. This is further substantiated by actual experiment with individuals and communities. There is, therefore, special necessity for physical education.

2. Will not this necessity be provided for in the discharge of the ordinary duties of life?

We answer, *Is it?* This necessity *may* thus be supplied, but is it in the ordinary business transactions? Are there no improprieties, not to say enormities, committed in allowing children to have their own way in physical exercises? Might not many of these irregularities be corrected in training children after a philosophical system? Are their physical powers, in ordinary education, developed to their fullest extent, dur- the time in which their mental powers are receiving attention? Are there not diseases rather, and sufferings, planted at a very early age in childhood, both in the school and in the family, which could be prevented by a proper knowledge of the means and skill to apply them? Are there any good reasons for supposing that man's physical powers would provide for themselves without this wisdom and special direction, any more than his intellectual powers would? Do they possess instincts or native intelligence to direct themselves in their development, which other powers do not possess? Finally, do they not seek activity, and in consequence of the urgency of this demand, and for the want of proper restraint and direction, do they not run into bad practices and adopt vicious habits that bring speedy destruction upon themselves and their possessors?

Until these and similar difficulties are disposed of, in such a way as to show the uselessness of system and arrangement in training these powers, we shall claim that there is just as much necessity for special education, in this department of man's nature as in any other; and especially is this true at that tender age when they are most impressible, and consequently most exposed.

3. Is there any necessity for connecting it with, and making it a part of, an educational system?

To this question we reply briefly, that since there is no incompatibility between physical exercises and mental activity, but that, when properly directed, the one promotes the other; and since there is no antagonism between any of the faculties and the forces that develop them; and since it does not become necessary to sacrifice one single physical power or one real enjoyment in order to educate the mind; therefore, we conclude that there *is* a special necessity for connecting physical training with, and making it a part of an educational system. All the departments of man's nature were made to grow, the one with the other, and not one at a time, much less that the development of the one should demand the sacrifice of the other, as the popular practice, in many instances, would seem to indicate.

It is a base reflection upon the wisdom and goodness of the Creator, to suppose that he made body and mind, and placed them in such intimate relationship, and yet that he demands that one should be sacrificed for the benefit of the other. It is a glaring inconsistency, whose parallel is not found any where else in the wide universe; and yet this very thing is practiced every day, in the family, in the school, and in the college. It is, however, an irregularity that a true and liberal system of education would correct.

We propose, therefore, in order to show the practicability and importance of exercising all the faculties harmoniously and simultaneously, with proper intervals of change and rest, to present the subject of Physical Culture first, as the surest means of meeting, not only the physical wants, but the mental and moral also. All three of these departments should be started

together, and kept together throughout the whole course of education.

PHYSICAL EXERCISES.

We shall proceed in the following order:

1. *Hand Culture*, its varieties and uses.
2. *Excursion and Labor*, their varieties and uses.
3. *Gymnastics*, the varieties and uses.

Section 1—Hand Culture.

The hands are the great instruments of physical labor and enterprise. Their great activity as well as the great demand for their services, indicate their utility, and the necessity of educating them. They are among the first of the physical powers (for they are instruments of power) in motion; and their continued and unwearied exertions, as well as the relation they sustain to matter and mind, as the instruments and media of tactual knowledge, should teach us the importance of providing employment for them at a very early day. Their activity, and consequent demand for employment, are incessant. And unless this demand is met, and appropriate employment furnished, they are pretty sure to find that which is inappropriate, or else to languish in hopeless idleness. In either case a lamentable injury is sustained.

It becomes necessary then, if we follow out the leading idea of this work, to inquire, 1st, into the nature of the educational capacity or want; 2dly, to seek the appropriate supplies; and 3dly, to make the proper application.

The first has been done briefly in the preceding remarks. Their further wants will appear as we proceed. It is pertinent, therefore, to inquire in the 2d place, what kind of employment is best suited to

satisfy these wants, and at the same time to accomplish the other results, viz.: their healthy development, keep them out of mischief, open the way to the mind, and, at the same time, train them to useful employment.

It has been remarked, that children are great imitators. And so they are. They not only imitate the actions of those with whom they associate, but they have an equal desire to imitate the forms of objects with which they are surrounded, at the same time that they are becoming acquainted with them; for the desire to become acquainted is the ulterior cause of imitation, in the great majority of cases. Nothing affords children greater pleasure, at the time when their hands become uneasy and anxious for employment, and sometimes very annoying to mothers and teachers, than for them to represent, by pictures and other means, the objects of nature and art, with which they are brought in daily contact. In other words, they love to make pictures. They are imitators, or mechanics; and though their first products are rude, yet age and practice will improve them. Their ideas of form, size and fitness have just been awakened, and like other newborn powers, exercise gives them pleasure. They love to give expression to these ideas; and this desire is so great sometimes as to lead to mischief, especially if not directed. Hence the propensity among boys, that have not had this desire properly cared for, to mark and cut, deface and even to destroy objects within their reach. This is only a perverted desire, the last being a distorted one. This may happen, too, very early in life; even before any other manifestations of a similar kind have

made their appearance. It is nevertheless the perverted desire. Who perverted it, is another question. It is enough for our purpose to know that it is so, and that even this bad state of the case can, in a great measure, be corrected.

There is a picture period, or a period of representative knowledge, into which every learner enters at an early age; and the acquisitions and development are more easily made through this source, than through any other. It is the earlier part of the Objective period. Tangible knowledge or objects themselves are first, second, their models and pictures; third, their names, etc. Every child that arrives at maturity, passes through this period. The same great truth is observable in the process of civilization and enlightenment of nations. They are first objective in their modes of representing knowledge, the object itself conveys the idea; then the picture performs the same office, then the word, etc. Hence the various stages of the development of written language. In the ruder stages of society we find first the pictorial; then, as civilization advances, the hieroglyphic, the verbal, the syllabic, and the alphabetic, or the highest and most philosophic mode of expressing thoughts. Thus it will be seen, that in respect to representative knowledge, a child passing from infancy through all the stages of growth, and a nation of people passing from Barbarism to Civilization, etc., have many peculiarities in common. But, in order to make the acquisitions more permanent and useful, they should be copied, or represented. This serves to fix it in the mind, and at the same time affords the right kind of employment.

Now observe the harmony and wisdom of the design. The hands, at this period, are full of activity, and must have employment, or they are continually running into mischief. The mind is in that particular condition, in which it craves that very kind of knowledge the hands alone can furnish. The hands therefore, ask to do the thing which the mind wants done, and which can be done by no other instruments. Why not then, let them work for each other, and prevent the countless evils that arise from their separation and consequent inactivity? But what exercises are best adapted to these wants? For the nursery and home training, children should have a plentiful supply of models, pictures, etc., as objects of imitation; and slates, cards, pencils and other conveniences, and opportunity for exercising their hands and eyes. This, in the end will be found to be a cheap and very profitable investment, for it will save both time and patience. But for the school-room, a classification like the following might be made:—

1. Blackboard exercises. 2. Slate exercises. 3. Card exercises.

Article 1—Blackboard Exercises.—It was a remark of a distinguished educator, that "Every inch of school-room wall, not devoted to blackboard, should be appropriated for a cabinet of common things and the curiosities of art and nature." This would be an admirable arrangement for the primary school as well as for the more advanced; for it would afford the right kind of facilities for experimenting and drawing. But a large amount of blackboard is also necessary for the use of children; so that when they became weary of their other lessons, and of their seats, as

they soon will, they may go to the board and amuse themselves, by drawing lines, pictures, maps, etc.

This would be a much better means of disposing of this superabundance of vital force and mental activity than to let it work off in the form of mischief, or even to attempt to crush it out by long confinement, and then to complain that the child has not capacity, when in fact he has just been deprived of what little he had. Scolding and whipping will only aggravate the evils by driving this activity into improper channels. Better direct it than attempt to crush it; for in doing the latter we are warring against the strongest element of power, planted in the human being. We venture to say that the effort to keep children quiet, all the time, in the school-room, as some teachers do, is more exhausting to teachers than all the teaching they do, simply because children were not made to be quiet all the time, any more than trees and plants were made to be moved every few days. Look at that child, teacher, as he writhes in the hopeless agony of idleness before you; and then tell me, if you can, that he must be quiet. Why, every limb and joint, and bone, and muscle, ligament, nerve, and fiber in his body quivers its negation to such a proposition, and says, as plain as language can say, *give me exercise, activity, and labor*. Will you, therefore, be dumb to these mute but eloquent pleadings? The children need the exercises of which the teacher strives to deprive them; and the teacher needs the force thus expended, to direct the children in their lessons and exercises. Let, therefore, the same harmony obtain here that exists every where else, in the departments of nature. Blackboard exercises may serve in part, at least, to exhaust that accumulation of vitality which is sometimes so annoying,

but which was never made to be wasted nor crushed out. For convenience, these exercises may be classified somewhat in the following manner:

1. *Copying, and forming lines, angles, and geometrical figures.* The perpendicular, horizontal, and oblique lines might constitute one class of exercises; and if the teacher can afford the time necessary to direct them, it would be well to have the whole class operate in concert. The combinations of right lines into angles and rectilinear figures might constitute another; while the curves and their combinations would constitute still another.

These exercises will cultivate close observation, and will train the judgment in comparison and in the apprehension and conception of forms of beauty, as well as the eye and the hand in tracing them. And when sufficient command of the hand and the muscles appertaining thereto, shall have been secured, a higher class of exercises may be attempted.

2. *Drawing pictures of familiar objects, etc.*, will be entirely compatible with the wants. Here it will be found that some children will prefer one class of objects, and some another. It may therefore be well to indulge them, to some extent, in their preferences, both for the purpose of encouraging them and of ascertaining their peculiarities. Better opportunities will also occur here for learning the disposition and capacity of the child, than will ordinarily occur in a whole term of the best instruction in A, B, C. Superadded to this will be the opportunity of encouraging talent in mechanical execution and æsthetical culture—departments of education too much neglected among the American people.

A classification of objects like the following, may

be of service to teachers: animate and inanimate objects; and of the first, the wild and domestic, with any subdivisions that may suggest themselves. Of the second, natural and artificial; and these again suggest their subdivisions as organic and inorganic, as vegetable and mineral—such as trees, rocks, etc.: and for the artificial; architectural structures, mechanical, agricultural and household implements, etc., etc. But it will be found best in most cases, at first, not to adhere too strictly to technical distinctions or classes. Let there be as much freedom in the selections as will comport with the nature of the exercises, it being sufficient for ordinary purposes to place the copies or models before the class, and allow them to make their own selections, except when the object is to secure concert of movement and dispatch, precision and accuracy in execution. In this case, the same forms should be selected for the whole class, and a regular drill given in the execution of them.

This mode of representing things will suggest the representation of localities or places. Hence, *drawing maps of familiar places* will follow as a matter almost of necessity; and the little urchins' eyes will sparkle as they trace the outline of the door-yard, the garden or orchard at home; or the school-room, the play-ground, or flower-garden, and little paths of the school premises; and I have seen the teachers' eyes sparkle too in such exercises, and a feeling of sympathy and love pervade the whole group of learners. How much better this, than that cold, forbidding crabbedness which freezes the very life out of children! This process will awaken mind as well as afford an outlet for vital force.

ART. 2—SLATE EXERCISES.—Another class of exercises equally important, though not so much of a physical character, may be named *Slate Exercises*. These may be practiced at the same time with Blackboard Exercises, and presuppose that children should be furnished with slates, the very first day they enter school. They are even more useful and necessary then, than their books are. It were no greater inconsistency to send a child to school without his coat or appropriate clothing or food, than to send him without a slate. He will need his slate and pencil as much as he will need any of these articles. It would be like sending a man to do a day's work without providing him tools with which to work; and the enormity would be still greater, if we should tie his hands and feet, and then require him to work. The analogy can readily be traced by those who have seen little boys and girls tied, as it were, to their seats throughout the long, dull hours of the school-day, with the hopeless task of nothing to do, staring them in the face. The best primary schools in the land now require the slate and pencil, as a necessary preparation for attending school.

There may be difficulty, however, at present, in securing this arrangement in the country school; and it is quite likely the same difficulty would exist one hundred years hence, provided there is nothing said about it. But a reform is necessary and *right*, and therefore should be put into operation as soon as possible. What, therefore, are the exercises with the slate? The child is supposed to be about learning the alphabet of elementary sounds, as a mental exercise. Now, of what advantage will this physical exercise be to him in this respect? For we have claimed for it that it is

useful every where, and in every way. It is a peculiarity of childhood, as well as of manhood, to set a greater value upon its own products than upon others. Hence the little boy will value the sled or top he made, or the little girl the doll dress she made, vastly more than he or she does any others, though the latter may, in reality, be ten times more valuable.

One reason for this seems to be that their attention has been called to every particular in relation to these things; they have felt an interest in every part and particle of them; their little ingenuities have been taxed, exhausted perhaps, in their production. Hence they have really cost them more; and a consciousness of ability to produce them, renders them a thousand fold more valuable. So in making a picture, a map or a letter. Its value to the child will be in proportion to the interest and ingenuity expended in its production. He will feel a greater interest in a letter or figure he makes himself, than in one he finds already made. All the letters of the alphabet, and the numerical figures may thus be made at the same time that children are learning them—all too, by just taking advantage of the desire and necessity for physical exercises.

Copying and forming letters and numerical figures may, therefore, constitute a pleasing and profitable employment for children while upon their seats, about the same time that they are taking lessons or exercises on the board.

But as soon as a child learns to make a few letters, he should be taught to combine them, so as to form words representing familiar objects. This now awakens in him the same idea that the real object or the picture did. Then his ambition and interest increase.

He begins to feel that he really is employed about some important business. And so he is. It is questionable whether, if he should live, he would ever be employed about any greater. Let him feel it then. Let his little heart swell to its utmost capacity; for he has actually accomplished wonders when he has acquired the ability to represent objects and words; and no wonder, if it become the proudest achievement of his life.

Hence, *copying* and *forming words* that represent familiar things, may constitute the second step in slate exercises, corresponding to the pictures on the blackboard or the slate, for they need not be confined to the board.

As soon, therefore, as words are formed, the propriety of connecting them will at once suggest itself; and little sentences composed of little words will soon grow up under this nurturing process. And hence just as fast as the child learns the elements in his mental training, he should use them in all possible relations until he is perfectly familiar with both their nature and use. Hence *composition* writing is commenced right here, on the principle that as fast as a child learns *facts* and principles, he should both *do them*, and *tell them.*

The advantages of the above named course can not fail to be seen and appreciated by every intelligent teacher. It might seem at first to be more of intellectual training than physical. Grant it: but it will be remembered that it is through the physical man that we reach the mental; so that while we adopt exercises to meet the wants of the hands, we are all the time feeding the mind most effectually.

ARTICLE 3—CARD EXERCISES.—These exercises are intimately allied to those last mentioned, and may be included under the head of Hand Culture, though they are not less efficient in the cultivation of the intellect, and the taste in particular. They may consist of two varieties, and are semi-intellectual in their application and effects. To be learned and appreciated they should be seen.

The first consists in the use of blocks or slips of pasteboard, or cards, with letters printed upon them; and grooves, or frames, or plain surfaces, into which, or upon which the children place these blocks, etc., so that the letters shall form words and sentences. This plan has been successfully adopted in teaching idiots. It aids them in the control of the muscles, and gives them precision and individuality of movement. The exercise is both physical and intellectual, and, if properly conducted, will suitably engage all the powers at the same time.

The other has reference to the use of blank cards or slips to be used in drawing, either linear or perspective. Painting or coloring pictures or maps, architectural drafting and sketching from nature are exercises in which the pupil will soon find great delight and profit, if he is allowed to indulge these desires here.

Special directions for conducting these exercises seem unnecessary here, since we have text-books upon most of these subjects. Indeed they scarcely need any direction. They will follow the other exercises, if the means are provided, just as certainly as reading will follow spelling, or as acquisition will follow experiment and study. And they may be continued all through the school period.

We close this section with these general remarks: 1. That teaching and learning become pleasant just in the proportion in which they conform to natural and philosophical principles. 2. That antagonisms and inconsistencies cease in the same ratio. 3. That while it is not the teacher's duty to relieve the child of any of its appropriate labor, not even to remove the natural obstacles from the way, but rather to teach it how to surmount them; yet when the way is entirely blocked up, and hedged about with error, it is his duty then to break the way and to remove the unnatural obstacles. 4. That it is important that this be done soon, since the miserable excuses now urged by some teachers, for clinging to the errors in teaching, will be likely to have as much force one thousand years hence, as now, provided no one steps forward and offers to remove them; and lastly, that it is the better policy always to educate the school up to a proper standard, than to degrade the standard to a level with ignorance and inconsistency.

Section 2—Excursion and Labor.

There is another department of physical culture or exercise properly belonging to school and family training, which should receive attention here.

For the want of a better name, we shall call it *Excursion and Labor.*

Its application to the school-room is not so immediate as that of Black-board Exercises; yet, there are many things connected with it that will render it highly useful for the same purposes for which the others are recommended, viz: 1st, In affording an outlet to the superabundance of vitality, and leading it off into useful channels; 2d, In developing, fortifying, and training the physical powers to manly vigor and useful employment; 3d, Of opening up the way for the most successful mental and moral development.

For convenience the subject may be classified as follows: 1. Field Exercises, etc.; 2. Manipulations and Experiments; 3. Manual Labor and Business.

These terms are not expressive of the precise ideas intended, and yet they come nearer than any others in *our* vocabulary.

The Field Exercises are used somewhat in the sense of *Field Notes* in surveying, etc.

They may include, 1. Botanical, Geological, and Mineralogical Expeditions; 2. Zoological and Entomological Expeditions; 3. Topographical and Historical Expeditions.

It is a truth well attested, we think, that nature, in her multiform varieties, teaches not only the first, but some of the most attractive and useful lessons. Her treasury of knowledge, for simplicity, variety, utility, and beauty, is not surpassed by all the accumulated stores of art. These stores, too, are well adapted to the purposes for which they were intended. Each season of the year brings with it its peculiar charms for childhood, youth and age. Hence, childhood and spring, middle age and summer, old age and winter, have ever been used, not only as the strongest types of physical and metaphysical resemblance, but as actually possessing mutual attractions for each other. But, however this last may be, it is nevertheless certain that the fields and the woods, the rocks and the brooks, the mountains and the floods, the flowers and the fruits, that are cast abroad in such profusion over the face of nature, possess a charm for the heart, for which we may seek in vain elsewhere.

This is emphatically true in youth. But what advantage can be derived from these dispositions in children, and their corresponding excitants in nature?

This marked conformity of want to supply and supply to want, indicates design; or else it forms an exception to the general rule.

Article 1—Field Exercises.—Botany is a science of great beauty and acknowledged utility; but its study is usually deferred until late in life. This, perhaps, is well, so far as the technicalities and more difficult parts of the science are concerned. But there is much of the beautiful and useful of this and kindred sciences that may be taught in connection with the school duties, physical exercises, and common duties, where they will be most readily seen and appreciated.

What is more lamentable than the ignorance that prevails among laborers, and indeed, among all classes, in reference to this and kindred sciences! And for what class of society are they more useful and befitting than for that which is brought in daily contact with nature's loveliness? But how shall the evil be corrected? Must they or their children spend their time in the pursuit of these branches in the ordinary way of studying them, when so many other things demand their attention?

Much, and perhaps all that is really necessary, might be done for children in these branches, while they are attending school, without at all interfering with their other duties. This is the age with them, when their bodies need the fresh and invigorating air from mountain and valley. Their long confinement in the school-room, perhaps in fetid and poisoned air, will render some change more necessary.

They need, also, the active exercise of limb and body. The long rambles, the excursions after fruits and flowers, etc., which will bring them in close proximity with the wonderful works and operations of nature, will afford this in due measure.

The waters and the air abound with life. The earth teems with myriads of living beings. Her bowels groan with untold wealth, intellectual as well as physical. Her surface is covered with a carpet of verdure, and starred and gemmed with flowers. Her products are full of strange variety, and the foot-prints of the Creator are visible upon every rock. Can she fail, therefore, to become interesting to the learner?

These objects themselves possess the same advantage over the mere description of them, in text books, that a view of a real scene or visible transaction possesses over the mere description; and, added to this, is the physical labor that earns it. Of course, these excursions and exercises will not supersede the use or necessity of the text book. They will render it only more attractive and useful, for reasons that have already been given.

What, therefore, will be the impropriety of stated rambles or excursions over the hills and along the brooks and rivers, in the fields and in the forests, to catch the glimpses of those noble forms of creation, that art can never equal, and which will plant great thoughts deep down in the soul?

Why not pluck the wild flowers, gather the fruits, or cull the specimens of shells and stones and ores, that abound in almost all localities? Why not hunt the beetle and the butterfly, and collect specimens in all the departments of natural history? Why not interrogate nature here in her own dominions, where

she will give sensible responses? Why not bound with light foot and lighter heart over the joyous earth, since our bodies languish, and our souls pant, and nature beckons us with her blandest smile? There *is* no impropriety in it, more than there would be, if a man were hungry, to feed him.

Let us suppose a band of blooming boys and girls sallying forth for an afternoon ramble. The understanding is, that they are to collect specimens in all the above named departments of natural history, for the purpose of forming a school cabinet.

They attack the first coal-bank that lies in their line of march, and make the necessary spoliation. The next may be a patch of wild flowers, or blossoming shrubs or. trees, and the shouts and exultations are prolonged and loud. Can you look at that excited group, teacher, without emotion? Why not? Because it is an exhibition of nature, giving a lesson to her children, a kind of recitation too rare in the schools.

Look again! There, they have found a nest of bees! And mark how that ambitious boy will risk the pain of an encounter, rather than lose his specimen of the hymenoptera. And see where yonder stream washes the pebbles from the mountain! What a busy crowd collect there! They are gathering shells and stones; and that fern along the sedgy lake or pond, must grace the herbarium of a loved sister or classmate. Even the fishes can not escape, and attacks are made on the brooks and streams. Thus they ransack nature through till tired, some sink down to rest, and cull their specimens; and some to ruminate, and drink in, the forms of beauty and grandeur of nature. And now the little group return to their school-house; tired, it may be, with the toils of the march, but laden with the spoils of science. Now they examine their stock, and prepare for the arrangement. They investigate and discriminate; they classify and arrange their specimens. And how sweet their sleep becomes, this night, because they have been exercising all their powers harmoniously; and think you they will not love their school and its exercises more and better, for this acquisition? Will they not, too, escape that ignorance, so common as to these sciences? Their stupidity must border close upon idiocy, if they do not.

ARTICLE 2—EXPERIMENT AND MANIPULATION.—The process of experimenting and manipulating may now commence; and it will be with that real interest that always invests a subject, when thus rendered practical. These exercises may be classified according to the amount of apparatus, grade of school, and elements used:

1. Chemical and Philosophical Experiments; 2. Preparation and Classification of Specimens; 3. Preparation and Arrangements of Cabinets. Every school-house in the land, might have a cabinet of some kind. The woods and hills and brooks, are full of the right kinds of specimens; and that teacher who is too indolent to collect them, or allow his pupils to collect them, ought not to be allowed to *keep school.*

Nothing perhaps would add more to the interest and profit of the school-room, than thus furnishing it with specimens in all the departments common to the locality, and with Chemical and Philosophical apparatus, by which other wonders in the natural world might be exhibited.

Enter two class-rooms with me. In the one, the

astute professor is lazily asking, or rather reading, questions to the class; or it may be, he is discoursing learnedly upon the various geological periods, the philosophical abstractions of Metaphysics; or he may be explaining the technicalities of Natural History, Language or Mathematics. The pupils sit with meek, blank submission. With folded hands and eyes upturned (if awake) it may be, half wonderingly upon him, but more likely staring into vacuity; their minds—it were easier to say where they are not, than to guess where they are. But thus they manage to endure the lesson. Every thing evinces the languor, stupidity, uneasiness and inattention of over confinement. Now at this point, propose a geological or botanical excursion with them, to the mountains; or a ramble or a scramble over the valleys and hills, as described above. Will not their eyes sparkle, their blank faces kindle, their forms straiten up, and every muscle begin to contract and to prepare for the encounter?

But enter the other class-room. The pupils are all fresh from one of those excursions. Each one holds his specimen, and is anxious for the test of experiment or examination. The teacher, no less enlisted than they, need but suggest a subject, and their willing minds grapple with it at once. They are all alive. The difference in the two recitations is quite perceptible. These latter have been shaking hands with the living, loving and speaking forms of nature; and their cheeks glow with health; their eyes sparkle with intelligence; and their minds kindle as they approach these life-giving subjects. The one process is *teaching*, the other is *stultifying*. Physical culture suggests the former.

Now there is no possible excuse why schoolhouses should present the barren and forbidding appearance that they do, so long as nature abounds with the very apparatus that is needed. And what renders this matter still more urgent is, that most, if not all that is absolutely necessary, may be collected in the immediate vicinity, by the teacher and pupils, in their rambles for needed recreation and health. What could not thus be collected, might soon be secured by exchanges.

Is this impracticable then? If so, then *education* is impracticable, because it involves the very first principles of education, viz.: development, discipline, acquisition and use. If this *is* mere speculation, and delicately elaborated theory without a possibility of practice, then education is a failure; and we must forever be doomed to unwelcome toil and drudgery, to vexation and ultimate disappointment, with the great mass of youth. But we are at liberty to draw no such conclusions. The experiments and successes already accomplished forbid this; therefore, the premise is wrong, and this *is not* mere speculation, but sound practical philosophy—the natural and most ready and legitimate way to accomplish the ends we have in view.

ARTICLE 3—MANUAL EXERCISES.—The topic of *manual labor* and exercise has been discussed in preceding chapters. It will not therefore be referred to again, except to show its connection with this part of the subject. The person taught after the manner indicated above, goes to his daily toils, feeling the dignity of labor. He not only feels that he is surrounded by the living and loving forms, but that he is handling

the very instruments that God has made for his use. He goes to his fields, not like the galley slave scourged to his duty, but conscious that he is there to meet with those welcome companions, those old acquaintances, that have contributed so largely to his happiness in early life.

The mechanic, the professional man, and the man of business, are equally benefited, in their several departments, from the knowledge of the forces of nature that have been thus early revealed to them.

Again: the chances for success in almost any department of business are more than doubled, by this early and practical acquaintance with Nature and her laws. Numberless occasions will occur, in the life of an educated man, in which he can not only enhance his own wealth and happiness, but can contribute largely to the enjoyment of his fellows. He sees beauty where others see deformity; and the grosser materials that are passed, it may be, with indifference by the vulgar, are made to contribute to his wants and enjoyment.

And last, but not least, these things have had a tendency to preserve health and develop the physical man. They have preserved him from a broken-down constitution; and now that he is a man, he has the feelings, the habits, the soul, the mind and the body of a man.

Section 3—Gymnastics.

The next subject to which attention will be called, viz., Gymnastics, is one so full of science, that we do not feel at all competent to do it justice. It has, however, such a practical bearing upon a symmetrical education, that its leading principles may be so

grouped and presented as to enable the teacher to apprehend them at once, and to put them into practice.

Text-books on this subject have been carefully compiled, which, if consulted, will enable the teacher to build up his own system. This subject is claiming much attention, in this way, in our best schools and among our ripest scholars; and the educational instrumentalities are considered by them, to be quite incomplete, if they do not embrace the means of physical culture.

Gymnastics, as it is applied by modern educators, has reference to the healthy development of the physical powers. It accomplishes this by means of various exercises which will be named hereafter. It proposes to correct the abuses commonly practiced, and to remedy those evils that have been imposed upon the body by improper management, as well as to strengthen and fortify it against the incroachments of disease. As such, it has been introduced into the schools, and is fast becoming a regular system of training.

ARTICLE 1 — ATHLETIC EXERCISES. — For practical purposes the following classification might be adopted. It may be made to include all, and perhaps something more, than can be practiced in the common school.

The Athletic Exercises may include Walking, Running, Leaping, Skating, Rowing, Balancing, Climbing, Vaulting, Fencing, etc. Most, if not all of these exercises may be practiced in connection with the school duties, provided there is some one to give direction to them.

Take the first one, for example. But it may be asked, "Do not our boys and girls of school age know how to walk?" "Why teach them what they already know?"

We ask, *How* do they walk? Are their manners in this particular what they should be? Take an example in some of our rural districts. Propose to the children to give a sample of their ability to cross and recross the room; to pass to and from the recitation seat; or to enter and retire from the room; and what are these performances like? We would be safe in saying they are like nothing else. They are purely *sui generis.* There would be limping, halting, swaggering, embarrassment, affectation, awkwardness, slovenliness and perhaps as many more varieties.

Now all of these faults become very annoying to a teacher of taste or refinement, especially in recitations. Can they be corrected? We maintain that they can; and that too, at school, and in the school-room—both the time and place to do this work. It is seldom ever done if neglected here. There is no time so favorable for refining the body, as when we are refining the mind, and when its organs and instruments are in a plastic state.

The first thing to be done in correcting the evils of this class, to which we are prone, is to cultivate an erect and easy posture in standing. Then some simple and graceful movements of the hands and arms—such as are commonly used in oratorical gesticulation; then of the feet in changing the position from right to left and the reverse; then turning, first, one quarter, then one half, and finally entirely round—each effort constituting a separate exercise, observing to make as little effort as possible.

These exercises should be practiced in concert daily,

and usually with the reading lessons, until the pupils acquire ease and freedom in the execution of all the movements.

Now the *step* may be introduced, which should consist, at first, of a few simple movements in concert; and may be timed either with or without music. Let them be easy, graceful, firm and elastic. For the school-room walk, as it is sometime termed (not the march), the toe should be last to leave the floor and first to approach it. This is done by a slight flexion of the knee forward, and also by throwing the body forward and over it, so as not to give the walk the appearance of a *strut*. It is not walking upon the toe entirely, since the bottom of the foot and heel are gradually brought to the floor after the toe or ball has struck.

A daily exercise at least should be practiced, and the boisterous, slovenly and uncouth habits of the boys and girls will soon undergo a change for the better, much sooner than if they were scolded for their noise and bad manners, for a whole term.

In all these exercises, care should be taken to avoid the labored or affected manner, such as reeling from side to side, or swinging the hands and arms, etc. Nature only needs assistance, in order to give the truest manners and the highest polish.

Here again it will be observed, the law of mutual adaptation is reaffirmed; for while these exercises are adopted chiefly for their physical benefits, they accomplish a very important part in the mental and moral development, and social refinement of the pupil.

The running, leaping, skating, rowing, etc., belong more appropriately to the play-ground and excursion, but may be rendered tenfold more serviceable by being

superintended by a competent master. And then again, those injurious excesses into which the pupils are liable to run, may be avoided.

We shall not attempt a description of these exercises here, but would beg leave to refer the reader to works on these subjects.

The climbing, balancing, vaulting, fencing, etc., as well as some to which reference has been made, belong to the gymnasium; and, where the school is furnished with an instrumentality of this kind, they should be under the strict superintendence of a competent instructor, by which the evils of improper and too violent or too feeble exercise may be avoided, and the healthiest, manliest strength and vigor cultivated.

How much wiser, on the part of the educator, to take advantage of this desire for active exercise, so common in childhood, and make it accomplish some important part in the child's education, rather than to allow it to be wasted in idleness, or upon corrupting and vicious games and trifling amusements, whose only effects are to degrade the man!

ART. 2—VOCAL EXERCISES.—Technically, gymnastics might not cover all the ground we have mapped out for it; but practically, we propose to make it include all that belongs to body culture, not included in hand culture, and excursions and labor.

Hence both Vocal Exercises and Calisthenics will claim attention. The human voice is the product of physical effort. Its organs constitute not only one of the most useful apparatuses, but, at the same time, one of the most delicate, complicate and wonderful.

We shall not attempt its anatomy or analysis here, but shall content ourselves with offering some suggestions on modes of culture, as connected with physical exercises.

One of the great obstacles to vocal culture is weakness and want of flexibility in the vocal organs. These should be the first things corrected. The habit of weak and indistinct speaking is one that annoys teachers much. Hence various devices have been resorted to, in order to correct it. Pupils have been coaxed, censured, and even threatened, for not speaking loud and plain enough in recitation, while it has been alleged as evidence against them, that they can speak loud enough in conversation, and on the playground.

But scolding, however much it may increase the *teacher's* quantity of voice (we do not think it can improve its quality), will have little, if any influence in improving the voices of the pupils. The only effectual way to induce them to give up their bad habits, is to give them good ones in exchange for them; or, in other words, to drive out bad habits by means of good ones.

Good reading and speaking, as a physical exercise, is made from good voices, and good voices are made from breath or breathing. Hence good elocution depends upon the breathing. The first step, therefore, in vocal gymnastics, is an exercise in breathing. This, at first, might seem unnecessary, since, in the language of the little boy who was caught whistling in school, if we let it alone, it will breathe itself; yet very few people really know how to breathe, so as to make the best possible use of their breath. If all did know, then would all have good voices, except those who have physical defects.

But suppose an exercise in breathing.

1. *Position.*—The pupils are arranged standing, and

it may be best, on a line, on each side of the room, facing each other. The posture should be erect, the hands resting upon the hips and waist, the fingers forward and pressing slightly upon the abdomen, the shoulders thrown back, but not strained.

2. *Inspirations.*—The inhalations should be in concert, and, at first, moderate, but gradually increased from time to time, until they become long, full, and deep, filling the lungs to their utmost capacity. They may be made either through the mouth or nostrils, or both; and, for the greater part of the exercises, they should be made without noise, or what is called loud breathing.

3. *Expirations.*—These should correspond with the inspirations. All the air should be expelled from the lungs, preparatory to another inhalation, gradually at first, but increasing in force and rapidity until the explosive force is reached. The passage of the air to and from the lungs, may, for convenience of concert exercises, be indicated by the upward and downward movement of the hand or index of the teacher.

The exercise should be daily at least—twice a day is still better—and should be continued each time until a sensation of dizziness is experienced. This sensation, however, will gradually subside. It would be well, in some instances, to accompany these breathings with appropriate motions of the hands and arms. These, thus combined, would give capacity to the lungs and chest; would develop and strengthen the muscles situated in and about them, and at the same time they would give command over the hands and arms. Another exercise, or rather a modification of the same one, may now be commenced.

It requires the same order and arrangement, and

the same exercise, except that in place of simple breath or breathing; we now use the voice while expelling the air from the lungs.

1. The long vocal sounds should be selected first, and delivered with all possible force, key and velocity; then *all* the vocal sounds in the same manner. It is best to practice on the deep tones first.

2. The sub-vocal and aspirate sounds may now be given in a similar manner, with the exception, perhaps, of some of the variations, observing always to secure full, deep, healthy sounds, as the physical benefits, as well as the success in training, will depend upon this.

3. Now take a word or short sentence, one having an easy flow of sounds, and drill the class upon it, in the same manner, through all the possible varieties of force, pitch, velocity and inflection. Then advance to more difficult sentences, and those having the most difficult combinations of sub-vocal and aspirate sounds.

The following system of marks has been used by the author, with some success, in drilling teachers at Institutes, and may be of some service to others.

The heaviest stroke in the following scale indicates the greatest force, or the loudest or greatest volume of voice; the next in size, a slightly diminished force, or loudness, and so on down to the softest murmur, and even the whisper, which might be indicated by a dotted line. Thus:—

In like manner pitch or key may be represented to the eye: the upper line in the following, indicating the high; the next below, the medium high; and so on down until the very lowest possible pitch is attained, being careful not to vary the general force. Thus:—

And thus again with velocity or rate of motion: the first or long intervals in the following, representing slowest utterance; the less intervals, the accelerated motion, and so on increasing, until the greatest rapidity of which the voice is capable is reached; being careful to maintain the same general force and key. Thus:—

And lastly the inflections and other variations may, for convenience, be represented to the eye; though but few of these can be thus represented with any considerable degree of accuracy. A rude sketch of them might be given as follows, commencing with the upward or rising slide, through all its degrees of abruptness; then the downward or falling slide in a similar manner; then the sweeps, waves and waving slides, as denominated by some authors; so the bend, the swell and emphasis (very imperfectly however), and every possible movement of the voice may, as a matter of convenience, in concert vocal drills, be represented to the eye. Thus:—

The advantage of this plan is, that it represents to the eye, what sometimes is too feebly represented to the ear, and for this reason, fails to reach the understanding. A person can lift more with two hands than he can with one. For a similar reason, a pupil will more readily apprehend a fact or principle when his eyes and ears both are addressed at the same time, than when addressed separately.

The foregoing plan possesses another advantage. It does not complicate the matter and confuse the scholar with a multiplicity of things at the same time. This is the prevailing error of the highly wrought systems and theories; and of those who teach them. But according to the above arrangement of the exercises, but one thing is attempted at the same time, and that is completed before another is commenced.

It is not claimed, however, that this plan is complete or exclusive, or that some other might not answer equally as well. It must be remembered also that it is only given as an exercise in vocal culture — as a means of strengthening and developing the powers of the voice, as a physical instrument.

EXERCISE.

A sentence may now be selected for an exercise in *Force*, and the class is drilled in concert on all the forces indicated, and as many more as may be thought best. It will be found best to commence with the medium, and ascend or descend from it. Frequent and rapid changes, from one degree to another, may be made as a test of the ability of the members of the class to control their voices. With the necessary variations, these directions will also answer for the other varieties.

The class may be divided into sections after the members have acquired some skill and confidence, each section reciting in concert, and these again into sub-sections, until finally, the individual exercise may be given.

Care should be exercised in these drills that the proper *force*, *pitch* and *velocity* are preserved, e. g., when the exercise is on force, the pitch and velocity should be preserved the same throughout; when on pitch, the force and velocity should be uniform; and when on velocity the force and pitch should be the same throughout; on the variations, all should be varied more or less.

These exercises, properly conducted, will certainly break up the most inveterate habits of weak voices and indistinct articulation. I have never known one so deep seated as not to yield, where a fair opportunity was offered.

But the excellencies of these exercises consist in their universal usefulness; for while they are practiced chiefly for their physical advantages, they constitute the very best means of teaching and training in that most useful of all arts, the art of speaking and reading.

Singing is nearly allied to these exercises, and when practiced in connection with marching, and hand and arm movements, as may be done in connection with the school songs prepared for these purposes, it becomes a very exciting and healthy physical exercise. But this would rank more properly with the next topic.

ARTICLE 3 — CALISTHENIC EXERCISES. — *Calisthenics*, as its etymology implies, is a science which has for its object the cultivation of beauty and strength of body and limb. As an exercise for this purpose, it perhaps has no equal. It proposes to meet the precise difficulties and diseases that arise from study and over-confinement, the exercises being so arranged as to bring into activity those parts of the body suffering most from inactivity, and resting those parts that may have been overtaxed with exercise.

We do not propose to give a full exposition of the subject here, it being sufficient for the present purpose to give the outline and allow teachers to consult text-books upon this subject, and to suit the particular exercise to the particular wants.

It may, however, be classified for ordinary purposes, in the following manner:

1. Arm movements.
2. Body movements.
3. Feet movements.

For a full and complete description, and special directions in those exercises, as practiced in our best schools, the reader is referred to Part Second, Chapter Fifth, Section III.

SYNOPSIS VI.

INTELLECTUAL CULTURE.

- OBSERVATION & EXPERIMENT.
  - NATURAL OBJECTS. — Properties of matter (external.) Motion. Sounds. General phenomena.
  - REPRESENTATIVE. — Apparatus. Models. Toys. Pictures. Numbers. Directions. Symbols. Simple combinations.
  - INITIAL AND NAMES. — Words (written) denoting things.
    " " " actions.
    " " " qualities & relations.
- CONVERSATION & DESCRIPTION.
  - INTERESTING NARRATIVE. — Tales. Sketches of travel and adventure. Incidents in biography and history. Description of common things and occurrences.
  - SCIENTIFIC FACTS. — Natural phenomena. Waking thought. Laws of life and health and growth. A knowledge of the arts and employments.
  - REHEARSALS, &c. — Maxims. Mottos. Sentiments. Rhymes. Poems. Lessons. Law. Correct mental habits. Order.
- INVESTIGATION AND GENERALIZATION.
  - PHYSICAL SCIENCE. — Relations. Adaptations. Chemistry. Agriculture. Natural and mechanical philosophy. Mathematics. Art. Natural history. Laws of life.
  - LANGUAGE AND HISTORY. — Practical grammar. Composition. Philology. Literature. Criticism. Philosophy of history. Politics.
  - METAPHYSICS. — Attributes of intelligence. Laws of thought. Existence. Duration. Infinity. Taste. Ideality. Theories. Creations.

CHAPTER VI.

INTELLECTUAL EDUCATION.

THE intellectual education of man ranks among the highest duties of the age. It has claimed more attention, however, than any other, since it has been thought that the intellect of man is about all there is of him, worthy of special cultivation; a proof this, of the high position it should hold in the scale of human elevation.

So great has been the desire for intellectual culture, that both body and soul have been sacrificed, and are to this day, in many instances, in order to secure it. But the relationship and sympathy between all the powers and faculties of man are such as to forbid that one department should suffer without impairing the health of the other. Hence the very plans adopted to *force* intellect, beyond the natural growth, have proved destructive, not only to other powers, but to the intellect itself, thus defeating the very object had in view, since upon the healthy condition of the other powers depends the harmonious and safe development of the intellect. No forced measures, however successful they may have been for a season, have ever done more than to show that the order of nature can not be disturbed, in the slightest degree, without deranging the whole educational system.

To the educator, it becomes a matter of the first

importance, not only to understand the nature and character of these powers individually, but to know their relative value, and modes of treatment.

The intellect has powers and faculties that have a mutual influence upon one another. The activity of one set of faculties induces a corresponding state in others; and the disease or inactivity of one, will induce disorder and abnormal growth in another. These powers do not all unfold or develop at the same time, nor in precisely the same order in different individuals. The same variety obtains here that exists every where among nature's works. Nor yet do they individually come to maturity at once. They require their full time for growth, just as essentially as trees and plants do; and no attempt to hasten them will be tolerated.

The order of development is a matter which demands consideration. There is first the bud, then the blossom, and then the fruit. But it would seem that this order is much deranged, and in some instances, almost inverted. There is a great desire to gather fruit from the blossom, and even from the buds. Man is too impatient of delay. And not only so, but he is disposed to search for fruit upon the wrong vines. This arises from an imperfect understanding of the nature and design of the faculties themselves, which results in a corrupt state of education.

The most popular classification of mental faculties recognizes the following grand divisions, viz.: Intellect, Sensibility, and Will. The intellectual powers, or those now under special consideration, have, according to their nature, and the offices they perform, been divided into two groups, viz.: the Primary and Secondary faculties. These have their subdivisions, as Perception, Consciousness (which, perhaps, is more a mental state than a faculty), and Intuition or Original Suggestion.

These again have their several functions to perform. Hence arises another classification based upon use.

Perception, for instance, may be classified according to the several organs through which it acts; and the knowledges or apprehensions of externality that such action gives: such, for example, as smell and odors, taste and savors, touch and texture, temperature, hearing and sounds, sight and color, form, size, etc.

These senses have also their interchangeable relations, as experiments in the apprehensions of the properties of matter would show. But it is not our purpose to give a strict analysis here.

Consciousness and Original Suggestion also have their subdivisions according to use; the first giving notice of the existence of the several mental states; the second taking cognizance of cause and effect, individuality and place, number and infinity, duration and power, right and wrong, etc.

The secondary faculties and their functions have been classified in the following manner:

1. Understanding, whose functions are, first the Notion-forming power, which gives us our common ideas of whatever we behold or think about. These ideas may be general or particular, simple or complex, correct or incorrect. Second, Reflection or the power the mind has to dwell upon its own operations or any subject of thought. It is usually preceded by attention and conception, which last may be true or false, vivid or weak.

2. Judgment, including, first, comparison or the power to detect resemblances, or to discriminate:

it deals with the notices furnished by the other faculties. Secondly, classification, which disposes of these, whether objects, facts or theories, according to their several peculiarities. Thirdly, argumentation or reasoning, which relates chiefly to terms, propositions and theorems, and the processes of deducing conclusions from premises.

3. Memory, the great treasure house of the mind, whose functions are to receive, associate, retain and reproduce, when called upon, the materials entrusted to it for safe-keeping.

4. Imagination, that pioneer of the mind, whose office is to enter into the ideal world, and to gather the raw material, or to take portions of that which may have been prepared, and to combine them into theories and creations, as the judgment or sense shall indicate, and the reason and taste shall decide.

Now any modes of culture that do not recognize these facts and principles or similar ones, is liable at once, to be at variance with the natural order of development. These faculties, all have their infancy, youth and maturity, corresponding severally, to the periods of growth recognized as the Objective, Transition and Subjective.

It is pertinent now to inquire into the manner in which these faculties may be developed, so as not to interfere with and disarrange this beautiful order and harmony of things.

It will be seen that Perception stands at the head of the list of Primary faculties, and Understanding at the head of the Secondary, and that these two are, in a great measure, concomitants, i. e., the notices furnished by the perception, are readily apprehended by the understanding, and passed on to be disposed of as the judgment may appoint. It will be observed further that the perception is furnished with a set of organs, through which it takes cognizance of the external world; avenues leading inward to the world of thought and abstraction.

Now the object of education is not to interrupt or cut off these communications either way, but to amplify and establish them, at the same time that the materials which go to awaken mind, are furnished through them. Hence intellectual education begins with the senses, through which early knowledge, the food for the mind, is received.

Section 1—Observation and Experiment.

This leads us at once to modes of learning and modes of treatment or teaching, which for the earliest periods may be denominated *Observational* and *Experimental*, because the senses are addressed first; and as soon as the observation or perception is complete, an inquiry as to what? what kind? when? how? etc., is begotten in the mind. This curiosity is planted in the human mind at this early period, for very wise and benevolent purposes. Were it not there, there would be no desire to know, and the child would be in a condition little better than downright idiocy. This desire prompts him to experiment, which is a second step in acquisition. Hence the ceaseless desire in young children to handle, and taste and examine objects; and these again present to them ever new and ever changing varieties, which keep their observational and experimental powers in a state of healthy activity. This early desire for observation is gratified only by indulgence. Color, size, form, temperature, texture and externality generally, constitute the first intellectual food for the faculties; and experiment is one of the first processes, or exercises of application.

The motions, sounds and general phenomena now attract the attention of the youthful learner, and he opens his eyes and ears upon the wonders with which this new and strange world abounds. The senses are astonishingly active in conveying their impressions inward, where they do their office work in awakening the incipient mind. But this subject, as it relates to very young children, has been alluded to in another place. This brief notice therefore must suffice. It is, however, a department of education, full of intense interest; and one with which the teacher should be very familiar. The more he knows of the infant, the better will he be prepared to know the man; and knowing him, to direct him.

Article 2—Representative Knowledge.—The next advance the child makes from the object world, where his faculties are employed chiefly with things and their properties, is into the picture period, or period of representative knowledge. This has also been described under the head of physical culture, which is so nearly allied to intellectual culture at this age, as scarcely to be distinguished from it. Indeed, about all the intellectual culture a child needs, he will receive in his physical training, if that is properly conducted. At this age his education is supposed to be directed by parents, and its chief object will be accomplished, if he is furnished with the necessary means for investigation—such as toys, pictures, etc., and the necessary facilities for imitating.

Too much special instruction will interfere with the natural order of growth, and discourage the child in his pursuits. The proper training of a young and tender plant does not consist in excessive handling, or in warping and bending it, but in furnishing it with the necessary means of natural growth. So in reference to mind, or the intellectual faculties. They need no overfeeding or cramming, nor yet do they require bending or incessant handling in order to secure their growth. They need the conditions of growth furnished them in due proportion, and then to be let alone. They grow from their own internal sources, appropriating the external as the means of growth. As much freedom, therefore, as is compatible with proper discipline, is a point to be aimed at here. For the school, however, it will be found that the exercises recommended in Chapter Fifth, Section 1—Hand Culture and those immediately connected with it—will be most effectual in cultivating the perceptive faculties, and in waking up other departments of the mind.

The following exercises are recommended as in harmony with those already given; and they may be used in connection with them.

1. Exercises in counting and numbering, in which the numeral frame or counters may be used; and exercises in pointing, in which not only the points of compass may be located, but all places with which the pupil is supposed to be familiar. The inaccuracies and blunders arising from defective knowledge in reference to direction and distance are most humiliating. They may be corrected as shown above.

2. Exercises in the combination of simple numbers, as addition, subtraction, and for those more advanced, multiplication and division, both oral and written, will be found useful in cultivating the power of attention, and quickness of apprehension.

ARTICLE 3—INITIALS AND NAMES.—Oral and written exercises on words representing things, actions, qualities and relations, may be introduced, in which the whole vocabulary of common words might be brought before the mind, and so connected with common facts and transactions, that both their meaning and use could be learned at the same time. The composition and analysis, the reading, spelling, and writing of simple sentences should go hand in hand; so that when a child learns a thing he may *know* it, *rctain* it and *use* it.

Thus it will be seen that the tedium of the school-room, which becomes so oppressive and distasteful sometimes, may be relieved by introducing these exercises along with others in common use. They are not designed to take the entire place of those now in use—except so far as the latter can be shown to be faulty but merely as auxiliary to them; so that that time which is usually spent in idleness, and that energy which is usually thrown away, and worse than thrown away, may be profitably employed.

If it be objected by any that time will not allow the introduction of additional intellectual exercises, it may be answered that if these exercises are as important as those now in use, they ought to share equally with them in time and attention: if they are more important, they should receive a corresponding amount of attention. And we might further add, that no teacher is worthy of confidence, who will persist in sacrificing the good of his pupils to public prejudice, when he sees and knows that his practices are wrong.

The most vigorous thinkers are those who have been taught thus early to make a practical use of their knowledge; and the best teachers are those who thus

recognize the necessity and the laws of intellectual activity.

Section 2—Conversation and Description.

That mode of teaching and learning which brings into activity the greatest amount of mental force, and at the same time does not interfere with the order of the faculties, may be pronounced good—nay, *the best.*

It is a well established fact that mental development is measured not so much by what a man knows as what he does; not so much from acquisition as from the ability to act—to act patiently, persistently, steadily, efficiently. Teaching, therefore, does not consist so much in the communication of knowledge, as in imparting, by a well directed train of influences, the ability to acquire knowledge, to grapple with and overcome the difficulties of life.

It should, therefore, be the constant aim of the educator, to develop man's mental faculties, so that they may harmonize in all their bearings and relations with one another; so that there be no friction in the mental machinery, no jarring, no lagging, no fitful starts or flights, no unsightly growth nor seeming death. To do this it is necessary to call into frequent and vigorous activity all the mental powers, and as nearly as possible all at the same time. This activity should not be merely the activity in acquiring, but in producing.

One of the best modes of inducing this healthy play of all the faculties is by *Conversation* and *Descriptions.* It refers more particularly to primary education, and includes both teaching and learning. A brief description of it may be presented in the following manner.

ARTICLE 1 — INTERESTING NARRATIVE. — Children from the ages of five and six to ten and twelve, are inveterate lovers of narrative, especially if it be of an exciting character. They are eager devourers of stories. Their literature is of an objective and descriptive nature. Hence it is a common thing for the little boy or girl to beset the mother or teacher for stories, etc. Their little minds do not seem to be satisfied with the stores of knowledge to which they have access—and this would be wrong if they were—they must seek it from another source. And during these recitals, mark the attention and the earnest expression. They are lost to all except the incident before them.

Now, this is one of the most educable points in the whole mental and moral constitution; and being most accessible it is assailed from all quarters. This very disposition which was given for the very best of purposes, is rendered sometimes one of the most dangerous, since through it the very fountains of the mind are corrupted: for this reason it should be most carefully guarded.

Again: the observations and experiments children have made, will have furnished them with sufficient stores to enable them to commence upon their own capital. Children delight to relate their own incidents and experiments; and in doing this, they are only pursuing one of the most effective modes of culture.

Tales, Sketches, of Travel and Adventure, form a large share of the literature of this age, but too much care can not be exercised in the selections. The characters and the incidents should be of an unexceptionable kind, since upon their good quality and the mode of presenting them, depends the success of the plan

The impressions made should have a refining and elevating influence, or it were better none were made. The ambition to excel may be a holy or an unholy one. If it is prompted by a desire to excel others for the simple pleasure of being above them, it is wrong. If, however, it arises from a desire to excel for the purpose of elevating others to the same point, it is right. This holy ambition may thus, by a judicious choice, be inspired to go forward, conquering obstacle after obstacle, until the aspirant has excelled even those whose noble deeds first inspired him.

Care must also be exercised both in the selections and the modes of presenting these topics, so as not to foster a morbid desire for excitement, which not unfrequently leads to an indiscriminate devouring of every thing that savors of the wonderful or the sentimental. Hence the desire for fiction and fancy. But incidents in history and biography, and in fact this whole subject abounds in that which is not only wonderful but true; and which, if properly presented, will be equally palatable with the overwrought fiction, so much sought after by the young.

These incidents etc., may be related in the school or family by the teacher or parent, and then at suitable intervals, they may be called up in review and recited by the pupil. This will cultivate the memory and the power of narration, at the same time that it will convey a knowledge of most of the important events in history and biography.

Another mode of cultivating the descriptive powers, and thereby training the intellect to habits of close observation and thought, is to require the pupil to give frequent descriptions of common occurrences. This will also afford an excellent opportunity for cultivating a habit of telling the truth, a habit quite too rare in all circles of society. Many suppose that, in order to make a story interesting, it must be embellished with all manner of superlatives and expletives; and hence they fall into the habit of exaggeration and falsifying to such an extent, that it becomes almost impossible for them to tell the truth, even when they wish. Though this is a moral evil, it may be corrected at the same time that these other important intellectual results are secured. The practice therefore, of frequently, and it may be at stated periods, requiring the pupil to give a plain unvarnished statement of common occurrences, will not only teach him to tell the truth on all occasions, but will cultivate his language, his power to reproduce, his habits of observation and thought, and will beget a desire for study and a love for the school. This will be perfectly natural; for whatever children can do well, they generally love to do. And instead of this practice interfering in the least with the ordinary school-duties, it will only invest them with additional interest, and carry into them the same accuracy and practical earnestness and utility, that characterize the Descriptions and Biographical Sketches.

ART. 2—SCIENTIFIC FACTS.—There is a large class of Scientific Facts which may be communicated at intervals and during recitations, without any interruption to the regular school duties. It is the most evident intention that these things should be learned early in life, since the mind then is in the most favorable state to receive them, and since ignorance of them often leads to accidents, ill health and fatal results. Those most useful, and at the same time most interesting, are those connected with Natural Phenomena, Vegetable and Animal Life, the Laws of Health and Growth, and a Knowledge of the Arts and Employments.

The air, for instance, is one of the most common substances, and yet its properties are, at once, most simple and most wonderful. Now a few brief allusions to these by the teacher, or what is still better where it can be done (and I know of no place where it could not), to give a few simple experiments, judiciously arranged, will usually awaken a greater interest in the study of Natural Philosophy and Meteorology, than half the text books in the land. These subjects themselves seem to be specially designed by the Author of nature, to evoke that kind of interest and mental development which, if left without these aids, oo frequently slumber throughout the whole period ›f life. Tell the group of wondering pupils, on some occasion when their minds are in an inquiring state, that the air once breathed becomes poisonous, and is hence unfit for breathing purposes again, until it is purified by natural processes; that this same air that is thus deprived of its animal vitality, goes to the vegetable world, freighted with the very pabulum of life for that department, where it is again purified, and fitted for the animal world; and you awaken a train of thought which may go on unraveling these mysteries until it arrives at the very threshold of Deity. Tell them that trees and plants do really breathe, and you at once beget the inquiry, "What, and where are their lungs?" What better opportunity could occur for a lesson in Botany? The uses of the leaves and flowers will at once suggest themselves. They will readily understand, that in addition to the grateful

shade and beautiful foliage they produce, they have an ulterior object, viz.: the growth and reproduction of the species. Tell them that trees not only breathe, but that they eat; and the wonder of these inquiring minds will amount to astonishment. Let them think over it, and talk over it, before you explain it to them, and perhaps in a few days the whole neighborhood will be aroused to investigation. Books will be purchased, authors will be consulted, and *mind* will be awakened.

Now is the time to describe to them the various kinds of soil, the processes of absorption from it, the ascent of the sap in trees and plants, its distribution to the buds and on the surface of the wood to form the new growth as in the case of forest trees: and, if the season is favorable, remove the cuticle, and the true bark, showing their uses and analogy to the cuticle and the cutis vera of the human body; and let them see this distribution of embryo woody fiber. Ask the boys, why they can not make their wooden whistles in midsummer and fall, as well as in the spring, and you will set them to thinking: you will throw an attraction about these subjects, which will make them the themes of constant observation and research.

Tell them that the burning of wood in the stove, the breathing of air in their lungs, and the rusting of iron when exposed to the moisture, are one and the same chemical process; and what better opportunity could you ask, in which to convey to them some of the most important chemical knowledge? It will beget a spirit of inquiry, that will result in more mental development, than is ordinarily secured by years of teaching in the hum-drum routine of

study and recitation, without these aids. And then again, there are the subjects of rain and hail, snow and frost, heat and cold, dew and fogs, winds and clouds, lightning and thunder, all these are common matters, and are fraught with intensest interest to children.

But the topics need not be confined to one or two departments of science. The earth and the waters, and the departments of Natural History abound with wonders that are no less entertaining and instructive. This is practical knowledge, and its value is greatly enhanced, when it is remembered, that in addition to the above named benefits, this process is calculated to inspire a love for the study of the natural sciences. Animal life itself is a mystery which, while it defies the wisdom of man, presents some of the most wonderful and pleasing phenomena that abound any where in the whole range of science.

The circulation of the blood, the digestion of the food, the processes of growth and elimination, of secretion and deposit, offer the same opportunities for waking up the mind. The flying of birds, the running of animals, the swimming of fish, and all the various phenomena, their habits, the adaptation of supplies to wants, of means to ends, seem fitted by the very hand of the Creator to inspire the young student of nature with a love for her walks.

Then, immediately connected with this subject, is that of a knowledge of the Arts and Employments. Children living in the city exclusively, are usually ignorant of the arts, employments and modes of life peculiar to the country. Many of them can not tell whether flour is made from wheat or corn, whether buckwheat grows on trees or vines, whether butter is a natural or artificial product, whether pumpkins, potatoes and melons are tropical, or the products of their native soil. And they are equally ignorant of the modes by which crops are produced from the soil, and how the various products are manufactured into the commodities of common use. The country children likewise, are no less ignorant of city life, and of some of the commonest arts and employments, such as the manufacture of the articles of commerce, etc.

Now if these things are worth knowing, they may as well be learned early in life, so that they may yield a profit; and then they are such essential aids to the practical study of the sciences. They enlarge the circle of human knowledge, and prepare the mind for the successful prosecution of the practical duties of life.

It will not be understood that these suggestions and recommendations shall form exclusive modes of culture. This is not their design. They are designed rather as aids to those already in use, and to suggest others more useful.

Article 3 — Rehearsals, etc. — There is another class of truths, more of a metaphysical nature than otherwise, which have a powerful effect in an educational sense, and which are not conveyed directly by the modes heretofore described, but which may be brought before the mind in the shape of maxims, mottoes, sentiments, rhymes, poems, etc. These are simple and direct, and by virtue of the style, are peculiarly adapted to the tastes and wants of the young.

Much solid truth as well as encouragement and precept, which might fail to make the proper impression if clothed in the ordinary style, may be couched in a pithy maxim or motto. And what renders this style still more useful is, that facts and principles in this form are more readily learned and easily retained. Simple poetry possesses the same merits, but great care should be exercised in the selections, so as not to corrupt the taste. All the above selections should be short, terse and not pedantic. Hence it is a good plan to have a large supply of these printed in large type, on convenient sized cards, to be suspended on the wall, where the pupils' eyes, while wandering about, will catch them; and, at times perhaps when we are least suspecting it, they will be drinking deeply of the sentiment. This will have the effect to familiarize the mind with some of the most noble sentiments and important scientific facts, and to inspire the learner with noble resolutions to exertion and perseverance.

It was upon this principle that the Israelites were commanded to "Teach these things to their children," (referring to the commands of God), "to write them upon the palms of their hands and upon the door-posts," where they would most frequently meet the eye. They thus became household words, fixed indelibly in the memory, and became the strongest incentives to thought and duty.

One of the grand objects of education is to learn to think, to train the mental faculties to habits of patient, persevering and persistent thought. The acquisitions are secondary to this, but most easily and readily made through it, and by it.

At the age of which we have been speaking, therefore, the *formation* of *correct mental habits* is a matter of the first importance, and should be kept constantly before the mind of the teacher. The education in the ordinary sense, is more than half accomplished when such habits are formed. The acquisitions then become a matter of pleasure.

Now, whatever may be said of the impracticability of these plans for awakening and training the mind to habits of thought and investigation, it is nevertheless true, that they correspond more fully to the order of development and the manner in which children learn, than the ones usually practiced; and that teacher that can not adapt the exercises of the school-room to them, should not teach. If these things can be shown to accord, both with the best philosophy and the best practice, no flimsy apology for not adopting them should be listened to for a moment.

Section 3—Investigation and Generalization.

In the preceding investigations and suggestions, we have kept steadily before the mind, the order of the development of the faculties, and the best modes of awakening and engaging the attention upon subjects of study. It might be well now to inquire briefly into the means by which this research can be continued without interrupting the harmony of action and order of growth.

The processes, or mental acts themselves, so far as they relate to acquisition and development, may be termed investigation—including analysis and generalization. And the sciences or subject in which they are employed may be arranged under the following heads, viz: 1. Physical Sciences; 2, Language and History; 3, Metaphysics.

The term investigation, as employed here, is one of more than ordinary beauty and strength. It may be made to include all the processes by which the mind makes progress in science. It is the permeating of the mental faculties into the substance of knowledge, tracking it out, through all its various ramifications; and so apprehending it, that the facts and principles become, not only familiar, but are assimilated to the mind itself, becoming a part of it, as the food by digestion and assimilation becomes a part of the living body. Knowledge thus nourishes the vital principle of thought. And in all vigorous and useful learning, the generalization processes follow, and even accompany the investigation as surely as digestion follows eating. It takes up the fragments as they are disengaged by analysis, and arranges them under their appropriate heads, referring individuals to species, and species to genera, until the whole superstructure is complete in all its parts. The power of generalizing is the chief distinction between an educated mind, and one in a rude, uncultivated state.

Again: two minds may be in the possession of the same amount of knowledge, and yet both not educated. The educated one will know how to use its knowledge; but the merely instructed mind, will be at a loss to know how even to retain its stores. Hence the difference in power and efficiency. The process of generalization is, therefore, of incalculable value to a teacher, since it gives him the power to arrange each topic of study in its proper order, so as not to disarrange the natural order of mental growth.

Article 1 — Physical Science. — The physical sciences afford ample scope for the exercise of a large share of the mental powers. We have spoken of the manner of introducing these sciences to the notice of the faculties, and the means by which they can be rendered attractive. It will be sufficient for the present purpose to point out a few of the relations and dependencies existing between these departments of science, and the intellectual faculties they were intended to nourish, and to leave the detail to the modes of study, recitation etc., Part Second.

Nothing has been made in vain. Even the smallest atom of matter performs its humble part in the great economy of Omnipotence, as well as the ponderous globe that rolls in ceaseless grandeur in its appointed orbit. The feeblest spark of intelligence has its appointed sphere, as well as the towering intellect of the tallest archangel. They all exist in mutual relationship. The one would not be complete without the other. They administer mutually to each other's happiness and even to their existence. So mind was made for science, and science was made for mind. God made both, and the one for the other. This is most conclusive, and it would be foolish, if not wicked, to suppose that there was any antagonism between them.

Mind lives and expands in science, while the latter, in turn is enlarged and extended by the action of mind upon it. The benefits are mutual, while the action and reaction constitutes one of the sublimest harmonies of nature. Not only is there a *general* adaptation of means to ends; but it descends to the minutiæ. There are grades or steps in the several departments of science, exactly suited to corresponding grades or steps in mental growth. If it were not so, then this order would be interrupted, and science would mock our hungry minds. But HE who made them, understood their relationship and wants, when he established this Divine order.

Now it is the duty of the educator to seek out this order, and so to adjust the two as to bring them together at points where they will harmonize; for unless they are thus brought together, there will be jarring and contention. The mind will rebel against the uncongenial labor and drudgery, while science in her turn, will yield but a meager bounty. She locks up her storehouses against all unwilling customers, and grants but a stinted dole to him, who seeks her treasures in unnatural channels. The questions therefore, to be settled at this stage of progress in mental growth, are, what is the extent or degree of development now existing in the individual, and what are the departments and steps in the same and different sciences, best adapted to carry it forward? These points can not always be determined by age, inclination, or by the opportunity enjoyed; nor yet are they the same with respect to any two individuals enjoying the same advantages. Hence the necessity of the most consummate knowledge of a professional character, on the part of the teacher, that he may balance those points nicely.

Perhaps, however, it is not given to human knowledge, in its present imperfect state, to avoid *all* errors in this adjustment, even were the materials furnished to our hands, in a perfect state; but the designs are nevertheless most evident. Because of corruption and consequent ignorance, we are incapacitated for this duty, is no argument against its existence, nor any excuse for not attempting it, any more than ignorance and neglect in observance of the laws would be excusable, because we were not all first rate lawyers. Much, therefore, should and *can* be done by intelligent effort, to render this subject plain, as the palpable errors now existing would abundantly testify.

For instance: if we could indicate the educational capacity or susceptibility by *a* and the degree of mental development by *b*, than *a b* would represent the mental condition or advancement of the individual. Now if *c* could represent the science or sciences, and *d* the department or departments in them, then *c d* would represent the educational force. In like manner, *n* might represent the power or true mode of application. Now when the first two sets of quantities or terms are reciprocally and individually equal,—as far as quantities so unlike in kind can be equal,—viz.: *a* to *c* and *b* to *d*, and *ab* to *cd*, each raised to the nth power, then would the educational problem be nearly solved.

But whether human knowledge shall ever arrive at that perfect state or not, is a question. It is nevertheless obligatory upon us to endeavor to reach it, since a perfect state of education can not exist without it.

We have two great departments of science, viz.: Physics and Metaphysics, each having subdivisions. These relate respectively to matter and mind.

Mathematics and Language are somewhat peculiar, having characteristics belonging, in common, to Physics and Metaphysics. They are, as it were, connecting links, binding the physical and metaphysical worlds.

The first, as a physical science, investigates the properties of matter, and the laws and forces of the universe. It also deals with truths in the abstract, as the numerical quality of magnitudes, and magnitudes in their relations to space, which give it a metaphysical character.

The second, or Language, sustains about the same relation to these departments; in that it gives expression to all these relations, and the thoughts, feelings and desires that arise in the soul; and it also represents the whole physical universe in its tangible forms, actions, qualities and relations. In these respects it is both metaphysical and physical.

Geography and History are merely local, temporal and descriptive, terminating within the limits of man's possible knowledge. The others reach far beyond. Purely professional science teaches only the right application of facts and principles, evolved from physical and metaphysical research, so as to promote the ends of life.

Here then we have the whole curriculum of sciences brought within this small compass. We might give the several subdivisions, did the necessities of a text-book require it. We therefore leave this part of the work to the learner, whose own investigations and classifications will be of greater service to him than any labored effort here.*

At the beginning of this section we have given a brief exhibit of the several departments of mind and intellect, the faculties and their functions. We have

---

* We take this opportunity, however, to refer the reader to a very ingenious classification of the Departments of Human Knowledge, given in a lecture to the "College of Teachers," at Cincinnati, by Roswell Park, and published in the proceedings of that body; also in the "Teachers' Indicator," a valuable collection of those lectures published by Moore, Wilstach, Keys & Co., Cincinnati.

also attempted a description of the general modes of culture, on through the primary period or that which relates to the perception, and through the secundo-primary, or that which relates to the primary understanding, judgment, memory, imagination, etc. The sciences and the several faculties now stand arranged, as it were, one over against the other. Neither can yield the full result without the aid of the other.

While it is true, that some sciences are more attractive than others, and some better calculated to develop certain powers of mind than others, it does not follow that each faculty elects its particular science, or is elected by any particular one. This would be at war with what has hitherto been advanced on this subject. But the mind, rather, elects departments in all the sciences—itself being elected by all — not however with the same strength of affinity.

It would not answer, therefore, to appoint one particular science to the task of educating a particular faculty, any better than it would to set one particular faculty at work upon one particular science. What could unaided perception or memory do, for example, in mathematics? or judgment or imagination in philosophy or history? or the reasoning powers in language? It requires, therefore, a combined action of all the faculties, as well as the combined influence of all the sciences, to produce the results anticipated by an education.

Natural and Mechanical Philosophy, Chemistry, Agriculture and the Arts, Mathematics, History and Geography, as far as they relate to matter, may be set down among the physical sciences as those well adapted to develop the understanding, judgment and memory, as well as to quicken the perception and reason. The understanding is rendered quick and accurate in its apprehensions and conceptions, by the study of these sciences, not one of which is without its influence. The judgment, in comparison, classification, and arrangement of facts, principles and theories is chastened, cultivated and refined. The memory has all it can do in receiving, associating, and storing away or retaining the material furnished by the united action of all the faculties, and in reproducing it, when called upon for that purpose.

ARTICLE 2.—LANGUAGE AND HISTORY.—It now becomes necessary to inquire briefly into the nature and influence of Language and History and kindred sciences. The harmony, mutual influence and benefits are even more marked here than in the preceding. All the faculties, including the imagination, to some extent, find ample room for exercise in Practical Grammar and Composition; Philology, Criticism, and General Literature; Chronology, Philosophy of History and Politics.

We will not undertake to decide upon the precise amount, or even upon the exact quality of the influence exerted by any particular branch of study upon the mental powers; for these results would be governed in a great measure by natural capacity, age, advancement, inclinations, and other modifying circumstances. But the fitness or unfitness of each will be determined by the existing wants. Neither will it be understood that if a pupil manifests a fondness for any particular branch that he is to be allowed uncontroled indulgence in it: nor yet is it the best policy to check him up entirely, thereby, it may be, putting an end to mental activity. The faculties may derive strength in all, or even in a few, of the sciences; but they seldom have a like preference for all. The course to be pursued, therefore, must be determined not by one or a few of these circumstances, but by all of them combined.

The course of study must be determined by the wants, and not the wants by the course of study. It should bend to the scholar, *i. e.*, the real wants of the scholar, and not the scholar to it. This perhaps is one of the greatest necessities connected with cou[illegible]op of study. Nature never bends to accommodate our whims. She often, however, permits us to go unrebuked for a time—justice often lingers long; but when she does call us to account, her reckonings are most fearful.

ARTICLE 3.—METAPHYSICS.—Lastly it will be proper to inquire briefly into the nature and influence of Metaphysical Sciences.

They stand, perhaps, among the highest for the cultivation of the Reasoning and the Reflective powers. Their influence, however, is not less potent upon the Imagination, and indeed, upon all the secondary powers.

The Attributes of Intelligence and Laws of Thought are intricate enough for the most searching analysis and the closest reasoning.

Existence, Duration and Infinity, are broad enough, deep enough, high enough, *vast* enough, it would seem, for the infinite mind, and hence for reflection of the highest order and the most far-reaching imagination. Man's feeble powers can but falter here; but they gather strength in efforts to fly.

Taste, Ideality, Theories, and Creations invite the imagination and fancy to revel in the exhaustless stores of their respective fields. They go forth, not alone in their excursions into the ideal world. All the powers accompany them, whence they return, ladened with the spoils gathered, it may be, in a hundred battles with science and art.

SYNOPSIS VII.

MORAL AND RELIGIOUS CULTURE.

- AFFECTION.
  - PHILANTHROPY — Love of kindred. Family ties. Love of the race. Sociability. Equality. Respect. Esteem. Friendship. Love.
  - PATRIOTISM. — Home attachments and influences. Nativity. Laws. Institutions. Love of right. True bravery.
  - RELIGION. — Love to God. Purity of heart. Reverence. Meekness. Submission. Adoration. Faith. Confidence.
- CONSCIENCE.
  - MORAL SENSE. — Ideas of God the basis of conscience. Ideas of right and wrong. Intuitions. The love of truth. Fidelity. Integrity.
  - MORAL DUTIES. — Relating to the family and Social compact Relating to country. Laws. Institutions. Relating to mankind in general. Honesty.
  - RELIGIOUS DUTIES. — To worship God in public and private. To love our neighbor as ourselves. To visit the fatherless and widow, &c.
- WILL.
  - MOTIVE OR PURPOSE. — Instruction in matters of right and wrong. Trust in the rectitude of a higher power. Energy and perseverance in duty.
  - CHOICE AND INTENTION. — Strengthening good resolutions. Obedience to superiors. Law. Submission to suffering. Privation.
  - EXECUTIVE VOLITION. — Direction and control by superior force. Encounter with difficulties. Temptations. Restraint. Moral suasion. Energy and perseverance in duty.

CHAPTER VII.

MORAL, SOCIAL, AND RELIGIOUS CULTURE.

THE moral Education of man is a theme which has engaged the attention of the educationist and essayist, for the past few years, to a greater extent than almost any other. Indeed, it has become quite an educational hobby. Long lectures, and earnest essays have been multiplied to such an extent, that one would think the world was fast approaching a revolution in its morals and religion. And yet we have a bad world. Notwithstanding Christianity has in eighteen centuries wrought astonishing changes in our civilization, laws and social refinement; notwithstanding she has wrested science, art, commerce and literature from the iron clutch of Paganism, and infused her life-giving spirit into our political and social institutions; yet I say, we have a bad world, too bad indeed, for unaided morality and human philosophy ever to reform. Indeed, vice and crime of every die seem to multiply right in the midst of all this light; and it is questionable whether the world would ever grow any better—nay it is quite certain it would not—under the brightest beams of the most exalted system of human philosophy, unaided by the gospel of Divine Truth. Man's *heart* must be reformed if the world is ever reformed, and *its* stains are too deep to be cleansed by mere human means. There must be a union of forces to produce harmonious results.

Now, most men are willing to admit these truths; but too many stop with the bare admission of them. But few seem to regard them, if we might be allowed to judge from the amount of attention bestowed upon them, in teaching, of any further importance, than a very fine speculative theory. Their practical results are very rarely tested, in connection with our systems of instruction. But the bare admission of the importance of a thing will never bring the thing to pass. The admission that drunkenness is an evil, and that stealing is a crime, will never punish theft or reform drunkenness. Our practice must, in all cases, correspond with our theory, if we ever expect to reform the world.

I have sometimes thought that if a being from some other world should pay our earth a visit, for the purpose of ascertaining what kind of creatures inhabited it, and should happen to alight in some of our school houses, and there form his opinion of our nature, exclusively from the exercises before him, he would wing his way back again, with the mournful intelligence, that man had no soul. For he would hear nothing about it, and see nothing. Nothing would be done, perhaps, from one week to another, to induce him to form a conclusion that man had a moral nature; but, on the other hand, there would be on the part of many teachers, a studied effort to avoid any thing that would lead to such suspicions, or betray the fact that man is endowed with an immortal nature—a living soul. Now, whether such teaching as this will ever effect any thing for the moral and social elevation of the race, I leave for candid and honest judges to decide.

Or suppose again, that we do recognize the existence of a moral nature in man, and teach the pupil a code of morals culled from the highest-toned moral philosophy, man's wisdom ever devised, and yet leave his heart untouched, save by the potency of human precept; think you, there would be the warm out-gushing of the living, breathing, loving spirit of Christianity in it? Think you it would restrain him, and sustain him in the dark hours of temptation and affliction? I tell you nay. The fact is, there is no sound and enduring morality without Religion. The best organized governments, and the best modeled social compacts testify conclusively upon this point. Religion, or piety is the basis of every sound principle and every redeeming feature in man's nature; and the attempts to make him moral without making him religious, are like the attempts to change the leopard to a kid, by feeding it with milk, or to produce a crop of roses from a growth of thistles. The adder's sting is not removed because he is petted like a harmless thing; nor the viper's fang, because he lies in your bosom. We do not say by this, that moral acts can not be performed, and from good motives too, by those who may be irreligious; but we do say, that just as soon as the motive which impels the act, proceeds from the right source, that moment the act approximates a religious act in the truest sense of the term.

Let man's heart be right, and then all the acts proceeding from it, will be right also; but let it be evil, and the issues can not be otherwise than evil; because "The same fountain can not send forth bitter water and sweet." "A corrupt tree can not bring forth good fruit, neither can a good tree bring forth evil fruit." "Either make the tree good and his fruit

16

good, or the tree corrupt and his fruit corrupt; for the tree is known by his fruit."

All the cold rules of morality you may hang about a man, if they do not affect his heart, will only gall him like so many chains, weighing him down with their unnatural burdens, and revealing more and more the corruptions of his heart. To throw the white mantle of morality over the dead carcass of sin, is like "painting the sepulchers of dead men's bones." To fill a wicked heart with moral precepts alone, is like the "parable in a fool's mouth," or the "jewel of gold in the swine's snout." True religion, and true morality, are therefore inseparable in their true results. The attempts to sunder them are like the attempt to separate the heat from the fire, the light from the sun, or the colors from the rainbow. The moment you do it, it dies. You paralyze every energizing principle, and the shapeless mass of morality, falls a cold, heartless thing. And the attempts to separate science and religion are not less destructive to the vitality of both, and are doing more, to-day, to destroy the effects they were designed to produce upon the human race, than most men are aware. They were made to go hand in hand.

When we shall come to recognize, in our practice as well as theory, the great fact, that man is by nature, a religious and social being, and that morality is nothing more than the legitimate fruits of the right culture of these natures,—or this nature, we might almost say; for they can scarcely be distinguished in their origin and effects, so intimately blended are they in the composition of human nature—then we may reasonably expect the improvements of which educationists have so long dreamed.

Man becomes circumscribed in his nature and influence, just in the proportion that he is deprived of any one or more essential ingredients or elements of character; and he increases in power, goodness and majesty, just in the proportion that he is allowed full and free scope to all his legitimate powers. If, therefore, it can be shown that man has a religious and social nature, and that upon the right cultivation of these natures will depend his true moral character and greatness, these being the true basis of morality, the way then will be clear for the establishment of modes of culture which shall be effective in moral training; for it is not to be supposed that these things are at all beyond the reach of educational influences. But just so long, depend upon it, as man is treated simply as a moral being, in the sense in which we usually apply that term, without attempting to purify the fountains whence issue the streams; these issues will continue to burst forth, leaping every barrier, breaking down all inclosures and soiling the whitest garments with which he can be clothed.

In making suggestions in reference to moral and religious training, we do not propose to usurp the authority or prerogatives of the church, or even to make theology a branch of study. This belongs to a separate branch of morality, yet not antagonistic to the former. Nor yet do we propose to dispense with any of the institutions of Divine appointment; for herein consists the whole merits of any mode of culture, which has man's true refinement for its object; but we simply mean to make use of means that spring up around man, by virtue of his nature and associations; or that seem, as it were, to be born with him; and which if not used for his moral elevation, will, from the very

same circumstances, be turned against him to work his moral degradation.

Section 1—Affection.

Man has *affections*, *conscicnce* and a *will*, as well as body and intellect; and the first three constitute the foundation, upon which chiefly rests moral and religious culture. Or, in other words, the proper training of these will result in a symmetrical moral character.

It will be necessary here to distinguish between good affections and bad ones, as the term, by most authors, is made to include the evil passions, as well as the good ones, or moral sensibilities. But all that is necessary will be accomplished by naming those to be cultivated, which cultivation will act as a check or restraint upon those that need this kind of discipline; so that the whole object will have been accomplished by the simple cultivation of the good affections.

The following classification of these affections will be found convenient and comprehensive enough, viz.: *Philanthropy*, *Patriotism* and *Religion*. These include the love of man, the love of country and the love of God, as the basis of all that is good in man's affectional nature, all that is worthy of cultivation; and out of which grow all the endearing relationships, social, political and religious, that appertain to man as such.

ARTICLE 1—PHILANTHROPY, in its most general sense means the love of mankind, that general benevolence that takes into its wide embrace the universal brotherhood of the race, which desires alike the freedom, development and happiness of all. It is antagonistic to human slavery, for philanthrophy rejoices in universal freedom and development of all man's powers, physical, intellectual and moral. Slavery teaches man to bind his brother in hopeless bondage. Or if it deny the brotherhood of the two races, it still involves a monstrous iniquity. It mingles those two races, and then allows a man to bind and sell his own race, and to make a chattle of the human soul. It teaches—nay it commands him to withhold the means of intellectual, moral and social refinement, which philanthrophy commands to be given him. Hence it is at war, at once, with the first and great principles of universal benevolence. But it is not our purpose to discuss this subject here. A simple statement of the general principles could not be avoided. This is all that is necessary, in order to teach our children to hate slavery and to love liberty; for, in accordance with our premise, just in proportion as we develop universal benevolence, we create a love for the one, and an abhorrence for its opposite.

But there are other evils of scarcely less magnitude, if not political, at least more general, crying right at our doors; which evils universal benevolence would seek to drive from the abodes of men. We refer to the needless and odious distinctions that prevail in what is termed refined society, by which the child is taught, in the most forcible manner, to respect and love one class of society, and to disrespect and despise the other. This is one of those polite, unobtrusive, yet insidious vices that makes its inroads upon us in the most stealthy manner, taking advantage of the very likes and dislikes of our nature, commencing at the very beginning of our intercourse with the world, and wielding a power over human conduct and human happiness scarcely equaled, and never excelled by any other vice. It is scarcely less criminal in its ultimate results than human slavery; since, when it ripens, and takes possession of the human heart, accompanied as it usually is, by a lust of power and gain, it teaches man to defraud, devour and oppress his neighbor. It is, therefore, the very root of bitterness in the sin of slavery. It is antagonistic to the law of God and the revealed character of God; for the first teaches to love our neighbor, and the other informs us that he is no respecter of persons.

When shall our people learn the true sources of happiness and greatness? When and where is there a better time, and a better place to teach these things than in the family and in the school, when and where the character of the man and woman is forming. If it is deferred until later years, that character will be warped by a thousand counter influences. A demagogue, and a hypocritical state of society, are the very worst teachers of morality and religion—except in a negative way—that could be employed.

The questions again recur, "When and where are the most befitting places, and who are the best teachers of these things?" We answer as before indicated, "In our homes and in our schools, and by our parents and by our teachers." The home influences and associations are the strongest. The school, which should be modeled, as nearly as possible, upon the same principles, so that it may take up the same course of training, is next in strength, and the stepping-stone from the family to the community of families. Both of these institutions, viz., the family and the school, are only preparatory to the great institution of human society, to which the pupil graduates at an early age.

Parents are the natural and rightful guardians of youth: and, by virtue of this relationship, they have an influence over them that none others can have. The teacher, by virtue of his office, is in loco parentis, for the time being, in which position the parent delegates to him all the powers he relinquishes, and even grants him rights and privileges in common with himself. Thus, in a proper state of society, the child is never without a guide—a constant text-book in morals. It becomes necessary now to inquire into the nature and potency of these educational forces, and at the same time, into the modes of applying them.

The love of kindred, or special philanthropy, is among the first affections of the human heart that shows signs of development; and hence demands the first attention. This is exhibited in the first answering tokens given from the child to the mother. The means of culture have been briefly described in the preceding chapters. It might not be inappropriate, however, to add that *the love of kindred or family ties*—the *affections*, constitute not only one of the dearest bonds on earth, but the basis also, or germ of universal benevolence. These affections embrace, 1. Parental love, or the love the parent bears to the offspring; and 2. The response to it, or filial love. The fact of its existence on the part of the parent first, is only in accordance with what is observable in every other department of nature, the former acting as a stimulant upon the latter, calling it out and giving it character. It might seem selfish at first, but not more so than all other early manifestations, relating to our sentient organism. The desire for food, for example, is among the first, and seemingly selfish; yet it has the most benevolent object in view. Here then we behold the buds of affection making their appearance among the very first manifestations of intelligence.

Now, if the dews and the showers, the sunshine and the shade of parental love, are shed upon these, in due proportion, they will unfold their tender leaves, revealing the morally beautiful, just as surely as physical beauty is developed under corresponding influences in the physical world. But how they wither and die, or take on some monstrous growth, when nipped by selfishness and neglect, or scorched and blasted by the hot breath of anger and revenge! Hence, those corruptions of the affectional nature, that manifest themselves in the form of the evil passions. They do not exist because they were planted there by the hand of the Creator: they are nothing more nor less than the fruits of a monstrous, perverted, or dwarfed growth of the good affections, produced by the poisonous breath of sin. The family, therefore, and school, which is only a generalized family, should contain all the nurturing elements that feed those tender plants, until they shall strike their roots deep in the soil of the human heart, and lift up their branches to the sunlight and the breeze, and shed their fragrance upon all the surrounding world.

It is wonderful to witness all the manifestations of a human being, even for a short time. In doing this, it will not be sufficient to take cognizance of the extraordinary occurrences alone: the ordinary events, and the common occurrences are the true indices to the nature and wants of the child. Every motion and every desire is significant of some passion which is destined to reign or riot in the human heart. They only appear insignificant because we do not comprehend their depth of meaning.

To an uncultivated mind, and an eye unaccustomed to trace the delicate workmanship of nature, a ledge of rocks presents nothing but a huge, misshapen mass. But the student of nature sees harmony and beauty in every part, and reads in legible characters the dates and names of the several geological periods. Both of these individuals may look upon a meadow, clothed in verdure; the one sees nothing but *grass*, the other sees a hundred beautiful flowers. They listen to the music of nature: the one hears a *noise;* the other listens, transported, to the rapturous hymnings of harps attuned to the sweetest melody. The one can scarcely bear the tedium of nature's walks, or the long, dull silence that reigns in her bowers: the other recognizes himself addressed by every sight and every sound; and if he had a thousand eyes and a thousand ears, he could find employment for them all, for every hour.

Thus it is with children and teachers. One person looks upon a child. He sees nothing but a rude, meddlesome, deceitful pest, and usually treats him accordingly: the other sees slumbering there all the elements of true manhood, nobility, and godlike power. The one sees in every look, and motion, and thought, nought but selfishness, craft and guile, and treats him with every mark of suspicion and disrespect: the other looks beyond the mere outward act, to the motive that impelled it, and by a word or look he anticipates his desires and checks the rising storm, or feeds the noble flame.

So one mother hears her infant when it cries, and she administers to its wants, as she does to the calf's or the pig's: another hears it even before it cries, and feasts it upon the pure milk of human kindness. The one hears in those torturing screams, nought but the rude expressions of selfish desire, or spleenish want: the other analyses those infant wails, and recognizes in them the tones of anguish or anger, of suffering or legitimate desire; and knowing, she is prepared to treat those desires judiciously. The one hears an angry broil among her brood, and rushing in with wicked words and maddening blows, dealt right and left, she assaults the contending parties, and succeeds in putting them to flight, and it *may* be to silence. But what a silence! Mark those flashing eyes, as they gleam, fiery red, each upon his antagonist from their lairs, and shoot their angry arrows into each others hearts. Think you they are subdued? So then is the tiger chafed by his prison bars. The other hears the contentions of her little ones, fierce it may be, but her heart swells, unutterably full of emotions, for the future of the man; and, with these struggling for utterance, she speaks, *but not in anger.* Her melting tones fall upon those hearts like oil upon the troubled waters; and the little ones, attracted by their sorrowful tenderness, glance quick into that tearful eye—their anger is forgotten. They hasten to their *mother's* arms—the asylum from the storm—to seek her pardon and a reconciliation.

Now we have drawn two pictures from real life, it may be one from each extreme; but the intermediate grades are scarcely less influential. We leave them to be filled out by the reader. Under the latter treatment, the elements and conditions are favorable for a vigorous growth; and as the processes go forward, these desires ripen into other forms of affection. The little children have been taught the first lesson, at least, in morals and religion, viz.: "to love one another:" and these affections, losing none of their essential characteristics, as a filial bond, go on widening, and deepening, and strengthening, until they embrace the whole human family. The very affections that cling so tightly about the mother, father, sister, or brother, gather sufficient nourishment and strength from these sources, to enable them to shoot out their branches and tendrils, and to entwine about other objects; and hence commences a more comprehensive growth—a *love for the race.* This prepares the way for *social culture.* We have spoken of the first, viz., General Philanthropy, or a love of the race, at the beginning of this section. We shall therefore devote a few pages to the latter, viz., *Social Culture,* as a means of securing the highest degree of moral and religious development. We shall commence by noticing some of the hindrances to the progress of religion, arising out of a want of social development.

One of the chief hindrances to the progress of morals and religion, is the cold and forbidding aspect these subjects *seem* to wear to the young. But these are by no means their natural garbs; they are only those that have been thrown about them by a mistaken idea as to the true nature and intent of these subjects. If any thing in the wide world should be attractive, it should be piety or religion, which has the same import as wisdom, as used in the Bible. "She is a tree of life to them that lay hold on her," etc. "Her price is above the price of rubies." "Her ways are ways of pleasantness, and all her paths are paths of peace." "The path of the just shineth brighter and brighter, unto the perfect day," etc. But it is unnecessary to extend evidence upon this point. The whole Bible is a mountain of testimony; and ten thousand living witnesses have testified to the same fact. Beauty and truth are inseparable companions. They are both equally attractive to the moral nature of man.

It will be necessary, however, to distinguish between the really beautiful or attractive, and that which is deceptive, having only the appearance—between sensual pleasures and those of a higher order. Religion or Wisdom ever represents the latter, and in that sense she should be held up to the young. She deprives man of no rational enjoyment. Indeed she hightens every earthly pleasure, and assuages every earthly sorrow. Every earthly blessing grows doubly dear, when piety throws her pure mantle over its enjoyment. It is true, she teaches us to deny ourselves of the sinful pleasures of the world; but in this we only exchange dross for gold. She teaches us to "take up our cross," etc., and to wage a continual warfare against sin; but in all this, we are more than compensated, not only by the peace of conscience, and the lively hopes and joys inspired within, but by the conscious strength we acquire; and the very air we breathe, becomes more precious, because of its source. Our friends become more dear, because we can love them with a purer, intenser affection. Our property is enhanced in value to us, because we can use it (in which consists the only pleasure we can derive from it) to promote the happiness of our fellow men, and to advance the cause of our master.

If any body should be happy, it certainly should be he who has a title to both earth and Heaven. If any body on earth should laugh, it should be the good man; if any body should mourn, it should be the bad man; for "the way of transgressors is hard." "The wicked are like the troubled sea that casts up mire and dirt." "There is no peace for the wicked, saith my God." "The lamp of the wicked shall be put out." All the family and social ties are rendered doubly dear, because they are hallowed by the sacred influences of piety. But while it is our purpose to show the nature and necessity of social culture, it seems necessary at the same time, to show that such culture will not be antagonistic to man's religious nature.

That man is a social being, no one but a hermit would deny. We have shown that he is a religious being, and a moral being. Now if his social nature is in *antagonism* with either of these, we at once discover a war among the constituents of man's nature, which criminates his Maker, and makes man the sport of contending forces. In assuming the foregoing position, it is not necessary to assert or deny that the good in man is continually waging war against the evil, and the evil against the good. This is entirely an independent issue, involving the circumstances and effects of the fall; and whatever views might be taken of that, would not at all interfere with the first position, viz.: that man has a social nature, demanding culture, in common with other departments; which culture, so far from interfering with the others, constitutes one of the strongest and the safest aids. Neither is it sufficient to say that this department will provide for its own necessities. The instances of lamentable deficiency, as well as perverted growth, prove an entire refutation of the position.

It becomes necessary therefore, to point out some of the modes of culture to be adopted, which will not interfere with, but will promote man's physical, intellectual and moral growth. And here it might be well to add that the chief, and perhaps, the only reason that modes hitherto adopted, have proved faulty or insufficient, is that they did not recognize all there is essentially in man; and the fact, that in order to make any one department of education successful, it must be accompanied by all the rest. And because they have failed, to some extent, the task has been abandoned as a hopeless one; or it has been handed over to those entirely incompetent, who have prostituted every power to pleasure, and the gratification of the senses. These have failed more signally than any others, since they have attempted to develop man's social nature, not only independent of his morals and his intellect, but in direct opposition to them.

Now we hold it as a cardinal point, that the good things of this world should be in the hands of the good, since none others seem so well fitted to enjoy and perpetuate them. It is equally tenable, that they should have the control and direction of the educational influences, since these are among the good things. The moment they relinquish their hold upon any one or all of these, they fall, from necessity, into the hands of the bad; since they must exist somewhere, and there are but these two classes of persons in the world, among whom they can exist.

Nothing, therefore, can be clearer to one having an unclouded perception, and an unbiased mind, than that the social nature of man does need attention, and that these influences should be looked after, since they invariably take one of these two directions. It follows also that the direction of man's social culture should be in the hands of the wise and the good, since it is a matter of such delicacy and danger, that it least becomes the hand of a novice or a knave.

The inquiry then arises, what shall be its nature and characteristics? In answering this question, it will be necessary to revert to man's original constitution and natural wants. These can only be determined by careful study, which will reveal the fact that he is a being of unabated activity, and ceaseless desires; that he invariably seeks companionship with his kind. He seeks *company* that he may give vent to those social desires and induce a lively activity of the faculties, since in their activity their pleasure alone consists. Now the questions arise, what shall be the nature of this companionship, and what employment shall engage his faculties; since upon the right or wrong determination of these points, will depend the success or failure of the whole thing.

In answer to the first, all will agree that the better the companionship, the better for the man. He would derive little benefit from the companionship with monkeys or savages. His habits and character will partake more or less of the influences surrounding him. Hence the higher, purer, holier and more refined those influences, the more beneficial the results become. And it is proper to remark here, that his regard, respect, esteem, friendship and love, all rise or fall to the same level, and will take their character, to a great extent, from the qualities of the objects upon which they are bestowed: i. e., the purer and more exalted the object of affection, the purer and more exalted the affection itself. Hence a man can not love a horse or a crocodile as he can love his own species. The seeming exception to this rule is accounted for on the principle of perverted affection.

It is equally manifest that if companionship of the highest order is withheld, man will seek that of a lower grade. But, that he should seek that of an inferior order, without some strong reason, would be as

strange as that he should love deformity and hate beauty, or that he should seek pain, and shun pleasure.

We have cases on record, it is true, of man's seeking and cultivating companionship with the inferior animals, and even with insects; yet this has always occurred, when he was driven by crime or other circumstances, from the society of his own kind. Here then, we have a true index to man's companionship. It should always be with his own kind, and should partake, as largely as possible of all the ennobling elements and refining influences which shall give a harmonious activity to all his faculties, intellectual, physical, social and moral.

Now the question arises, since man has found his companionship, and since this calls for employment, what shall this employment be: shall he do good; or shall he do evil, are *the* questions to be decided. We have spoken in preceding chapters, of the various kinds of employment, suited to man's several wants—such as labor, study, recreation, etc., but have not spoken particularly of social amusements.

That the desire for amusement does actually exist in man, no one can deny. But whether it is there by command or consent, is a question that might trouble some. In either case, we are under equal obligation to provide for it, or for its removal. We infer that it exists by command, since God has made such abundant provision for its gratification, and since it is, in itself, both innocent and useful, as we shall have occasion to show as we proceed. Now if God has created nothing in vain, then the desire for amusement is for some purpose. If it is for some purpose, that purpose is either a good one or a bad one. To admit the latter would be to charge God with evil.

Says Dr. Paley, "We never discover a train of contrivance to bring about an evil purpose. No anatomist ever discovered a system of organization, calculated to produce pain and disease; or, in explaining the parts of the human body, ever said, 'This is to irritate; this is to inflame; this duct is to convey the gravel to the kidneys; this gland to secrete the humor that forms the gout.' So in relation to the faculties of the mind. Who has ever discovered faculties there designed to demoralize and debase us? Who in explaining them ever said, 'This is to make you profane, this to make you intemperate, this to make you cruel, and this to make you dishonest.'"

This is a very fair exposition of the argument, and shows conclusively that God has not only not made anything in vain, but has made every thing for some wise and useful purpose. He has made man just right, and the world in which he has placed him, just right. All the wrong is chargeable to man himself. Another proof that the desire in man for amusement, is a natural desire, is found in the fact that he has, from time immemorial, sought after it; and where attempts have been made to deprive him of it, they have resulted in disaster to some of his powers by entire abstinence, or driven him to excess in an opposite direction; as the monkish asceticism on the one hand, and the shameless abandonment to pleasure on the other, are but too sad commentaries.

Again: The laws of God, as revealed in his written word, as well as upon every object of nature, and especially in man's own body, as well as upon his mind and morals, all testify, as with one voice, that man needs amusement, just as essentially, as he needs his food and sleep; and that if he is deprived of it,

though the disasters are not so visible, yet they are no less certain.

And again; the young of all animals play. It is as natural as that the sun should shine when it arises, or that plants should bloom and thrive under his genial influence. Children need it all for their physical and social development. Without it, they would become a race of drones and misanthropes. If there is any thing in this dark world, calculated to make glad hearts, it is the merry sports of childhood and youth.

But the old need it also. It will not answer to say, that this is all well enough for the young, but that the old should abstain from such frivolities. They need its life-giving influence; if not to engage in it themselves, at least to witness it. It is the sunshine of life. It makes them live over again, their youthful days, and infuses new vigor into their bodies. It were as grave an error in philosophy, that would teach that the aged and middle-aged did not stand in need of amusements, though they might be of a graver sort, as that would be, which would teach that the sunshine and the showers were all well enough for the flowers and the tender plants, but that the giant oak and the ripening grain, had no need of such light and trifling things. How long would the oak live without sun or rain? When would the grain ripen? We have an answer to these questions in the untimely death of mortals, and the unripe condition of mind, body, and morals.

The question, therefore, is no longer "Shall we have amusements?" that is decided. It is now, what kind? And who shall superintend them? The first would involve a longer description than the limits of this chapter would allow. We would simply remark, however, that some of the best and most ennobling of these amusements, have been discarded by the religious world, as vicious and contaminating in themselves. And because they have thus been driven out of the best society, and all moral restraints removed from them, they have sought refuge among the vile, and have hence become contaminated.

Whether, upon the whole, it would be wise to attempt to purify and reinstate these amusements, is an open question. It is nevertheless certain that they either should be, or else others of equal merit should take their places. This conclusion is inevitable from the nature and constitution of the human race, as well as from the sad abuses to which amusements have been prostituted. One of the most popular of these social amusements, and the only one to which we shall call attention, is that of dancing, a science at once and an amusement, in itself entirely innocent, when properly conducted; as much so surely, as singing, or walking or talking, yet unfortunately, like poor Tray, it is suffering from being found in bad company.

Now since men and women, and boys and girls, will, and must from necessity seek society, and since this institution is organized for the benevolent purpose of refining the feelings and manners of its members, as well as to contribute to their enjoyment; and since when thus assembled, the time either drags heavily and uselessly on, or else is filled up with vain, insipid and trifling conversation, or what is still worse,—since all the powers want activity—with boisterous plays, and rough and uncultivated and uncultivating conduct; and since health, intellect, morals and physical development, grace, ease and dignity in bodily movements, as well as a healthy flow of good nature, all seem to entreat for some employment and cultivation; and since, in the great majority of instances of intercourse, the usefulness, and consequent happiness of the individual are measured by, and are dependent upon his ability to make a proper use of *all* his powers, especially those that relate to personal address; therefore, it does seem necessary that some amusement, having the greatest possible number of these objects in view, at once simple, cheap, harmless and attractive in itself, should be adopted for the benefit of all classes.

If it be objected, that dancing would lead to balls, routs, masquerades and all that giddy dissipation which now form the chief, and indeed, almost the only valid objection to it; let it be answered, that these are mere accidents, and mostly traceable too, to the neglect of those who complain; but that they are not the necessary results, any more than the extremes or excesses in other employments are necessary. It is not a valid objection against singing, for instance, that it happens to be prostituted to base uses; nor yet against language, because it is employed by the vile to convey bad thoughts. What would be thought of the moralist, for instance, who would not talk, because somebody had made a bad use of language.

But if any thing better than the dance can be adopted, *let it be done:* no good man or woman, certainly, would object; and the bad might thereby be the more easily reclaimed. But there is that about the dance, when conducted to the sweet strains of music, which renders it at once the most pleasing, soul-cheering, and refining, both to body and mind, of any mere social exercise. In saying thus much we are not pleading for, nor apologizing for the miserable abuses of this practice, the objectionable forms which have obtained in the most corrupt classes of society. It is no more necessary to include these in this science, than it is to admit all the vulgar songs in music, or all the obscene and profane words in language. The fact is, all those irregularities and abuses would gradually disappear, if the science were cultivated, and the practice recognized and superintended by the wise and prudent. It is questionable whether any exercise, whether social, religious, or otherwise, would survive long, in its purity, were it subject to like abuses; and it is quite likely that many of the social and religious exercises, if not all of them, would be liable to as fatal extremes, were they submitted to as rude hands.

This leads us to remark, in the second place, that this exercise, in common with all other rational amusements, needs regulating; or like all others committed to the young and inexperienced, it will run into fatal extremes. And first, it should be regulated as to time, place, and freqüency. Let us glance at the present practice. Notice is given that in six weeks there is to be a grand Fourth of July or Christmas Ball, at such a place, and so and so. Tickets of invitation are circulated, but not always to the most worthy. Of course, it will be a grand time, and the excitement begins to rise to the neglect of other duties. Preparations are to be made, and a needless expenditure for clothing never again to be worn, must be ventured. The time arrives: and the parties, illy clad it may be for the season, assemble; and under the most exciting circumstances the exercises commence. But the room is illy ventilated (yet it must needs be closed), and the air soon becomes vitiated. The youthful revelers become intoxicated, mad with pleasure, and heated with excitement. No one is there to check them—no father, no mother to chide or counsel, no minister of grace to mingle his seasonable advice,—they are all young, and anything like moderation would be treated lightly, or with suspicion at least.

Father or mother, do you see your daughter there, whirling in that giddy throng? Do you see your son there, reeking in excitement? Look, but tremble for their safety. The soul and body are both in danger. . . . . But attend longer. It grows late in the evening—Nine. . . . . Eleven. . . . . it is One; and they may have been thus engaged from One or Three of the preceding day. But, "on with the dance," and dissipation now becomes more bold; and dissolute conduct and the vulgar jest mark the demeanor of that young . . . . . . But we quit the scene. The hour is now four in the morning, and the youthful revelers repair to their homes; but think you with light hearts? The past to them appears like a dream; but it will not soon be forgotten. They go to their homes, amid the exposures of inclement weather and poor protection, to spend a blank, unhappy day, dreaming in morbid sentimentality over the last night's revel.

Now, is this physical culture? Is it intellectual culture? Is it moral culture? It is neither. It is downright murder of body, mind, and soul! Yet, who is to blame? Who but those who have the power to correct these abuses, and will not use it? Who would be to blame if you, parent, kept your child in such a situation, that his physical powers had become so reduced by hunger as scarcely to possess vitality, and the mind judgment; and in this starving state, you should turn him loose to a table loaded with all the delicacies and dainties of a refined restaurant, if you should find him in a few hours a bloated corpse? Who would then be to blame? Nothing but necessity and ignorance would excuse you in the eyes of the law. But neither of these would excuse you in the eyes of God or the world. And yet your conduct, in reference to your child's amusement, has been perhaps precisely of this character. He has been deprived of the privilege and benefits of it at home where it belongs, it may be for months at a time; and then, on some extra occasion, he is turned loose without any restraint, except the feeble resistance offered by his own judgment, to glut himself to repletion upon that which is most intoxicating. What could be expected but excess! It were far better not to indulge at all, or to get a beggarly subsistence upon that which is thrown out by the wayside, than thus to abuse our powers.

But this is only a faint sketch of the evils of modern dancing. What remedy shall be proposed? What but that which should be prescribed for any other natural want? *Regulate it*, both as to *time*, *place*, and *frequency*. *Regulate it, or abandon it altogether!* The time should not infringe upon the hours of labor, devotion, or rest. No midnight revels should therefore be tolerated.

The place should be free from all the objections described in our picture, and should, if possible, be at *home;* because it is a home and family amusement, as much so as family devotion is a home exercise, though both may be practiced abroad. And here allow me to ask, what impropriety there would be in bringing these two exercises together, or at least in close proximity? For if amusements of this kind are worth any thing—if they are right, they are worth asking God's blessing upon: if not, it were better to abandon them.

The same regulations with regard to frequency, should be observed, that obtain in other habits—as in sleeping, for instance. The objects will not be attained by resorting to them once a week, or once a month, or only on extra occasions, any more than the objects of eating and sleeping could be secured by resorting to a similar course in reference to them. Other regulations might be offered, as to mode and degree of exercise; but they will readily suggest themselves, if amusements of this character are entered into, with a proper spirit, and having a proper object in view. As to the former, however, we might add that all modes or figures that have the slightest tendency to excite undue levity or mirth, or to awaken evil desires, should be studiously avoided. No crazy waltz or giddy polka, or any other objectionable figure, should ever be allowed a place in the social circle, much less in the family training of boys and girls.

But who are to be the superintendents of these exercises? We have just seen that it is no more safe to intrust this department of education to children themselves, or to wicked and designing men, than it is any other department. The answer then to the question is this: *The leading minds in education and religion.* If the wise and the good do not regulate them, the wicked and profane will; because they *must exist*, and it is for the former to say, whether this important educational force shall be wrested out of their hands or not.

If amusements were under the strict surveillance of the parent, the teacher and the preacher, just as other departments of education are, and treated in as rational a manner, we submit, would not the evils arising out of them speedily disappear? But until these functionaries shall come forward and proclaim a reform in them, instead of standing off, at a respectable distance, and hurling their anathemas at them, the probabilities are, they will continue where they are, or perhaps will retrograde.

This mode of suppressing the evils resembles the ridiculous farce of Dame Partington, armed with her mop, disputing the right of the sea to the possession of her own humble dwelling. And it is reported that the sea beat the old lady in that memorable contest, notwithstanding her excellent mode of warfare. So we are apprehensive, the battle with these amusements will most likely terminate, unless the mode of attack is changed. The fact is, any attempt to suppress these amusements without providing a rational substitute for them, is too much like the attempt would be to remove all food or exercise from man, because it so happens that some food and some exercise are not profitable, or that some men become gluttons, and others kill themselves at hard work.

We have spoken candidly, frankly and somewhat pointedly upon this vexed question. We have tried to show the absolute necessity for safe and wholesome amusements; and we have pointed out the errors and excesses and shown the necessity for moral and religious restraints, as the only corrective. We were compelled, from absolute necessity, to take this ground, however reluctant; because we conceive it to be wrong to attempt to conceal any part of the truth.

18

We therefore leave the reader to form his own conclusions after weighing carefully the testimony pro and con.

Article 2 — Patriotism. — The next topic under moral and religious culture, claiming attention, is that of *patriotism.*

It may not readily be understood how this subject belongs to morals; but it will be seen, upon closer examination, that the influences that cultivate a true love of country and inspire the spirit of bravery, are of a purely moral character, and can be traced back, in most cases, to home attachments and influences.

Again: it might not at first be easy for every one to see how this virtue can be cultivated in the school or family; but a little reflection will disclose, not only its true sources, but the surest means of development. Home, if it is a home in the truest sense of that word, is the most hallowed spot on earth. With what fondness we are accustomed to revert to scenes of early childhood! Our weary pilgrimage in life may have cast a shadow over our brightest prospects; and our present abode may have become anything but desirable; but there is usually one spot on earth, about which the memory lingers with a dreamy fondness. That spot is the dear old home, where the world first revealed its wonders to us.

The traveler, far from his native land, when night closes in upon him, instinctively turns to gaze upon the setting sun; and quick as thought, visions of the past and of the dear native home flit across his mind, and he lives over again for a few brief moments his childhood days. The soldier, dying in a foreign land, breathes in his comrade's ear his last faint accents of home and the loved ones there. The mariner struggling upon the wave as his gallant barque goes down, catches glimpses of home, and his last sad wailings, mingling with the crash of waters, tell but too feebly how he loved his home. If this were not sufficient to prove the love of home to be an affection, worthy to be cultivated, that inimitable ballad, "*Home, home, sweet, sweet home,*" etc., is sufficient of itself to canonize the feeling, and to render it ever a matter of pleasure to think of home. There is therefore a home affection, and this constitutes the basis of patriotism. It only needs, like other affections, the fostering hand of the true teacher, to give it its proper direction, and the home affections expand and embrace the whole country.

Now just in proportion as home, the mother of patriotism, is made home-like and happy, will these attachments grow and become, not only among the strongest barriers to the incroachments of vice, but a sentiment, when fully expanded, that will be one of the strongest ties to fatherland. It will soon go out and attach itself to country, laws and institutions, and become the strongest motive for the defense of the right. This presupposes, of course, that these laws and institutions, etc., be based upon sound principles. Otherwise there might be alienation and rebellion, instead of attachment and patriotism.

It will readily be seen that when the home and its surroundings are such as to inspire these warm attachments, the individual not only derives the greatest enjoyment from them, but he is cultivating those affections which constitute the basis of true bravery; for what is that patriotism worth which has no stronger incentive than mere mercenary motives, or the lust of

power? The spuriousness of such patriotism has been fully tested, and the genuineness of its opposite fully established in contests between parties actuated—the one by mere passion or the lower propensities, and the other by those lofty sentiments of honor and affection which arise from this early home attachment, and from a consciousness of right. Our own country affords examples of this, while all history abounds in similar testimony.

Let home be made the pleasantest spot on earth, and children will instinctively love it; and in indulging this natural desire, they learn to love their country, laws and institutions.

ARTICLE 3—RELIGION.—Nothing is more apparent than that man is prone to pay religious adoration to some being, either material or spiritual. There is both a contrivance, which indicates design, and a sphere of action to suit the mechanism of the human soul, which clearly point out its destiny.

When man was first created we can easily imagine him to have possessed all his faculties in a state of perfection. Every power glowed in an ecstacy of delight, and moved in perfect harmony with the world of beauty into which he was introduced. Not a jar, nor a discordant note was to be heard in all the glad anthems that ascended on high "when the morning stars sang together, and all the sons of God shouted for joy." Man walked abroad in all his innocence, majesty and beauty. And such was the exaltation of his powers—even the same powers that he now possesses—that he held direct intercourse with his Maker. But in an evil hour he put forth his hand to disobedience and fell from his exalted position. A moral night ensued, more dense and terrific than that, when the Spirit of God moved upon the great deep of chaos, and brought light out of darkness, and order out of confusion. A blight came over the whole face of nature, and the ground was cursed for man's sake, requiring additional physical toil to subdue it. His faculties partook of the general blight, descending to a fearful depth of depravity. He goes forth to struggle with his fortune and to finish his career, but not without hope; for no sooner had the fiat which drove man from the garden, gone forth, than preparations are made for repairing the breach. Even the command which is supposed by some to contain the heaviest curse, to wit., "In the sweat of thy face shalt thou eat bread all the days of thy life," etc., is big with mercy, and contains the very preservative element of the race, viz., labor; for without it, man would sink into imbecility.

No sooner therefore had man fallen than infinite goodness and wisdom set about devising his redemption. A ransom is provided and promised in the fullness of time, but a struggle for his faith here was necessary, as well as sweat from his brow in the physical world. The first should win life to his soul, the second bread for his body. In this we see not only man's redemption, but his education epitomized, and religion, or a reunion with his Maker and a renovation, and a reinstatement of his faculties are most clearly recognized; for "As in Adam all die, so in Christ shall all be made alive." Christ, or the second Adam therefore, becomes the medium through which man is again to approach his Maker—the link that is to reunite that which was alienated by sin and wicked works: for Christ who knew no sin became sin for us,

i. e., satisfied the demands of a broken law, and thereby reconciled believers to God. "He took upon himself not the nature of angels," but assumed our humanity and God's divinity, that he might effect this reconciliation, which seemed impossible on any other terms.

Now, if this is the nature of religion, why should we either fear it or be ashamed of it? Why should we esteem it lightly or even a sacrifice, since it confers upon mortals the most exalted relationship and honor that can possibly exist, even the relationship of sons of God, and heirship jointly with Jesus Christ the Son, to "an inheritance incorruptible, undefiled and that fadeth not away." Such in brief, is religion, and as such, it now becomes necessary to inquire how it can best be inculcated in the hearts and minds of children.

By referring again to man's original or natural constitution, we find him possessed of certain marked peculiarities, which render the inculcation of religion a matter of necessity, in order to cancel all the claims his own desires have upon him. Man's whole affectional nature is but a living and perpetual commentary upon religion; and one of the most interesting features of the home attachments and love of country, etc., as described above, and of philanthropy or the love of the race, both general and special, as described further back, is the ripening or culminating of these affections into the purest, holiest and loftiest sentiments that can actuate the human mind—I mean the love to God—the crowning excellence of all love and all affection.

The student should be careful while investigating the nature of man's affections, not to confound their use with their abuse. For instance, we speak of philanthropy or love of the race, and patriotism or love of country, etc. Now the legitimate sphere of these is diametrically opposed to that inordinate affection or lust of power or gain, which is denominated in holy writ, the love of the world, which is enmity against God. This is the very antipode of those affections which we should seek to cultivate. We believe the world and all that is in it (sin excepted), are legitimate objects of love instead of hatred; that when properly loved, they lead us to the great source and fountain of love, and the object of adoration. God so loved the world that he gave his only begotten son to die that he might redeem it. And shall we hate it?

The very fact that those things that were made for our comfort and happiness, and which should be the means or instruments of leading our affections outward and upward, are made objects of suspicion, dread or aversion, by a misguided apprehension of sanctity, constitutes the strongest reason why religion, the true source of all happiness, wears, to some, such a repulsive demeanor. In consequence of our ascetic notions, we often defeat the very object we wish to accomplish, viz., the inculcation and development of religious sentiments and feelings in the hearts of children. We do not make it a matter of every day duty and conversation. We only bring it forward on extra occasions, and allude to it in the most *awful gravity of style.* This makes children dread it.

Now I would not divest it of any of its awe or majesty, or give it any other character than what it really has; but I would invest it with its own lovely character. I would connect all our happiness with it. I would make it one of the most attractive subjects of conversation, instead of one of the most forbidding. I would make all other interests and exercises bend to this. I would hallow life's duties with it. Indeed I would make it the one great object of life, and mingle it with every earthly enjoyment. It would thus sanctify every other blessing and defend its possessor against the encroachments of vice. It should be worn as a shield, rather than as an amulet. It should defend man, rather than that he should defend it. It should be his strength, rather than his weakness. It should be his delight, rather than his aversion. It should sanctify him, rather than that he should sanctify it. In a word, it should be the star of his hope, and the crown of his rejoicing.

But we can not better illustrate this point than by quoting a few pungent passages from a little work recently published, entitled, "*Life Made Happy.*" The author is laboring to prove that religion is happiness, not misery, when he remarks, in effect, that "there is one aspect in which asceticism is still more destructive to the cause of Christianity than almost any other one thing. I allude to that strange feature in the character of the great body of Christians that their religion does not seem to set pleasantly and happily upon them. They do not wear it as they would a precious jewel, where it may be observed by all that meet them. They don't clothe themselves in it as a garment every day. How seldom is religious conversation ever ventured upon on ordinary occasions! How seldom is it brought forward, except when it *must be!* How seldom do we see a man who enters into religious conversation as freely, as easily, and apparently as happily, as he discourses about his business! Why is this? The reason is obvious. Religion is made a very solemn and a very gloomy subject. Is is not so? Does your pastor, does any one address you on the subject in the same tone of voice, with the same joyous countenance that he addresses you on other subjects? Is not the introduction of religious conversation a signal to hush all joyous sentiments, and to call in all the smiles? Is it not required? Can it be expected that our religion will be worn by us every day, if it must be done with a cloud on our brow? Or can we be expected to obtrude it upon others if the effect of it is to cloud their brows also? No! Religion can never be an every day matter, can never enter into our common conversation: it can never be a part of our lives, while it assumes its present gloomy character.

The gospel of Christ can never command that success that it is calculated to meet with, and will meet with, until that ascetic dead weight is removed. No man willingly chooses to be gloomy and sad himself, or to be the occasion of it to others. Why is it that the Gospel of Christ has made so little progress in the world? Why were the apostles, with their limited means, so much more successful than their successors with steam-presses? Do you not believe there is a defect somewhere in presenting it? I submit, is it not in this gloomy feature of it? Why should not a Christian be the happiest man in the world, and wear the happiest countenance, and talk joyously about the blessed abodes beyond the skies? Can we expect that religion will be generally embraced until Christians are so?

Why should religion and religious subjects be so gloomy a matter? What is there in them to call for it? Are they any thing more than discourses about a final and a happy home, and the way there? Ought we not to look upon those distant abodes as a child looks upon his distant home, when far away; and thinks of it, dreams of it, talks of it to his companions, and finds the theme ever bursting from his lips before his superiors? Compare him, as with eye brightning and countenance beaming, he discloses his young anticipations of delight, when emancipated and suffered to fly to that home of bliss, with another child, his brother, perhaps, who is alike exiled from home, but who is studiously silent on the subject, when excited at all with enjoyment, and only brings it forward at set times, when he must do it; and then it is done with a countenance and a tone of voice betokening any thing but enjoying it. Which of those children would soonest interest you in that home of his? Which of them would soonest tempt you to partake with him of its hospitalities and joys? and which of them would give you the most lively evidence that he so loved that home that nothing would tempt him to forfeit his title there?"

Such are the views of this author: and we might add, that while we would not be willing to become responsible for all the interpretations that might be put upon them, yet we are willing to vouch for the general sentiment of them.

Having thus pointed out some of the characteristics of pure religion in the first part of this article, and called attention to some of the obstacles that impede its progress, it were sufficient perhaps to add, that it does not consist in creeds, formulas, confessions, doctrines and dogmas, however excellent they may be, but in that love to God, and purity of heart which an unclouded belief and a living faith alone can inspire.

Its results are the peaceable fruits of righteousness, and its life is the life of the soul. "Pure religion and undefiled before God and the Father is this, to visit the fatherless and the widow in their affliction, and to keep himself unspotted from the world." It is not all faith, nor yet is it all works, but a happy and consistent blending of the two. It may not be amiss, therefore, to allude briefly to the manner in which it may be inculcated.

It has been shown that true religion can flourish to its fullest extent only when the affectional nature of man is fully developed: that universal benevolence, and the love of home, country, and kindred which characterize the individual while subject to these influences, may, under proper training, be made to converge all these energies in the one great object of affection—the God of the universe—thus bearing the whole tide of man's affectional nature to the great central point, where culminates every virtue, and around which clusters every grace that adorns the Christian character. Under these influences man's esteem ripens into veneration for the character and goodness of the Creator; his reverence into adoration, and his friendship into love, while purity of motive, meekness, submission under the provocations of life, and faith and confidence in God may characterize and possess the whole soul of man.

The manner in which this may be encouraged may be briefly summed up or indicated thus: The child loves its parents; but by conversation, teaching and pure example, its little mind may soon be brought to realize the fact that God is its father and the direct source of every comfort that administers to its wants, and every delight that swells its heart; and all this, too, without at all diminishing the strength of the parental bond. It loves its brothers, sisters, kindred and friends; and all these, including its parents, are the legitimate objects upon which the affections are first drawn out; but by a mere gratification of a spirit in man—a desire for an object of worship higher than mortal—these desires take on a higher development, and attach themselves to the elder brother, even Jesus, and to kindred in the skies. It may love the brotherhood of the race; yet this is not weakened but strengthened by a love that purifies and exalts all others—the love for the Redeemer and the redeemed. It may love its home and country; but these are only types of that better land where there shall be a full development and fruition of every noble sentiment that now swells in the human heart.

Now we have shown in another place that these things are teachable, and that just so far as they are, they are placed in the hands of parents and teachers: and we here add, that that system of education that does not recognize them as cardinal principles, will never meet the wants of the human race as it is now constituted. And since it is unsafe to defer the teaching of these things until their opposites become established in the heart; we must therefore look to the family, the Sabbath School and the Common School, to take charge of these matters. And since the whole subject is thus teachable and thus committed for the most part to these institutions, it is their duty, at once, to set about classifying and arranging these subjects, so that they may be taught and inculcated in the hearts of children at an early age. Let lessons be given regularly, and in due proportion, on those subjects; and what is still better, let them be mingled with all our teaching of whatever character; so that every lesson may make the child better just in the same ratio that it makes him wiser; and let every word of instruction, point upward to man's higher and holier destiny, for which alone this life is a preparation.

Section 2—Conscience.

The next topic for consideration is *Conscience*. And however diversified and conflicting the opinions are in reference to this department of man's moral nature, it is universally conceded by all, that man, in his normal condition, has a conscience, and that it is subject more or less to the influences of education. It is a significant fact also, that while conscience is the peculiar guardian of the sanctity of the soul, it is itself subject to some of the most violent abuses, from a want of education, or rather from a wrong education. It will therefore be seen, that whatever may be its ultimate ingredients or nature, as a basis, it is, nevertheless, subject to great modifications in its manifestations, and only acts in proportion to the light received, and is always true to its own nature and capacity. Taking all things in reference to it, into consideration, we are warranted in the assumption, that it rises no higher in its decisions than the ideas upon which it is predicated. It becomes an infallible guide to right and wrong, no further than the light shed upon its path, shines from the orb of truth. Therefore, the more accurate this light, and the more exalted these ideas are, the more exact and exalted will be these decisions. God being the highest possible object, therefore, in him all ideas of perfection center; and from him all light shines; and these become, by virtue of this exaltation, the true basis of conscience. Hence again:

the more exalted and correct our views of the Divine Being, the more elevated our conscience and conduct.

Article 1—Moral Sense.—The ideas of right and wrong themselves, seem to originate from this source; and it is not claiming too much for them, when we say they derive their peculiar force from these ideas of God: though I know, they seem to exist from the earliest dawn of intelligence. They would appear, therefore, in reference to some of the more direct operations of reason, to be almost intuitive: but our feeble powers fail, doubtless, to take cognizance of all the subtle influences that, we have reason to believe, operate to produce these strange results; so that we shall be safe in concluding that all these manifestations are referable, either directly or indirectly, to the causes named above. And we might add, with equal plausibility, that from the same source also, proceed our *love for the truth*, *fidelity*, *integrity* and every thing in fact, that relates to the moral sense. And that these can be cultivated, we shall now proceed to show. For if they can not be taught, then must truth be left to wage unequal warfare with falsehood, and to struggle against the combined influences of false teaching and false doctrine.

Our ideas of God being the true basis of conscience, it might be necessary to inquire how these ideas can be brought to as perfect a state as possible. A knowledge of the true God is therefore necessary. It will not do to believe in *any* god, nor yet to believe *any* doctrine concerning the true God; for our moral acts partake more or less of, and are affected, to a greater or less extent, by our belief. A corrupt doctrine is sure to beget a corrupt life. Wrong theory leads to wrong practice. Believing a thing will never make that thing true; and universally, the greater the error in belief, the greater the crime of believing it; and hence the more disastrous the consequences following such a belief.

Now, that our belief, so far at least as doctrine is concerned, is almost without exception, the product of education, is proved by the fact that children, who have received any parental instruction at all, adopt the belief of their parents; and though they may change that belief in subsequent life, yet relics of it will remain; frequently too to the torment of the believer. A belief in ghost stories and hobgoblins, early contracted, is an example of this. Again: the child often receives wrong impressions of God, both from bad precept and bad example. Our parents and teachers teach such low, human ideas of God, that he comes to be regarded by the child, scarcely above a human being, and hence the attachment rises no higher than the human standard. It is comparatively weak. Some err perhaps as much in an opposite direction, by teaching that God is so much a God that he never meddles with human affairs, but regards man and all his actions with a stoical indifference. Hence there can be no ready attachment; for an object to be loved must not be a myth, but a reality, and possessing lovely attributes. One teaches that God is all mercy and forgiveness, without considering his attributes of wisdom and justice; another that he is all inflexible sternness and vengeance, according, usually, to the predominance of the sentiment of love or fear in the mind of the teacher. This results, on the one hand, in an undue indulgence and a careless indifference, as to obedience; and on the other hand in a harrowing dread of the vengeance of God, which, unaccompanied by love or mercy, must produce a secret aversion in the mind of the child, and a desire to be free from such slavish restraint.

Now the truth is doubtless found in neither of these extremes, but in the happy blending of both into that harmonious character which is both the wonder and admiration of angels and men. The child should be taught to fear as well as love; but it should not be a slavish fear. He should fear to offend as a ground of willing obedience: he should love to obey as the best possible means to promote a healthy fear; and both these sentiments, in their interchangeable relations, should, as far as possible, be induced without extraneous force. The child should be taught to love the right, for right's sake, and not for pecuniary reward; and to abhor the wrong for its own inherent wrongness. He should be taught to love the truth for truth's sake, and to hate a lie for its native deformity. He should be taught to be honest, not because it is the best policy, but because honesty and uprightness are excellencies far above reward; notwithstanding they carry with them their own reward.

But in all this teaching, it will not be necessary to attempt to conceal the rewards by any artifice, much less should they be held up as motives to induce action, but only as the inevitable result. The child therefore should be taught to do right, to love the truth, to be honest and to worship God from principle, and not alone from impulse, let the consequences anticipated be what they may. Such teaching can be done in every family and every school, by simply taking advantage of the common occurrences and every day circumstances connected with other duties.

ARTICLE 2—MORAL DUTIES.—It will not be necessary to enter into a discussion upon this topic, since the nature and bearing of *moral duties* have already been alluded to; and, were it not that their connection with the conscience should be pointed out, they would not be referred to again.

1. Those relating to the family and social compact are prominent, and constitute the basis of all the rest. If these are observed, if the child is taught not to violate his own conscience in reference to the social ties, he will be more likely to regard it as sacred, when he comes to operate in a wider sphere.

2. The next class of duties of a purely moral nature, are those that relate to country, laws and institutions. This arrangement is in keeping with the natural order of the development of the affections; and it will be found that these affections, under a right system of education, will exactly keep pace in development, with the demands made upon them.

3. The next relate to mankind in general, and will be found to be no more nor less than a generalization and a little different application of those existing in the family and the school.

Now any violations in the antecedent relations of any of these duties, will only pave the way for a more extensive depredation in subsequent relations. For instance, if it is esteemed a light thing to infringe the rights of conscience in the family and in the school, such infringement will be comparatively easy when applied to society and country; and if with these, then with nations and with the world; and hence wars and national difficulties.

Now we submit this question for candid consideration, viz.: Suppose that all these antecedent relations were guarded carefully, and every infringement anticipated and apprehended; and suppose honesty and uprightness in their largest and most critical sense were taught and enforced as carefully and as rigidly as the rules in grammar and arithmetic are, would not the wars and contentions among nations, as well as the petty differences that arise among neighborhoods and individuals, cease, or at least be very much circumscribed? Would it not hasten the long-looked-for Millenium, as much as all the theorizing of theologians upon this subject?

Again, the little deceptions and hypocrisies which so often escape the eyes of the teacher or parent, and which are sometimes practiced by teachers and parents themselves, are the very beginnings of depravity of a monstrous growth, that develops itself in later years in the form of thefts, fraud, murders and such like crimes. How much better "to nip these things in the bud" than to allow them to attain their full growth. But with this brief allusion, we leave this part of the subject to notice, lastly under this section:

Article 3 — Religious Duties. — These have also been discussed to some extent, and will therefore claim but a brief notice here.

Unless religion becomes a matter of conscience, and not merely of convenience and commerce, its genuineness and existence are of doubtful standing, to say the least. The duties she imposes have a higher claim upon our attention, than a mere matter of policy. The discharge or neglect of them will affect the conscience either for good or for evil.

These duties may be enumerated under the following heads, viz.:

1. Those that relate to public and private worship, including secret devotion, reflection and self-examination. And here it might not be amiss to remark, that there should be a portion of each day set apart to these duties, thus rendering them periodical; for any exercise to be profitable must be thus. But he who attends to none but periodic duties, will seldom grow in the christian life; while he who does not attend to such, will soon lose all life. Hence there is necessity for both.

2. There is another class which relates more particularly to the religious obligations we owe to our neighbor. "Thou shalt love thy neighbor as thyself," is no less a command than "Thou shalt not kill;" and so far from its being a mere moral obligation, it is easy to understand that a man might be strictly moral, in the light of the human law, and yet be entirely indifferent as to the claims of this command. Again, we are commanded "to love our enemies, to bless them that curse us, to do good to them that hate us, and to pray for them that dispitefully use us, and persecute us:" all of which demands are more than the merely moral man can do, for it clearly presupposes a heart deeply imbued with the principles of piety.

3. There is still another class of religious duties, which seem to be somewhat distinct from those described above, viz., those that relate to the poor and unfortunate. The nature of this obligation is briefly summed up in the 27th verse of the first chapter of James, quoted in another place.

Now, whatever may be the tone of public sentiment upon these subjects, it is nevertheless certain that they embrace the great mass of the principles and duties of Christianity, and that their inculcation and practice will, to a great extent, depend upon the vigilance and fidelity with which they are taught in our schools and in our families. They must not be left to chance or the uncertain influences of the world. That policy would not be regarded as sound, which would leave the intellectual training to so uncertain influences. Well, the moral nature of man is not less subject to control. "He that soweth to the flesh, shall of the flesh reap corruption: but he that soweth to the spirit, shall, of the spirit, reap life everlasting."

Section 3—The Will.

The nature and offices of the will, as a motive power, are so intricate and diversified, that its strict analysis will not be attempted here. Its general characteristics are so well known, as to render such an analysis useless. Nevertheless, its relations, to the thinking principle, and its influence as a moral force upon the actions of men, are such as to render its cultivation, at once, an object of great solicitude.

Perhaps as clear an idea of the office of the will can be gathered from the following extract,* as from any other source. "It is the monarch of the mind, ruling with despotic, and at times with tyrannical powers. It is the rudder of the mind, giving direction to its movements. It is the engineer giving course and point, speed and force to the mental machinery. It acts like a tonic among the soul's languid powers. It is the band that ties into a strong bundle the separate faculties of the soul. It is the man's momentum: in a word, it is that power by which the energy or energies of the soul are concentrated on a given point, or

* "The Will as an Educational Power," by Rev. J. B. Bittenger.

in a particular direction: it fuses the faculties into one mass, so that instead of scattering all over like grape and canister, they spend their united force on one point."

But it will be sufficient for our purpose to consider its several functions under the following heads: 1. Motives and purposes. 2. Intentions and choice. 3. Executive volitions; and we shall content ourselves by pointing out some of its prominent characteristics, in connection with some modes of culture.

It will readily be seen that the operations of the will are intimately allied to, and somewhat dependent upon the action of other mental powers; that while it is itself the motive power, it awaits, in its executions, the light of the understanding and judgment, itself moving these powers to action, at the same time that it is dependent upon them for the light that guides it. It is, in one word, that power which the whole mind, as a unit, has to direct its own energies, bringing all the powers under its control, and making the body, as well, its special servant. Viewed in this light, the mind itself, according to the author just quoted, assumes the following threefold functional classification. "The intellect is the legislative department, the sensibilities are the judicial, and the will the executive." But it will be necessary to understand this with some latitude: for it may not be easy to see how the sensibilities, for instance, aid the understanding and judgment, the two faculties most concerned in forming conclusions. Viewed in its automatic relations, however, the will is the blind Samson of the mind, which must needs have other eyes to guide it; or else like him, it knows not where to exert its strength. It is like him in another essential respect. When it tamely and basely surrenders its power to appetite or passion, it is soon shorn, like Samson in Delila's lap, of its locks of strength, and then like him again, it becomes itself the slave, bound hand and foot, powerless to remonstrate successfully, against the imperious demands of the passions.

How important, therefore, that the will be educated, and that the perception, understanding, judgment, imagination and memory, the natural eyes of this faculty of the mind, be trained with reference to their psychological relations to the Will!

ARTICLE 1—MOTIVES AND PURPOSES.—No intelligent act, however trifling, is ever performed without a motive or a purpose. These do not constitute the energizing principles of the will, nor yet are they the food: they only serve as the occasion for action. And the more exalted and intelligent these motives and purposes are, the more definite and determined become the operations of the will. Hence, *instruction in matters of right and wrong*, at least, becomes a necessity in order to secure an intelligent and harmonious action. This need not be different, at least in manner, from ordinary instruction. It would comport perhaps with "moral suasion," and thus afford the necessary light to the executive functions.

There must also exist *a desire to promote the right and the general welfare.* This will be induced in right instruction, and will thus become not a mere blind impulsive distemper of the mind, but a noble sentiment characterized by intelligence and wisdom. But in order best to promote right motives and right purposes, especially in the youthful mind, it is necessary to induce a *trust* or *faith* in the *rectitude* of a Higher

Power. Here seems to be the very point, most accessible to the teacher, and upon which he should seize, in order that he may become master of the will. Children are themselves dependent. Parents or instructors are usually the objects in which such dependence centers. The main object, therefore, is to so mold and fashion these motives, etc., as that they shall superinduce the proper volitions. This will apply to the intellectual culture as well as to the moral. But the modes of culture, as far as they relate to the motive power of the will, in directing the application of the intellectual faculties, will be noticed in part second of this work, under the topic of "*Modes of Study.*"

ARTICLE 2—INTENTIONS AND CHOICE.—No sooner are motives judiciously placed before the mind, and the proper desires and confidence inspired, than it at once sets about forming intentions which, under the influence of the reasoning and judging powers, soon ripen into determinations and well-defined choice, one of the primary functions of the will. These may exist at first in the shape of half-formed purposes of action, and may be weak or strong, according as the cast of mind varies and as the motives have been feeble or powerful. In a mind uncultivated and unused to grapple with the difficulties of contending interests and forces, the great danger will be that the will will be tempted to yield those determinations or resolutions, without making the necessary effort to maintain them. Hence, such a will needs encouragement and strengthening by every laudable inducement that can be placed before it. Nothing is more disastrous to the will than the habit of forming, or rather half forming resolutions and then breaking them. It soon refuses to give heed to the calls of those premature and irresolute determinations, and grows weaker and weaker at every successive attempt and failure, until finally it ceases to act at all; and the intentions fall to the ground as fast as they are formed. The moral effects of this practice are ruinous. See to it then, that no resolutions are formed, whose fulfillment will be doubtful, and that those that are formed are carried out at almost any sacrifice.

It often becomes necessary however to interpose authority: and here the will should be taught to bend to a higher power. Stubbornness and willfulness are as much to be deprecated as feebleness and vascillation. Obedience to law should be a cardinal point in all instruction, since a willing submission to properly constituted authority, is as essentially a noble act of will, as resistance to tyranny and oppression.

Another mode of cultivating the will, as a moral force, should not be overlooked, viz., the *submission to suffering and privation.* Nothing, perhaps, has a happier effect upon the human heart, than the lessons affliction and suffering teach, provided we show proper submission. To rebel against these has the opposite effect. It creates a petulance that very much aggravates our difficulties. To bear the ills of life patiently, is one of the noblest virtues; and one, too, that requires as vigorous an exercise of will, as to resist the encroachments of wrong. The virtue of endurance is nearly allied to that of perseverance. Children should be taught to bear the yoke in their youth.

Article 3—Executive Volitions.—We come now to consider the will in that sphere of action where it exhibits some of its strongest characteristics, viz., its volitions. These constitute its executive force, and are the great motors in all the operations of mind and body. To regulate these forces would seem to be one of the first objects of education. Some possess this power in a very feeble state, while others are gifted with more than would appear to be necessary for ordinary purposes. Hence, there is a necessity for both restraints and stimulants. These of course should be administered judiciously. It will not answer for us to interpose our restraints or stimulants too freely, where the voluntary volitions act in reference to opinions and belief. While it might, in general, be denominated *direction* and *control* by *superior* force, it would imply, of course, nothing more than the regulating influence which a wise teacher would throw around his pupil.

But one of the most powerful educators of executive volitions, is the actual encounter with difficulties and temptations. The will, or executive volitions of the child, can no more be cultivated while the teacher or parent studiously avoids bringing him into actual contact with trials, than can his mathematical powers be developed without calculation. The child will no more become a strong, determined man, under these circumstances, than he would become a good soldier, while he was always kept out of danger. But to cultivate this power, he must enter the field and engage in the actual conflict with difficulties. He must grapple, single handed, with trials and hardship. He must meet temptation face to face, and conquer his own desires to sin, if he would realize all the glory of a conquest.

This brings us to notice energy and perseverance in duty, the last topic which we shall attempt here, and the crowning excellence of a well regulated mind.

The necessities for these virtues are sufficiently obvious, as their opposites, irresolution and indolence, are notorious. To cultivate these virtues requires care and patience. It should be commenced early in life, and continued gradually until the habit is established. Nothing should be demanded which can not be performed; and nothing that is attempted, should be abandoned unperformed. It may require encouragement and even absolute authority, as incentives; but the energies should never know they could yield except to impossibilities. That which seems difficult will thus often prove easy; and the list of impossibilities will be reduced to a mere "shadow" provided the energies of a living soul are aroused and arrayed against them by an indomitable will.

For further and particular modes of culture of this department of man's nature, the reader is referred to modes of study, recitation and government, as described in Part Second.

SYNOPSIS I.

PRELIMINARIES.

- OPENING EXERCISES.
  - Reading the scriptures.
  - Singing. Chanting.
  - Prayer.
- ORGANIZATION.
  - Enrollment and seating, etc.
  - Examination and classification.
  - Order of exercises.
- ASSIGNING LESSONS.
  - Definiteness. Extent. Not too much assigned at once. Points of interest and difficulty.
  - Manner of recitation named

PART SECOND.

CHAPTER I.

SCHOOLROOM DUTIES.

INTRODUCTION.

We come now to consider that part of our general subject, that relates more particularly to school keeping, or special Didactics: that part in which the special applications are shown: that part for which the previous chapters have in some degree, it is hoped, prepared the mind of the student.

It might be thought by some to be sufficient had we confined ourselves exclusively to this department of the subject; but it must be apparent to any one, on mature reflection, that to commence the subject here, would be to commence it in the middle; it would be to take things for granted, whose truths had never been demonstrated. It would be downright empiricism. It would be as though the merest charlatan should attempt to establish a science upon naked assumption, or upon a limited number of experiments: and it has been shown in another place, that experiment is no science or any part thereof. What is true in the individual case, is of no determinate value until it can be shown that all possible cases, falling under the same head, are true also. Individual facts, therefore, prove nothing conclusively in establishing general truths, until they can be generalized. Experiments are useful chiefly in discovery, and as far as they go, they give good testimony; but their employment in the establishment of general principles, would prove rather tedious for this utilitarian age. Hence we must have general truths in all sciences whose principles are susceptible of demonstration. From these we may deduce specialities.

This seems to be the precise character of this science. It answers to all the conditions. The fact is for every operation in nature there is a cause; and every step in growth or education, has its antecedents. Every act performed is either right or wrong. There are no indifferent ones; and every thing done in school is either of one class or the other. If the act is right, there is a reason for it, which may be sought out, generalized, and made a guide to subsequent acts and investigators. If it is wrong there is also a reason for it, which may be demonstrated and developed in such a way, that it may become a warning to all who pass over that same way.

The whole subject of special didactics therefore, may thus be referred to general laws, whose principles underlie the whole superstructure of human culture. Every step in practice, if it is a right step, is only the application of a general principle to a particular case, and can therefore be referred back to theory or general principles for authority; so that there may be as much definiteness; nay *certainty* in the art of teaching, when once it is thoroughly apprehended, as in any other art. The very existence of the science of education and art of teaching, as has been before shown, is predicated upon this truth. But this discussion will not be continued further, than merely to show the connection and mutual dependence of theory and practice, or general and special didactics.

In presenting the practical part of this subject, special attention will be given, not only to methods of teaching and learning, but to the reference of these to the general principles discussed in part first; so that nothing may seem to be taken for granted, or adopted without authority. The whole therefore, will have the *appearance*, at least, of a perfect system.

The Home and Miscellaneous Duties have already, to a great extent, been disposed of. As far as it will become necessary to refer to them again, they will be blended with those of the Schoolroom, since their nature and influence are so similar.

The topics for consideration have been named in the introduction to Part First, and may, we believe, be made to include every thing pertaining to the duties of teaching and managing schools; and what is one of the most interesting features is the exact coincidence of the two parts, or of the science and the art. Not a single application in the latter, that does not find its principle in the former. Not a stroke in art that does not find its counterpart in science. The one is the echo of the other.

The topics for investigation are the following, which we propose to take up in the order in which they occur: 1, Preliminaries; 2, Study; 3, Recitation; 4, Business; 5, Recreation; 6, Government.

In the discussion of these topics we propose to consider the young teacher about to assume, it may be for the first time--the duties and responsibilities of his office. We shall attempt to meet and dispose of every duty and difficulty that he will be likely to encounter.

Preliminaries.

Under this head we propose to consider every thing that relates to the organization of schools, the opening exercises, and the mode of assigning lessons and making preparation for study.

ARTICLE 1—OPENING EXERCISES.—We place these first, because we think, in point of time, they stand first; and because we believe the organization and other duties can be much more easily conducted after those exercises have been disposed of in a proper manner.

I believe it is universally admitted that those persons succeed best in their pursuits, of whatever character they are, that attach the greatest importance to them; that their success is usually measured by their devotion, and the estimation in which they hold their employment, other things being equal. So, to apply the same principle to teaching, I have found, almost without exception, that those teachers who were actuated by a deep and abiding sense of the responsibilities of their calling have succeeded best. The fact is, that Providence, however provident she may be, does not usually help those who do not help themselves. Much less will she help those who ignore her existence, and consequently will not apply to her for aid. A great many of our teachers fail for want of earnestness. They do not take hold of their work as though they felt their souls wrapped up in it. They set a low estimate upon their duties and labors, and it can not be expected that their scholars will do more. They fail to command that respect for themselves and for the school which is so necessary to success. The stream will rise no higher than the fountain. To make others feel, we must feel ourselves. To warm their hearts the fire must burn within our own bosoms. An iceberg emits no rays of heat, however majestic it may stand. The north wind seldom breaks the fetters of winter and wakes the young flowers to life; but the silent, unobtrusive rays of the sun penetrate the very heart of nature and start the warm currents of her life-blood through every vein and artery in her broad bosom. So that native earnestness and undeviating honesty that finds its rise in a heart deeply imbued with a love for the calling, will usually melt down the hardest cases and surmount the most inveterate difficulties, though other qualifications may be by no means extraordinary.

Again; others fail for want of system. I am persuaded that the errors and failures in teaching are more the result of a want of system or ability to use knowledge than from any want of knowledge itself. It is said that "knowledge is power," and in the sense in which that maxim is generally understood, it is true; but knowledge is not power any further than it can be wielded to accomplish results, any more than a huge, overgrown body void of sense or reason is power. It is powerful perhaps in the sense that the earthquake, the volcano or the hurricane is powerful; powerful for mischief and destruction; powerful, it may be, like the locomotive, unable to accomplish one single good result, until directed by the skillful hand of the engineer. Such is mere knowledge without system.

I am persuaded also, that without system, at least one half of the teacher's power is as good as thrown away, since it is expended, for the most part, in misdirected efforts; that with the same amount of scientific knowledge now possessed by the profession of teachers, twice the amount of good might be accomplished, were this vast force directed by some well-digested plan of operation. No one can succeed in any department of business without a system or a plan by which to work. If farmers, merchants, mechanics and business men generally, manifested no more concern about their employment, and worked as objectless and aimless as many teachers do, there would be universal failure and bankruptcy all over the land. System guides and gives success to the military general in his battles and campaigns. It guides the scholar in his investigations, and the statesman in his legislation. In a word the worlds are guided by it, in their ceaseless whirl in space. The seasons go and come according to the plan laid down for their observance; and day and night are perpetual in their round. System reigns in every department of nature and of successful art. It is the secret of success every where else, and it would not seem probable that teaching forms any exception, save that the necessity seems greater here, in proportion to the greatness of the duties and responsibilities.

This want of system in teaching comes, in the great majority of cases, from a want of a clear understanding of the intention and importance of the duties, and a frank acknowledgment of them in the presence of the school. No school can succeed well, when there is not this clear understanding and cordial reciprocity on the part of all concerned. I know of no better way of bringing about this state of things, than for the teacher to lead off in the matter, not waiting for parent or pupil, but to show by his conduct and conversation, that he is deeply in earnest in this matter.

But earnestness without prudence, will avail but little. Great energy without skill, would resemble the locomotive without a hand to guide it; and great powers, minus humility, would become offensive and nugatory where great interests are at stake.

Let us instance two cases to illustrate the point. One teacher, with hat in hand, and blustering, it may be, from his recent exertion, enters the schoolroom about the time to open the school. Presently a rapid succession of heavy raps, or the loud ringing of the bell is heard in the vicinity of the teacher's desk; and through all, and above all, the stentorian voice of the teacher is heard calling to order (?). By repeated effort, and great exertions, this is so far accomplished at length, that one accustomed to such scenes would hardly be mistaken as to the *intention*, at least. Order thus far secured, without one moment's reflection, to say nothing about opening exercises of a formal character, the classes are called, and teacher and pupil rush into the arena of duties, to contend and toil, to fret and sweat (I will not say swear), over the day's difficulties.

Now, we submit, are the minds of teacher and scholars in a proper frame to encounter such perplexing duties as will most likely meet them? If for no other purpose, than merely to afford time for a few moments' reflection, and opportunity to call in their minds, and to place them on the duties in which they are about to engage, it would be desirable to have a portion of time set apart for some formal opening exercises.

Take another example. The teacher enters the room quietly, unobtrusively, and in ample time to take a general survey of persons and things before the hour for opening the school arrives. Presently a gentle, but well-known signal is heard, and all are quietly seated in their proper places. A moment or two of silence elapses, during which time all are listening and expecting; and then there break forth from the stand in subdued but earnest tones, the blessed words well chosen from the Bible. The teacher reads, but his soul is full of the inspiration from that holy book, and he bears the shafts of Divine truth to the hearts and consciences of those that hear. His remarks are pointed and mostly bearing upon the duties and difficulties of the day. But hark! a hymn of praise now rises from that little band, and echoes from the hillside and the forest. And now all is hushed again, save one earnest pleading voice devoutly imploring Divine favor. The scene closes, and the sunbeams of joy steal in unconsciously upon those confiding hearts, and all their anger and dark suspicions, if they entertained any, have melted away like frost-work before the sun, under the beam of Divine Truth. Now, are not these hearts, these minds, in a better condition for study and recitation than those in our first picture?

There may be those in the school who would affect indifference to these things, and so they might, were the heavens to fall; but that affected indifference would not screen them from the influences thus brought to bear upon them. These things will commend themselves to their sober judgments; and if consistently and persistently prosecuted, they can not fail to produce the happiest results. But it is not our purpose to dictate. We only wish to present the case fairly, and allow teachers to chose for themselves. To this end, we suggest the following exercises, any one or all of which may, as shall seem best to the teacher, be adopted as appropriate opening exercises.

1. *Reading the Scriptures.*—The reasons for this exercise might be briefly summed up as follows:

1. The children need moral and religious instruction as has been shown, and as everybody admits. This is a most favorable time, when their minds are clear and vigorous to apprehend those truths.

2. It offers the best possible opportunity to make impressions. The words of inspiration have more force than any others, simply because they are inspired. No mere human words or composition can have the effect that these have, when read and felt by the teacher himself.

3. It prepares the way for successful study and instruction in other departments. It opens the heart and the mind to receive and impart the truth, which will grow all the better for being watered thus daily by the dews of Divine Inspiration.

4. It offers the very best opportunity to smite down some of those vicious habits that may be making inroads upon the school. It would not be wise, perhaps, to take special pains to make it bear upon these points; but the silent influence of the Word itself will prove sufficient, in most cases, to work the reform.

The manner of conducting this part of the opening exercises, will be left to the judgment of the teacher, with these simple suggestions, that while some would succeed best with one plan, others might adopt a different one and succeed equally as well. I have known most charming results produced in primary and secondary schools, by the whole school's repeating the Lord's Prayer in concert. The same may be done with portions of Christ's Sermon on the Mount, and selections from the Psalms. Then again, I have seen a whole school, teacher and all, affected even to tears, by a careful and earnest reading, explanation, and application of some of the most interesting portions of holy writ. The historic parts of both the Old and New Testament are suitable. Others again I have known to succeed best by joining with some or all of their pupils in reading. But whatever may be the form, children should be taught to regard the reading of the Bible with more interest and earnest attention than they do other books. Otherwise there is great danger of their coming to regard it, by and by, of no greater value. It may become unto them "a savor of life unto life, or of death unto death." It is a sharp, two-edged sword for good or ill. It is an educational instrumentality, of such force that no teacher can afford to do without it: and it is to be devoutly hoped that the time is past when its use will be objected to. It is suitable for all conditions of the human race, but is used to greatest advantage when the passages are carefully and wisely selected for the occasion. It then acts like a charm upon the heart. There are storms of troubled passions there. But Christ's words, "Peace, be still!" that echoed from wave to wave over the troubled waters of the sea of Galilee, were scarcely more potent to produce a calm, than these passages will become, when properly selected and read with the right spirit.

2. *Singing* is an exercise, at once, so appropriate and so common, that it needs no argument to recommend it. There is scarcely any excuse for not practicing it in school; for if the teacher can not sing, some or perhaps all the pupils can, and all that is necessary is to grant them permission, and the thing is done; perhaps not in the most approved style, but

time and practice will improve it. Of course, it need not be confined to the opening exercises. It may mingle with all others. It will gladden and enliven all. All know the magic power of music to subdue the passions, to cultivate the voice, and refine the feelings. Let its sweet strains therefore, mingle freely in all the exercises of the schoolroom. For the opening exercises, such selections should be made as shall comport with the occasion, and should be so arranged, if possible, as to allow all to participate.

There is one particular mode of singing, fast coming into use in the schools, which seems to possess merits for opening exercises, surpassing all others, viz.: the chant. It does seem that nothing can be more appropriate than this, when the whole school can unite in chanting the praises of God, morning and evening, for what we have said of opening exercises is mainly true of the closing.

3. *Prayer.* After what has been said of reading the Scriptures, and singing etc., the arguments in favor of prayer or some form of devotion might be inferred. It is the crowning excellence of all the rest, as it is a virtual acknowledgement of allegiance to God, and of dependence upon him. It more than all others, will show the teacher to be deeply in earnest. Of course, it presupposes that every teacher should be a good man; for who else should teach? Not the bad man surely! And there are but these two classes. Therefore the argument runs thus. All good men pray; none but good men should teach; therefore teachers should pray.

But it is not our purpose to proscribe those who do not; for we believe that many excellent teachers do not presume to pray, for conscience' sake, or because

they do not make a public profession of religion. I honor and respect such; but I can not avoid the conviction, that their excellencies would be very much enhanced, could they consistently add this other grace also. It would sanctify and intensify every other power. And it would seem, on a careful examination, that if there is any one duty in all the wide range of human duties that demands prayer, it is that of teaching. If there is one position in life in which a man needs Divine guidance, that position is the one in which the training of human beings is concerned. Add to this the moral effects of prayer upon both pupil and teacher, and its claims are set beyond a shadow of a doubt.

Now, if this form of opening exercises be objected to by any on the plea of want of time, let such be answered as follows: That if these things are of the importance claimed for them, then they have as much claim upon the time of the schoolroom as any others; and it would be just as unreasonable to quibble about the time devoted to recitation in Grammar or Arithmetic, as about this. And when it is considered how much these exercises really add to the sum total of education, not only by preparing the minds and hearts of pupils, etc., but in actual instruction in matters of the most vital importance, it will readily be seen that so far from being any loss of time, it is actually time saved. "To study well is to have prayed well," was a maxim of one of the greatest students and reformers the world ever knew; and it is not without its application here. But the time thus employed need not occupy more than ten or fifteen minutes at the outside, and often it can be brought within the compass of seven or eight.

Organization.—The organization of schools is a matter of so much importance, that its claims to a separate hearing can not be set aside without very much impairing the completeness of the plan we have marked out. The efficiency and success of the school depend so essentially upon a thorough and systematic organization, that teachers should study this subject with as much care as they do any other, relating to the school.

At the commencement of a term of school, the great anxiety of the teacher seems to be, to get to hearing classes; but it will be found that time may be saved, as well as perplexity avoided, by a little care and attention at the outset. A week, or even ten days may be spent to great advantage in organizing and trying the machinery, before starting off for the term, especially if the school be a new one. This will be found to be much better than to commence the first or second day with an imperfect organization, only to run into difficulty, and expose the teacher and pupils to the mortification of a reorganization and perhaps a failure. The examinations and other general exercises which will be described by-and-by, will afford ample employment for both teacher and pupil, until the regular exercises begin.

Another reason why teachers should not be hasty in completing the organization of their schools, especially if they are unacquainted with their pupils, is found in a want of a mutual understanding between the parties. Teachers need time to observe and study the capacity, advancement and natural inclinations and dispositions of their pupils; and they, in turn, stand equally in need of time to make a similar acquaintance. The exercises about to be recommended afford these opportunities in due proportion.

I have sometimes made this remark to teachers that were about going out, perhaps for the first time, to engage their schools; and the recommendation may not be inappropriate here, viz.: that if they can spare the time, they should spend at least a week in visiting the families of the neighborhood or district, for the purpose of getting acquainted with the parents and children, and with the influences that have been, and still may be operating upon them; or in other words, to learn their antecedents; for no teacher is prepared to give direction and instruction to a child until he knows something of its capacity and antecedents. In the ordinary way of organizing, he is left without any means of knowing, except that which is afforded by a very imperfect acquaintance, acquired in the ordinary recitation.

Let him not go on these visitations however, as a pedagogue, or as one whose special business it is to instruct; or he may not find those who are willing to learn from so green a disciple. Let him not go to lecture the parents upon their duties, etc., and to frighten the children and old ladies with his immense learning; or he may breed contempt in the minds of those who are as wise as himself. But let him go, rather, as a friend to converse and counsel with, and receive instruction from them, in reference to their labors, daily duties, habits and wishes; and he will acquire more valuable information in a half-day's friendly intercourse, than he would in a whole week's recitation, simply because he then comes in direct contact with the real boys and girls, which is not always the case at school. He may thereby avoid errors, which if committed, will lead to the defeat of his most sanguine purposes. How often has the

teacher had reason for sorrow, and repentance for his treatment of children, after learning what those poor little ones have to contend with at home! Teacher, look well to your children's homes, if you would educate them.

Again; a thorough and systematic organization of the school, before starting off, will do much to convince the pupils, both of the importance of their duties and of the ability of the teacher to conduct them. A few master strokes here (I do not mean *strokes from the master*) will give him a greater ascendency over his pupils, than any or all the other kinds of strokes he may employ subsequently. Whereas, a few mistakes will have a tendency to sink him correspondingly low in their estimation.

Many teachers fail from this cause. They come before the school, perhaps for the first time in their lives, without any definite or well digested plan. The consequence is, they are embarrassed. They hesitate and halt in the performance of their duties; and however wise they may pretend to be, and however earnestly they may labor, nothing will conceal from the lynx-eyed children (and they read motives by intuition), the lamentable deficiency, or save him from exposure. He may struggle, but his embarrassment will increase; and at every successive blunder, he will sink lower and lower in their estimation, and deeper and deeper into difficulty, until his resurrection becomes impossible.

But take an example of a teacher well versed in didactics: one who has a plan and wisdom, and dispatch to execute it. He comes before his school, without ostentation or embarrassment. He knows what is the first thing to be done, and the second,

and the third, and so on. He disposes of them in their proper order, and in such a manner as to convince his pupils that "knowledge is *indeed* power." The whole is completed with that eminent ability which proves him to be a master workman. And what is the effect upon the pupils? They yield their willing and unqualified submission; and the teacher rises, at each successive step, until he stands before them an embodiment of power. Such a teacher can *teach*. Such also is the effect of system, or a studied plan of operation. This alone is argument sufficient to convince any one, that there is something more than mere familiarity with the branches of study necessary to secure success in teaching. No amount of mere scientific acquirements can compensate for this deficiency in professional skill. This must be learned somewhere, either before or after the teacher commences his duties. It were better far to learn it before, since this may save him from a world of mortification and perhaps failure, and his pupils from a still worse calamity.

The opening exercises disposed of in a manner similar to that described under that topic, the school now is supposed to be in a condition to favor a good, thorough organization.

There is, however, one thing common to the rural districts, which usually operates against such an organization. It is the want of a full attendance of the pupils, the first few days of school. But the plan proposed will, in some measure, meet that difficulty and greatly relieve it; since it delays the complete organization until a greater number can be present. It is to be regretted, however, that parents can not see the utter hopelessness of a respectable organization, where the children are delayed in their attendance until the second or third week of school. It is of the utmost importance, therefore, that the children be present on the very first opening of the school. Parents ought to know, and feel too, that every hour that every scholar delays in entering the school, is not only so much time lost, and worse than lost, to him, but that he actually inflicts a wound upon the school, in interrupting and delaying its organization.

What, for instance, would be thought of the wisdom of a neighborhood that had adopted as one of its regulations, that no one should be allowed to commence the spring plowing, until every other one was willing and ready to commence also; and that if some few of them had taken advantage of the pleasant weather, and had actually done a part of their work, that they, forsooth, because their lazy neighbors were not ready, must *unplow* or *unsow* that which their industry secured? And yet this policy resembles in no slight degree, the wisdom and justice of sending pupils to school after the school is organized, and compelling the reorganization to accommodate them.

Or what would be thought of the wisdom of that farmer, for instance, who was about sowing his wheat, but, forsooth, because he had not seed enough prepared, when the time came for sowing, instead of preparing more, should go on and sow what he had, over the whole field; and then wait a week or two, until the grain sown had got fairly growing, and then sow another sowing and harrow it in, right among the tender shoots of the growing grain; and then again, along in May of the next year, when the crop began to spring, he should discover that it was not quite right yet, and should sow the balance of his grain and

harrow it in as before, right among the growing grain? Why, such a man would be thought a fit subject for an insane asylum, and so it would seem; but a policy very much like this is practiced in nearly all our country schools. What kind of a crop would that man reap, if he reaped any at all? It would resemble very much the intellectual and moral harvests that are too frequently gathered in many of our schools. That growing grain thus mutilated by repeated additions, is but too apt a type of many of our schools disturbed and rent asunder by a fresh arrival of pupils every few weeks. But until parents can see this evil in its true light, it were better perhaps to endure it for a time, and provide for its removal as soon as possible.

One of the first steps in the organization of the school, is the *enrollment and seating of pupils.* This, though apparently a small matter, offers an excellent opportunity for the teacher to exhibit that skill and wisdom which are to give him command over his pupils. There is a right way and a wrong way in everything, and the principle descends even to this small duty. If the teacher do those duties well, the pupils will give him credit for it; if he do them ill, they will place it on the debit side, and woe be to that teacher, if, when the balance is struck, the debit should exceed the credit.

It is not our purpose, however, to recommend any particular method of doing this duty, to the exclusion of all others. The great diversity of the form and manner of seating the schoolrooms, and other circumstances, would forbid this. But we shall indicate a few plans which will, most likely, prove suggestive to teachers.

1. The teacher needs a general roll, for reference and other purposes, and it should be arranged in alphabetic order. He therefore makes this announcement to the school, explains its use, and says, "All whose names (meaning the family name) begin with A, will please arise." As fast as their names are called and recorded, they take their seats. The letter B, is called in a similar manner, and so on of all the letters.

This exercise also offers a fine opportunity for the teachers to learn the names of his pupils—a matter of no trifling importance—to make general remarks, and to become somewhat acquainted. A similar course might be pursued in forming class rolls also. This matter well done, will impress the school with the idea that order prevails everywhere; that it is one of the first and firmest laws of nature; and its appearance here will be greeted with respect, to say the least.

2. The next step, perhaps, is *seating* the pupils. In this matter the teacher will have to be governed somewhat by the form and size of the room, and the position and arrangement of the seats. In most instances he will find it to result in the greatest convenience, to seat the larger pupils in one part of the room, and the smaller ones in the other, placing the larger ones back, and so grading the school forward that the smaller ones shall occupy the seats nearest the teacher's desk. This will give the school an orderly appearance. No one likes to see a large boy and a very small one occupying the same seat. It is out of proportion and disorderly. It resembles too much a team composed of one very large horse and a very small one, or a mule harnessed with an elephant. The objection, that this plan would prevent children who wish to

study together, or who wish to be together for any other purpose, is not a valid one. Since to prevent this is the very thing aimed at, it is the chief excellency of the measure. Children should not be permitted as a general thing, to assist each other in their lessons, but should be taught to rely upon their own individual exertions, as we shall have occasion to remark more at length when we come to notice the topic of study. The practice of studying together, and assisting and prompting each other, is ruining thousands of scholars in our schools. It destroys that self-reliance and independence, so necessary to make a man.

Again: this plan would prevent any noise and mischief, which are sure to be the result when the practice is allowed to any extent. It will be found also where children are allowed to select their own seats, without any general system, that if there happen to be two or three mischievous ones (and such cases, I believe, are not unsupposable) they will be sure to get together "to have a good time." Now all this may be prevented. All these evil combinations may be broken up, by a judicious arrangement; and the teacher should have the entire management of the seating of the pupils in the school. The effect of this arrangement may easily be anticipated. The pupils will see, at once, the propriety of it, and will say within themselves, if not audibly, "well, I guess there *is* going to be something done this term." "I wonder if it would not be best for me to fall right in ranks, and assist in carrying out these plans?" "I see plainly that the teacher knows something, and that mischief and idleness will not pay, this term." Such will be the mental cogitations of the pupils.

The matters of enrollment and seating disposed of,

the next item of importance will be the *examination and classification* of the pupils. This will constitute the great burden of the organization. Too much pains, therefore, can not be taken with it. It requires the greatest care and discrimination, combined with the most unflinching integrity, to perform this duty well. A hundred and one reasons will, perhaps be offered, both by child and parent, showing why "*so and so*" should be put into this class or that; all of which are to be heard and disposed of. And, while I would not encourage obstinacy or self-conceit on the part of the teacher, yet I would have him distinctly to understand, that it is his exclusive prerogative, to determine the position, in classes, of every scholar in school. He should not assert this prerogative, however, without duly considering all the circumstances, cautiously consulting the wishes of all parties, and receiving all the instruction possible from whatever source. The teacher is supposed to know better than any one else, what will be the best for the child in school. If he does not, he ought not to teach.

Again: some one must have the general direction of affairs. If that person is not the teacher, pray, who should it be? What would be the condition of the school, for instance, provided every little Master or Miss, every fond mother or doting father—to say nothing about the grandmas, aunts, and other functionaries interested—should "have a say" in the arrangement of affairs at school? No two opinions would agree, and anarchy and confusion would reign.

But in rendering these decisions, examining the pupils and arranging the classes, respect should be had to the following points:

1st. To give the pupil credit for what he thinks he knows, as far as possible.

2d. To give him credit for no more than he knows, proved upon careful examination.

3d. To reserve the privilege of correcting any false notions in reference either to capacity or acquirements, and the right to determine his standing and position in class.

This course will most likely disclose the following facts: that some scholars place too high an estimate upon their abilities; that others, again, place that estimate too low; and still another class that need special attention, viz., those who through pure indolence, or a desire at least to escape from hard labor, will select classes and studies far below their abilities. Such need a special spur.

The main point to be observed is, so to dispose of every member of the school, that as few changes as possible will be required after the school once commences in earnest; for all who have had any experience in these matters, know how demoralizing it is to all concerned, to be obliged to rip up the organization of classes, and to make changes, or to form new ones. To those pupils who have to be turned back in their studies, it becomes a matter of severe disappointment and discouragement. Their aspirations and anticipations have been raised by an unwise step, only to be dashed to the ground; and in too many instances, all hope perishes, and with it, the desire for study. Now a teacher has no right to treat a pupil in this manner. Hence the greater necessity for knowledge upon these points. And then again, to those who have to be set forward, the evils are sometimes scarcely less ruinous.

Their pride and self-conceit, are often pampered, and indolence and superficial habits take the place of honest industry and frugality.

In conclusion upon this topic, it is but justice to remark, that most of the evils here pointed out, are amply provided for, and the recommendations happily anticipated in our best organized union or graded schools. But the object of this work is, if possible, to bring the common district school up to a level with the union or graded school.

The examination of pupils and the formation of classes completed, the scholars will begin to cast about them for some employment. This should be furnished them in exact measure. No time should be lost by the teacher, in furnishing them *with an Order of Exercises.* Much valuable time is lost, and much mischief concocted, from not providing for this want, from the beginning. Pupils may not really desire to be negligent or vicious; indeed, very few, if any, do; but in consequence of their not knowing exactly what to do, and, in some instances, not exactly caring about doing any thing, or not feeling the special necessity of labor, their duties are therefore neglected. But if a general order of exercises, stating the exact amount of labor, and the precise time of every recitation, and of every other duty, were placed in such a position that every pupil might see it, and learn just what to do; and when to do this, and when to do that, these temptations would be, to a great extent, removed. There would be less excuse for illy prepared lessons, for the lessons and time to prepare them, would all be measured and balanced. The scholars have a right to know this arrangement; and it will do more to form and strengthen the habits of regularity and industry,

than any amount of lecturing and scolding that may be bestowed upon them; and then the very habits formed here, are the ones that will follow them into the workshops, on the farm, into the office, counting-room, pulpit, bar or schoolhouse. They are the ones that will render them successful or unsuccessful throughout an eventful career of life. The fact is, a great many of the evils we complain of most bitterly, in the school, are the results of some such mistakes, in not providing the scholars with the means for prosecuting these duties.

Another recommendation equally worthy of adoption, at least by all the larger members of the school, is the construction of a separate *order* for individual use, in which every hour and half-hour of the day, shall be provided for. Let one be written out by each individual pupil; to meet his particular case; and, if need be, let it be revised by the teacher, and compared with others of similar character. This will cut off the last possible excuse for neglect of duty, and will have a tendency to make orderly and successful men and women, in whatever department of life they may chance to labor. But this plan will be described more fully, under the head of "Special Order of Daily Duties."

ARTICLE 3—ASSIGNING LESSONS.—There is still another duty which may be regarded as preliminary, though not in the sense in which the organization and opening exercises are. The first, it will be observed, is a preliminary which, if once disposed of properly, does not need repeating; the second is periodical, occurring each morning; but the third, or *Assigning Lessons*, is a duty that may occur every half-hour or even less; it is preliminary or preparatory to study and recitation, and hence is not without its importance.

It is laid down as a fundamental principle, in another part of this work, that the scholars will be governed in their estimate, and consequent discharge of duty, by the estimation in which these duties are held by the teacher himself. If therefore, carelessness and indifference are manifested by the teacher, in assigning lessons, the same disposition will most likely be manifested by the pupils when preparing and reciting those lessons. For instance: after a hurried recitation in which, perhaps, not more than one-half or two-thirds of the previous lesson has been recited, the teacher says—hastily turning the leaf of the book and glancing hurriedly at the contents, for the bell has rung and, being a little behind, the next recitation is pressing hard upon him—"Here! your lesson commences somewhere in the neighborhood of the —— or —— page, and may extend—let me see—how far can you go?" (to which not very satisfactory or unanimous answers are given) well, go as far as you can." "Next class!" and the books are hastily closed and the pupils hurry to their seats, and make busy preparations to———do nothing, absolutely nothing! for the teacher most emphatically announced to them that task, by his failing to circumscribe the limits of their work. He said in the most forcible manner: "*Do just as you please;*" and they *may* please to do nothing.

Now what kind of a recitation will that teacher meet when he next calls the class? He ought not to expect any thing more or better than he gave; and since he gave nothing, he should expect nothing. If he be thus modest in his expectations, he may not be disap-

pointed; but he is apt to expect more. The recitation is about to commence. One says, "Why, *I* thought the lesson commenced here;" another says, "No, there," a third, "I don't know where;" but a fourth, with more roguery than honesty may say, "*I didn't know there was any;*" and so it goes. One is called upon to recite. The question is asked, but the answer comes complainingly: "*I didn't study that.*" "How perplexing!" (fortunate if nothing worse escape him,) sighs the poor teacher, chafed and worried by a succession of such difficulties. Well, whose fault is it, teacher? Who set the example? If you want your pupils to be precise, prompt and faithful, you must be so yourself. If you would have them do the work, you must mark it out for them.

What would you think of a carpenter, for instance, who was about erecting a house if he should go on the ground with a score of green hands, and commence in this wise, "Here boys are the timbers. Well, I want you to bore the holes, make the mortises, fit the tenons, square the beams, trim the braces and ties, make the doors and windows, and in fact do as well as you can; now go to work." And they go to work "with a vengeance," every one doing what he thinks best (?) The frame is erected and such a frame! What would you give gentle readers, to see that house? I venture to say you would give one groan at least. It might be no idolatry to fall down (if *it* didn't fall first) and worship it; for it would not have its likeness either on the earth, under the earth, in the sea or in the heavens. But bad as it is, it would be but too correct a likeness of the mental and moral fabrications that are sometimes erected in our schoolhouses. The comparison can be readily carried out.

Now in such a case, a good workman would take a square and compass, and passing carefully from timber to timber, would mark off, here a mortise, there a tenon, here a brace, there a tie, here a door, there a window, etc., until all was completed; and then he might say with some propriety, "Here boys, go to work." So a good teacher would take a book and pencil in hand, and calling the attention of the class, would carefully mark off the lesson. He would say in the first place, "The lesson commences precisely with the —— article, and extends to the —— article; and every word and sentence is to be studied and recited." Hence *definiteness as to place and extent* is a matter first to be considered. The pupils should know just where a lesson commences and where it ends, and every thing else that will be demanded of them. This may be tested by actual examination by the teacher before the class leaves the recitation seat, if there is any doubt about it. They then will have no excuse from that quarter, for neglect of duty. It brings the matter under their immediate notice, and fastens it so upon the memory that there will be no escape from its claims.

Again: Care should be taken not to assign too much or too little. The tendencies are to err in the first extreme. In this case the mind soon wearies of fruitless endeavors to encompass much, and the result is that nothing is done well; superficial habits are formed. The effects of this mania, "to get through books," are very discernible in all departments of business, especially in the Western country, where the evil prevails to the greatest extent. It shows itself in fast living, in overweening desires, in hasting to become rich, in living beyond the means, and often in

open bankruptcy. I have thought also that I could discover the results of too long lessons given in school on some of our Western farms, where an attempt is made to cultivate 200 or 300 acres of land, with means hardly adequate to cultivate 50 well. The results are broken-down fences, dilapidated buildings, inadequate cultivation, poor crops, briers in the fence corners, and a general appearance of slovenliness pervading every thing; while in New England, where, to my certain knowledge, the lessons given in school are not more than one-half so long, the farms and the way-side, and every thing, seems to wear an air of neatness and finish, which have been the subject of just praise by the traveler. May we not seek for the cause of this in the foregoing? Indeed I think we may safely conclude, that whatever of error or excellency we behold in the walks of society, are but the reflections of the school and the family. The child's capacity should therefore be exactly measured, in assigning a lesson, and just enough given to keep his powers in active exercise, for the requisite length of time, and then the labor should be remitted or changed. This, it is true, would require skill and wisdom; but it is *their* claims we are trying to enforce.

Again: to make the matter sure, there should be a distinct understanding, that *no lesson is to be assigned twice* for any cause, save the most unavoidable accidents. One of the prevailing errors in the present mode of teaching is the one of allowing the pupil to have two or three trials at the same lesson. They come to think, by and by, that they can not get a lesson the first time, and their efforts seldom exceed their expectations. The evil is brought about in this way: teachers give too long lessons in the first place;

in the second place, they do not take sufficient precautions to secure the study of them; and in the third place, if the lessons are imperfect, as they most surely will be under these circumstances, they are assigned a second, third, or even a fourth and fifth time, before they are completed. Now, any one can see at a glance, that this is nothing more nor less than a bid on laziness. The pupil will console himself with reflections like the following: "Well, though this is a pretty hard lesson, yet there is this consolation, that if I don't complete it now, I shall have another trial or two." "The master will be easy with me, and what I do not understand, he will explain." "I will therefore get but a portion of it, or the whole imperfectly, and complete it at another time."

Now any one can see where this would lead; and it would be safe to say that a very great part of the poor recitations, as well as of poor scholarship, may date existence to causes like these. There should therefore be a distinct understanding, that no lesson is to be assigned a second or a third time, and that if a lesson is accidentally or carelessly lost, its loss falls only upon the unfortunate or guilty one. (The cases that might be regarded as exceptional will be noticed in another place.) This, I imagine, will do more than almost any one thing, to correct the evil habit of careless and superficial study.

Another matter relating to preliminaries deserves attention, which, perhaps, will be more clearly understood by first showing the evils to be removed, and the benefits to be secured by its adoption.

In almost every lesson, there are some interesting points that may not attract the attention of the learner, unless such attention is particularly called to them. They exist sometimes in a kind of undefined state, but only need to be pointed out, not explained, in order that they may be apprehended, and thus become strong incentives to study. History and geography abound in such matters, and no branch of study is, perhaps, entirely wanting in them. Again: there are also, in most studies, a greater or less number of points of difficulty, to which it may be well to direct the attention of the learner, especially if the lesson is a new one. Pupils are not unfrequently brought in contact with those things in a manner calculated rather to discourage them than to excite their energies. It would not be wise, therefore, to remove them entirely out of the way, but, rather, prepare their minds, as far as possible, to encounter them. The practice of merely defining the limits of a lesson, and saying to the pupil, "There, now study," is too much like taking him up to the border of a seemingly impenetrable forest, through which he is required to pass, and saying to him, "There, now pass through the best way you can." Would he not be more likely to accomplish this feat, more to his own pleasure and profit, and to the satisfaction of all parties, were the teacher to give him a little instruction, such, for instance, as the "points of the compass," the direction to go, etc., and to point out to him a few of the difficulties he will be most likely to encounter, giving him directions how to avoid them, rather than allow him to blunder through without such aid?

Would he not be better prepared to meet those difficulties, and to enjoy those pleasures also, if the teacher should say, "At such and such a place, you will come to a steep mountain; but its hight has been scaled, and *you* can ascend. The top affords you a most beautiful prospect. That passed, and you descend into a most delightful valley covered with a carpet of the richest verdure and flowers. You will not tarry nor rest in its borders, lest night overtake you. Next you will encounter a deep and rapid stream, bounded by high ledges of rocks, and flanked by deep ravines. But by the aid of some hanging boughs* that nature has kindly furnished for the traveler, you may safely swing yourself upon a platform† on the opposite side, erected for your accommodation, from which your passage will be easy. You next pass into a beautiful plain that ends ere long in a most dismal marsh. Here it will be necessary to exert the greatest caution, lest you plunge into some of those pools of water, or sink into some of those filthy quagmires that abound throughout its whole extent. But by carefully observing, and by making good use of that light‡ you hold in your hand, you will discover a narrow, graveled walk that leads to the opposite side, where your journey will terminate."

Now, would not the prospect of pleasure and of daring adventure animate and nerve his limbs like steel to plunge into that forest, and to explore its wonders? So in reference to assigning lessons. The pupil knows but little of the difficulties, dangers and pleasures of the way. The teacher has been over the ground; and, if he has been observing, he has marked all those points, and by pointing them out to the pupil, he prepares him also to encounter them. Or, to refer to our forest again—which, by the way, is a very good representation of a difficult lesson—let the teacher plant, as it were, a light at some distance from

* Common sense. † Definitions. ‡ The rule.

the border, but within sight, so that the pupil's eye may catch its glimmering, and it will serve as a mark to guide him thither; and then another beyond, and so on, each one affording him light enough to carry him to the next, until the goal is reached. This, in effect, will be following the annexed direction, viz.: *To note the points of interest and difficulty, and give some general directions how to treat them.*

Again; pupils are sometimes perplexed to know how, or in what manner the lesson is to be prepared, and recited, and the result may be a failure to get the lesson in the manner intended by the teacher. They may succeed, as they think, but when they come to recite, they are surprised, disappointed and chagrined, to find that they have entirely misapprehended the nature of the recitation. Now, it is their right and privilege to know the manner of recitation before they commence the study of the lesson. In the several branches, ample scope is afforded to point out how the lesson is to be recited. In reading, for instance, pupils should be apprized beforehand what particular feature of it will be made the special topic for the next recitation—whether loudness, distinctness, the high or low keys, or whatever variety may be named: or in grammar, whether it be analysis or synthesis, whether of words or sentences, and how; and so of other branches. Hence the *manner in which the lesson is to be recited should be distinctly named.*

And lastly, it would not be wise to name or require all the things that relate to the various kinds of recitations at once. Suppose the teacher should say to a class in reading, for instance, "Now I want you to read this lesson to-morrow with the right degree of force or loudness, on the right key or pitch, neither too fast nor too slow, to articulate distinctly, to give the proper emphasis, to observe all the pauses, circumflexes, sweeps, bends, slides, closes, and every other variation." What would be the result? Most likely, that not one of these things would be observed, and the reason is quite obvious. It would be about as reasonable as to demand that a child should do as many different kinds of work, and to do them all well. Suppose you wished your boy to remove a pile of stone to a different quarter of the yard. He goes to work, but on your going to inspect the progress, you find him tugging and toiling to remove the whole pile at once. You remonstrate with him; but he says, "Why father, you told me to remove this *pile* of stone, and I am doing the best I can." "So I did," would be your reply, "but common sense ought to teach you that you could do it more easily and quickly, by taking one or two at a time." So common sense ought to teach teachers, that if they expect or even wish to accomplish anything, they must attend to one thing at a time.

It could hardly be expected that the pupil could remember even the one-half the list named to him above, much less that he should accomplish it. But if but one, or at most two things be attempted at once, and then, for the time being, all the energies of the body and mind be directed to them, the difficulties will melt away gradually, and more surely than if the teacher should open a whole battery of abuse against the scholar.

Now it is but justice to say, that in order to follow these directions and recommendations, it will require time; but if this be offered as an objection, we reply as on a former occasion: that if they are right they

have as much claim on the time as any other duties. But it will not be inferred, that all that has been said of the last topic, for instance, will be required at every lesson. The probabilities are, that not more than one-half or a fourth will ever be required at any one time; but they are nevertheless all necessary, and all demanded in their proper places. It will be found, that from three to five minutes will be amply sufficient to dispose of all that will be really necessary for any one recitation. That much time can not possibly be better spent. It will be ten times that amount saved in a very few weeks, and success instead of failure in the end.

SYNOPSIS II.

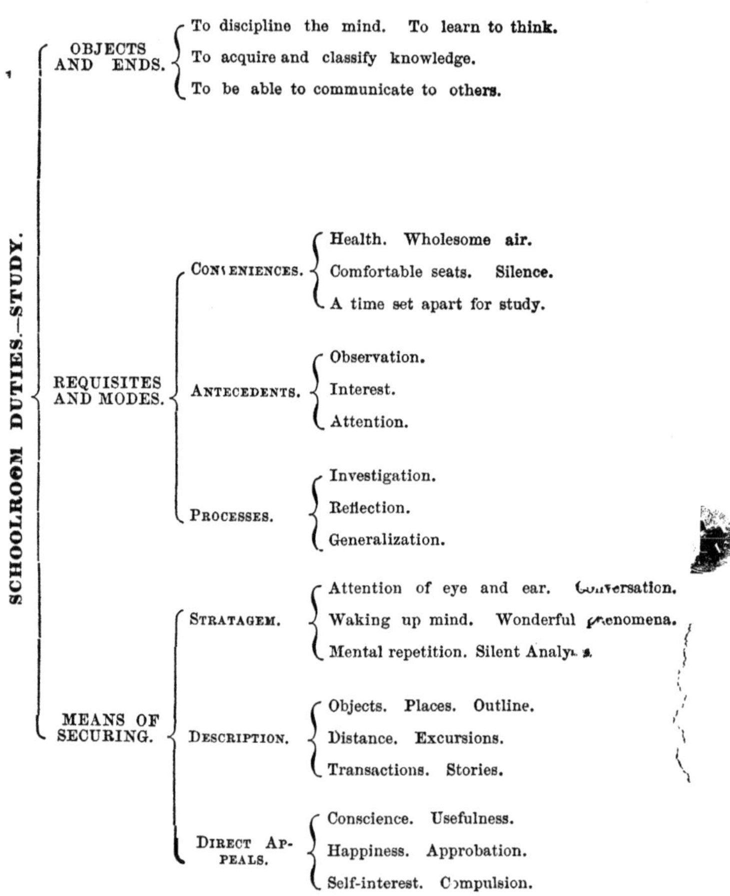

SCHOOLROOM DUTIES.—STUDY.

- OBJECTS AND ENDS.
  - To discipline the mind. To learn to think.
  - To acquire and classify knowledge.
  - To be able to communicate to others.
- REQUISITES AND MODES.
  - CONVENIENCES.
    - Health. Wholesome air.
    - Comfortable seats. Silence.
    - A time set apart for study.
  - ANTECEDENTS.
    - Observation.
    - Interest.
    - Attention.
  - PROCESSES.
    - Investigation.
    - Reflection.
    - Generalization.
- MEANS OF SECURING.
  - STRATAGEM.
    - Attention of eye and ear. Conversation.
    - Waking up mind. Wonderful phenomena.
    - Mental repetition. Silent Analysis.
  - DESCRIPTION.
    - Objects. Places. Outline.
    - Distance. Excursions.
    - Transactions. Stories.
  - DIRECT APPEALS.
    - Conscience. Usefulness.
    - Happiness. Approbation.
    - Self-interest. Compulsion.

CHAPTER II.

STUDY.

The claims of this branch of the subject to special consideration, are such as scarcely need argument. Study, with recitation, constitutes the great staple of the school. Without it, there could be no real progress or development. It is a condition of growth in the intellectual world, as essentially as cultivation is in the vegetable world; and the condition of the mind without study or discipline, is not inaptly compared to an uncultivated field, over-grown with brambles and unsightly weeds. Study keeps the powers from stagnation, and the mind and body both in a healthy state. If they are left without this regulating force, either one or the other, or both, take on a monstrous or diseased growth. It has been remarked already, that if good seed is not sown, bad will be; if good habits are not formed, bad ones will be; and if the harvest is not garnered by skillful hands, it will be trodden down by the feet of the wicked and dissolute. This is true in an intellectual sense as well as in a moral.

But there are difficulties in the way of study that must be removed, before any successful labor can proceed. These difficulties are of such a nature, as often to defy the unaided efforts of the young. One of these difficulties exists in the form of weakness, or natural inability to study, arising from extreme youth. The mind, like the body, needs practice, before it can

perform its functions properly; and like it too, its motions at first are awkward, feeble, and confined chiefly to the simple operations; and they are of short continuance.

Again: the difficulty may arise from constitutional dullness or stupidity. This also finds its similitude in bodily weakness and imbecility. Hence the same amount and kind of study should not be demanded of all alike, any more than the same amount of food and labor should be apportioned to all, without respect to age or constitutional differences.

The early formation of bad habits is another fruitful source of difficulty. These, like an incubus, weigh down the mind, and divert it from its proper channel. The mind, in its natural or unobstructed state, possesses no aversion to study; but by wrong treatment and misdirected effort, early prejudices are formed, which become serious obstacles to healthy study; not only so, but habits of superficial study are formed, which, in the end, are scarcely less formidable, than aversion itself.

Again: willful obstinacy is a condition of mind that must be met and provided for; for among all the obstacles, none will demand greater patience or skill to overcome. From these, and various other sources the mind is hindered in its approaches to progress and development; so that we would be safe in saying that from one-half to two-thirds of the time devoted to study in the schools, is employed to little or no purpose, or perhaps to positive disadvantage to the pupil. This would seem like a grave charge against the institutions of our country; and yet the facts, as carefully deduced from experiment, will justify the assertion. The very time and energies that were intended for the most benevolent purposes, are most

shamefully perverted, and turned against the child, as a shaft of self-destruction. They are squandered, and worse than squandered, at a time too when they can least be spared. This is too fearful an expenditure for the morning of life; and the loss is much aggravated by the reflection, that what is lost here, only prepares the way for subsequent losses. But we propose to notice. 1. The *Objects* of study: 2. The *Requisites* and *Processes*; and 3. The *Motives* and *Means* of securing study.

Section 1—The Objects and Ends.

It is necessary that we have clear ideas upon these points; otherwise our efforts may be entirely misdirected. It will be found also, upon the examination of pupils, that they possess very inadequate notions with regard to the true objects and ends of study—many of them ranging no higher than a mere desire to recite the lesson well, to keep up with their classes, or to receive as high a credit as possible. Now all of these may be well enough in their places; but any one can see, that they are not the objects that should be held before the mind, to guide it in its development. They are selfish; and their attainment would defeat the very object the teacher should have in view in requiring study. They circumscribe the limits of thought, and confine the mind to the mere drudgery of selfish toil.

Again: others get the idea that the highest object of study is to acquire knowledge, in whatever way they can. Hence they come to regard the mind as a kind of warehouse, or lumber room, into which they may deposit their knowledge and ideas for safe-keeping, rather than as a fruitful field to be cultivated, that

it may yield a continuous supply of these, all fresh and vigorous, and unlike the musty and withered warehouse ideas, dragged forth from where they may have been molding and rusting for years.

ARTICLE 1—DISCIPLINE.—The chief object of study, therefore, is *to discipline the powers of the mind, or to learn to think closely, accurately, methodically and continuously.* The Americans—perhaps justly—are styled a nation of talkers; and if there is truth in the maxim, that "He who talks much must talk in vain;" this is no very flattering tribute to our talent. The compliment would certainly be more acceptable if it included thinking also. We maintain that it is just as necessary that we learn to think, as that we learn to talk; not that talking is antagonistic to thinking; but that we learn to think independently of talking. There seems to be more need of sound, sober thinking and study, than for the proclivity to which allusion is made. For this reason, there should be a portion of the time set apart for the cultivation of this talent.

It will also be found, upon the examination of pupils, that few possess the power to think or study closely and accurately. They do not dive into the depth of a subject, but skim upon the surface. Their thoughts are not distinct and well-defined, but in a blurred and indefinite state. This may be called superficial thinking or study, and affords little or no discipline for the mind.

Others again may possess the power to elaborate clear thoughts; but they lack system or method. Their thoughts are in a chaotic state. They rush on in a confused and disordered manner. Their force is expended without accomplishing the desired results.

They resemble the disconnected links of a chain, lying scattered round. The links themselves are all well enough, but there is no connection. Now, it is the business of education and discipline, to regulate and bring into line this untamed and scattered force, and harness it into the car of consecutive thought; to give point and efficiency to the efforts of the mind; not only to arouse thoughts in the mind, but to wing them, and send them on their mission.

Another difficulty or hindrance to successful thinking or study, is the want of the power of concentration or continuous effort. Some seem to be able to think for a few moments, vigorously, but are unable to protract the process at will, to any considerable length. They resemble those birds that fly rapidly for a few rods, but are unable to continue long upon the wing. Such persons must, necessarily be circumscribed in their efforts; for it is only by continuous and protracted efforts that great results are produced. There is a vast difference between the mere passage of thoughts through the mind, and close consecutive thinking. The one resembles the fitful glare of the meteor,—the other, the steady blaze of the summer sun. The one dazzles the eye for a moment, and then disappears in darkness, the other pours down a continuous ray, until the whole firmament is in a blaze. Few are thus capable of holding their minds upon a given point, until it has mastered it; or of commencing at the beginning of a subject, and thinking it through without stopping, or allowing the mind to wander. But it is the province of education and discipline to impart this power; to arm the mind with strength to grapple with and overcome difficulties; to subdue and chasten it, and bring it under such

control, that it may, at pleasure, bend its energies upon a given point, until that point yields. This is discipline, one of the first and most important objects of study. Every lesson assigned should look to this object. It is not so much the mere acquisition and possession of the facts in science that educates, as it is the exercise and labor of acquiring.

There is, therefore, this difference between acquisition and discipline, between instruction and education. Acquisition and instruction collect the materials, discipline and education dispose of them in their proper places. The first feed the faculties of the mind, the second exercise them; the first constitute the means, the second the ends; the first develop knowledge, the second power; acquisition is learning, discipline is wisdom; instruction affords nourishment, education begets strength. Knowledge is the accumulation of facts and principles, wisdom is the ability to use them. An instructed man is a man of knowledge, an educated man is a man of wisdom. Instruction is a condition of education, knowledge of wisdom, acquisition of discipline. Instruction and acquisition afford the opportunities of improvement; education and discipline make use of these opportunities for the accomplishment of the duties of life: so that they are all as essentially necessary to perfect development of mind, as food and exercise are for the growth and perfect development of the body.

ARTICLE 2—ACQUISITION.—The next object, therefore, of study is *acquisition*, which, while it does not rank as high as that of discipline, is nevertheless, no mean object; and one of the most fortunate circumstances connected with this subject is, that the very best modes for discipline are the very best for acquisition, and vice versa. That acquisition which does not call into exercise, more or less, all the powers of mind, should at least be distrusted. This is evidently the intention of acquisition, that while it feeds the mind, it should also work it, and make it strong. The mere acquisition, without the discipline, would produce the mental dyspeptic, whose powers, rather enfeebled than otherwise, would sink down under the unnatural burden.

ARTICLE 3—COMMUNICATION.—But suppose the individual, if it were possible, should stop with mere discipline and acquisition; would the objects and purposes of study be fulfilled? In this case, he would resemble the miser who had hoarded away his silver and gold, to canker and corrode on his hands. We despise such a creature. We say of him, "There goes a man that has robbed the world—the widow and the orphan of their dues." Thousands may be dying of want, and yet he clutches his illy-gotten gain, still more tightly. He becomes an object of detestation and loathing; and he ought not to expect more, for he has no right to human sympathy, since he gives none. No man has a right to deprive his fellows of the necessities of life, without sufficient cause. But how much better is an intellectual miser, one who has hoarded away his intellectual treasures, while the world may be dying for them, than the merely physical miser? Rather, we should ask, how much worse? If depriving men and women of that which merely feeds the body, becomes a crime, what must the enormity of that offense be, which deprives them of their mental food?

Here again would appear the harmony and economy of right modes of education; for while the individual learner is most actively engaged in disciplining the powers of his mind and acquiring knowledge, he is at the same time throwing off rays which enlighten others. Man, when he lives right, lives not for himself, but for others. His chief advantage, as well as his chief happiness (and they are never separated) consists in doing good to others. The very best way of disciplining the powers of our own minds, and of acquiring knowledge, is to make use of those powers in giving away our knowledge, as fast as we acquire it. What we give away, we keep; what we keep, we lose. This is a seeming paradox, but it is no less than one of the benevolent designs of the Creator; for if a person is free in the use of his knowledge and intellectual powers, he not only keeps what he has, but is constantly acquiring more; whereas, if he attempt to retain it, without using it, he is sure to lose it. Hence, "To him that hath (and uses) shall be given, and he shall have more abundance; but from him that hath not (improved) shall be taken away that which he hath." This is the reason why the profession of teaching, when properly pursued, offers larger opportunities for thorough, full-orbed development of soul, body and intellect, than any other in the whole range of professions. It is the Heaven-appointed means of perpetuating knowledge and of educating the race; for when and while an individual is educating himself, after the true mode, he will furnish the conditions whereby all within the circle of his influence, may be educated. All are, therefore, to some extent, teachers, but some more than others; and the more fully they act in this sphere, and fulfill the conditions of

the true teacher, the more exalted are their privileges and powers. By the very nature and design of this profession, it furnishes these privileges in larger measure than any other; for while it gives it receives, and while it exercises, it strengthens. Who ever heard of a teacher becoming demented by teaching? When this happens (but it never happens from real teaching), the teacher is no longer fit for service. "He is thenceforth good for nothing, but to be cast out and trodden under foot of men."

A third object of study, therefore, is *to learn to communicate to others what we have learned ourselves.* This object should be kept constantly before the eye of both teacher and learner. The understanding should be, that the lesson is to be so well prepared, that it may, with ease, be communicated to others. This completes the discipline and renders the acquisition more rapid and certain.

Section 2—Requisites and Modes.

There are certain conditions necessary, in order to secure the results anticipated under the head of *Objects, etc.*, which are clearly entitled to consideration. In addition to those named in the introduction to this chapter, there are others of a more special character, which will be treated under the topics *Requisites and Modes.*

ARTICLE 1—HEALTH, ETC.—Among the conditions necessary to secure good study, the physical health should not be overlooked. The body should be in a sound condition, and the surrounding circumstances should all be favorable. No child can study well, when it is suffering from disease, or when it is placed in an unnatural and uncomfortable position. But to attempt to consider all the conditions of the body necessary to healthy study, in detail, would require a treatise on physiology and hygiene. We shall content ourselves, therefore, by noticing a few of the more general points.

1. The air should be in as pure a state as possible. It is terrible to witness the suffering that arises from breathing impure air. It vitiates the blood, which, in its turn, acts upon the brain, causing disease there, and rendering it utterly impossible to secure any thing like a healthy action of that organ. Healthy thoughts must proceed from a healthy brain, and a healthy brain is dependent upon healthy blood, and healthy blood can not exist without pure air, and pure air can not exist in poorly ventilated school-rooms. Hence, healthy thoughts depend, in no small degree, upon the condition of the schoolroom.

There has been much said and written upon this subject lately, and yet people have not more than begun to open their eyes upon the enormity of the evils arising from the want of pure air, in the growth and education of children. Teachers and pupils are yet confined in small and badly ventilated apartments from two to three hours at a time, with scarcely breathable air enough to supply the demand for fifteen minutes. The results are pale, sallow countenances, headache, colds, indisposition, languor, fretfulness and bad temper, and a general dislike to the school and all its exercises; and if we add to this vitiated atmosphere, a dusty and filthy schoolroom, which is too apt to be its accompaniment, we have all the conditions necessary to produce permanent disease, and sometimes death. No pecuniary considerations should be weighed against the provisions for furnishing a

constant supply of wholesome air to the inmates of the schoolroom.

ARTICLE 2—SEATS.—Again: comfortable seating is a consideration of no small importance. It is plainly a condition which ought to be considered in connection with study. No successful study or thinking can be carried on, when the body is constantly tortured by confinement in uncomfortable positions. The energies of the mind are exhausted in devising ways and means for escape or diversion, while those of the body are either exhausted or wrongly directed in efforts to endure the pain, or to evade it. This is true of adults: what then must be the effects upon those who are far less able to bear suffering? Children need all the minds they have for study; and it seems strange that any other means should be devised for disposing of them.

But these evils are fast disappearing from our schools. People are coming to understand more fully the physiological and psychological nature of man: that there is really a connection between body and mind, and that it is not necessary to torture one in order to develop the other; but that when any injury is inflicted upon the one, it is transmitted to the other.

ARTICLE 3—OPPORTUNITY.—There is another class of conditions or requisites which we shall call *opportunity*. We often require of children, what they are incapable of performing, until we have provided them the means, or removed some of the difficulties from the way. Their little minds are weak, and, like their bodies, require the most careful treatment, until they acquire strength. They are incapable, for the most part, of any protracted efforts in study or thinking, and yet it is not an uncommon thing to hear teachers give orders like the following: "Now I want you all to be *perfectly* quiet all this forenoon, and *to study* all the time." Now if the teacher really means what he says, in this requirement; and if it were fulfilled to the letter, for a series of days, there would soon be a fine job for the undertaker. The teacher in this case has demanded next thing to an impossibility, even allowing the necessary movements for breathing, &c. What, *children* to be perfectly still for two or three hours at a time! Why, it is monstrous! He might with about the same propriety have said: "Now don't you breathe:" or "Don't you think a single thought." Does he think that education consists in being still? Does he know that motion is a law of the universe, and a necessity for children? and that what he has demanded, viz., study, requires motion? that he has interdicted this law and this necessity? Does he know, in fact, that he has given them a lesson in disobedience? that they must necessarily disobey him? and that the force of his commands, however reasonable in other respects, is thereby weakened?

Now if children were vegetables, and required to be kept in one position all the time, to insure their growth, there would be some propriety in this requirement. But they are animals, thinking and rational animals that require alternate rest and motion. Education is not confinement; it is freedom and activity of body and mind. It is not torture and pain; it is pleasure and enjoyment. It is not weakness and decrepitude; it is strength and vigor. It is not sickness; it is health. It is not death; it is life, glorious, active, busy, buoyant life, with the largest liberty and most perfect development of all of man's rational and legitimate powers. Why then should the teacher make such an unreasonable demand? And then he has required them to "*study all the time.*" He might, with about the same propriety, have required them to eat all the time. It is impossible for them to study all the time. Hence, the probabilities are, they will study none of the time, since no particular portion has been assigned them.

Children are incapable of thinking upon one subject more than a few minutes at a time. Now provisions should be made to suit this want. One of these would be a time set apart and devoted exclusively to efforts, to call out and develop thought. The ordinary recitation will accomplish this in part; but it is not sufficient. There is one kind of thinking—and the most useful kind, too—that it does not necessarily promote, viz., the silent thought, so necessary in preparing lessons. Children do not know how to study or to think, until they are taught how. There should, therefore, be thinking exercises, in which nothing else is done but pure thinking or study. This will afford opportunity for the formation of the habit of thought and self-control, which is so valuable in every pursuit in life. It will be described under "Means of Securing Study."

ARTICLE 4—SILENCE.—Again: the circumstances should be favorable in another respect. *Silence* is a condition necessary to this kind of study. No pupils, unless they possess extraordinary powers of concentration, can study with a continual noise and buzzing about their ears. Their powers of voluntary attention are necessarily weak; hence, whenever any thing from

without, having a stronger attraction for them, obtrudes itself upon their notice, their attention is drawn from those things having less attractive force. There should, therefore, during the time set apart for thinking or study, be no unnecessary noise, not so much as moving the lips. Children should be taught to think with their mouths shut. Their lips are not the necessary appendages of thought, any more than their fingers or toes are. Hence, during the time of study, which should not exceed five or ten minutes at a time, children should not be allowed to interrupt one another by studying half audibly or "buzzing," as it is commonly called. The "loud school," as it is termed by some, or the practice of studying aloud, is an anomaly, and should never be countenanced. Whatever may be said in palliation of this practice, can never redeem it from the objections which have been offered above. The silence there recommended, will afford opportunity for the formation of the habit of close consecutive thinking, which will do more to strengthen the power of attention than all the loud study that can be practiced. Whatever excellency this mode of study may possess as a means of cultivating the ability to think in the midst of confusion (and it may possess merit in this respect), is more than counteracted by the loss of time and dissipation of thought (to say nothing about the inconvenience and annoyance to the teacher), by the noise and confusion arising from it. And then, to say the least of it we can, if it is not absolutely disorderly in itself, it offers one of the greatest temptations to superficial study, and for carrying on mischief that could be devised.

ARTICLE 5—INTEREST AND ATTENTION.—The *modes*

of study are also worthy of notice. All valuable study is accompanied with *interest and attention.* Attention is the key to investigation. It may be either voluntary or involuntary. The former is the genuine, but it often becomes necessary to resort to the latter as a means of securing it. Children, however, seldom possess sufficient self-command to force attention. It therefore becomes necessary to "bait them" with a little interest, and the more the better, so that it does not amount to undue excitement. The two things, viz., interest and attention, are so nearly allied to each other, in the process of study, that it seems difficult to separate them; and that study (?) which is secured at the expense of either is of little or no value. Children may "say their lessons over" from morning till noon, and from noon till night, without securing the discipline which it is the design of study to give.

There is a kind of attention which is not desirable. It is that which forces the lesson for the time being upon the memory, and charges it to keep it, until after recitation; but further than that, it does not concern itself. This kind of attention and study seldom leaves the mind any better than it found it. Indeed, aside from the little knowledge that may accidentally have clung to the walls of memory in its rapid passage through (for it does not remain there), the mind is rather injured than otherwise, by the formation of a bad habit. Just as soon, however, as any thing having the properties that possess attraction for the mind, is presented to it, interest is excited, and attention is elicited. The mind is now in a favorable state for progress. A series of inquiries are at once begotten, which result in *investigation* and *reflection.* These may be, at first, in a feeble state—scarcely noticeable indeed.

For instance: take the young child in the nursery. Give him some pleasing toy. His interest and attention are at once excited. This must be the case, or he would not even notice it; much less become absorbed in it. Now mark the process that follows the interest and attention, just as surely as the thunder follows the lightning, or as light is the result of the rising of the sun. He, in all probability, breaks, tears, or bites his toy; for his hands are his instruments of apprehension, and his mouth is his test-tube, retort and crucible, into which he introduces all his substances for examination and experiment. But in all this, is that boy doing nothing more than merely amusing himself? It would seem so; and he can give no further account of it, himself. He perhaps, is unconscious of any further motive. But watch him. What prompted that desire and that movement? They must have a cause; and their existence indicates design. They could not have been given for the purposes of mischief and destruction alone. This would be impeaching the wisdom and benevolence of the Creator. But there is the wisest and most benevolent design connected with all this. What therefore, shall we call all this manipulation and experiment? *It is investigation* in its nascent state; and though it may scarcely bear a mark of that exalted mental operation, as it appears in manhood, yet that little boy is investigating, just as essentially as the chemist in the laboratory, or the mathematician at his formula, or the astronomer as he sweeps the heavens with his telescope. They are all investigating, the one as essentially as the other, with this difference, that in the latter case, the process is guided by judgment and will; in the former by mere impulse. The first is investigation in embryo; in the second, it is ripened into a purer and higher type. In the first, it is investigation to gratify an apparently idle curiosity; in the second, to answer the highest aims of life; but it is easy to trace back this higher form, through all the various stages, until we arrive at the very threshold of intelligence; or until we find it in its incipient state, in the nursery and among the toys. Hence it will be seen, that investigation becomes a second step in learning, and therefore a mode of study. The process itself has been described in Part First.

But with pure investigation alone, the mind would not receive the full benefits of study. It is followed by memory and reflection, as surely as that investigation follows interest and attention. The memory gathers up the thoughts and fragments of thoughts, as they are disengaged from the subjects of study. Reflection is the power which the mind possesses of reviewing its own conclusions for the purpose of ascertaining more certainly their truth, and of fixing the facts and principles more permanently, in their appropriate place. Just as soon, therefore, as the mind becomes active in the pursuit of truth, these several processes commence, as surely and essentially, as that the several wheels, bands, cranks and spindles, all start off in motion, when the power is applied at the water-wheel, or at the engine. How vain, therefore, to attempt to put this tremendous machinery in motion, by tugging at some of the bands, or twisting at some of the spindles! And yet this is the process, when we attempt to secure study, without Interest and Attention. But let the engine move; and, if the gearing is perfect, the whole machinery will move also.

ARTICLE 6—ABSTRACTION, GENERALIZATION, etc.—There are yet other processes, following or accompanying investigation etc., which while they may be regarded as a part of it, nevertheless have some distinctive characteristics, worthy of a separate notice. Their importance also to teaching and learning is such, as to entitle them to a brief recognition.

As the mind advances, step by step, from the simple notices and apprehensions, on through the several stages of investigation and reflection, it arrives at a point, where there is an evident need of other operations, growing out of its own relations and the existence of matter. It is not our purpose to investigate this feature of the subject, further than to show the character of this want, and the mode of supplying it.

For instance: if the mind should halt in its progress, when it had investigated or tracked out all the facts and apprehensions, it would resemble its condition, should it pause with simple acquisition. It might not be able to appropriate its acquisitions to the purposes for which they were intended. Abstraction, or that power which enables it to separate and consider apart, particular and distinct properties or species, arising out of general or complex subjects, becomes necessary. Children, for the most part, are incapable of doing this, to any great extent. Care, therefore, should be taken in the arrangement of their studies, not to perplex their minds with those studies that require too much abstraction.

The process of generalization, or the power to arrange under their appropriate heads, the facts and principles elicited in the process of investigation, is indispensable to learning and teaching. It completes the modes or processes of thinking, just as communication or the art of expression, to which it is preparatory and an indispensable prerequisite, completes the object of study. It will be observed, therefore, that the *objects* of study and *requisites* are concomitants, the one answering to the other in points of mutual coöperation. Thus: health and convenience, interest and attention, being indispensable to discipline and thought, investigation (including the other mental operations), to the acquisition of knowlege, and lastly abstraction and generalization to that of communication or the art of teaching. The application, or process of making use of knowledge constitutes, within itself, a mode or process of culture; but its claims have been considered elsewhere.

It will be necessary to keep the objects, requisites, and modes of study distinctly in mind, while investigating the means of securing it, since the success of the whole system, and indeed of any system, will depend upon the closeness with which we adhere to the principles involved in it. For this reason we have been more particular in describing some of the mental processes concerned in successful study.

Section 3—Means of Securing Study.

It might be well now to inquire after the means whereby this valuable mental exercise can be elicited and conducted. In doing so, we shall have recourse to the following classification of means: 1. By *Stratagem.* 2. By *Narrative and Description.* 3. By *Direct Appeals.*

ARTICLE 1—STRATAGEM.—These terms will need a little explanation, since it is not claimed that they convey any particular direction in and of themselves; nor yet is it claimed that they are the best that could be used: they are only the best we could find. We shall hope, therefore, to receive some indulgence, if we succeed in making their use intelligible in this connection. For instance: it is not intended by the use of the word "stratagem," that we may resort to deception and low tricks in securing study; but rather, a judicious employment of means and motives that have been furnished us by the Creator, for the express purpose of calling out and adorning the minds of the young. It is employed in the sense of tact, skill, wisdom, prudence, forecast, or strategy, which last, perhaps, would be a better word. Narrative and Description are used to indicate that mode of inducing thought and study, by calling out and making use of the knowledge already acquired, as a means of inciting to further acquisitions and use. The Direct Appeals have reference to a class of motives that may be used, according to circumstances, with a higher grade of development, such as we usually find in the intermediate and high schools.

In describing the various devices that may be resorted to, in leading children into habits of thinking, we shall consider the simpler modes first, on the supposition that we are operating with small children, and thence pass to the more advanced. It was stated in the article on the "Object of Study," that to discipline the mind, or to learn to control its powers, is one of the first and most important objects; and in the article on "Requisites and Modes," that health, convenience, opportunity, interest, and attention are requisites that could not be dispensed with. It is not within the province of a work of this kind, to descend to the particular modes of fulfilling the first three conditions, further than they are described in the preceding. These being complied with, as far as possible, it will be necessary to inquire after the best modes of eliciting *interest*, and cultivating *attention*, that vagrant of the mind, which, when once tamed, becomes the engineer of investigation—the key that unlocks the storehouses of knowledge.

In order to possess ourselves of the citadel of attention, we must besiege the outposts and gain admittance through the open gates; for to batter down the walls and force a passage (even were this possible) would yield no advantage, since by committing this outrage, we render useless all the engines, ammunition and energies of the besieged. It is desirable, therefore, that the entrance be made through the natural gates; and since these are open during all the waking hours of the mind, the difficulties of admittance are much reduced. Again: to render success certain, we must approach these outposts, not as enemies, not as a belligerent force, but as friends, seeking the peace and happiness of the inmates. This citadel is rendered still more accessible, from the fact that the sentinels on the outposts are continually on the alert, and seeking some one to enter, that will give them exercise and pleasure. They however, persistently refuse to admit any that will not give promise to this effect.

The eye and the ear are the two grand gateways or highways to this citadel of thought; since, if these, with one other, which is a kind of subterraneous passage—the sense of touch, or the avenue of tactual knowledge—were closed before any impressions have been made through them, however perfect the organism in other respects may be, the individual would be incapable of the exercise of thought. The teacher should, therefore, first avail himself of the command of those avenues, that he may direct their energies upon proper themes, or rather, he should so operate upon them, and the mind through them, that their notices and the whole attention shall be as nearly voluntary as possible. Take, for example, the eye, the window to the mind, which, in childhood, is ever on the alert, ever seeking gratification and food for the mind. The object should be to train it, not only to the appreciation of the beautiful, but to habits of close observation, and continuous application for a given period.

Many children are incapable of confining even their eyes to observe anything closely, for a minute at a time. Hence, when the eye wanders, the attention wanders also. The weakness of mind in this respect on the part of children, is truly remarkable. They may be induced, it is true, to look at a beautiful picture, a flower, or something novel or wonderful, for a greater length of time, and even here the observation is apt to be superficial; but to confine the attention at will, and make it do the bidding of the mind, are matters of such difficulty, that few children can accomplish them, without special assistance. Many, indeed, spend half their time in weak and ineffectual efforts to study; while others, from the same want of discipline, spend still a greater portion of theirs in mischief.

Now, this error can be corrected, and this fearful loss and abuse of time and energy can be saved. This squandering was never intended; and if the common schools can not correct the evil, then they are not the proper instrumentalities for the education of the people. What we wish to cultivate in the children is the power to fix the attention at will, and to hold it upon a subject, until the object for which it is held, is accomplished; or in other words, *the power to study their lessons and to think.* The ordinary mode, or that which children, if left to their unaided efforts, are apt to adopt, does not do this; since it is no uncommon thing, to see a whole bevy of children actively engaged in what they call study, while perhaps not one in ten is exercising his thoughts upon the lesson. Such study is a positive injury.

A little expedient, to which I have resorted, on some occasions, may be suggestive of means that may be adopted for correcting these evils, and of fixing the attention. Holding up my watch to the school, I have said, "How many of these little boys and girls can look at it, for one minute at a time?" The idea perhaps is a novel one, and their little voices and hands will respond, anxious for the experiment. Some will say boastingly, "I can look at it an hour!" "*Two hours!*" responds another little captain who is anxious to make a display of his prowess. At this juncture, I ask, "How many would be willing to make the experiment of one minute continuous looking, provided I should give you five dollars, if you should succeed?" At this announcement there is a shower of hands and a shout of voices raised to the highest pitch. "Well, I will not promise you the five dollars; but let us try." "All ready!" "Now!" and their forms straiten up, and all eyes are bent with intense earnestness upon the watch. It grows very quiet, and every one listens and looks. . . . . . . Presently it occurs to half a dozen or more of them, that they are doing it about right. "I wonder if John, or Charles, or James, or

Mary, or Jane, or Ellen is looking too?" "Wonder if they all are doing as well as I am," and their thoughts leave the watch and the promise, and wander after Charles or Jane, and the temptation to look away becomes so great that in about a half a minute or less, you will see an occasional pair of eyes glance hurriedly to some convenient quarter of the room, and back quick, to the watch again: others, still less cautious, will turn the head, and look carelessly away; others again, will drop off entirely, and cease to look; while some, more resolute and determined and careful than the rest, will not remove their eyes for a moment, and at the expiration of the time, will announce their triumph with evident satisfaction. At the close, some will insist upon a new trial. It may be granted; and then others will succeed: and here it might be well to vary the experiment. The question might be asked: "If you are capable of holding your eyes fixed upon that watch, can you, with equal success, confine them to a picture or mark upon the board?" This experiment may also be made and repeated, accompanied with such explanations and variations, as may seem desirable.

"Now if you can look at a watch, a picture, or a mere chalk mark upon the board, for a given time, can you look at your books as long, without change?" The intention here, perhaps, will be discovered by some; and they will begin to see the force of it. Let the experiment be made, however, and repeated with the book, without attempting to study. Indeed I would not allow them to study, for the first few trials. They must simply *look*. And if they succeed well, suggest that if they can look upon one page of the book, they might study that long, without looking away. And here it might be well to explain the whole matter to them, and pledge them to an exercise of this kind, once or twice a day. This would be applicable, of course, only to those who can read or spell; but it may be varied to suit any grade. And if they can thus confine the attention for one, two or three minutes, they can also, by practicing, continue it to five and six. But it will be found that young scholars are not able to endure more than three or four minutes, even after weeks and months of practice.

A similar stratagem may be employed for the purpose of securing quiet, for a limited time, and then it should not be insisted upon, beyond that time. All noise may be hushed for a minute at a time, and then for two, three, four, etc. Here it might be well to suggest, "What an excellent opportunity for study!" Show the importance of quiet in study; the advantages of doing but one thing at a time, and of doing that *well*. Pledge the children to the trial; and experiment patiently with them, until the results are secured.

Now the question arises: Can they think of their lessons for the required length of time? for there is such a thing, all are aware, as watching and mouthing lessons, without study or thought; or at least, while the thoughts are busied about something else. The object now is to induce the mind to follow the eye. This, a few weeks of practice will usually accomplish, yet it can be greatly facilitated by a few special exercises, similar to those described for the eye, only the object now is to confine the mind upon the subject of experiment. Suppose this to be the watch, as before. "Now how many can *think* of the watch, for one minute, or during the time that the eye and the ear are giving attention?"

It will be better here, however, to select some object about which it will be easier for them to employ their thoughts. The pictures of animals will form good subjects, since their nature, habits and the anecdotes respecting them, will form excellent topics of thought while suitable experiments are made. These experiments should be repeated, both with and without the looking exercises, until satisfactory results are secured. At first the novelty of the thing itself will prevent, to some extent, the accomplishment of the object; but by and by, if the practice is persisted in, the habit will become a matter of ease and pleasure.

Now it is not maintained that these are the only modes of cultivating attention. They only constitute a class that may be varied to almost any extent, and are useful chiefly in preparing the way for study. If five minutes of each day were thus employed, even if nothing more is attempted than merely keeping quiet and looking at the book, it would be worth practicing, since it would then exceed what many children do, without such an exercise. The habit of idling time away, in fidgety attempts to study, or of gazing into a book, pretending to study, in order to deceive the teacher, is not only a shameful waste of time, but it is ruining the morals of the pupil; for what is it but downright hypocrisy and lying? And yet I have known it to be practiced from morning till night, and from week to week, and term to term, with scarcely a variation. Can it be expected that boys and girls, taught after this fashion, will do any thing else than deceive whenever occasion is offered? Like will not produce its like, if they will not. And let it be borne in mind, that a lie can be acted, as well as be told with the tongue.

But this practice of devoting just so much time of each day, to silent thought and study, strikes at the very root of this evil. It has a tendency, not only to break up the bad habit, but to form its opposite; and the lessons which cause hours of anxiety, perplexity and dread, not to say sin, may be disposed of in a few minutes. Then the books should be laid aside, not kept as tormentors of the little folks, or to hide their mischievous faces behind, but laid aside, to be taken up again when the exercise is to be renewed, or a recitation is to be heard: laid aside, and their little busy hands and brains furnished with other employment. This will not only keep them out of mischief, but will use up all their mischievous desires in profitable labor.

Not to be tedious in description, we only add that there are other means of inducing children to think, which may be treated under the head of *Conversation.* These appeal more to the voluntary than the involuntary attention, and may include all the exercises that were described in Chap. VI., Intellectual Culture, to which the reader is again referred. Conversation possesses a power over the minds of children, amounting almost to magic. Here is the place to make use of it, in inciting the incipient thoughts to action, and in putting in practice what has been heretofore recommended. The exercise may, by way of distinction, be called *waking* up *mind* by a recital of interesting narratives, etc., and a description, or rather an allusion to some of the wonderful phenomena of nature—such as described in the chapter alluded to above.

Still another mode might be described here; though it is not strictly strategical. We shall call it *mental repetition*, and append a brief explanation; but first the difficulties it is intended to remove. Many children, as has been remarked, are incapable of carrying forward a series of mental operations, without some extraneous aids; and unless these aids are furnished, they too frequently remain in this state of inability. They need something to cling to, until their minds acquire strength to move without the "props and stays." In some instances, the evil manifests itself in the want of power to reproduce what may have been understood. This acts adversely upon the ability to think independently; for if a person have the power to call to mind a connected series of words and sentences, and to follow a train of thought furnished by another, he will find less difficulty in his independent efforts, since the efforts thus made, produce the required discipline; hence the utility of mental repetition, or the practice of frequently and statedly calling to mind the words, sentences and thoughts of others. It should be commenced gradually, and something after the following manner:

Let a brief, simple sentence composed of three or four words, be read in the hearing of the class, requiring each member, as soon as it is completed, to call all the words to mind, in the order in which they occurred in the sentence. When completed, let it be announced by the uplifted hand. Then let the same sentence be repeated, compelling the mind, without the aid of speech, to examine every word carefully, as it passes before its vision. Another of greater length may then be introduced and treated in the same manner. And so on, until by practice, say five or six minutes per day, the class will, in a few weeks or months, be able thus to call to mind the consecutive words of sentences composed of twenty, thirty, and in some cases fifty words.

This cultivates close attention, and the pupils that can thus hold the mind upon the words of a sentence, will soon learn to make use of the same power, in the pursuit of other subjects. It is learning how to think consecutively.

The same thing, with slight modifications, is practiced in many of the best schools. A sentence is read to a class, and then the members, in consecutive order, are required to spell the words as they occur in the sentence, without the teacher's repeating them; and it is astonishing to witness, not only the accuracy and rapidity with which they will reproduce the whole, but the extent to which they will carry it, often spelling sentences composed of thirty, forty and fifty words, after hearing them once pronounced.

Now, children taught in this way are not so apt to forget what they hear and read. They are not compelled to read the same page a half-dozen times before fixing it in mind; and, hearing a discourse or lecture, they will be more apt to remember it, in the order in which it was delivered.

Still another method, which we shall call *Silent Analysis*, may be employed with success. Its chief use, however, would be confined to pupils who possess the power of calculation, to some extent. It may be described thus. The teacher reads a question like the following: "If three oranges cost fifteen cents, what will seven oranges cost?" The class is now required, not to give the answer, which could be done, perhaps, almost the instant the question is announced; but they are required to pass quietly over the whole example, bringing vividly before the mind, and examining every step of the analysis; thus, in thought, "If three oranges cost fifteen cents, one orange will cost one-third of fifteen

cents, which is five cents; and if one orange cost five cents, seven oranges will cost seven times five cents, which are thirty-five cents," examining every step and word as they pass along, and when the conclusion is reached, to announce it simply by the uplifted hand; then, at a given signal, all are required to review the process and report as before. Another question or example may be given in a similar manner, and repeated again and again, till the pupils acquire the power to fix the attention, at will, upon whatever point they please. Not a word is to be spoken during the whole exercise, except the mere reading of the question by the teacher, or some member of the class.

It will be observed that this is a purely mental exercise. It is compelling the mind to take cognizance of its own operations, which will be found, at first, a more difficult task than a mere announcement of the result, after a brief survey, and then giving the analysis orally, which is the common mode of recitation in mental arithmetic. The former mode secures by far the greatest amount of discipline. But this will be described more fully under Recitation.

ARTICLE 2 — NARRATIVE AND DESCRIPTION. — These modes have been briefly described under the head of Intellectual Culture, Chapter VI. Their use, as means of inciting to study, will be further illustrated here.

It will be found upon a careful analysis of the modes and processes of thought, that they continually seek a tangible expression. We shape our thoughts, in some degree, after the objects of nature and of art, with which we are most familiar. The mind is continually seeking comparisons, similes, metaphors, etc.

Hence all the figures of rhetoric. This peculiarity obtains more strongly in the earlier stages of thinking, as well as in earlier stages of civilization. The feeble powers continually seek some sensible object, through which, and by which to give expression to the ideas. In other words, thinking is done by the aid of sensible objects. The simple, touching, forcible, and sometimes almost sublime expressions of childhood, will abundantly testify to this fact. Hence the narrative and descriptive modes are the processes they employ.

Now it is the policy of every wise teacher to take the thought, and the mental strength already developed in children, and to use it as a means of acquiring or developing more, to use the present stock as a principal, from which a continual annuity arises; for these thoughts, accurately expressed by their possessor, will awaken other thoughts, which become in their turn, antecedents to others yet unborn. The advantage that this exercise possesses over many others, is that the thoughts must proceed in consecutive order, or the beauty of the narrative or description will be destroyed.

A plan like the following might be adopted. Let a certain portion of the day be set apart by general consent, as a time in which everything of importance which occurs, is to be carefully noted in the memory, in the order in which the several transactions take place. These are to be related in the same order, by the pupils, at the appointed time. Or the whole day might be apportioned out to the whole school, in the same manner, each one having a certain alloted part,—the incidents to be reported at the proper time. This, I apprehend, would have a powerful effect upon the order of the

school. It should be guarded, however, from any system of espionage. The object is an entirely different one. Or the subject of narration or description may be some particular incident: in all of which cases, care should be taken that everything be related in its proper order, and be strictly true.

An excursion after specimens in natural history, would afford one of the finest opportunities for cultivating this power of observation, of attention, and of the ability to think in consecutive order. Different departments might be allotted to different members, one taking the objects of one particular class, and another, another. The occurrences and events might constitute another theme which could be disposed of in a similar manner. It will be amusing, as well as instructive, to listen to all the minutiæ. If circumstances are favorable, these things might be committed to writing. This will also prepare the way for composition writing, which certainly should be preceded by some exercise, to give or induce thoughts, since the want of them seems to be the principal deficiency. If a child is capable of telling a straight story, it is pretty good evidence that he has thought it straight beforehand, which is just what we want. And if he can think a straight story, he may make a ready transfer of this power to his books and lessons.

Again: *Objects and places* form another class of excellent exercises for this kind of practice. For instance: an object of some kind is named or exhibited to the class, and each member is required to give a description of it, including the size, form, weight, color, and all the properties belonging to it, including history and use. The object may be a chair, a block of wood, a fragment of rock, a lump of earth, a branch of a tree, some part of an animal, or it may be some kind of grain, fruit or flowers: what a theme for conversation and description opens up here! What an endless variety of them!

Places may be the theme. In such case, it may be well to commence with the place occupied by the pupil, and then advance to those whose peculiarities are well remembered, such as the door-yard at home, the garden, the orchard, the meadow, the farm, the neighborhood, etc., etc.: or take the dwelling-house, and what a fine subject is offered in the description of the several apartments!

A description of *outline* and *boundary* is an excellent exercise for inducing thought. Let the simple outline of some well-known field, farm or forest be given as a lesson for description. Let a person be supposed to pass round it. The objects and places passed or approximated, should be named in the consecutive order, commencing at a given point.

Way or *distance* may be described in the same manner. The pupils are requested to note every thing worthy of description, that they observe on the road to or from school; or to describe accurately the road from their homes to the schoolhouse door. Such exercises will not only make the pupils close observers of nature and art, but will make them close thinkers and describers, which latter acquisition is fully as valuable as the former.

Now it will usually be found, that the first efforts in narrating and describing, will be rather rude and indefinite, which rudeness and indefiniteness are sufficient reasons in favor of this practice: for what is our education for, if not to make us able and exact? Practice, however, will soon remove the inaccuracies.

26

Let these exercises be repeated, day after day, at regular intervals, in connection with other duties, taking up the topics in some systematic order, and teachers will be astonished at the accuracy that will in a short time be acquired. Lessons will be studied and recited with ten times the care and accuracy that would obtain, were no such aids used. For, if a pupil can tell what occurred within a given space of time, during the school hours, he can certainly study and remember the events and incidents recorded in his history lesson, with greater ease; and if he can describe the one, he can the other. If he can describe the outline and boundary of a field or farm, with accuracy, he certainly can apply the same to the study of geography. If he can gather up, and treasure in his mind, the several incidents as they occur by the wayside; if he can describe objects accurately and fully, he has already taken the first step in the study of language. He may, therefore, with greater ease, apply the principles and rules of grammar, or follow the solution of a problem or the demonstration of a theorem.

Such are some of the advantages of narration and description; but their chief importance, as means of inducing thought and study, can only be estimated by their use. A fuller description of these modes will be given under the head of Recitation, in connection with others, bearing more immediately upon that subject.

ARTICLE 3—DIRECT APPEALS.—1. We shall now proceed to notice another class of means, intended more immediately for a grade of pupils, capable of appreciating the higher motives, which we shall endeavor to present in their natural order, beginning with the highest.

It is a well-established principle in ethical philosophy, that a desire to do right, simply because it is right, or from purely conscientious feelings, ranks, if not the highest, at least among the highest motives of human action. Hence, an appeal to conscience for a faithful discharge of duty, would be the highest appeal that could be made. It will be understood here, that we mean conscience, as developed by reason, and founded upon the most exalted ideas of God and a future state. These appeals then become a potent instrumentality, not only in the discharge of the duty itself, but in cultivating the conscience.

Motives of this kind, however, could avail but little, with children of the age and advancement of those for whom we have been recommending the other two classes of means. It would avail but little, for instance, to say to a child that could not understand the right clearly, or comprehend the motive, or feel the obligation, "Now you must study, because it is your duty; it is an obligation of the highest possible force." The child thus addressed, might have no ill designs, but on the contrary, the impulses might be of a generous order; but the force of that appeal would scarcely be felt, simply for the want of a proper understanding and appreciation of it: and yet I have known teachers and ministers to talk to children, just as if they could be moved by the same class of appeals which are appropriate for adults. Their lucid illustrations of right and wrong, would make the children stare, but would leave them wondering at such profundity, or reproaching themselves with ugliness or stupidity, when, in fact, the stupidity, at least, was

on the other side. But with a class of pupils who are capable of appreciating appeals of this nature, to connect their duties thus with their highest destiny, and show their intimate relations and certain dependence, would act with a force measured only by the power of conscience.

2. The *appeals* to a *desire for usefulness* are closely allied to the appeals to conscience. This desire, it will be seen, is purely a benevolent one, and the appeals to it become, like those to conscience, both the means of securing study, and of cultivating the desire itself. This desire, we maintain, is a natural one; for no one, exept a fiend, or one greatly depraved, could desire the misery of human beings, or even of brutes. We see this desire exhibited among children in a remarkable manner, in the sympathy they so readily manifest in each other's joys and sorrows. When properly cultivated, it leads them to desire the welfare of all their associates and friends, and when more fully developed and Christianized, it ripens into that holy ardor for usefulness that burns in the bosom of the missionary of the cross or the true philanthropist. This desire will also be found to exist in various stages of development in the minds of pupils, and often sadly mingled with selfishness. When, however, it can be shown that true usefulness depends upon faithfulness in the discharge of duty, especially that of study; that the power to do good is measured by development and discipline, no healthier stimulant can be applied. It is free from all those excesses to which so many of the ordinary motives are subject.

3. *The desire for happiness* is another powerful motive. It is intimately blended with the preceding one, since usefulness and happiness are inseparable. The

desire for happiness is like the desire for existence itself. It is a universal desire. It pervades all ranks, ages and conditions in life; and it even reaches beyond this life, and becomes one of the leading motives to impel a preparation for the life to come. It can hardly be said to be strictly benevolent, since it seeks self-gratification or enjoyment; and yet even this may be regarded as a species of benevolence. Indeed it becomes a very high order of benevolence when it is so regulated in its actions as not to mar the happiness of others in seeking its own. A purely enlightened selfishness, in this sense, would lead a man to do right; for, since the happiness of man depends upon the fulfillment of the law of love, or "to do unto others as ye would that others should do unto you," he would necessarily seek the fulfillment of that law. The amount of virtue, however, that such actions would involve must be determined from another standpoint.

It may be clearly shown that the enjoyment of the faculties of the mind, and hence of the mind itself, depends upon action, development, and discipline of those faculties; that a lack of healthy activity would impair the growth; that a sickly development would beget feeble enjoyment; that imperfect discipline would involve precarious happiness; and again, that the entire happiness depends upon usefulness, since, according to the well-known laws of mind and matter, just as soon as a man ceases to be useful to his fellow man, he ceases to be happy; that there is no such condition in the economy of things, as a man's carrying his happiness outside of his usefulness, since they both lie precisely in the same line; and that if he loses the one he loses the other also.

What a merited rebuke upon sordid selfishness! If

the poor, blind devotee of gain, or power, or pleasure, could but open his eyes upon this path, how soon would he recognize the folly of his course! God has made it impossible for any human being to be happy, outside the path of duty and usefulness; and the degree of pleasure is usually measured by the devotion to this course. What stronger, healthier, higher, holier motives can be employed in the schoolroom than these? Does any one ask, "When and how they shall be applied?" We answer, by appealing to them in every lesson, recitation and duty, by making every word of instruction point to this great object of existence.

4. *The love of approbation* is a motive that may be *gently* plied in the schoolroom. The affections which sometimes exist, and which should always exist between teacher and pupil, can be wielded with powerful certainty by those who understand their business. It exists in various degrees, from the simple cold respect, up through all the various grades of regard, esteem, veneration, reverence, friendship and love. The higher the grade of affection, the more potent the influence becomes. Now, if the pupil feel any or all of these generous emotions for the teacher, whatever of approbation he receives, will tell just so far, as a motive to duty; and whatever of disapprobation is shown, will sting the conscience and self-respect to active exertions, to repair the losses and regain favor.

But in the use of approbation and disapprobation, the greatest care should be exercised. There is great danger, on the one hand, of fostering pride and self-conceit, and a morbid desire for praise, which, if not bestowed, results in jealousy, envy and childish whims, and on the other hand, in discouragement, petulance, and churlishness. The approving smile and look of love will do far more to elevate, purify and stimulate the desires, than all the fulsome praise and idle flattery that can be bestowed; and on the other hand, the look of sorrow and disappointed hope, the gentle but earnest reproof, will do more than all the censorious fault-finding and angry threats that can be employed, in the government of children.

5. *Self-interest*, as a motive for study, is one that admits of two interpretations. If it is meant by it, that regard for self which leads the individual to seek his own happiness from the highest sources, and without interfering with the rights of others, or in a manner described under "*Usefulness and Happiness*," there certainly can be no objection to it. But, if by self-interest, is meant the mere gratification of selfish desires, without regard to the feelings or rights of others; or to rise by pulling another down, or to acquire at another's sacrifice; or if it be the mere gratification of self for self's sake—it is not only of doubtful utility, but radically and unequivocally wrong.

The practice, therefore, of giving prizes or rewards of merit, can scarcely be free from these objections. To say the least we can of the principle, as usually practiced, it is apt to engender an unwholesome spirit of rivalry, to discourage the backward and timid, to provoke jealousies, to stimulate inordinate ambition; and above all, and worst of all, it is setting a paltry price on learning. The practice is therefore wrong in principle, when it proposes to pay a pupil for benefiting himself. In accepting, he takes that for which he has rendered no equivalent. He gets all the benefits of study or obedience himself, and then expects

to be paid for it besides. Too much care can not be taken to teach children that they should, as far as possible, render an equivalent for every thing they obtain. There can, however, be no objection to giving tokens of approbation; but the practice of holding out the idea, that for so much study, so much pecuniary reward will be given, is at once to degrade study or obedience in the estimation of every right-minded pupil.

And then again it is accompanied with this difficulty, that when the incentive is removed, when there are no more rewards to be received, the mind having been fed on such motives, there will remain no wholesome desire. It is apt to cease to act, when the false stimulant is removed. And yet we will not undertake to decide, that there can be no system of prize-giving, free from these objections. We will only say we do not know of any.

6. Now, in conclusion, allow us to add, that it is altogether possible, that cases will arise in school, that none of these appeals, nor yet any of the artifices heretofore described, will effectually reach. Such cases are not only supposable, but doubtless have an actual existence; and it would not be granting too much, perhaps, to say that various degrees of laziness, stupidity and stubbornness exist throughout all the grades here described. But what shall be the resort in the extreme cases? The question is a plain and fair one, and is entitled to a courteous and frank answer. We therefore reply definitely and distinctly, that, when all other means have been exhausted, or where the probabilities are that they would be insufficient, if applied, that recourse may be had to absolute compulsion: that forced obedience is better than rebellion. "What," says one, "force a child to study?"

"Would you force a child that is not hungry, to eat?" No; but I would force a diseased person to take medicine or nourishment, if the disease were of such a nature or malignity as to deprive the patient of judgment and reason; provided that food or medicine were the prescribed remedy. I would confine a patient by physical force, to submit to amputation of a limb, if I were satisfied that that course is necessary to save his life: so I would compel a pupil, on the same principle, to submit to study; for I would consider him dangerously diseased *mentally*, if he could refuse all the means heretofore described; and the sooner treatment of this kind is resorted to, the better, since the disease is apt to become aggravated from delay. But if a dose of silent study, administered by compulsion, once or twice a day, and an occasional amputation of a bad habit were performed skillfully, it is more than probable that the patient would soon show signs of convalescence; whereupon milder measures might then be employed.

With these suggestions, we close the chapter on Study. But before leaving it, it is but just to say, that it is not claimed, by any means, that the list of motives which may be employed for teaching children how to think, has been exhausted. The fact is, we have only just approached the subject. It will be found, also, that the ordinary means will be sufficient for the great majority of cases; that resort to special efforts will only be required where special difficulties exist; and that with proper study, by the teacher, upon these points, no difficulty can arise, but that a remedy will be suggested.

27

SYNOPSIS III.

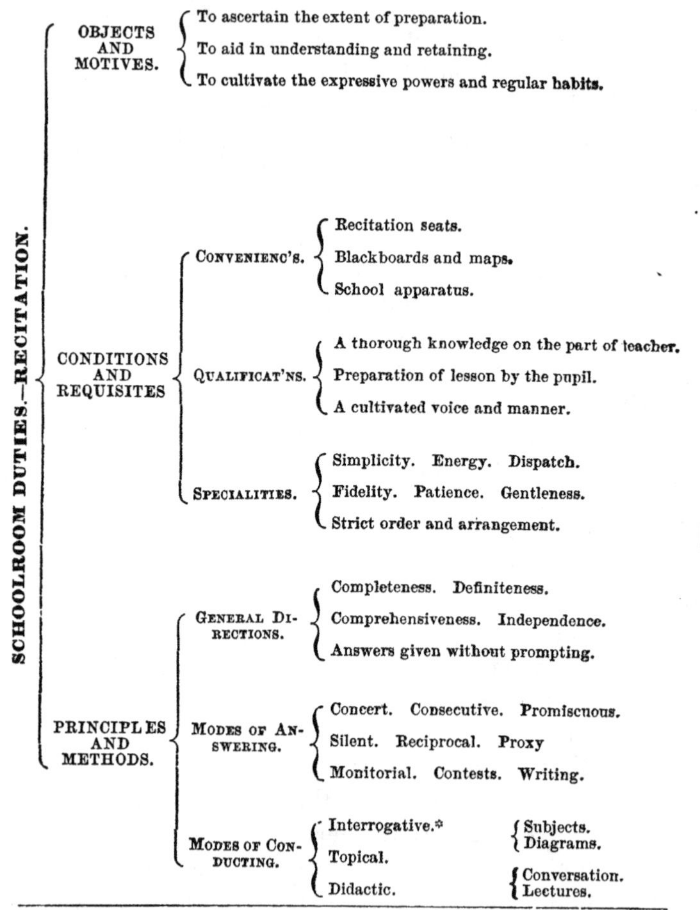

*See Modes of Answering.

CHAPTER III.

RECITATION.

We now approach that mooted and much belabored subject—*Recitation:* the one which forms, perhaps, the great burden of treatises on teaching; but which, important as it is, is entitled to no higher consideration than many others. From the fact that it has long been regarded the *summa summarium* of teaching, its claims have been considered paramount to all others; but upon a careful study of these claims, and a comparison of them with some others, recitation in many respects will be found to rank even below study. For instance: recitation is an instrumentality chiefly in the hands of the teacher; and may be wielded by him as a powerful force in the education of the child; but study, so far as it relates to the actual duty, belongs to the child himself, and hence is more direct and potential. It constitutes the chief means of learning and discipline. Recitation, however, may do much to facilitate study; and in this sense its importance increases.

We shall proceed to examine this topic, first, with reference to its *Objects* and *Aims;* secondly, its *Conditions* and *Requisites;* thirdly, its *General Principles,* and their *Application.*

Section 1—The Objects and Aims.

It will be found that there is a lamentable deficiency among teachers, as well as among pupils, in reference to the objects of recitation. Many have taken no further pains to inform themselves upon this point, than merely to acquaint themselves with *some* of the leading modes. They take it for granted that the practice of reciting is all right, of course, since it is customary. But the time when it was not customary, except in a few branches,—such as reading and spelling,—still lingers in the memory of many of the present generation. But modern improvements have wiped out many of the old usages, and brought about a radical change, and with that change many inconsistencies. It is but reasonable to suppose, however, that in so great a revolution, there should obtain many errors, mostly of an opposite extreme. And so we find it in recitation. From the extreme of no recitation, or scarcely none, we find all recitation, or nearly all. From no explanations, it is all explanations; and the pupil has only to place himself in the *receptive* attitude, and the mental pabulum is dealt out to his taste. The process of deglutition is scarcely necessary, to say nothing of mastication, since the acquisition is made so easy by dilution, as not to require much effort on the part of the scholar. His delicate nerves are not to be disturbed by any such vulgar process as that of thinking. That is already done to his hand. The processes of simplification have gone on, to such an extent, that the various subjects of learning have become exceedingly simple—so simple indeed, in many cases, as to be absolutely silly. But these errors will be noticed in due order in the course of this chapter.

We shall not attempt an exhaustive list of the objects of recitation, since they are so numerous as to forbid any such effort. It is due the subject to say, however, that the knowledge upon these points should be very definite. Both the teacher and the pupil, should know why they recite, and the objects to be gained by the recitation, or the probabilities are, that the lesson will neither be assigned nor studied in a proper manner. Among the objects to be kept before the mind, while conducting a recitation, the following may be named:

1. *To ascertain the extent of preparation*, on the part of the pupil. According to the principle laid down in reference to "assigning lessons," no more labor should be given, than can be thoroughly mastered by the pupil; and then, when time for recitation arrives, every thing assigned should be demanded, when the aforesaid object can be ascertained. When a lesson is assigned in a proper manner, the pupil is laid under the most binding obligation to prepare it. Any failure to fulfill that obligation, should be regarded as an act of willful disobedience, and treated accordingly. Indeed, I would never suffer a pupil for any cause, save that of unavoidable hindrance, to enjoy the benefits of the recitation, if he had not spent the required amount of time and effort in preparing the lesson. I would at once send him to his seat as an offender. I am aware that this might seem like a harsh measure; and yet what are our recitations for? Are they to cover up the faults and defects of the pupil, or are they to expose and correct them? Are they to pamper and indulge laziness and disobedience, or are they to cultivate habits of industry, and prompt and willing obedience?

A great many pupils are accustomed to drag themselves along in recitation, by depending upon their neighbors, or their shrewdness in guessing, good luck or some other equally reprehensible expedient; and

sometimes, too, through excess of assurance, they even make a fairer show than some others who have been diligent in the preparation of their lessons. But all this is wrong—*morally* wrong,—since it is lowering the standard of industry and order, and offering a temptation to others to neglect their duties likewise. Such scholars should at once be informed, that their progress in education is measured, not by their good luck or shrewdness in evading its duties, but by their faithful discharge of these duties.

It may be asked by some, "What shall be done with an offender who persists in disobeying—one, for instance, who would rather rejoice than do otherwise, at an opportunity to be released from recitation?" To this, I would answer, that if the additional labor of preparing and reciting two or three lessons at once, failed; and if confinement to study or recitation during the hours of recess did not work a reform, I would treat it as I would any other act of disobedience of similar import; and I would bestow upon it such a punishment as would soon convince the offender, that it is no light thing thus to trifle with duty and authority.

To ascertain how well the lesson has been prepared, I would have recourse to something like the following. The class being called, a question like the following might be asked: "As many as have complied with the conditions of study will please to rise, or manifest it by the uplifted hand." These conditions should be well defined and well understood beforehand. It may not be necessary for all to study the same length of time, or even to go over the lesson the same number of times; but there should be a standard for every one, either individual or general, by which

pupils are to be guided in their reports; or there might be several standards, and those who could not reach the first, might reach the second or third, and so on.

Now the next thing will be, to test the correctness of these reports by actual examination or recitation. If they prove correct, all well: if not, then the pupil should be called upon for an explanation. This will be making a serious matter of recitation, and the scholars knowing that they will be called upon to report themselves thus accurately, and then be obliged to submit to the test of examination afterward, will be less likely to spend the time allotted to study, in idleness. They will not be over-anxious to expose themselves in the presence of their companions and teacher, in the ridiculous attitude, either of deception or failure.

2. A second object of recitation is, *To aid in a more thorough understanding of the subject matter of the lesson.*

The appositeness of this object will be seen at once: but there are some things belonging to it that need attention. For instance: some teachers seem to regard this as the only object of recitation; and that it is most readily accomplished by rendering the labor of the pupil as light as possible. Hence they make it a point, either through pride of display, excess of good nature, or a misdirected zeal, to do as much of the reciting themselves as possible. Having, perhaps, a tolerable knowledge or understanding of the subject matter of recitation themselves, they seem to regard it as a sacred duty to lecture and explain the lesson all away, leaving the pupil nothing to do but the delightful (?) task of listening and learning (?), or, more properly feeding upon the mere husks of knowledge.

Now it has been frequently remarked, in the progress of this work, that the pupil's advancement is measured by what *he does*, more than by what *he hears*, or sees somebody else do. The teacher, therefore, has no more right to deprive the scholar of his recitation, than he has to deprive him of his food or clothing; and he would be regarded as rather a suspicious character, if he should be caught, plundering the children's dinner basket, or purloining a convenient article of apparel, occasionally.

It is proper to remark, however, in this connection, that much additional information may be given during recitation, and it is relevant to inquire just how much assistance should be rendered. To this, we would reply, that nothing should be told directly, that the pupil can find out for himself; that the glory of conquest belongs to him, by sacred right; that he should not be deprived of the luxury of thinking; but that where light can be thrown upon a subject, either by word or act of the teacher, in the recitation are both the time and place, in which to do this. If difficult points have been laid over for future consideration, or experiment, the recitation affords the proper opportunity. It is one of its special objects to afford opportunity to dispose of these things ; and all such cases as demand special attention, should be reserved for recitation.

3. Another important object of recitation is "*To aid in retaining the knowledge, or cultivating the power of memory.*" In this it becomes disciplinary, as indeed are all the modes of recitation, as well as those of study. It is a well-known principle that repetition aids the memory. The very process itself serves to fix facts and principles in the mind; and at the same

time trains the pupil in the use of language. This matter is worthy of some consideration, since so much of the success in learning depends upon the memory. It is a constant complaint among scholars, that they forget so easily. But the memory was not made to be forgetful, but ready and obedient. It was not made to be treacherous any more than the reason and understanding were. There is no more necessity for forgetting any thing that is properly learned, than there is for failing to understand a thing. When people complain of a bad memory, it is certain evidence of bad treatment, unless there is a natural deficiency, which is seldom the case where the organization in other respects is good.

The memory is a true and faithful friend; and it only asks to be treated with the same consideration with which other friends are treated, and it will prove as trusty. Many things, however, that are committed to it, or supposed to be committed, are disposed of so carelessly, that no particular responsibility rests any where: hence when the memory is called upon to report, it answers very justly and innocently, "that such and such things never passed this way; or if they did, their stay was so transient, and the acquaintance so slight, that no permanent impressions were made; consequently, we are not responsible." It should, therefore, be the especial object of every recitation, to fix securely and permanently in the mind, every fact and principle in the lesson.

4. The fourth and last object that we shall name, is the *cultivation of the expressive powers.* This will be inferred from what has been said upon this point in other places. Perhaps there is no higher object in reciting, than this. Recitation is the place in which

we should correct inaccuracies of expression; where we should cultivate clearness and accuracy, strength, beauty and richness of language—should call out the knowledge the pupil possesses, in the best possible forms of expression. But it is a well-known fact, that our pupils usually fail in this part of their duties; and the inference is just as clear as the fact is notorious, that the difficulty arises, in a great measure, from careless and hasty recitations. Teachers are too prone to take for granted, that a child knows a thing, either because he pretends to, or thinks he does, or makes some halfway, blundering answer that may be tortured into a remote reference to the point in hand.

But it is not assuming too much to say, that a pupil does not know a thing as he ought to know it, until he can tell it as he ought to tell it; and it is equally certain, that he can not tell a thing as he ought to tell it, until he knows it as he ought to know it. One of the special objects of recitation, therefore, is to afford time and opportunity for the cultivation of the expressive powers. This relates to clearness, distinctness, and loudness of utterance, as well as perspicuity and comprehensiveness of style. The manner is of scarcely less importance, as an educational object, than the matter itself. They aid each other, and are both equally susceptible of cultivation.

Section 2—Conditions and Requisites.

These departments of the subject assume considerable importance, when it is remembered that they involve, to some extent, the preparations and qualifications of teachers. A brief allusion must suffice, however, since but one class of qualifications can be considered, and since those of a more general character, have been discussed in former chapters.

There is, however, a class of conditions and requisites, to which we propose to call a brief attention, under the head of *conveniences,* before considering those which belong to the teacher. 1. The size of the schoolroom is a matter that ought to be considered. Of course, it should be ample. One of the chief objections to our present style of building and architecture, is a want of room. Teachers are perplexed, discouraged, and absolutely prevented from adopting some of the best improvements in recitation, simply for the want of room. They can not bring their classes to the recitation seat, or dismiss them from it, in any kind of order; nor yet can they arrange them in convenient forms while there. Every thing has to be huddled together, in the most confused manner, in order to afford space for the occupants of the seats. A teacher in this predicament, has about as much chance to do his duties well, as a ship-carpenter would have in a cellar-kitchen. There must be room,—room to breathe, room to walk, room to stand and room to talk; room for motions of body and *mind;* for *this* too, must have room. The world is wide enough and high enough for all that is on it, and much more, without crowding. The policy therefore, of huddling children together like sheep in a pen, and that too, for the purposes of *educating* them, is too much like burying a few bushels of corn in one spot, for the purpose of planting it. It is horrible! Half the corn would rot under such circumstances; and we should hardly expect that the children would fare much better, in some of our schoolhouses. The enormity is so great that it should not be tolerated.

There should be, at least twenty square feet for every pupil, which would make our rooms from thirty to forty feet square, or about those dimensions.

2. The *form* of the room is another condition that increases or decreases the pleasures and benefits of recitation. It would be impossible, however, to give special directions here, that would apply to the various styles of school-furniture, order of seating, and other conveniences. The arrangement of the desks and other furniture, should be such as to allow the greatest freedom of movement, and other conveniences in reference to ventilation, heat and light. There should also be a large open space or court, for physical exercises, usually situated just in front of the teacher's stand, and near the recitation seats. The propriety of this arrangement will be seen, when we come to speak more directly of modes of reciting.

3. Recitation seats are necessary, as we have intimated above. A schoolroom without them would be like a dry-goods store without a counter. When an examination of the goods is to be made, the customer is obliged to visit all the shelves and drawers, much to the disadvantage of all parties. So, when the members of a class for recitation, have to be arranged, one in one part of the room, and another in another, their attention is correspondingly distracted; and the teacher's force is often expended in fruitless efforts to collect and concentrate the scattered fragments of mind, that this arrangement has a tendency to dissipate.

4. As a general thing, the recitation demands blackboards, maps, globes, charts and other apparatus. The first of these are so necessary, that no teacher can do without them. One should occupy a position near

the teacher's stand, and fronting the class, so that explanations may be given with as little inconvenience as possible. The others, for the use of the class, might occupy all the space between windows and doors, not needed for the cabinet of "common things," but as convenient to the recitation seats as possible; and they should be ample enough to allow twenty pupils to operate upon them at the same time.

The use of maps, globes and other apparatus, will be readily inferred, and is best learned from actual observation and practice. They add much to the interest and benefits of recitation, since they render tangible many things that otherwise appear difficult and abstruse.

5. For small children, a *cabinet of common things*, composed of collections of as many of the objects from the three great kingdoms of nature, as can be procured, together with artificial objects, pictures and models of those that can not be had, forms the best conditions and requisites to their peculiar mode of recitation and study, that can be devised. The object lessons described in another place, demand these.

6. *Previous preparation by the pupil*, is a requisite which has been alluded to in another place. No pupil, therefore, should presume upon his ability to recite the lesson, without having assured himself of that fact, by careful study beforehand.

7. A thorough knowledge of the lesson by the teacher, is a condition of the first importance. He should know, before the class is called, what the lesson is, and what is in it. The mode of assigning it will aid much in this respect; but in the majority of cases, the lesson should be carefully reviewed by the teacher, on the previous day. Other text-books beside the one

used, should also be consulted; for there is great danger of his becoming opinionated and circumscribed in his views, unless he is accustomed to take liberal surveys of men and things. This will also give greater freshness and accuracy to what is taught, to say nothing about the collateral matter with which he may enliven the exercise.

No teacher should presume to hear a class recite, in the common branches at least, where he is compelled to hold a book in his hand to guide or prompt him, either in the questions or answers. Unfortunately, in many of the text-books, the questions which the author *thinks* ought to be asked (a presumption on his part without much foundation), are placed in the margin of the page, or interspersed for greater convenience (?) through the entire lesson. Now, if the teacher is compelled to resort to these questions, he becomes a mere parasite. He teaches merely with a reflected light; and often the orb whose rays he borrows, is a feeble one. Judge then of the feebleness of the light he sheds. He becomes to the pupil what the moon is to the earth, a pale, sickly orb, whose light is only the faint reflections of the sun. It might shine upon the earth for a million of years, and never cause one single bud to start, or flower to bloom, or a spire of grass to grow. The earth would grow colder and colder all the time, just as some scholars do, intellectually and morally, under this secondhand teaching. But it is the sun, the warm, mild, yet energizing rays of the sun, that penetrate the bosom of nature, and cause her great heart to beat with emotions of life and joy. So with the true teacher: he should shine with no reflected light; he should warm with no borrowed heat; but should vitalize every principle of

intelligence in the child with his own native born vigor.

If the teacher is allowed to consult the book in presence of the scholars, during the recitation, for the purpose of asking the questions, or, as it frequently happens, of refreshing his memory on the answer, I see no good reason why the pupil should not have the same privilege. But whether he has such a right or not, he is very apt to take it; since the absence of the teacher's eye, in chase after *his* question or answer, offers a fine opportunity for the scholar to take that liberty; and he will be possessed of more than the ordinary share of virtue, for such a school, and with such a teacher, whose every act gives the lie to his profession, if he will not improve it.

The teacher should have the lesson and all its bearings well fixed in mind, before recitation commences; so that he may deal out as occasion demands, and not be perplexed or embarrassed with hunting up questions and answers during recitation. He needs all the mind with which he is favored, to direct the recitation, even if he is perfectly familiar with it; without having to chase it up, or borrow it, as he goes along, and, at the same time, watch a set of unruly scholars that may be nearly as bad in this respect as he is himself.

There is another evil practice that deserves notice in this connection: it is that of marking off a certain portion of the text, or so much of it as is supposed will satisfy the question. Neither scholar nor teacher should be allowed to indulge in this whim, since it destroys all connection of the subject, and gives the knowledge, if it give any at all, in piecemeal. If the text-book needs any abridging, it should be done by

general consent of the profession, and not mutilated by every bungler that sees proper to tinker at it, and hack it to pieces.

8. *A cultivated voice and manner*, are requisites of the first importance. This qualification applies, of course, to both teacher and pupil. The powers of the human voice, as well as its mechanism, are most remarkable. Its tones may soothe the wildest passions to rest, or rouse them into a flame. They may wake the purest and loftiest desires, or provoke the very demon of hate. There is no gift to mortals, save that of mind itself, whose interpreter the voice is, that possesses such wonderful properties. Its meek, subdued, and patient strains are readily distinguished from the harsher tones of petulance, anger, or revenge, not only by man himself, but by beast, bird, and reptile. If joy gladden the heart, and sparkle in the eye, the tones of the voice swell out in sweet liquid strains, or in merry shouts. If sorrow depress it, the mournful cadence tells of the grief within. If joy and holy desires swell it, the deep music of its earnest tones awake the loftiest emotions of the soul. If hatred, and diabolic rage lurk in its secret chambers, the rough, dry, sharp, sudden, half-formed intonations grate like saws or files upon the delicate sensibilities. If deceit, guile, and hypocrisy harbor there, the telltale voice is sure to reveal the fact. If treachery, cowardice and guilt, its very accents speak it all. If fidelity, bravery and innocence, the noble, manly tones of the voice speak the sentiments within. A man need not tell that he is heroic, highminded and pure; his voice and manner reveal it all: nor yet need he strive to conceal his meanness of purpose, his little soul, his base designs and cowardly spirit; for lo! his

voice, true to the instincts of nature, has stamped him with his true value.

The voice is the harp of the soul; the music it plays is the exponent of the inner life; and the world's ears the interpreters of the song. I know that hypocrisy may be "skilled to grace a devil's purpose with an angel's face;" and that the tones of the voice may affect the purity and sweetness of the dulcet, when the most fiendish designs inspire it; but these designs can not be long concealed; for the voice, in its own machinations, will betray to one skilled in human nature (and children are no mean judges in the art), the most subtle and determined efforts. I know too, that many a noble purpose is misjudged and defeated, for the want of culture of voice and manner, but this only argues more strongly the necessity of cultivation. It therefore becomes the teacher, above all other persons, since he deals with the young, since his voice is continually sounding in the ear of childhood, to cultivate that voice to the highest possible degree of excellence; to cultivate it not to dissembling, not to sycophancy; but to give the true utterance, and potency to the pure thoughts and sentiments within.

There are four things that should be kept in mind in the cultivation of the voice: 1. The naturalness of the voice. 2. Its quantity or loudness. 3. Its quality or pitch. 4. Its variety or flexibility.

1. Some teachers seem to think it necessary to address their pupils in an assumed voice and manner—in some affected, dignified or commanding tone. Scarcely any thing will sooner render such teachers ridiculous in the estimation of the shrewd and observing. No assumed voice or manner should ever be tolerated in the schoolroom. Of course, if there are

natural deficiencies in the voice, these should be corrected; if there are obstructions, these should be removed; but this can all be done, without interfering with or destroying, in the least, the naturalness of the voice, but rather rendering it more natural. Let the teacher, therefore, use his own voice, but make that voice as perfect as possible.

2. Many teachers are in the habit of speaking too loud. This arises more from habit than from any thing else. I remember that I once visited a school of some reputation, in which the teacher was addicted to this fault. I was invited to take a seat upon the stand, to listen to a recitation in geography. The members of the class were called, and took their seats within six feet of the teacher's desk. All things being in readiness, the teacher arose, and, having naturally a stentorian voice, he pronounced the first question with such startling loudness that I, supposing him to be in jest, began to laugh. But I soon found out my mistake. I was sadly out of order. The sober faces that confronted me from every quarter, and the earnest demeanor of the teacher, soon convinced me that it was all in sober earnest. Question after question followed, in such thundering peals, that I began to seek for an explanation by supposing some to be deaf. But this supposition was soon abandoned, for, when addressing the pupils on other points, the teacher dropped his voice down to a moderate tone. And what was still more surprising, the pupils in answering the questions were about as far on the opposite extreme. The contrast was most striking and amusing. First, there was an almost deafening scream which, I am confident, could have been heard a half mile, and then the response would come in a faint whimper,

which, both taken together, reminded one of the deafening roar of the lion, followed by the faint squeaking of mice.

Now, no one need be told that this is wrong. The children's ears, in this instance, however, seemed hardened to it, so that it produced apparently little or no sensation, except a slight scowl which showed, doubtless, the remains of an ancient sensation, such as I experienced. And thus it is. If it should thunder all the time in continuous roar, we should cease to notice it. It would fail to produce an impression. It would be just as if it did not thunder at all. The teacher, therefore, who expects to make an impression with the powers of his voice, should remember that it consists more in the richness of its tones, and in pleasing and appropriate variety, than in either pitch or power. The teacher is very apt to err in excess of loudness, for as he warms in his subject, the animation unconsciously leads him into loud and boisterous talking. Let him remember, however, that a teacher can be animated without being boisterous; and that the tones of his voice can be impressive without being loud.

It is hardly necessary to add that the teacher should speak sufficiently loud, and with sufficient animation to be heard and felt by all who may be listening. A lazy, dull and lifeless teacher, has no business to work with children. He might, however, be of some service where a soporific is needed; but where minds are to be energized, thoughts to be developed, and general activity to be induced and directed, something more is needed than the prosy cogitations of a drone. The teacher must be *himself*, in actions and thoughts, what he would have his pupils become.

3. Another fault to which teachers, especially females, are liable, that of choosing too high a key upon which to speak. This, when accompanied with loudness and boisterousness, as it is most likely to be, becomes exceedingly disagreeable. I have seen a whole school wrought up to a pitch of the most unhappy feeling, just by the harsh, squeaking, cat-like voice of the teacher. Mischief, uneasiness, discontent or stolid indifference, was visible upon almost every face. No one seemed to know why he felt unhappy. No one suspicioned the instrument of torture; yet all felt it. Mischief and rebellion seemed rife; and the teacher's voice, threats, or entreaties, were so far from having any tendency to allay this feeling, that they only aggravated it. But let the rich, subdued, mellow, luke-like tones of voice, inspired by the deep, solemn earnestness of the soul, fall upon those ears, and a change will come over the spirit of their feelings. You can almost see the tears start to their eyes. These sweet tones are the melody of the soul, and they touch the soul, which yields responsive to their wooing. If teachers could only estimate the mischief and unhappiness their tones of voice inspire, they would be astonished; and if they could only realize a tenth part of the good they might accomplish, they would at once set about cultivating this powerful instrument of good or evil.

4. *Variety* is a quality of voice, that should be cultivated. A teacher who talks upon all topics with about the same degree of force, and on the same key, soon becomes monotonous, and will lose both the power to make impression and to control his school. There are occasions that demand the loud, terrible tones that shake the very soul; and then from that on down, through all the pleasing varieties, to the

gentlest murmur that falls upon the ear, like the sweet zephyr. There are occasions too, that demand the deep, solemn, awful gravity, that searches the very depths of the heart; and on from that to the tripping merriment and humorous glee, that shake the very sides with laughter. All these varieties are necessary, and will constitute one of the teacher's strongest forces, both in governing and in teaching.

There is still another quality which properly belongs to requisites, though it refers more to the language itself, than to vocalization. We mean the style of expression. This may include, in addition to what has already been said, clearness, distinctness, simplicity and purity. We propose nothing further here, than a bare allusion to these properties, and simply to urge upon the student the necessity of studying them from some of our best authors.

Many teachers, in their efforts to use good language, overreach the matter, making use of terms in explanation, which are really more difficult to comprehend, than the things they were intended to explain. All definitions should be plainer than the things defined, or they cease to be definitions. All explanations should be couched in language precise and definite, and not difficult of comprehension.

Some again, are very careless in their use of language, not unfrequently making use of expressions, not only of doubtful signification, but often meaning the opposite from what they intend. Their language lacks perspicuity. Others again, have a labored style, and fail to render themselves intelligible for the want of simplicity and purity. While I would not contend that the teacher should descend to the level with his pupils in the use of language, or that he should resort to the mere common-place expressions, and never strive to elevate and purify their language; yet I would have him make use of no terms or expressions, in his explanations, which the pupil can not readily comprehend. I would have his language plain without boldness, exact without stiffness, rich without superfluity, elegant without affectation, pure without poverty, simple without being silly, and child-like without being childish.

The manner and personal appearance of the teacher have much to do with his success, and hence are requisites to be considered in this connection. We shall speak, however, of those only which concern recitation.

The foundation of all good manners is a good heart, without which all outside culture seems to be thrown away, since it is often used to cover up wicked designs, and to dress vice in a most attractive garb. But the good heart without the good manners is often incapable of exerting a good influence, from that very fact. Therefore the personal appearance and the demeanor of the teacher should be as attractive as possible, since his influence for good is often lost, not only from a repulsive air and demeanor, but from a want of neatness, cleanliness and appropriateness in style of dress, etc. But a bare allusion to those points must suffice here, since we propose to speak only of recitation. They have been pretty thoroughly discussed in the popular treatises of the day.

We remark, therefore, that the manner in recitation should be guarded from, at least, two extremes, viz.: too great reserve on the one hand, and too great familiarity on the other. Perhaps more err in the first direction than in the second. Some teachers get the idea that in order to be dignified they must affect an air of dignity, when in fact nothing is more destructive to true dignity. It will soon render them ridiculous. Then again, the cold reserve which some teachers assume, when communicating with their pupils, is utterly destructive of that sympathy which is indispensable to good teaching. Such teachers repel rather than attract, and freeze the feeling and thoughts, rather than warm them into life. True, earnestness and honesty are the foundation stones of true dignity; for, whenever a teacher becomes too solicitous about his dignity, he is apt to lose it. Take care of the children and the teaching, and let the dignity take care of itself.

On the other hand, if too great familiarity is shown, the pupil soon loses a proper respect for the teacher. It is not necessary, however, for him to descend to any low familiarity, in order to secure the confidence and love of children. Indeed they usually become suspicious of, or hold in absolute contempt, any mock sympathy or forced familiarity. He should, therefore, manifest on all occasions, no more interest in their welfare, and no more willingness to sympathize with and assist them in their duties, than he really feels. Let him rather show by his actions that his goodness exceeds his professions, if he would exercise an unlimited sway over the hearts and minds of his pupils. This continual fussing with and flattering of children, are detrimental both to mind and morals, while a mock sympathy will deepen and settle the convictions of dishonesty in them; and to run at the beck of every pupil and assist him whenever his whims may demand it, will not only make a slave of the teacher, but will destroy all the self-reliance and manly independence of the pupil.

The teacher should avoid all rough and coarse expressions in class, all ambiguous and unchaste allusions, or anything that may be construed into vulgarity, or lead to bad inferences. His intercourse should be that of a gentleman, without forced pretensions, and his refinement should be of the highest and purest order. He should also avoid all bodily postures and gestures that partake either of waggishness or of foppishness, such, for instance, as sitting with feet elevated upon the stove or desk. The place for the feet is on or near the floor; and they are sadly out of place when they stray to other positions. Some teachers again, seem greatly at a loss, unless their hands are busied either with pen, pencil, knife, or possibly toying with a button, while engaged in recitation. While I would not urge that the teacher put himself in a straight jacket, during recitation, yet he should avoid the habits alluded to, as much as possible. He should have control of his body as well as his mind.

Most of the leading characteristics of the teacher have been alluded to in different parts of this work. We refer to some of them in this connection,for the purpose of showing their application in recitations.

1. *Order* and *arrangement.* Every one must have noticed that some teachers accomplish a great deal more than others in the same length of time. They do not seem to be in a hurry; yet everything moves with certainty and precision. No false steps are taken to be retraced, and every stroke tells. Others again are continually in the midst of business and excitement. They are pressed beyond measure. They are in furious haste, but do not seem to accomplish much. Now the simple difference is this: the first have *order*

and *arrangement* which they carry into the recitations; others lack these qualities. The first dispose of one piece of business before they commence another; the others have a dozen things on hand at once, all calling loudly for attention; and the poor, distracted beings fly from one to the other, without the ability to concentrate their forces anywhere.

2. *Energy* and *Dispatch* are characteristics that ought never to be separated. Both classes of teachers above described, possess energy; but the distinctions are sufficiently obvious. Energy, without boisterousness, and dispatch without haste or confusion, should mark all the movements of the teacher.

3. *Honesty* and *Fidelity.* The occasions for dishonesty in recitation, on the part of both teacher and pupil, are very numerous. Some of these have already been noticed. It is sufficient, perhaps, to add that any thing like deception in recitation, has a tendency to lower the standard of morality, and to breed contempt in the minds of the pupils and teacher, for each other. If a mistake has been made by either party, duty, honesty, morality and policy demand that it be frankly and candidly corrected, and as publicly as it was committed. If the teacher is so unfortunate as not to understand a thing, the moment he is called upon for information or explanation, it is certainly no dishonor for him to say so. Nothing will be lost, but much gained in the end by telling the truth. Lying is monstrous, and always out of order. There never was an occasion for it, and it is safe to say there never will be. Not the remotest good can come of it, because the whole universe is opposed to it. The very laws of mind and matter are predicated upon the supremacy of truth, and they rebel at falsehood. What

good, even the remotest, then, can come from violating these laws? To pretend, either by word or by inference, to know a thing when ignorant of it, to put off the scholar with the plea, "I did know it, but forgot," or "I have not time now," or "Wait till to-morrow;" or to attempt to palm off an error upon them, to screen ourselves from blame; or to hide our ignorance behind a multitude of words, argues a state of depravity too low to be tolerated in the teacher for a moment. The state of public and of private morals will never improve, until teachers and parents learn to tell the truth, and teach their children the same lesson. I would not make a confessional of the school, for I think it has a higher mission to perform; neither would I make it an instrument for instilling falsehood and deceit in the minds of the young.

4. *Integrity* and *Fidelity* in the discharge of duty, are other matters of great importance to teachers. It is not an uncommon thing for teachers to make large promises to pupils, either by way of encouragement, or to rid themselves from present obligation, without the remotest prospect of ever meeting them. Children, in their innocence of the faithlessness that obtains in higher (?) circles, expect the fulfillment of these, and their sense of right and wrong is shocked if they are not fulfilled. It is a notorious custom also, for teachers to threaten and banter with their pupils. This is not only a shameful impropriety, however thoughtlessly it may be committed, but a sin of most disastrous consequences. It is sufficient for the present to say, that teachers have no right to elevate the hopes or to excite the fears of their pupils, needlessly. This practice, however, soon fails to do either; but the immoral tendencies, which may be easily inferred by the

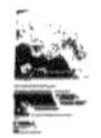

reader, are still worse. Nothing, therefore, should be promised that can not be performed, or delayed that can be done now; and no threats at all should be made. Threats and promises, for the most part, are out of place in the schoolroom. The ready-pay system works better both ways.

5. *Gentleness and Patience* are in constant demand. Gentleness, with refinement, is a virtue of such captivating merits, that it commends itself to the regard of all. In this sense it is the opposite of violence and vulgarity. What the sunshine and rain-drops are to flowers, gentleness is to the heart of childhood. It winds its certain way into the affections of youth, and even into the corrupt and depraved nature of the dissolute and abandoned. It stirs the fountains of love in the one and opens the door of repentance to the other. Nothing seems more out of place than harsh and brutal treatment of children. But there is no virtue for which there is greater demand in recitation, than patience or forbearance. Some children are weak and timid, others are bold and self-conceited. Some are dull and stupid, and some are willfully and incorrigibly vicious. All these cases, and a great many more that might be named, demand different degrees and qualities of patience. Indeed, there must be no impatience or petulance. These are always out of place.

It is related of the celebrated Dr. Adam Clark, that when a child, he was remarkable for nothing but his seeming stupidity. His mother had undertaken to teach him some verses, supposing, as most mothers do, that the only evidence of intellectual promise consisted in a liking for books and progress in learning. She had labored long, faithfully, patiently, and seemingly to no purpose; when the father of the lad, a

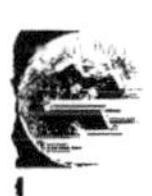

witness of the scene and of the mother's final triumph, having long before lost all patience, exclaimed: "But how could you have patience to tell that blockhead the same thing twenty times before he learned it?" "Because, my dear," was the meek but laconic reply, "if I had stopped with the nineteenth time, I should have lost all my labor."

This example of patience and perseverance is worthy of imitation. The teacher is too apt to bestow praise where it is least deserved and least needed. He is pleased with the smart scholars; and it seems natural that he should be. But early development is little evidence of intellectual greatness, as the subsequent history of our smart boys and girls too often proves.

Grace Greenwood tells a story which is to the point here. She was visiting an esteemed and talented friend of hers, who, unfortunately, had fallen a victim in early life, to books and colleges; but who had escaped to the country to mend his broken health and save his family from a like calamity. During a pleasant summer afternoon, a little boy some eight years old, the son of our friend, was having a frolicking time with a large Newfoundland dog. Witnessing their playful gambols upon the green sward before the door, Grace, who, it is said, has a natural fondness for children, remarked to her friend, "Why, what a fine, noble boy you have there!" "Well," coolly remarked the friend, "he is not pretty, nor very smart; but he is honest and healthy: he is innocent and good-natured he is affectionate and obedient; he never tells lies and, thank God, *he dont know his letters!*"

Now this needs no comment; but it is a severe commentary upon the popular opinion that children are smart only when they give early indications of aptness

to learn from books, the excess of which is rather an unfavorable omen than otherwise. I should ask no stronger indications of future mental imbecility, than precociousness, or that a child should abandon his hoop and ball, his sports and romps, and betake himself to books and moping study. The boys and girls that give the least promise, those upon whom we are accustomed to look in school, as the dull ones, or the mischievous ones, very frequently make our best men and women. Let patience then have her perfect work, and do not nip the tender bud by petulance or misjudgment. "The race is not always to the swift, nor the battle to the strong:" but to the faithful, patient, toiling ones. They need our patience, sympathy and love, to smooth the asperities of their way, and to encourage them in their labors.

Section 3—Methods.

We have thus far spoken only of the objects and requisites of recitation. We shall now devote a few pages to the consideration of methods, that least important part, since every one well versed in the philosophy of education will, to a great extent, be the manufacturer of his own particular plans. Nevertheless, there are some general plans and principles that obtain everywhere. They are matters of universal application. These become the common heritage of all who enter the profession, and are no less practical than they are peculiar. Hence the experience of those who have been successful may be of great service in aiding those who are less experienced, to form their modes, etc., and as such we give these methods, repeating the caution, used in another part of this work, that "no one can be successful if he copy

the entire plans of another." "That a teacher's success must be the product of his own skill." "He must be the architect of his own fortune." "That particular methods are serviceable only so far as they can be generalized; and are thus suggestive of others." There are, however, a few general directions which logically precede the special modes; and indeed all that is really worthy of special notice in the methods of recitation, may be discussed under these. They have reference more immediately to the manner in which lessons should be recited, and therefore apply more directly to the pupil than to the teacher.

ARTICLE 1—COMPLETENESS—is a condition in recitation that should not be overlooked. There is a very common failing among teachers of all grades, respecting this one thing. It shows itself chiefly under the two following forms: First, in fragmentary answers; Second, in insufficient answers in other respects. It is no common thing to hear questions and answers like the following:

1. "In what part of British America, near several lakes, does the Mackenzie river rise?"

Answer. "Central."

2. "What mountains in North America, extending from the northern part of British America, in a southern direction, through Washington and Oregon Territories, in the United States, separating Nebraska and Kansas Territories from Utah, and thence branching off in several divisions in New Mexico; and terminating finally in what are called the Sierra Madre, near the southwestern boundary of the United States?"

Answer. "Rocky."

3. "What town in southeastern Virginia, celebrated

for a remarkable battle, fought there in 1781, by the Americans and French on the one side, under the command of General Washington; and the British, under the command of Lord Cornwallis, in which the latter was defeated and captured, surrendering the whole force under his command, to the Americans?"

Answer. "Yorktown."

4. "Suppose you wish to calculate the interest on a note for three years, six months, and twenty-seven days: after you have found the interest on one dollar, at the given rate per cent, and for the given time; what do you do with this,—divide or multiply it by the principal?"

Answer. "Multiply." And the same course is pursued in other branches.

In an example like the following, the evil may be seen in a slightly different light.

5. "Where does the Mississippi River empty?" The pupil having perhaps associated the words "Mississippi," "empty" and "Gulf of Mexico" together, the latter would be the answer. But on reversing or changing the questions thus: "What flows into the Gulf of Mexico?" or "What took place at Yorktown?" "What mountains in North America?" it has been found, in many instances, that no intelligent account could be given.

Now we do not claim that all of these are the exact words copied from the text-books upon these sciences; yet they are but fair samples of them, especially of some that have been manufactured or distorted by the teachers themselves, in order to render them more easily answered: and the answers are just what children would ordinarily give, the fault being more with the questions than the answers; since they circumscribe them to one or two words. All the pupil really has to do, in such cases, is to commit to memory a word or two, usually under each question, and to be careful not to get the answers confounded, one with another. The evil exists in all stages of development, from the very worst, on till it can scarcely be perceived.

Now any one can see the evil tendencies of this practice. It is destructive of all progress, since it removes, in a great measure, all obligation from the pupil, to say nothing about the bad habits it fosters. Instead, therefore, of the questions containing so much of the information, which belongs properly to the answer, it should only call up distinctly the points upon which answer is demanded, leaving the pupils to reply to them. And instead of these mere fragmentary answers, or scarcely any answer at all, each one, as a general thing, should be a complete sentence; and in most instances, should include the question itself, or so much of it, as shall be necessary to make an entire sentence. Thus in the first instance: "Where is the Mackenzie river?" Answer. "The Mackenzie river rises in the central part of British America (naming the lakes etc.), flows in a north-western direction, and empties its waters into the Northern Ocean" (giving the length and tributaries, etc., if desirable).

Take a case in arithmetic. Thus: "How do you multiply a fraction by a whole number." Answer. "To multiply a fraction by a whole number, we either multiply the numerator by the whole number, and under this product write the denominator, or, when it can be done without a remainder, we divide the denominator by the whole number, and write the quotient under the numerator, and reduce, if neces-

sary," etc. The same course should be pursued with all rules and definitions, except, perhaps, in rapid reviews, or when the pupil is known to be familiar with them. The clearness, distinctness and completeness of utterance, adds very materially to the clearness and comprehensiveness of the understanding.

Now compare the answers given in the first instances with those in the last, and tell me which conveys the most intelligence, which the most discipline, and which will make the readiest and most exact scholars. Which of the two methods is the easier for the teacher,—the long questions (especially when they have to be read from a book, during the time in which the teacher's eye must be upon the class, to prevent them from a like calamity), or the short questions and long answers, throwing the burden of labor on the pupil where it is needed? Which contains the greater force,—a half sentence, or a whole sentence? Which the most beauty? Which will cultivate the mind to the greater extent,—a part of the truth, or the whole truth? Which would be of the greater demand in a Court of Justice? The one is just as much more forcible than the other, for the purposes for which it is intended, as a whole charge of powder is than a half or a hundredth part. Every answer therefore, should be an entirety, and should have some immediate connection with the question.

The case of *insufficient answer* is one not so marked in its effects. It differs from the one just described, in that it attempts completeness as to extent, but omits some important points. It is usually the result of weakness, want of culture, or carelessness. It applies, of course, as well to the incompleteness of articulation and vocalization, as to the poverty of

language or expression. About the only remedy for this difficulty is practice. If a child fail to give a complete answer in relation to this feature of it, it should be repeated even to the twentieth time, or until it is correct. Let it not be passed over by the teacher, with this excuse: "O, he knows, I guess; only he can't tell it." "His power to express himself is so poor, that I do not require much of *him:*" while, in fact, this is the very reason why he is entitled to extra attention. This is one of the objects of the recitation, viz., to cultivate the power of expression. If the child were perfect, so far as further improvement is concerned, he need not recite; and the same principle holds good with any imaginable degree of perfection: the nearer perfect, the less need of recitation; and the further from it, the more, so far as that perfection which the recitation can impart, is concerned. Hence the child that halts the most, and makes the poorest recitation, should recite the most, however agreeable it may be to listen to the prompt ones recite. The recitation should therefore, be distributed among the pupils, according to the age, advancement and capacity.

It will be found that many scholars require frequent repetition before they can overcome their difficulties. It will not usually remedy a deficiency to tell the child his answer is insufficient, or even to correct his errors for him; he must mend his own errors if he would profit by his labor. We can not correct bad habits by merely exposing them; neither can we establish good ones by mere precept. We need the actual practice. It will not make a boy a good accountant, merely to show him the mistakes of others; nor yet will it to show him the beauty, order, and arrangement of the day-book, journal and ledger. He must have the actual practice. To drive out a bad habit, we must establish a good one in its stead; and to establish a habit of any kind requires practice and repetition. Hence, if a mistake is made by the pupil, it is not enough that the teacher say to him, "No; not that way: thus;" and then pass on; but the error should be corrected by the scholar himself, and the correction repeated, and re-repeated, in class and out of class, in concert and alone, until it is thoroughly established; or, the probabilities are, the very next time the thing is used, the same error will be committed.

I recollect that I once listened to a recitation in elocution, by a class in one of our best colleges, when something like the following took place: The word "persist" I think occurred three times in the same few paragraphs. The student read to the first, and pronounced it "perzist." "No," said the teacher, "that is pronounced 'persist.'" The pupil read on until it occurred again, when he pronounced it as before. "Persist," remarked the teacher. "Persist," responded the scholar, and read on, until he came to it the third time, when it again became "perzist," which was again corrected by the teacher. I then called upon the young man to read the same paragraph again; when all three of the "perzists" came on in their regular order. I then called his attention to it, and requested him to pronounce it with me three times. He did so. I repeated that process with him several times, after which I requested the whole class (some forty in number) to pronounce it in concert, for a successive number of times. I then turned to the young man, and asked him to pronounce it, and it was "persist" every time after that. The word *beneath* (subvocal "th") was corrected in a similar manner. The same thing is true of sentences, rules, definitions, and answers to questions generally. If they are not complete, they should not be passed over until they are. It would not be well to tax the time of the recitation to a very great extent, in this repeating process; or this may induce some to defer learning the lesson until they come in class. But this may easily be prevented by care.

The same principle holds good with problems, questions, examples, and all slate and board exercises. They never should be left or called right until they are complete in all their parts. Not a decimal point or the most apparently insignificant sign or mark should be understood; for, in business transactions, it would not be considered satisfactory in a note of $1300, to say that the decimal point is understood between the digits and ciphers. The difference, however, between $1300 and $13.00, is not greater than the difference between right and wrong, morally speaking, in any other respect. Let the most scrupulous care be exercised, therefore, in order to secure completeness, at least in those two particulars named; for "Whatever is worth doing at all is worth doing well."

ARTICLE 2—DEFINITENESS AND EXACTNESS are qualities that should be cultivated. We have spoken already upon some topics nearly allied to these, while discussing the objects and requisites of recitation. Their application to methods, however, is peculiar. Definiteness and exactness, as used here, differ from completeness in its two phases alluded to, in that while the latter remedies the two evils, viz., fragmentary and insufficient answers, and relates to fullness and integrity of answer, or to quantity; definiteness and exactness refer to precision and perspicuity in the use of language, or to quality rather than quantity.

It is not claimed that the terms here used have the exact logical or metaphysical meaning in themselves, that we have attached to them: but it will be remembered they are used simply in a technical sense, and for the purpose, chiefly, of distinguishing and describing practices, etc., that are nearly similar. Teachers are not sufficiently careful to secure plain and precise answers; and the pupils come to think, by and by, that almost any answer will do; often depending upon the fortune of the occasion for manufacturing one, or resorting to the guessing process, by which they are enabled to slide along somehow. Their knowledge exists in a kind of chaotic state. It lacks system and arrangement. Now it is the business of education to regulate this mass of vagrant matter, to point it, and energize it, to make of the seemingly dead carcass a living soul.

One particular form of indefiniteness will be pointed out, from which others may be inferred. It exhibits itself at the blackboard, in some instances, where pupils have not had the advantages of early training in the use of marks and figures, such as described in a former chapter. They have been accustomed, it may be, to express themselves, both at the board and in other recitations, in so vague and indefinite a manner, as to pay little or no attention to the size, form, position and arrangement of the figures and lines; and hence it is not an uncommon thing to see pictures like the following, upon the board during recitation.

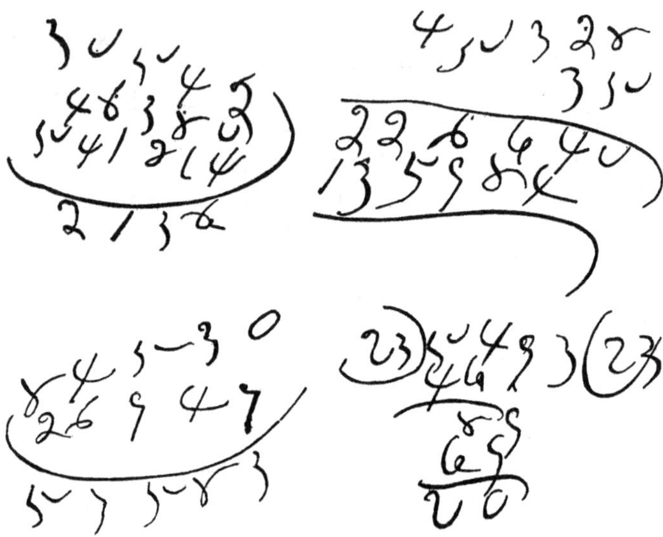

Perhaps some teachers will recognize the above picture as a familiar acquaintance; for it is but a fair transcript of what may be seen upon blackboards in all parts of the country; and it is a fair inference to suppose that it presents a very just view of the state of the mental discipline of the children who formed it. Now how long will it require a child to lose himself and become discouraged in working an example after this fashion? I presume it would not be too much to say that nine-tenths of the mistakes and failures which occur at the board, find their origin, either immediately or remotely, in some such indefiniteness as the foregoing exhibits. How long a time will it require to acquire clear and definite ideas upon grammar and the use of language; upon the geography of his country; or, in a word, to acquire a fund of knowledge

that will be permanently serviceable to him, if he is thus indefinite in all his recitations? It is true, this general "mixing up" and vagueness of expression might, in time, wear itself down to something like an understandable shape; but it is the object of education, and especially of recitation, to save this time, and to correct and refine, to trim and prune this misshapen mass, just as specifically as it is the business of the gardener to trim and prune, to bend and straiten, the crooked, gnarled and unsightly branches of the tree. Instead, therefore, of the suspicious-looking characters in the foregoing examples, and the glaring want of order and precision in the arrangement of them, the following will in all respects be preferable.

3465
5829
310
57482
―――――

4589
27
―――――
32123
9178

27 | 8953 | 33
81
――
85
81

Now the child will take a thousand times as much interest and pleasure in these examples, because they are more beautiful and more orderly.

Article 3—Comprehensiveness.—Every recitation, definition, rule and application should be rendered as comprehensive as possible, both with reference to a clear and explicit understanding of the matter, and in making it as specific as possible. This part of teaching is too much neglected. Teachers are too easily satisfied with the mere repetition of words, or with the bare recitation, without giving it a sensible or life-like

turn, without making it comprehend the business transactions or apply to the life-duties and the realities to which the lessons frequently refer. Hence it is not difficult to find those among pupils (I will not say among teachers) who, though they have "*ciphered* through the book," yet do not possess a dozen clear and well-defined ideas upon arithmetic: or those who, though they have "*said* all the grammar in the book," yet are incapable of writing or speaking without making the most ridiculous blunders.

Again: there are those who, though they may be able to answer all the questions *printed* in their geographies, are nevertheless profoundly ignorant of distance and direction in general, or the relative position of places on the globe. When, for the sake of testing their comprehension of local geography, I have requested them to point toward the different places and things about which they were reciting, such, for instance, as Spain, Iceland, or California; the Andes, Alps, or Alleghany mountains; to Constantinople, Cincinnati, or St. Petersburg; or to places, lakes, and rivers in the more immediate vicinity; almost all imaginable directions have been given; some up, some down, some to the right and some to the left, representing nearly all the points of the compass for one single place. In a very few instances, indeed, has there been any thing like correctness or uniformity; showing a most lamentable deficiency in comprehension. Their ideas of geography had not been localized. They had learned the answers to the questions, which in itself, is all well enough, but they had not got beyond that. Their ideas were of books and maps and not of the earth; and when they thought of these places (or their names rather) they at once called to

mind the book, and their position and appearance there. One boy, and one of my own teaching too, contended stoutly with me, that the waters of the St. Lawrence ran toward the south-west, since, as he affirmed, the water could not run up hill—as he supposed from the position of the map upon the wall, from which he had obtained much of his geographical knowledge, would be the case, if they ran toward the north-east. Others again have told me that Indiana is red; Ohio, yellow; Kentucky, green, and Pennsylvania, blue; that the rivers and lines representing boundary are black, since these things are so represented upon the map. Sometimes, on my asking these simple questions on local geography, there would be a vacant stare, or a half-suppressed laugh, as much as to say, "Why, that question is not in the lesson or book."

Teachers, therefore, can not be too careful to localize, or transfer the ideas from the book to the things intended. In geography, for instance, in speaking of mountains, instead of confining the mind solely to the dark or light spots upon the map, the pupils should be carried in imagination to the base, or plain below. They then should cast their eyes up along the sides to the hight of two or three very tall trees (if the children live in the country), or church steeples (if they live in cities), to the jutting rocks or cliffs that hang ready to tumble from the side: then to a bright cascade glittering in the sunshine a half mile higher up the side; then to the forests of evergreens that skirt the sides beyond, and last of all to the towering peak that lifts its head above all these, and against which the clouds strike and crumble to pieces as they pass along; or if the subject is a river, instead of confining their minds to the dark lines upon the map, exclusively, let them see the banks, low and marshy, beautiful and fertile, or high and rocky, and the farms and foliage in the distance; if a state or country, instead of the various, and variegated colors upon the map, they should behold the hills and valleys, the plains and forests, farms, grainfields and meadows, houses and barns, roads, cities and villages, and every thing, in fact, that belongs to local geography. A similar course may be pursued with the other sciences.

Article 4—Independence.—Again; the child should be taught to manifest a due degree of *independence in recitation.* There are, however, two extremes here, and chiefly attributable to the practice of the teacher. We shall endeavor to guard him against both. The one is a blind adherence to books and customs, and a cowardly or indolent dependence, which forbids every attempt to think for one's self: the other is an egotistic assurance, or self-conceited effrontery that sets aside all books and definitions. It is a disposition and a habit some teachers fall into, of finding fault with authors, and every body else whose opinions do not agree with their own. They seem to think it a mark of wisdom to quarrel with definitions and rules. They build up their reputation with the bones of their demolished (?) adversaries; and often build upon their follies and weaknesses. They live by plunder. They are wiseacres. They are continually making discoveries, that others have made long before them, but which *their* better judgment led them to see were no discoveries. They can see but one side of an argument, and that is their side, and unfortunately it is too frequently the wrong side. Such, for example, are those who must live by excitement, always inventing some new thing, and straining to make the world believe that everything has been going wrong, until they happened to be born. They do not spend their time and energies so much in teaching the sciences, as in finding fault with them, and hence weaken the confidence of the scholar that needs strengthening; unbend the energies that need stimulating, and unsettle and distract the purposes and knowledge that may have been half formed.

The other extreme is scarcely less detrimental to true progress, but not so dangerous. The one is absolute destruction, the other is simply a barrier. While the first cuts loose from all mooring, carries no anchor and ignores all faith, save what its own dogmatism invents; the other remains bound fast to the ancient customs, and dares not believe and practice anything that does not conform to the creed. The one is rabid radicalism; the other is rank conservatism. The one is meteoric or gaseous; the other is fossiliferous. Both are destructive to healthy growth of mind.

The effects of either of these extremes upon the pupil can easily be imagined. They either become pedantic, self-conceited and opinionated, or obsequious, stupid and parasitical. But there is a happy mean between the two extremes, and that the teacher should endeavor to follow. While I would not recommend a blind subserviency to the old usages, and to texts and definitions, as laid down by authors; yet I would say, agree with authors just as far as possible, lest your distrust and skepticism lead those who have less judgment, too far from a settled belief; and lest you distract the interest and attention so necessary to progress.

There is still another feature of independence worthy of consideration in this connection. It aims to correct a prevailing practice, among teachers, which, for evil results has scarcely a parallel. We speak of the practice of rendering undue assistance, or of prompting the scholar during recitation. This evil is so general and has so many slightly different phases, that it will be almost impossible to guard against all of them in the short space allotted here.

The case of pupils' prompting each other, in recitation, prevails in many schools to a very great extent. And what renders it still worse, it is winked at by many teachers, or at least no very vigorous attempts are made to break it up. Now I can hardly conceive of a greater insult, except open violence itself, a pupil could offer a teacher or fellow pupil than if, when a question is asked, he should clandestinely communicate the answer to the pupil about to recite. To say nothing about its criminality, as a species of falsehood, the effects upon the progress of the pupil upon which it is practiced, is most ruinous. I have known several instances where pupils have been disgraced by this vice, to such an extent that they had lost all confidence in themselves, and they were content seemingly to remain in this state of abject servility. I have known others again, who had practiced "telling in class" so long, that it seemed almost an impossibility to break them of it. I know of no remedies other than those used to prevent other crimes of like magnitude.

But the worst form of this vice is exhibited, when the teacher himself descends to it. It then becomes as it were, a public pest, and it is as if all barriers to laziness and deception had been thrown down. It is usually practiced by the use of what are called *leading questions*, which may be classified in the following manner. 1. By asking questions in such a form as only to require the assent or dissent of the pupil. 2. By arranging the questions in such a manner as to make them embrace all the answer except the last few words, that may be readily inferred from the preceding. 3. By suggesting the answer either by a significant word, tone of voice, look or gesture. 4. By open assistance, or preventing the pupil by untimely assistance. All these forms have a tendency to weaken or destroy independence in thought and study, as well as in recitation. They can be best illustrated by giving examples in each.

Suppose, for example, that a class in arithmetic is called upon to recite, when the following dialogue takes place—

Teacher. You can not add fractions that have not a common denominator, can you?

Pupil. No, sir.

T. Well, when you wish to add fractions of this kind, they must be reduced to a common denominator, must they not?

P. Yes, sir.

T. Very well! Now to reduce fractions to a common denominator, you must multiply all the denominators together for a new denominator, must you not?

P. Yes, sir.

T. Well then; to find the several numerators, don't you have to multiply each one by the product of all the denominators, except its own?

P. Yes, sir.

T. Then, to add, you must find the sum of these, must you not?

P. Yes, sir.

T. And then you place the common denominator under this sum, do you not?

P. Yes, sir.

T. Then, if the resulting fraction is an improper fraction, it may be reduced to a whole or mixed number, may it not?

P. Yes, sir.

T. *Very well!* (flatteringly), and all parties seem well satisfied with their progress—the teacher in exhibiting his knowledge, and the pupil in saying *Yes, sir:* for any one can see that the teacher did what reciting was done, only asking the assent or dissent of the pupil, as he advanced, which, of course, was readily granted.

2. The second variety of prompting, or that in which the questions are so arranged, as to embrace all the answer, except the last few words which are suggested by the preceding, or "answers made easy," may be described in the following manner. Take an example of a recitation in Grammar.

Teacher. The part of English Grammar which treats of the modification, inflection, composition and classification of words, is called what?

Pupil. Etymology.

T. That part which treats of the agreement and government of words, and their arrangement in sentences, is called what?

P. Syntax.

T. When words denote objects—or the names of all persons, places or things, they are called what?

P. Nouns.

T. Nouns are classified into two general divisions

or classes, the one including all general or *common* names, the other all particular or *proper* names: now, what are these called?

P. Common and proper.

T. Very well: now that property of the noun, which is used to distinguish the sexes, is called what?

P. Gender.

T. When the word denotes a male, what gender is it?

P. Masculine. (So of all the genders.)

T. That property of nouns and pronouns, used to distinguish the person speaking, from the person or thing spoken to or spoken of, is called what?

P. Person.

T. There are three persons used in English Grammar; the first denotes the person or thing speaking; the second, the person or thing spoken to; the third, the person or thing spoken of: now, what are they called?

P. First, second and third (so of the definitions of the several persons).

T. That property of the noun and pronoun, used to show their relations to other words in a sentence, is called what?

P. Case.

T. When the noun or pronoun is used as the subject of a proposition, or as the agent, actor or doer of a thing, in what case is it?

P. Nominative case. (So of all the cases, etc.)

The faults alluded to above, are much aggravated if the questions are printed in the text book. The pupils may in this case be hunting up the answers while the teacher is reading the questions. This they have a fair opportunity to do, since the answers are so much shorter than the questions. This mode, however, is less objcctionable than the first, in one or two respects, since it *does* graciously grant the pupil the privilege of slight variations. He is not obliged to say, " *Yes, sir*," all the time; but may make his selections, and guesses from at least a dozen words. But it is more general in its use; and hence, in the main more baneful than the other. The first is so glaring in its absurdness, that it would seem, no one would practice it. Yet it is not difficult to find cases in our schools precisely parallel; and then it has almost all possible shades and degrees of inconsistency ranging from this extreme, until we scarcely find a trace of it, or merging into some other practice equally reprehensible. We find the other in some of its forms and modifications, in nearly all the schools. But it will be seen at once, that it virtually deprives the pupil of the benefits of the recitation. He acquires none of that discipline in thought and style which is contemplated in the objects of study and recitation. He is put upon the stand as a mere piece of furniture. His principal business is to give mechanical responses. In this respect he resembles the piano at his side. He is for the benefit of the player, or for the teacher to exhibit his skill upon, in asking and answering questions. It is just so much answer for so much question; and when the teacher ceases playing his questions upon him, he is as quiet, so far as recitation is concerned, as the dumb piano. The teacher himself is on exhibition, in such recitations as these, and he only uses his scholars as instruments to aid him in making a display: and for all practical purposes, they might almost as well be so many posts or pegs.

3. The third case, or that in which the answer is

suggested by peculiar arrangement, significant word, tone of voice, look or gesture, is one of most frequent occurrence; and like the others, it may enter every grade of recitation. It is more difficult of description, however, since the tones of the voice, gesticulation and manner can not be represented to advantage, upon paper. Suppose, however, we have a recitation in geography.

Teacher. Is the earth a flat plain, or is it *round* like a ball?

Pupil. It is round.

T. Is there more land or *water* on the surface?

P. Water.

T. Is there more land south or *north* of the equator?

P. North.

T. Are the Balkan mountains in Australia or *Turkey?*

P. In Turkey.

T. Is the surface *hilly* or level in New England?

P. Hilly.

T. Does the Rio Grande flow into the Pacific Ocean or the *Gulf of Mexico?*

P. Into the Gulf of Mexico.

T. Is the temperature in the frigid zones higher or *lower* than it is in the torrid?

P. Lower.

T. Where is the Colorado river, in Maine or Mexico?

P. In Mexico. (?)

Or suppose the lesson is in arithmetic.

T. To multiply a ratio, must you multiply the antecedent or *consequent?*

P. The consequent.

T. If in a proportion, the answer ought to be greater than the third term, do you place the greater of the two remaining terms in the first or *second* place?

P. In the second place.

T. To reduce fractions to their lowest terms, do you multiply or *divide* those terms?

P. Divide them. Etc.

It will be seen that this mode is subject to all the objections of the second one, with an additional one, viz.: that of offering a choice between two answers, and that choice always determined either by the position of some important word, or the tone of voice in which it is pronounced. But its worst form consists in look or gesture.

Suppose a class to be reciting, and a question like the following is asked:

Teacher. Where does the Mississippi river rise, which way does it run, and into what does it flow?

Pupil. "It rises in the northern part of the United States, and"—(hesitates). *T.* "In what lake commencing with?" (pointing to his eye). *P.* "In lake Itaska, and runs"—(hesitates and looks at the teacher, who makes a mistake and points the wrong way)— "north." *T.* "How?" (correcting himself). *P.* "*South.*" *T.* "Well, into what does it flow?" *P.* "And flows into" — (hesitates) — *T.* "Into what gulf?" *P.* "Into the Gulf of St.—(hesitates and looks at the teacher, who shakes his head) "California!" *T.* "Where?" *P.* "Mexico?" *T.* "Yes! very well!" And other questions are disposed of in a similar manner.

Take a lesson in parsing. Example: "Careless girls soil their books."

Pupil. "Careless is a verb." *T.* "No." (Pupil looks desponding, evidently waiting to be told).

T. "What part of speech is it that expressed quality?" *P.* "Oh, the *adverb!*" *T.* "No, that modifies the verb," etc. *P.* "Well then (inquiringly), an adjective?" *T.* "That is it!" (flatteringly): "Now go on;" and he does *go on* in the same halting, half-guessing, half indifferent manner to the close of the sentence, when he knows but little more than he did before he commenced.

The practice that pupils sometimes fall into of closing each answer with the rising slide, or as if they asked the teacher if it were not so, is one falling under this head, and should be carefully guarded. This might be called the guessing process, since the scholar by a shrewd bantering way manages to guess his way along, and to call the answer out of the teacher. For instance, a child commences a definition, rule or explanation, and progresses until he arrives at a point where he is not quite certain. He hesitates, and glances at the teacher, who is also watching and ready to respond. He proceeds cautiously, and perhaps makes about a half mistake, when a shake of the head, a knowing, significant look or wink from the teacher, arrests him, and he quickly changes and glides off in an opposite direction; or after hesitating and telegraphing the teacher, to know whether he is right or wrong, upon receiving an affirmative reply, by nod, wink or any other sign, he moves on, assured that all is safe.

Suppose, for example, that the class is spelling orally. The teacher pronounces the word "*independent.*" The pupil spells "in-de-pend-a"—— (The teacher looks the knowing look), "ent" is quickly pronounced by the pupil. *Teacher.* "Ceremonial." *Pupil.* "Se"— *T.* "How?" "Cer-i"— *T.* "Cerē-monial, not Cerĭmonial" (accenting and rendering *long* the second syllable). *P.* "Cer-e-mo-n"— (hesitates and looks inquiringly at the teacher), "e"— (slight shake of the teacher's head), "i" (an approving look and nod), "Ceremoni-el." *T.* "How?" *P.* "al,—Ceremonial." *T.* "That's right;" and another word is guessed through in a similar manner. Now who spelled these words, the scholar or the teacher? The teacher, of course; and he might, with a great deal more propriety, have told the pupil in plain, unequivocal terms: and the latter might, with a great deal more honesty, have asked the teacher in a plain, frank manner, for the answer, than for both of them to deceive each other.

4. There is still another bad practice that deserves notice here. It is that of telling the pupil outright as soon as he hesitates, or before he has time to answer. This practice prevails to the greatest extent in reading, though it extends to all other branches. It will be readily recognized in the first by a reference to a common practice with young beginners. Some teachers are in the habit, as soon as a child hesitates upon a word or sentence, to pronounce it for him at once. I have seen whole recitations conducted in that way, the teacher pronouncing at least three-fourths of the words, and the child drawling them out after him; after which both would seem satisfied, the child that he had *said* his lesson, and the teacher that he had *said* it to him. But the practice is carried into other branches. We shall give but one illustration.

I remember listening once to a recitation from a class (or teacher rather), in what was called a High

School. The lesson was in Physiology, and on those most interesting topics, "Digestion and Circulation." The teacher commenced by asking the questions from the book; and having a good verbal memory, a ready tongue and more self-conceit than judgment, he, in almost every instance, before the pupil had time to respond, would commence telling him the answer, sometimes graciously condescending to ask the pupil at the close if it was not so. And though the lesson lasted over half an hour, I am sure there was not a half-dozen questions answered by the pupils without an interruption from the teacher; and at least five-sixths of them were answered by him alone. A few of the pupils, judging from appearance, had prepared the lesson with the evident intention of having the pleasure of reciting it. To them his officiousness seemed annoying; for, when the question was asked, and they were about to respond, and when the teacher, either fearing lest some one might suspicion his knowledge, or wishing to astonish some one with it, would strike in and crowd them off, there were evident manifestations of disappointment. Others, less sensitive, seemed to take it patiently, probably from greater respect for the wisdom and learning of the teacher, or possibly because it was a very easy way of reciting the lesson. Now, this case is by no means an exception; others could have been selected equally faulty.

Again: the habit that some pupils have of waiting in recitation until they receive "a start" from the teacher, falls properly under this head, as the practice is most probably induced by the failings last alluded to. A distinguished educator in Ohio, in speaking of this class of pupils, compares them to an old rickety pump, into which a few pailfuls of water must be poured before any can be pumped out, which, when obtained, is but a sickly stream; and as soon as the pumping ceases, the connection is broken, and all efforts to obtain more are fruitless, until more water is introduced from above. The comparison is a good one, since the ability of these pupils to recite seems to depend almost entirely upon the extraneous efforts of the teacher.

Now, all these forms of prompting exist, and perhaps many more slightly different. Their deleterious consequences may be readily seen. Some of them pander to the laziness of the pupils, some to their pride. Some cultivate deceit and falsehood, some superficial habits. Some, again, are absolutely annoying and even insulting, while the whole brood are destructive of manly independence and progress. The remedy for all these forms of evil is short and simple, and perhaps has been anticipated already.

1. For the first, in asking questions, avoid, so far as possible, all that admit of the answers, *Yes* or *No*. Let them be put in such a shape that the pupil shall have the entire benefit of the answer. This is his by right; and he just as certainly languishes without it, as the tender plants do without the showers. Take the first example, for instance, under the first case. Instead of the labored and childish repetition there exhibited, the question should stand simply thus: "How do you add fractions that have not a common denominator?" And the answer should follow without a single word from the teacher, until the pupil has done with it; then, if it become necessary, let explanations and illustrations follow. For beginners, or those less familiar with the subject, it might be staked off something after this manner:

First Step. The reduction or changing of the terms. This consists of two operations: 1. Those relating to the denominator; 2. Those relating to the numerator.

Second Step. The addition of the numerators.

Third Step. The disposition of the denominator.

Fourth Step. The reduction of the fraction, should it be necessary.

2. As to the second case of prompting: in asking questions, let them be as brief and pointed as possible, neither offering nor denying a choice of words, and conveying no allusion whatever to the answer. Take the example given under the second variety of prompting. Instead of the strained effort to make the answers as short and easy as possible, let it stand simply thus: "What is Etymology?" "What is Syntax?" "What are nouns?" "Name the different classes and define them." "Name the properties of nouns, and define them," etc.

3. As to the third case: after the question is asked so as not to allow the child to choose between two things, let the teacher mind his own business until the child has answered, or at least made an effort to answer it—*i. e.*, let him not, by word, tone of voice, look or gesture, convey any knowledge to the pupil as to whether he is right or wrong until he has either finished the entire answer or failed; in which latter case it may either be corrected by the teacher—though this should be rare—or passed to another pupil, and when answered, should be returned to the one making the first mistake for his answer as corrected, and so of all the others. Take the first question under the third case. Instead of what is there stated, let it stand thus: "What is the shape of the earth?" etc. Take the one on proportion. Let it stand thus: "State the

rule for proportion: 1. When the answer ought to be greater than the third term; 2. When it ought to be less, and the reasons for," etc. For the other form of this variety, take the question given under it, viz.: "Where does the Mississippi rise?" etc., which is a proper enough form for the question, the difficulty here lying in the mode of answer. Let the answer be given without any intervening questions or suggestions, either by word or by act. And in cases like that given in analysis or parsing, let there be no guessing, no "drawing out," no hesitating for suggestion from either teacher or pupil, no rising slides on the part of the pupil, no suggestions, no winking, nodding or negating, to indicate to the pupil whether he is right or wrong.

4. In reading, and in all other recitations, avoid the practice of assisting the pupil whenever he hesitates upon the pronunciation of a word, or the utterance of a sentence, making it a positive injunction that the lesson is to be so well prepared before recitation, that, especially in reading, all the words can be named at sight; for if they can not, the child should be remanded at once to easier lessons, even to the "cards" or word and object lessons, until he acquires the ability to pronounce readily. It accomplishes little or no good, for a pupil to drag his slow length along in reading, where not only the meaning of the words, but their connection is lost by his long intervals or pauses. Again: avoid the practice of showing the pupil how well you can recite yourself, at least until he has had the first trial, which by right and duty belongs to him. This practice is so annoying, it would seem that no one who had witnessed its evil effects would ever tolerate it, much less resort to it. In addition to the annoyance, it discourages all effor

on the part of those who desire to learn, and pampers the laziness of those who have not the desire. The elocution exercises may form an exception to this rule.

Lastly : the practice of assisting pupils to the first few words of the answer, is doubtless the offspring of the last mentioned evil. To correct it, never allow yourself to be guilty of the practice yourself, and never allow your pupils to presume upon your indulgence in this respect. The understanding should be, that the first word is just as important for the pupil to learn, as the second or third; and that the integrity, as well as the usefulness of knowledge, will be much impaired, if it is based upon as uncertain a process, as that described under this head.

Section IV—Specific Methods.

It only remains now to speak of the several modes of recitation, in which an application of these specific directions may be made. For convenience, they may be classified as follows:

I. The Interrogative Method.
II. The Topical Method.
III. The Didactic Method.

The first is one of almost universal use, and the one in which most, if not all the directions given above, will apply. We shall speak of it under the several forms in which the answers are given.

Article 1—The Concert Method, or that in which all recite at once, is one in general use, and is not without its uses and abuses. 1. It is useful in awakening an interest in class and in school. 2. It aids those who may be too timid otherwise to recite, to overcome their diffidence. 3. It gives all an opportunity to recite the

whole, or a greater part of the lesson, in the same time. 4. It offers the best opportunity to secure uniformity, and to cultivate the voice; and it shows a school off to better advantage: though, whether this last is really a desirable object, will depend altogether upon the style of exhibition. If the object of the *show* is to secure answers to the greatest number of questions, without any reference to where they come from, it would then be objectionable. If, however, the display consists in better-drilled voices, greater uniformity, and more promptness in manner, etc., all of which may be secured by this method, then it becomes a decided advantage. The chief benefits of this method, however, are confined to reading and spelling, which have been described elsewhere; but it may be used to advantage in reciting rules and tables of currency, weight, measure, and in accurately arranged definitions, and in the declensions and conjugations of words.

Some of the more important abuses of this method, are the following: I. It offers an opportunity to any that do not know the lesson very well, to attach themselves, as it were, to those that do, and thereby appear to a better advantage than they really deserve. 2. It affords an opportunity to those who may desire to conceal mistakes, intentional deviations and ignorance, to effect their purposes; though an experienced ear will generally detect any thing of this kind. 3. Unless carefully guarded, it has a tendency to cultivate an unnatural and monotonous style. 4. Those who have been in the habit of reciting too exclusively in concert, are for the most part, unable to recite alone. They do not acquire the strength and confidence, to enable them to stand without the "props and stays" of other voices. Therefore, while this method possesses unquestionable merits, and many advantages, it should be used with great caution, never exclusively, and never to usurp the place of other forms.

ARTICLE 2—CONSECUTIVE METHOD.—This method is one of long standing and perhaps of universal adoption. It is that in which the members of the class are so arranged that the questions or exercises uniformly commence at a given place in class, and pass on in consecutive order, from head to foot. This plan is not without its merits and demerits.

1. The labor of conducting recitations after this mode, is less than in most others, the teacher having no other special care than merely to ask the questions, and to see that they are answered properly.

2. It has the advantage of order and system; and for advanced pupils, or those who can resist the temptation of inattention, may be used with safety.

3. It affords an opportunity for pupils to compete for position—if indeed this is an advantage; and we think it may become useful under proper restrictions.

But the objections to this method, when used with a certain class of students, and without great care, will more than overbalance the benefits arising out of it.

1. It affords an opportunity for the pupil to neglect certain portions of the lesson. They will prepare only such portions of it as will most likely fall to them to recite. Hence, it is no uncommon thing to see pupils, even after arranging themselves in class—if they are allowed their books in recitation—first ascertaining their location in class, then measuring off a place in the lesson corresponding to it, and then commenc-

ing a vigorous preparation of that part of the lesson, paying little or no attention to any other part.

2. If this custom alone is adopted, after a pupil has once recited, he is apt to feel no further responsibility; and for all practical purposes, might almost as well be excused from the class, after he has "said" his part of the lesson.

3. In large classes, where a fixed arrangement is observed, there is danger of slighting some altogether, and hence of inducing them to slight their lessons until such time when they will be most likely to be called upon for recitation.

It was the misfortune of the writer once to be a member of such a class of about 50 members, arranged in alphabetical order. The lessons were of such a character, that it was not absolutely necessary that more than about half a dozen pupils should recite at one recitation—and that was about the average number—so that each one of us had the privilege of reciting as often as about once in ten days. And I well remember the demonstrations that were made by some of the class after passing the ordeal of "their turn." The book would be thrown aside with the exclamation, "There, I shall have nothing more to do this week, sure!" One can easily see that the knowledge and discipline obtained in this way, are worthless.

ARTICLE 3.—THE PROMISCUOUS METHOD is one which, perhaps, has more merits than either of those just described. It consists, as its name implies, in asking questions of any member of the class, irrespective of time, place or order. It has these advantages:

1. It compels all to get the whole lesson, since no

one can know how much he will be called upon to recite, or when or where.

2. It checks any disposition on the part of the pupil to be inattentive, since each one is liable, at any moment, to be called upon to recite.

3. It forces all to keep in mind the connection; for, where the method is properly followed, the teacher may, at any time, and at any stage of the answer, arrest it, and require some one else to complete it.

4. It acts as a kind of a check upon most of the evils described in the foregoing.

It has, however, the following objections, if not properly administered.

1. When the pupil, after having been once called upon, feels sure he will not be called upon again, he is tempted to inattention in the remainder of the lesson. In this it is similar to the second method, only in *that* the inattention may occur both before and after being called upon; while in *this*, only after, since the pupil is obliged to keep a sharp watch for his turn. But even this abuse can be obviated by taking advantage of such pupils, and calling upon them three or four times in succession, in the same recitation.

2. It requires more care on the part of the teacher, in order to distribute the lesson rightly among the members of the class. But this can hardly be called an objection, since the benefits thence arising, will more than compensate for any additional care. On the whole, this variety of the Interrogative method, in its many applications, and with proper care, is subject to fewer objections than almost any other.

ARTICLE 4—THE SILENT METHOD.—Another variety closely allied to this last, deserves special notice. For the sake of distinction we shall call it the *Silent Method*. It is described thus: The question is asked the whole class, and all are required to answer mentally or silently —not merely to call to mind the answers, or to think of the conclusions, but to examine carefully the processes by which they are reached; and when this is done, to indicate it by a given signal. When all the members have thus signaled, or after the lapse of a reasonable time, let some one of the pupils be selected to give the oral or written answer, or solution.

This method is thus described: The question is announced distinctly to the whole class. The time elapsing between the asking and answering should resemble that which usually occurs between the flash of the lightning and the report of the thunder. It should be impressively still. This gives every one time, not only to get the full import of every question, but really to answer every one mentally, and then to review it, when the oral answer is given, which, if correct, may be indicated by the pupils' assuming the proper posture; but if incorrect, and as soon as incorrect, the signal should be repeated, when the one reciting is arrested in his answer, and another called upon to complete it, etc.

This plan brings more minds into active and vigorous exercise than almost any other. No one can really escape, since in case of a failure, the plan itself reports the delinquent; and if false reports are given, they may soon be detected by the teacher. If he have suspicions of this nature, let him require the pupil thus suspicioned to recite; and a few exposures will generally cure the worst cases of this species of falsifying. The only objection that really operates against this variety, is that it requires a little longer time. But the additional discipline, in most cases, will more than compensate for any loss of this kind. It requires also a considerable previous culture and discipline to make it work well; but it may then be used in nearly all kinds of recitation.

ART. 5—THE MONITORIAL METHOD.—Another variety called the *Monitorial*, has been adopted by a few with success; though the experience of the best teachers, I believe, has condemned its general use. The only instance in which I remember to have seen it employed with any marked success, was in the Model Department of the Connecticut State Normal School; and in this case it was not strictly monitorial. A class of about twenty girls was reciting in history. One of their number (the monitress) sat upon an elevated seat, immediately in front of the class, holding in her hand a set of cards, numbered and corresponding with duplicates held, one by each member of the class. As the teacher asked the questions, the monitress drew a card from her pack, not knowing herself what one, called out the number to the class, and the pupil holding its duplicate, arose and recited. The teacher, in this instance, did nothing but simply ask the questions. The class was responsible for the balance, even the correction of any errors that were committed. There are other forms of this variety differing slightly from any hitherto described; one of which, by way of distinction, we shall call *reciprocal*. It is nearly monitorial, only every member of the class is a monitor, at the same time all are pupils. The peculiarities of this variety consist in placing the whole recitation in the hands of the pupils, each one, according to pre-arrangement, asking such questions as come within the scope of the lesson

or review, and to whatever member of the class he may choose. Sometimes there is connected with this, some incentive—such, for instance, as contesting for the head, in which case, the pupil standing anywhere in class—say No. 7—may question any member above him, and in case he ask a question that can not be answered by the one of whom he asks it, on answering it himself, he takes his place.

This plan is both amusing and instructive. The interest it awakens in class, and the incentives it adds to the preparation of the lesson are surprising; since it must be learned not only to be recited well, but so well that the pupils themselves may teach it. This plan but slightly modified, works well in performing operations at the board, especially in the simple operations in arithmetic where long columns of figures are to be added, or in any others, where practice and rapidity are required. Let the pupils contend in a similar manner, or simply take turns in performing rapidly various parts of the operation.

ARTICLE 6—MISCELLANEOUS METHODS.— (a) One of these varieties, though somewhat limited in its application, is worthy of notice. For want of a better name, we shall call it a *method by proxy*. Its chief use is to cultivate ready and close attention, and it may be used occasionally, in nearly all the branches. It consists in a repetition and transfer of the question as it comes from the teacher, requiring answer in most cases from those least expecting it. For instance, the question is announced by the teacher, when the pupil to whom it is directed rises and repeats it to the class, and calls upon some one to answer it, who may also be required to repeat it, and if unable to answer, may call upon some one else, etc. This mode, of course, can never be rendered general, its chief use being to cultivate attention and the ability to ask and answer questions under a variety of circumstances.

(b) The practice of reciting by *contests*, or better known as "*choosing sides*," though of somewhat ancient origin, has but few superiors. As a means of exciting and sustaining attention, it has few if any equals. Many, doubtless, can yet remember the excitement that used to prevail at the spelling matches, which in fact constituted about the only attractive feature, belonging to the old usages. The same interest may invest almost all other branches of study, by only submitting them to the same influences. For instance, let the class choose sides to remain chosen for one, two, three, or four weeks at a time. Let a careful record of the losses and gains of both sides, be kept by the teacher, or some one or two of the pupils, and reported to the class once a week, or at the expiration of the time, if that be deemed best. There are many other modes of keeping tally, besides many other incentives that may be used with this plan. This practice also cultivates the power of criticism, since pupils criticise each other. It also enables the pupils to follow demonstrations or answers of any kind, exercises them in the practice of asking and answering questions, all of which are of great utility to every one, and especially those who expect to teach.

(c) The plan by *written questions and answers* is one that ought to be practiced more than it is, since many that can answer very well orally, are nevertheless incapable of doing so by writing. The questions, in this variety, may be written on the board or on slips of paper, and distributed, and answers prepared by the pupils. Of course, care should be taken to prevent communications. In this manner, a great deal of time may be saved, since the teacher may be employed about something else, while the class is preparing answers, etc.

ARTICLE 7—THE TOPICAL METHOD.—This method, for intrinsic merit, perhaps, has not a single equal in the whole list. It levels in one bold stroke nearly all the evils and inconveniences attached to the other varieties, and aims a death-blow to superficial habits of recitation, since it throws the whole responsibility upon the individual pupil. This is just precisely what is needed to make independent and self-reliant scholars. Its chief benefits, however, are confined to advanced classes. It also admits of several varieties, a few of which we shall name.

(a) The mere announcement of the *subject* or topic, while reciting, is one. Instead of the enunciation of the whole question, as in the case of the preceding, the teacher simply assigns a topic—embracing more or less, to suit the capacity of the class—upon which the pupil is expected to recite. For instance, instead of saying, How do you multiply a fraction by a whole number? A whole number by a fraction? A fraction by a fraction? etc. The teacher simply says, or writes, "The multiplication of fractions;" and the pupil proceeds, at once, to discuss the whole subject, naming and describing the several cases in their order. Instead of asking all the questions as in the example given in grammar, he simply says, "Etymology," "Syntax," "Noun," "Properties," "Relations," etc.; and each one of these topics is then taken up and disposed of, without further assistance from the teacher, except slight explanations, as they may be needed.

In geography, where this plan is peculiarly appropriate, in describing the mountains of Europe, for instance, instead of asking the position, altitude, name and other peculiarities of each range or spur, the topic would simply be, "Mountains of Europe;" and so of the rivers. In describing the seas, lakes etc., it would be "Bodies of Water." In describing a particular state or territory, the following list of topics might be suggestive enough. 1. Position, in reference to Latitude and Longitude; 2. Boundary; 3. Area; 4. Population; 5. Bodies of water; 6. Rivers; 7. Surface, including mountains etc.; 8. Soil; 9. Climate; 10. Productions, including the three kingdoms of nature, etc.; 11. Chief towns and Capitals; 12. Employment; 13. Education: 14. Internal improvements; 15. Curiosities, and any others that may be desirable.

The following are some of the advantages. 1. The labor on the part of the teacher is less, while the advantages to the pupil are greater. 2. It presents a connected view of a subject. The knowledge thus acquired is available. 3. It strengthens memory and cultivates the powers of the understanding and judgment. 4. It cultivate good manners, and the powers of expression and description. It teaches to tell straight stories, and to describe accurately. 5. It cultivates independence, originality, completeness and comprehensiveness of thought and style. 6. It corrects nearly all the abuses incident to the other modes.

The objections to it are few, weak and readily removed or prevented. 1. Its use is confined chiefly to pupils somewhat advanced, the Transition and Subjective. 2. It will require time to initiate pupils into this method, especially if they have, as Mr. Page says, been subject to the "Drawing-out and Pounding-in system."

(b). Another form or use of this method consists in the use of *diagrams* and *analyses*. This variety embraces the practice of mapping out subjects, giving the generic terms and placing their specifics in order, giving, in many instances, the entire analysis, by a process of generalization; and it is questionable, whether any other practice is more useful to advanced pupils, or those who wish to teach. It is the very key to investigation of a higher order, since it arranges the materials of knowledge and thought—the tools of progress—in such order, that they become available in further researches.

The advantages of this variety are similar to others just described; and the only objection I am able to urge against it, consists in its abuse. Some teachers, seeing its beauty and utility in a few things, foolishly attempt to apply it not only to all subjects, but to all grades of advancement; while it is strictly a subjective process. And further, they multiply divisions and subdivisions to such an extent, as rather to confuse and confound, than render intelligible the subjects to which they apply it. They should not only remember that facts come before their philosophic arrangement, but that they confuse the mind, rather than enlighten and strengthen it, when they are presented in such masses.

ARTICLE 8.—THE DIDACTIC OR LECTURING METHOD has already been described. Its use in recitation is somewhat limited; though, for certain classes and certain purposes, it produces, when properly employed, most remarkable effects. There are two principal varieties, viz.: *conversation* and *lectures*. They are sufficiently explained elsewhere, to be comprehended without further description.

Both these varieties, however, are subject to great abuse. The excessive talking and lecturing in which some teachers indulge, are alike ruinous to their own usefulness and the pupil's improvement. The teacher who makes the least ado, in conducting the exercises of the school, is the one who will, in the end, have accomplished the most for his pupils, provided he so dispose of these exercises, as to secure the greatest amount of thought and action, upon the part of pupils.

But as this topic has been discussed elsewhere, we close this chapter by a brief reference to the importance of every teacher's having a variety of methods, and that he study the philosophy of them, so that he may wisely apply them. Every one knows, that the teacher who has but one plan, and that perhaps, an old edition stereotyped, soon renders his subjects monotonous, wearies the patience of his pupils, and circumscribes the limits of their progress. By the very necessities of the case, he can only reach a few, and call out but that limited amount of talent, for which his "plan" may be peculiarly fitted; while he who has a variety, and that variety based upon philosophical principles, may wisely suit his plans to every individual case.

We have therefore presented, under three general heads as generic, some twelve or fifteen varieties. But it will not be inferred, of course, that this exhausts the list; for, while it will be found that all the methods and varieties here described, as well as others practiced by the profession generally, are referable to some one of these methods, or some of their varieties; yet each one of these again admits of a great many slight modifications in the applications, which, of course, would be too tedious for description here. The teacher who acquaints himself with their nature and design, and also with the peculiar wants of his pupils, will find little difficulty in making his own applications of them. We have therefore avoided as much as possible the multiplication of special modes, believing that the few given are not only distinct enough in their characteristics, but comprehensive enough to admit of all necessary changes, and to embrace all possible varieties.

SYNOPSIS IV.

- **SCHOOLROOM DUTIES.**
  - **BUSINESS.**
    - OBJECTS, ETC.
      - Habits of neatness, order, promptness
      - Punctuality. Time. Place. Manner
      - Aid in other duties and emergencies.
    - REQUISITES.
      - Change of classes. Communications.
      - A written order of duties, etc.
      - Close attention. Self-denial.
    - MANNER.
      - Dispatch, without haste or confusion.
      - With a moderate degree of stillness.
      - With scrupulous care and accuracy.

CHAPTER IV.

SCHOOL BUSINESS.

The object of the present chapter shall be to show, in as brief a space as possible, some of the uses of the school life. It might be a question with some whether there is any necessity for such a topic in the "*School-room Duties;*" but, since there is a class of duties that do not really belong, either to study or to recitation; and since, if they are not provided for, they are either constantly interrupting those exercises, or else neglected entirely, it therefore seems proper and right that such a chapter be introduced.

It is a fact well attested by the opinions of our wisest men, as well as by common observation, that school training, notwithstanding its many excellencies, falls short of meeting all the demands of education. It does not, in the great majority of cases, prepare the young for the duties, dangers, and responsibilities of life. Too many leave school with thoughtless, slovenly and disorderly habits, notwithstanding they may be mathematical, philosophical, *learned* in the knowledge of books.

Now it is not proposed that the school should do every thing for the pupil, such as furnishing him with a trade, or employment, or even giving him a very large stock of practical knowledge. Indeed, this can not be expected; for nothing but the actual struggle with the life duties themselves will ever give that *thorough* preparation which these duties demand. But that the school duties might be rendered more effective in this respect; that they should become a kind of foreshadowing of these duties, and, so far as possible, the actual preparation, are conclusions inferable, both from their nature and design, as well as from the lamentable deficiencies that exist in reference to such culture. That the education of the child and the man should be a life preparation for life's duties and destiny, is a truth that can not be too thoroughly inculcated; and that the school life should, so far as possible, be an epitome of that world life upon which the child is soon to enter, is another truth of equal significance. We shall therefore treat the above named subject under the following heads:

1. *The objects* or *necessity* for such an application of school duties.
2. *The requisites and means* for carrying it into effect.
3. The *mode* of conducting this department of school duties.

Section 1—Objects, etc.

If it be true that the schoolroom does afford opportunity for this life preparation, etc., then indeed does it follow, that its exercises should look to that one great object as a central and leading idea, about which, or rather to which, all others should bend; for it is scarcely possible, and by no means probable, that unless some special pains are taken, these results will ever be secured. It is pertinent, therefore, to inquire, in the first place, after the habits and traits of character that render children and men and women useful; and, in the second place, how far these duties can be rendered efficient in the formation and development of these habits and traits.

ARTICLE 1—HABITS OF NEATNESS, CLEANLINESS, AND ORDER.—These are habits of acknowledged merit, but at the same time, subject to woeful neglect. How far then, can the actual duties of the school be rendered efficacious, and how far can special duties be introduced that shall not conflict with these, and still be the instruments in the formation of these habits, are questions that ought to be considered.

The position is assumed in Part First of this work, that neatness and cleanliness, and indeed all forms of outward refinement, as well as heart culture, keep exact pace with the march of intelligence, provided always, that the subject of culture is a fair one, and the system philosophical. This position is true beyond controversy, or else education is a failure; and we add here, that when these effects are not produced, the teacher may be sure that something is wrong. It follows, therefore, that with every increase in knowledge and development, there should be a corresponding improvement in the personal appearance—in the habits of neatness, cleanliness, order, etc. But how is this effected? Will the simple acquisition accomplish this, without special direction and application? We answer, not to the full extent, any more than plowing the ground, and sowing the seed will produce the harvest. There must be a nurture, a careful cultivation, and a husbanding of the stores, before the precious grain can be rendered serviceable to man. It is thus with the processes of education. Its full rewards are never realized, until the uses of knowledge are fully established. But how shall pupils be made to feel the force of this general development, in this special direction? What special exercises can be adopted that will increase the point and power of gen-

eral acquisition? We shall now endeavor to answer these questions.

1. Every child's desk or seat and its premises should be considered his home. He has, or ought to have, books, papers, pencils, slates, and various other apparatus, which are essentially his utensils and instruments for carrying on his employment. In this it is like home. He has duties to perform; he is in this respect, imitating, to all intents and purposes, the scene that will soon open before him on a larger scale, on the stage of active life. Every child's domain in the schoolroom being his home, it should be considered under his special charge, while the teacher has the general supervision. The pupil is responsible for the order and neatness of this charge, *and this responsibility should be just as binding as that of recitation.* There should be therefore, in every school, a standard of order and neatness, just as there is in recitation. The position of every article of his stock of implements, should all be decided upon. One great reason, and perhaps the chief, that children are not neater and more orderly is because they have no standard, hence no ideal nor ideas, as to what constitutes true order, further than what they may have gathered from very uncertain teaching. Let these standards and tests be furnished, and contended for, in the same manner as other excellencies are, and it would not be long before the whole face of education and of nature would be changed.

What is true in reference to the domain of each scholar, and of the whole schoolroom, each one being responsible for that portion of it in his vicinity, is also true in reference to each pupil's clothing and personal appearance; and as no litter of any kind should be allowed to collect upon the premises of any one, so none should collect upon the person of any one. If the house should be clean, so should be the housekeeper. Let both be insisted upon with the same pertinacity with which other duties are, and it will not be long before these same habits will reproduce and perpetuate themselves in dress and personal appearance. The boys will not leave mud or filth upon their feet and clothing any more than they would upon the floor or in their desks. The girls will not permit their dresses to appear in a slovenly and slattern way. The schoolhouse and yard will soon show signs of improvement. The window-blinds will be more neatly adjusted. The shawls, bonnets, and hats will be disposed of in a more orderly manner. The floor will be kept clean and the furniture will be dusted. The smaller pupils will catch the spirit, and will soon learn that a spot of mud or dirt upon their clothing or their premises, is out of order; that a tattered garment, unwashed hand or face, and uncombed hair are disorderly; and that filthy and slovenly habits, vice and suffering are all of the same species of disorder. What a world of happiness is thrown away by those who neglect those little things! How our homes might rejoice under the transforming influence of this genius of order, provided the same attention were bestowed upon these things that is bestowed upon arithmetic and grammar! Just as if these *alone* would make people neat and tidy, contented and happy! The happiness of the world does not depend half so much upon these as upon the little things we overlook in our rage after the "mint and cummin." Roses might bloom where naught but briers now:

life and beauty where naught but desolation reigns; happiness where naught but misery.

In addition to this standard of order and neatness in the schoolroom, there should also be, at least a daily inspection, and a report on the conditions of things, which report should be considered of as much value in determining the standing of the pupil, as that of study or recitation. This would invest these duties with the same degree of interest that others have. It is unreasonable to suppose that our children will attach any effective importance to them, unless they are brought into prominent notice. It is a rare instance indeed that children become what we propose to make them, merely by preceptive instruction. In this, as in all other departments, they must actually engage in the duty, and feel its responsibility.

ARTICLE 2—PROMPTNESS and PUNCTUALITY are traits of character which this department should especially cultivate. These are of such vital importance, that it may be said with truth, that all permanent success in every department of business, depends upon them. True, the exercises of study and recitation, properly directed, have a tendency to cultivate these virtues; but it is proper to inquire how far promptness and punctuality depend upon special efforts.

1. As to *time*. In the transaction of these and all other duties, special attention should be given to the time. If we expect our pupils to be, in this respect, what our precepts would indicate, and what we expect of them, they must have these traits of character cultivated by the same process that others are. There should therefore be an exact and definite time in which all these duties should be conducted—exact to a min-

ute—as much so as that a definition or rule should be to a word—and no ordinary excuse should justify or excuse a departure from it.

2. The place and manner of disposing of these things should be just as definite. Every article of furniture about the premises of every pupil should have its appropriate place, and should be arranged in its appropriate manner, and with as much care as if they were words in a sentence, or figures in the solution of a problem. The one will have no greater effect upon the habits and happiness of the future man or woman than the other. Instead of books, etc., being thrown about the desk or room in that confused manner which usually costs the pupil and teacher so much perplexity, they should be arranged in just such a place and in just such a manner; so that when the pupil has need of any of them, he need not disturb the whole school, rummaging in his confused pack, asking a dozen needless and impertinent questions about this thing and that, before finding what he wants. How frequently is this the case! And how unhappy, not to say miserable, this makes a school! And then this habit is carried right into whatever business or employment the pupil may select in after life. If he become a mechanic, with these evil habits clinging to him, his tools and materials will present the same disorderly appearance. His saws and files, and nails and hatchets and hammers, will be thrown confusedly together, to be injured by the contact; and square and compass, augers and bits, planes and chisels, will be lost in a heap of rubbish, while his nice patterns and plates will be greased and soiled—the whole a fair transcript of his desk in school.

If he become a farmer, his fields will be out of pro-

portion. An unsightly stump or tree will be standing where it ought not to be, and a dozen will be cut down or marred where they ought to be cultivated. His fences will be thrown down, or overgrown with brambles. Little patches of ground will be left uncultivated here and there, about the stumps and wet or stony places. His door-yard, if he have any, will be bleak and naked, the object of constant depredations from pigs and geese. His cows and sheep, hogs and horses, will all herd together; and his barn-yard will become the common rendezvous for the vagabond animals of the neighborhood. His buildings—well, look there! You may see them all out of repair, and bleaching in the sun and rain. The saddle and rakes are on the porch—a roosting-place for hens—while bits of broken harness, and remains of harrows, ornament the piazza. Old barrels and benches lumber the barn, and pitchforks and plows, scythes and sickles, the house and yard. If he become a professional man, his office and study will present a similar picture; if a merchant or banker, his books and ledgers will be crowded and confused; his accounts unsettled and uncertain.

But careless and slovenly habits are not alone felt by men. They visit some of their worst woes upon women. The young lady (?) of disorderly habits, perhaps becomes a wife and a housekeeper. Her house— But we forbear. We will not uncover the secrets within. Over this sad picture we would draw a vail. We fain would hide it from mortal sight. It were enough to say, that in too many instances, squalid wretchedness, angry broils, unhappy households, dissipated husbands, children driven from what should be a peaceful fireside, to seek a gratification of the social nature, amid scenes of dissipation and vice, all testify but too strongly against the neglect to cultivate habits of neatness, order, promptness and punctuality, in connection with social and æsthetic training.

Article 3—Aids to Duties and Emergencies.—Another object, which alone should be sufficient to secure the special attention to these habits, is the aid they would afford in the performance of other duties, and the ability they would impart to ward off danger. No one can estimate the value of the time lost in fruitless attempts to prosecute business, under circumstances where everything is out of time and place. This evil is felt severely in the schoolroom, but not more severely there than on the stage of active life. When a book is wanted, for instance, from which to prepare a hurried lesson, it is lost—"somebody has taken it." An impatient search commences, during which an inkstand or two are upset, the contents besmearing the books and furniture. Pupils in the vicinity are annoyed. Much time and patience are lost, and above all the peace and order of the whole school are disturbed by one such pupil. What, then, must be the fate of that school, composed—teacher and all—of such? It is more easily imagined than told. But another object, connected with this article, deserves notice here. It is the provision or preparation that may be made, while in school, against the emergencies, accidents and casualties incident to human life.

In this uncertain world, accidents will happen. While their number and severity may be much reduced by an enlightened and highly liberal education; yet it would be vain to expect to escape all of them. It were, therefore, wiser to provide for them. It is a well-known fact too, that few people possess sufficient self-control, in cases of severe accidents, or in places of imminent danger, to enable them to do any thing available, either for their relief or rescue. In fact, in the great majority of instances, the dangers and mishaps are aggravated for the want of coolness and self-possession in the hour and article of imminent peril—such, for instance, as in cases of fire, of drowning, of poison, or in the case of asphyxia from any cause. The man who climbed to the third story of a burning house and threw from the window a mantle-clock and looking-glass, down upon the pavement below, and then caught up a feather bed, ran down two flights of stairs and carefully deposited it in the street, is but too apt an illustration of the want of sense that usually prevails on such occasions. A few noble exceptions, I know, we have on record, but these only show us what could be done, provided the masses could be imbued with the same spirit, and these noble traits of character cultivated.

What an awful calamity was that which occurred a few years since, in one of our Eastern cities, where hundreds of children were precipitated down two or three flights of stairs, and crushed in one mangled mass below,—and *all* from a false alarm of fire! Now, without reflecting the least blame upon those teachers, allow us to ask, could not these children have been saved? Could they not have been taught, by rigid and careful training, to master their feelings by their judgment? Could they not have been taught to sit quietly in their seats and await the orders of their teachers, in such cases of danger? I *know they could*, provided they had been taught lessons on the dangers of precipitation, as carefully as they had been in reading and arithmetic. I say *taught*, because I believe children should be shown, by actual experiment, that they only endanger themselves by haste in such instances. Let the experiment be made with the children in going out in a disorderly and hurried manner —of course avoiding danger—and then, in a quiet and orderly manner, and the difference in time noted. Let it be made frequently, and practiced for the express purpose of providing against accidents, etc.: and it will be found that from one-half to three-fourths of a minute is sufficient time for all to quit the premises of an ordinary building. Let them see that one minute and a half at most, are sufficient time to allow all the inmates to escape from a burning building, provided all are orderly; and that it will require ten times as long if they are not; and that no fire is likely to occur which would destroy egress in one minute of time; and that should this be the case, disorderly haste only augments and aggravates the delay.

This imperturable coolness and calculation in moments of peril or emergency, will prove of infinitely more service to the pupils in their lives, perhaps, than nine-tenths of all their learning, and will not, meanwhile, interfere at all with it. And then in cases of that most frequent and frightful, yet most unnecessary, as well as too frequently fatal class of accidents, the explosion of lamps, and burnings from the clothes taking fire, how many might be saved if they had only been taught how! Not only how to extinguish flame, but how to possess their wits at such times. But let it be shown also, how the flames can be extinguished under such circumstances. Perhaps, it would not be good policy or even safe to set any one on fire, for the benefits of the experiment; and yet the whole process might be shown in a very short time to a class of children, which, but for this timely instruction, might not only always be ignorant upon those points, but the actual sufferers themselves.

And so in reference to poisoning, or suffocation from any cause, severe wounds, freezing, etc., etc., all these things and their remedies and modes of treatment, should be discussed in a few practical lessons in every school in the land. The antidotes and remedies for these are usually forgotten in the fright that occurs under such circumstances; but if children are taught in a series of lessons as before indicated, and these things made the subject of frequent reference, the occasions would be rare indeed, in which they would either be forgotten or neglected from any other cause.

This part of the subject might be continued at great length, but the information upon these points is abundant. All that seems necessary is that the teacher prepare himself to make use of the means; and we might add, that no teacher who neglects these things, does his whole duty.

Section 2—Requisites, etc.

We shall now devote a few pages to the consideration of some of the requisites and means, for carrying forward this species of culture. We have endeavored to show, in connection with the objects and necessities, the manner in which the habits of neatness, order, etc., may be established in early life. It might be well to inquire further as to the advantages and opportunities, the schoolroom affords for such a course.

ARTICLE 1—CHANGE OF EXERCISES.—Aside from the advantages of convenient schoolrooms, plenty of apparatus, etc., etc., which have been noticed in another place, there is this additional one, rising out of a necessity for a change of employment, which is continually recurring. It will be seen, furthermore, by a reference to the close of this chapter, that a certain amount of time is appropriated to the several duties of each day. The changes from one duty to another, therefore, afford the very means we could desire for the cultivation of promptness and precision, both as to time and manner.

1. There is a necessity for change of classes, occurring periodically. These changes should not only take place precisely at the same time each day, but should be conducted with strict uniformity as to manner, etc. Children should be taught among the first things, to pass to and from the recitation seat with the utmost care. But there will always be more or less noise on such occasions. It would not be wise to insist upon the usual quiet during these changes. But this time should by no means be lost. It may be devoted, by pre-arrangement, to the transaction of any business that might require the pupils to leave their seats.

2. It may, and in most cases it is necessary to keep up fires, or to attend to ventilation. This is the time for these duties, and they should not be allowed to usurp any other. How unpleasant and unreasonable it is to have a boy rattling at a stove, or banging at a door or window or a ventilator (if the school is fortunate enough to have any), while the teacher is engaged in hearing a class of pupils that may be troubled with weak voices and weak nerves. Rather let there be a fixed time and a distinct understanding in reference to these duties, and let them be attended

to when there will be the least loss of time, and the least interruptions in other directions.

3. Again: *communications* are necessary. Aside from the fact that children are eminently social beings, and hence ought not to be deprived of this privilege entirely, there are duties and labors which render it absolutely necessary that pupils should communicate, both with one another, and with their teacher. There should, therefore, be a time set apart for this purpose. It might be called whispering or business moments, and should occur at least once an hour, but should not exceed from three to five minutes in length. All communications between the pupils, and all questions to the teacher, that do not require lengthy answers (most of this latter class come in recitation), should be reserved for this time, and not allowed to mingle with and obstruct other duties. This arrangement will very much facilitate business generally, and besides it will be the surest means of suppressing that troublesome practice, among pupils, of communicating at improper times. Perhaps no one evil has been more universally dreaded, or more stoutly opposed with poor success; and the chief reason for this is found in the fact that, in the great majority of cases, no provision has been made for an outlet of this superabundant and pent-up vitality and sociability.

Let there be a time set apart for this, just as for any other necessity, and let no communications (except cases of extreme necessity) be permitted at any other time, not even the simplest question. It might be a little inconvenient and seem a little hard for a boy or girl to be compelled to wait half an hour before he or she might be permitted to ask what seemed a very necessary question; but it should be remembered that in a school, as well as in a larger community, individual interests and preferences must yield to the public good. But in most cases, it will be found that the business, or request, is not so urgent that it may not be delayed without damaging any one; and not only so, but that a very wholesome lesson may thereby be taught the delinquent, in reference to attending to these things at their proper times.

Suppose a pupil, for instance, has neglected to note the lesson assigned on a previous day, and that when he takes his book for the purpose of preparing said lesson, he has forgotten where or how it begins; but his companion next to him knows all about it: now may he not obtain permission to inquire after said lesson? No: rather let him suffer the ill consequences of a failure, so that he may avoid a like calamity in future. Or suppose he has neglected, at the proper time, to get a book that lies within a few yards of him, and that that book is necessary for the preparation of the next lesson, may he not ask for it? No: let him suffer the consequences, rather than establish a bad precedent. Let the penalty fall upon the guilty one, and upon no other. This constitutes an additional reason, why there should be a set time for all these duties. A few weeks' practice will teach the pupils to dispose of all their items of business at the proper time. How much better thus than to suffer the constant annoyance of an attempt to carry on all these departments at once! The communications should all be disposed of here, the study and recitations at their respective times, and practice will soon insure all this. How much better thus than to mix them all together! And how much better than to

insist upon constant quiet, and perhaps obtain nothing more than constant disturbance. Therefore, provide whispering moments, and let these be observed as scrupulously as any other duty.

ARTICLE 2—AN ORDER OF DUTIES.—Every child should be provided with an *order of duties*. Those who are able to write, should prepare these, in which every duty shall be provided for, and every moment of time employed. These orders after being prepared by the pupils, might be submitted to the teacher for inspection and improvement, as before directed. For the younger classes, they should be written out upon the board, or upon cards, and so arranged that, with the aid of the teacher, they may direct them in the disposition of *their* time also. This measure thoroughly adopted and carried out in all the schools, would, of itself, do more to systematize labor, and hence remove the many evils complained of by teachers, and at the same time assist the pupils in their duties, than almost any other one thing. And then it is just what is wanted to form and establish good habits and prepare our pupils for the practical duties of life.

This *order* should differ from the "order of exercises," described in another place. That is general, or for the whole school; this is particular, or for individuals and classes.

ARTICLE 3—CLOSE ATTENTION.—Another requisite is *close attention*. In order to meet the claims of this severe regime, there must be no inattention or idleness. The system admits of none. The moment the child indulges, he is lost. He is out of his place, and falls behind. The system itself will either correct him, or, in time, banish him. While there is ample time given for communication, recreation and amusement (and these duties should be encouraged just as others are), there is no time spent without a purpose or an object.

Now let a child, or let all our children remain from five to seven years under this severe drill, in which they acquire the habit of making use of all their time, and what will be the probable, nay almost certain effects upon them? Time and existence would not then become a burden. They would not be sent adrift from the school, to become a prey to idleness and the dupes of vice. Their *education* will have fortified them against these calamities, instead of exposing them to them. The world would be rid of a race of vagabonds; virtue and innocence would be comparatively safe; and comparative peace and plenty would reign in all the walks of life. Would not this be worth a trial? Are not this rigid discipline and order more to be desired, than the mere acquisition of knowledge, especially, since they are the safest means of accomplishing even this?

Again: *self-denial and frugality* will be required. As before remarked, the pupil's personal preferences, will, in many instances, have to be sacrificed to the general welfare; and he will soon learn to make use of the allotted time for the performance of each duty. Here again, he will only be cultivating feelings and habits that he will be called upon to exercise in the drama of life. How much evil does this world suffer from indulgence and indolence! Might not these be arrested here, before they find too deep root in the habits of life? Might not the school assist in this preparation? Is not this its legitimate object? Would not the discipline and order necessary to carry on this exact training, meet the demand exactly? In one word, is it not the most evident intention of all education to regulate man's forces, and to give him entire command of all his powers? Let the school then be the instrument of earnest and wisely directed labor; not a mere farce, or a place where a few feeble, sickly exercises, are engaged in, day after day, for the purpose of filling up the time. No wonder that the children turn with loathing, in many instances, from such tame and tasteless humdrum, such irksome and aimless toil. But we leave this part of the subject, to consider for a moment,

Section 3—The mode of Conducting, etc.

This part of the subject will require but little attention, since the manner of conducting these exercises, will readily be inferred from what has already been said. We might add a few directions, however, by way of completing the outline.

1. *Despatch*, or haste without confusion. 2. *A moderate degree of stillness* in the transaction of the various items. 3. *Scrupulous care and accuracy* in reference to the arrangements of books, apparatus, etc., and also in the movements of the body; all of which topics we shall discuss in the same connection. They are all important features in the transaction of business of any kind; but when we come to apply them to the schoolroom, and to make them the type or standard of the whole life business, their importance is very much augmented.

It will be found, upon the introduction of the plans and practices here suggested, that much that has been assigned, will be neglected for want of time; and this

will be the standing excuse for nonperformance; for children, if left to have their own way, will usually consume twice or three times as much time as is really necessary; besides, they are not always aware of how little *noise* is really necessary, and of how much real advantage scrupulous care and accuracy in the arrangements are, in the transaction of the various duties of the schoolroom. Hence these things should be shown to them, in a series of special exercises, and then practiced in all the regular duties. One class of such exercises might be called "*Handling books and apparatus.*"

For the special drills in this exercise there might be a "word of command;" such, for instance, as is usual in Calisthenics. The first might be, "*Preparation for study;*" in which every book, paper, etc., not to be used should be put away in proper order in the desk. Let it be done too, in the speediest manner possible, and with no unnecessary noise, and the proper position assumed, *with books closed* and eyes turned toward the teacher; because it often is necessary for him to give some directions and explanations about the recitations at such times, when it is very annoying to him, for the pupils to be giving their attention to their books. On such occasions, when the books and slates are brought out for use, there will necessarily be a rustling, caused by the great number of movements of this character, at the same time; but there need be none of that obstreperous slamming and banging, so common on such occasions, caused perhaps by a half-dozen slates let fall upon the floor, or two or three desks upset, on making the change from one posture to another. If the first trial is not successful, let the books, etc., be replaced, and the experiment repeated again and again, until the proper movements are secured.

A second word of command might be, "*Preparation for recitation*," in which every thing not needed in recitation shall be disposed of in a similar manner. It is customary to give a signal for rising, before coming to the recitation seat, and one for advancing, and sometimes one for being seated, and for proper arrangement. With scholars undrilled, the first few attempts will be unsatisfactory. A part will not be quite ready; hence some will rise after the balance are up: others perhaps, not having obeyed the first summons, will be occupying such positions as will very much interfere with their graceful movements; hence in rising they are apt to make a disturbance. Others again, will slowly unbend themselves from a circular posture which they may have assumed, and will occupy about as much time in rising as an old superannuated ox would. Others will perhaps bound to their feet with a quick, nervous movement, that will be equally objectionable. All these movements must be regulated. In coming to the recitation seat, some perhaps will dally with some trifling amusement by the way; some will lounge lazily along, and swing themselves into the seat, as if it were a place of torture — and perhaps it really is to some. Others again will jostle a book or slate upon the floor, or upset a desk or an inkstand; and altogether there will be about as much noise as a four-horse team, or a drove of cattle would make in the passage of a bridge. But let the experiment, in all the necessary variety of movements, be repeated for the express purpose of improving them. In rising up and sitting down, for instance, if it be not in good taste, let the class be politely requested to be seated, the error pointed out, and the whole process repeated; and so of advancing, seating and retiring, until satisfactory results are secured. A similar opportunity occurs for cultivating these habits of neatness and propriety at the opening and closing of school, and at all the regular recesses. Let the same exactness and care be exercised in these as in others; and it will not be long before the pupils will begin to regard all the exercises of the school-room with a new degree of interest. They will look upon them as the means of improvement, and their diffident, uncouth and vulgar habits will give way for those of refinement and order.

The following scheme for the division of time and labor will be found suggestive, at least. While it is not claimed that this, or indeed that any could be devised, that would meet all the circumstances of every school, yet it is claimed that the time and duties of every school in the land may be arranged in a manner *similar* to this; and the benefits arising from such a disposition of affairs would more than compensate for any difficulties that might be experienced in putting it into practice. Let it be written or printed in large type, and so placed that all in the room may be able to read it. It will be necessary also, to have a clock, and a small bell, in order to mark those divisions of time. Some teachers have found it a good plan to appoint monitors daily to take charge of the bell, and to mark by slight strokes upon it—just enough to be heard by all the school—the several divisions of time as they occur. Others again, have found it best to take the entire charge of it themselves.

Order of Daily Exercises.

FORENOON.

From	9.00	to	9.10	Opening Exercises	10 min
"	9.10	"	9.20	Study	10 "
"	9.20	"	9.40	Beginning Class	20 "
"	9.40	"	10.00	Reading (C)	20 "
"	10.00	"	10.05	Business	5 "
"	10.05	"	10.25	Reading (B)	20 "
"	10.25	"	10.35	Recess	10 "
"	10.35	"	11.00	Arithmetic (A)	25 "
"	11.00	"	11.20	Arithmetic (B)	20 "
"	11.20	"	11.25	Business	5 "
"	11.25	"	11.45	Arith. (C) (M. & W.)	20 "
"	11.45	"	12.00	General Exercises	15 "

AFTERNOON.

From	1.00	to	1.10	Study	10 min.
"	1.10	"	1.35	Reading (A)	25 "
"	1.35	"	1.55	Beginning Class	20 "
"	1.55	"	2.00	Business	5 "
"	2.00	"	2.20	Grammar (B)	20 "
"	2.20	"	2.45	Grammar (A)	25 "
"	2.45	"	2.55	Recess	10 "
"	2.55	"	3.20	Geography (A)	25 "
"	3.20	"	3.40	Geography (B)	20 "
"	3.40	"	3.55	General Exercises	15 "
"	3.55	"	4.00	Closing	5 "

The above is more to show the necessity and practicability of a *Plan*, than to describe one. For the want of something of this kind, the energies of the teacher and the time of the pupils are spent in useless attempts to perform the duties of the schoolroom.

It will be observed that no provision is made for Writing and Spelling. A part of the former, and perhaps all the latter may be done in connection with Reading, and other lessons, as practiced in our best schools. Neither is there any provision made for the higher branches; but it will most frequently occur that *some* of the classes provided for above will not be needed. In that case the higher branches may take their places. If not, then the other exercises will have to be shortened.

The limited number of classes may be objected to by some, but we venture to say that the Reading and Arithmetic classes may be classified in three divisions each, with a beginning class, etc., and the Geography and Grammar may be classified in two divisions. The needless multiplication of classes to accommodate either parents, pupils or *publishers* is ruining the order and efficiency of many schools. Teachers should be *competent* to judge, and should have the authority to say what and how many classes there should be in the school.

SYNOPSIS V.

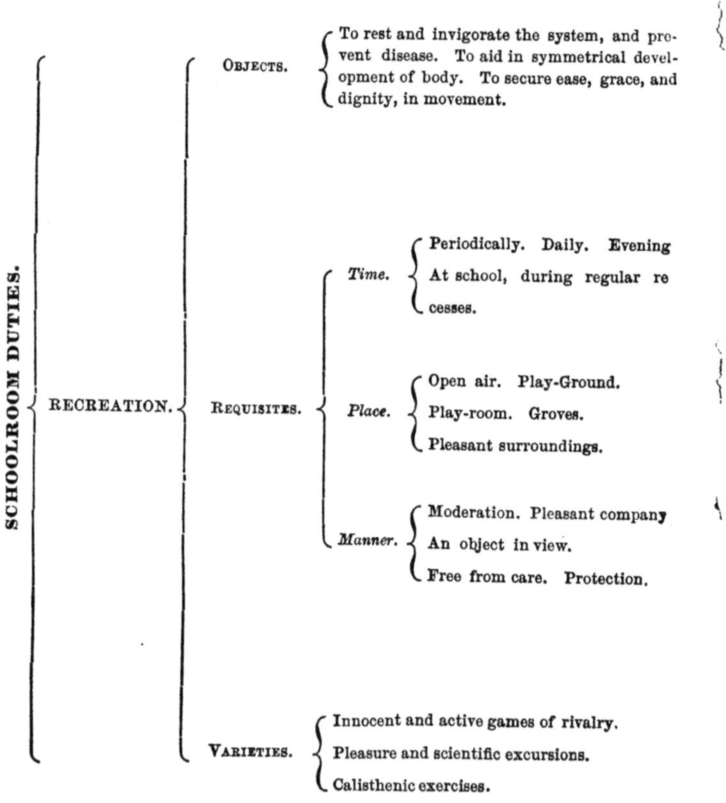

SCHOOLROOM DUTIES.

- RECREATION.
  - OBJECTS.
    - To rest and invigorate the system, and prevent disease. To aid in symmetrical development of body. To secure ease, grace, and dignity, in movement.
  - REQUISITES.
    - *Time.*
      - Periodically. Daily. Evening
      - At school, during regular recesses.
    - *Place.*
      - Open air. Play-Ground.
      - Play-room. Groves.
      - Pleasant surroundings.
    - *Manner.*
      - Moderation. Pleasant company
      - An object in view.
      - Free from care. Protection.
  - VARIETIES.
    - Innocent and active games of rivalry.
    - Pleasure and scientific excursions.
    - Calisthenic exercises.

CHAPTER V.

RECREATION.

It has become necessary to refer to this subject so frequently in the course of this work, that its separate treatment here would not be demanded, were it not to show the relation it sustains to the special duties; and further to set forth that part of it which relates to those duties, in as condensed and as connected a form as possible.

The very nature of education is such that recreation enters into it, just as essentially as water does into the composition of plants. Indeed there is no education, and there can be none; neither can there be life or growth in the animal world, without it. It is, as the etymology of the term implies, the *re-creating* or renewing process, by which, in the animal world, the old and worn-out particles of matter in the system are removed, and their places supplied by new ones. In this respect, it is a highly useful process, since the health and happiness of the individual depend so essentially upon it. These particles, if not removed from the system, become obstructions to a healthy vitality, and hence are the fruitful source of disease. And if new particles are not supplied, as the old are removed, there is consequent emaciation. This truth has also an important bearing upon the intellectual and moral man. The mental powers need the renovating influence of activity and rest, since their operation is through a physical organism.

Now, the whole thing is reduced to this: to recreate there must be both exercise and rest—exercise and activity or motion of the several parts, in order to throw off the waste material, and to aid in the deposition of the new—rest, to allow time for settling and fixing the deposits, and renewing and invigorating the weary powers. The question now arises, are the exercises of the schoolroom prejudicial or beneficial to this natural and necessary process? If necessarily prejudicial, than there is antagonism between man and his own happiness—an inconsistency so glaring as to forbid belief; if unnecessarily so, then the health and happiness of the race would demand an immediate reform. If recreative exercises are beneficial, then they should be encouraged and practiced. These reasons, and others that might be given, are sufficiently apparent to warrant their introduction and practice in the schoolroom. For further evidence upon this subject, the reader is referred to those sections where its claims, as an *educational force*, are treated more at length.

Section 1—Necessity and Objects.

In accordance with the views expressed above, among the first necessities, objects and uses, would be that of *resting the mind and body*. It is a well-known fact, that change of employment rests and invigorates or renews the system. This is effected chiefly by changing the position of the exercise from one point to another. It is equally well known that in the confinement necessary for protracted study, certain parts of the system suffer more than others: certain parts are brought into almost constant exercise, while others remain in comparative inactivity; and that some powers are exercised almost constantly, in the same employment, while a simple change in the direction would relieve them. At such times there will be a desire for either motion, rest, or change.

Article 1—To Invigorate the System.—Now it should be the care of the teacher not to allow any of the desires to end in evil, or even to run to waste. They are all needed in educating the child. The object, therefore, of all recreative exercises, should be to confine, as much as possible, the exercises to those parts most needing them, to rest those which have been overtaxed, and to change or reverse the movements of those parts which suffer most from continuous exercise in the same directions. These principles apply to the mind and body, considered as two reciprocal agents; for the one may be rested by the exercise of the other: but their chief application belongs to the interchangeable relations existing between faculties and sets of faculties, belonging to the same particular structure. The main object of recreation, therefore, in the school, should be to equalize and distribute wisely the exercise and rest necessary to produce the most harmonious results, both in body and in mind.

Article 2—To Prevent Disease.—A second object, though scarcely removed from the one just described, *is to prevent and to cure disease.* It is said by anatomists, that there are two contending forces in the animal structure; the one organizing in its processes, the other disorganizing: the one is life, the other is death; and that we exist between these two forces, the one building us up, the other tearing us down; and that we actually live by the process of dying. Now it would seem that when our vital forces become so exhausted and weakened, either from over-exertion or want of exertion, that the disorganizing processes become the stronger; that actual disease then fastens upon us, arresting for the time being, the entire process of organization: hence both the suffering and emaciation caused by sickness.

It therefore becomes a matter of the greatest importance, to preserve, as nearly as possible, the balance between these forces. Especially is this necessary in childhood and youth, when, from natural causes, the building-up processes should excel the tearing down. At this period *—as we have shown in other places—owing to the peculiarly flexible, and continually changing nature of the substances, the liabilities to contract disease are greater. But these tendencies to disorganization may, from the same cause, be more easily counteracted, since the subject is in a formative state, and liable to either direction, determined by the stronger force. It should therefore be the chief object of the teacher to fortify those points most exposed, whether they relate to the body or to the mind, and to build up a superstructure of the greatest possible strength and durability.

It is also true that disease may be arrested, even after it has made considerable progress, provided the treatment is such as to assist the building-up processes to such an extent as to throw the balance in their favor. The lungs, for instance, may be suffering, or may be diseased; but pure air is their element and nourishment. By wise and judicious breathing therefore, the disease may be thrown off and the parts

---

* Transition, and perhaps the same is true of the objection.

healed. The stomach, and consequently the whole system, may be suffering from indigestion. There is, perhaps, a demand for additional fluids, or motions that will produce them, less stimulating food, or healthier blood. If these demands are complied with, and the derangement has not become too deep-seated, the powers soon regain their accustomed vigor; and so of all the vital organs. Sometimes exercise, sometimes rest is required. But since many of the duties and exercises of the school, unless carefully guarded, invite disease; and since many diseases are already formed from this and other causes, it should be one of the special objects of recreation to remove the obstructions from the path of human progress and happiness. For what other purpose could this desire for amusement, diversion, change, etc., have been given us? Surely not that it might torment us, or lead us estray! Let the teacher, therefore, seize hold of it, and use it, not only to guard his pupils against the encroachments of disease, but for its actual removal.

ARTICLE 3 — TO FACILITATE GROWTH. — Another prominent object of recreative exercises, is the valuable aid they render in the symmetrical development of the body. One of the saddest pictures our sin-smitten race presents, is the distorted, sickly and insufficient development of body. The world resembles one great hospital, and its inhabitants the inmates, with here and there an exceptional case. The great majority seem to be suffering from some malady. Weakness of limb and lungs, of body and brain, sunken chests and crooked backs, diseased livers and distorted spines, poor digestion and poorer powers of endurance are but the common heritage of our race.

Indeed it is in the rarest instances that the adage of the ancients, "*Mens sana in corpore sano*," is realized in the present day, yet education is the boast of this same generation. In the very jaws of disease, we lift up our feeble huzzas for human progress. We boast of our national and internal improvements, and at the same time hug our bodily complaints and maladies as evidences of our refinement. But away with such an education and such refinement from the face of the earth! They are a moral pestilence and have no business among a race of *men*.

If sunken cheeks and sallow skin, if hollow eyes and emaciated forms, if physical debility and suffering are evidences of education and refinement, then, O, give me blissful ignorance, and the life of the savage! If the broad shoulders and stalwart frame, the ruddy cheek and plump rounded limb, the firm, elastic step and bounding form, the sparkling eye and the joyous laugh, must yield to the narrow chest and pinched up dandy form, the spindle shanks and lily hand, the sickly, sentimental face and its usual accompaniment, a shallow brain, the languid walk and almost breathless sigh; if cotton must take the place of muscle, sound, healthy muscle—and paints and powders the place of the roses and flush of health; if these and more than these must become our heritage, then close up the school-houses and colleges, and let the races, yet to come, escape their horrors.

But these calamities are only the results of inadequate education. They constitute no part of a sound system of culture, any more than a failure in bank stock, constitutes a part of political economy. Education makes a strong body as well as a strong brain. It makes a good heart as well as a wise head. It gives a symmetrical development to every limb and muscle, as well as strength to the understanding and judgment. It gives beauty and elasticity to the human form, as well as acuteness of reasoning and brilliancy of imagination.

Now the question arises, what are the instrumentalities rejected from the list, that have caused this breach in a symmetrical growth? We shall not claim that recreation and rational amusements have been the only ones, for a thousand other abuses have wrought their inconsistencies into this tangled web, until, with all its excellencies, it seems to be inadequate for the demand. But, however much we attribute to other sources, it must be admitted that, if every encroachment of a physical nature, occasioned by close confinement or study, were met and repelled by the appropriate physical exercise; the bodies of our boys and girls, if free from constitutional disease, would grow up, sound and healthy at the same time in which they are acquiring knowledge, and expanding their minds. This, therefore, is a cardinal principle in every sound system of education. But it has been contended for at every step in the progress of this work.

ARTICLE 4—GRACE IN MOVEMENTS, ETC.—Another object of a similar nature to the above, is accomplished by recreation, viz.: *ease, grace and dignity of movement.* This would be but the natural result of the preceding course of training. The healthy and full development of body and limb, gives command of all their motions, while neglect gives awkwardness and ill manners. What a symmetry and beauty, in the complete human form! No art can equal it.

Power's Greek slave, is but the impersonation of the perfect ideal of a great artist; but every teacher has perhaps, fifty real, living beings, of the originals of which this is only the copy. Every one of these is of more value than a hundred "Greek slaves"; and though he may not make models of all of them, yet he may make all much better; and he does not educate them, unless he does this.

Again: what poetry, what magic, what majesty, in the proper movements of this human form! There is sublimity in the sweeping torrent, as it leaps from the precipice to the abyss below. There is majesty in the oak, as it sways in the storm; there is grandeur in the tread of an army, or the rush of battle. There is beauty in the swoop of the eagle from his mountain eyrie, or in the gliding of a ship upon the ocean. There is grace in the stately movements of the bending pines, and ease and elegance in the bounding of the nimble deer; but man combines them all in the well directed motions of his body. He possesses within him all these elements. They should therefore, be brought out, and cultivated to the highest degree of perfection that circumstances will allow. Much of usefulness, as well as of pleasure, especially among teachers, is lost by neglecting to cultivate the grace and poetry of motion. However much children may differ as to natural ability, these graces are brought to perfection in any, only by careful practice; and since the young body is most impressible, these gifts are most readily incorporated in their movement by early training,—by taking advantage both of the necessity and desire for exercise and amusement, and making them subserve the double purpose of convenience and refinement. Hence it should be the object of all recreative exercises, to cultivate the easy, graceful and dignified, in movements and manners.

Section 2—Requisites, etc.

The requisites to recreation may be considered under three heads: *First*, in reference to the *time*: *Second*, in reference to the *place*: *Third*, in reference to the *manner*.

ARTICLE 1—THE TIME.—We remark, in general, that all recreation, and especially that kind which includes exercises in the shape of amusements, must be regulated with regard to time. It will no more answer the purposes of recreation to engage in it occasionally and at irregular intervals, as convenience or even as inclination in all cases would indicate, any more than it would to pursue the same policy with eating and sleeping. The reason that we experience greater inconvenience from abstinence in the latter cases, is because the blessings conferred by these are more directly essential to life; and also, because the processes of recreation are carried on even by these, and other independent modes. But the actual benefits of recreation are just as essentially interrupted by neglect or irregularity, as those to which allusion has been made would be, by a similar course pursued with them: therefore, these exercises must be regulated, and must occur, as nearly as possible, at regular intervals.

But it will not answer to make the intervals too long or too short, or the occasions too seldom or too frequent. Not being of that class of necessities which are regulated by nature or instinct, they are subject, more or less to the control of the judgment. If too frequent, they either cloy or become a passion, and thereby interfere with other duties. If the intervals are too great, the exercises lose their effects, and keep the powers in an unsettled state. As the day seems to be appointed to labor, and the night to rest, and since recreation stands as a necessity about where labor does, and since each day, for the most part, embraces the whole routine of essential duties, these things would seem to indicate its frequency. We would be safe, therefore, in saying that it should be *at least daily.*

The next inquiry would be, What time in the day is most appropriate? In this we should be guided by judgment again, though the inclinations point in the same direction. Since the powers become weary through toil, and since the quiet repose of nature invites, the evening, between the hours of labor and rest, would seem to be the appropriate time, though of course this could not apply so well to the school. It will therefore become necessary to select other times for the department of recreation that relates to it: and since the regular recesses are not employed with other duties, a part, at least, of this time should be devoted to some regular and well directed physical exercise.

It is a well known fact, that in a great many instances, this time is spent to little purpose, comparatively—usually in some trifling amusement, or idle gossip, without any reference to the wants or the suffering of the body. If a game of any kind is selected, it is just about as likely to be injurious as beneficial. Little or no attention is given to direct the exercises to those parts of the body that need them, much less to restrain or distribute them in due proportion. These and other circumstances seem to point to the regular recess as a proper time when a part, at least, of the great objects of recreation could be secured. This arrangement would render necessary a little direction from the teacher, as we have remarked in another place. His presence and influence are also necessary; first, because if recreation is worth anything, it is worth directing; secondly, it should be guarded from excess and abuses from other sources; thirdly, the teacher's presence, or influence otherwise, will have a tendency to restrain evil passions and vulgar and profane words; fourthly, it gives him the best opportunity to become acquainted with the dispositions and habits of the pupils; fifthly, the teacher himself needs the exercise. It will clear his head and heart both, from the brooding cares and perplexities incident to the profession, and will in no measure detract from his dignity. But it will be found necessary to employ a small portion of the time outside of the regular recesses. This will fall under what we have denominated business moments: when the books and study should be laid aside for a few moments to engage in the hand, arm and body movements, such as described at the end of this chapter, under the head of Calisthenics.

ARTICLE 2—THE PLACE.—For general exercises, such as games and sports, the open air is, by all means, preferable; first, because of the purity of the atmosphere—an indispensable condition to recreation; secondly, because of the greater freedom of motion that may be secured. Every school-house should have a play-ground, and this should be arranged with reference to its uses, just as the schoolroom is with reference to its uses. Where a play-ground can not be had, or *will* not be had, as is frequently the case in cities and large towns, a play-room should be fitted up with special reference to the wants of the children. This is a very desirable appendage in all cases, since in inclement weather the play-ground would become useless. But in no case should the schoolroom be used for games and sports, much less for general romping. It *may* be used, however, for regular calisthenic exercises.

Again: the places of recreation and amusement should be free from mud and filth of every kind; and should be far enough removed from any public highway, place of general resort, or dangerous precipice, rocks, rivers, lakes, ponds, or any thing that would endanger either the health or clothing, lives or morals of the pupils. Too little attention is paid to this matter. A dingy, dark prison-house of a place for play, is about as objectionable as it would be for study or recitation. A muddy street or forlorn highway, or dirty yard or pen is not much better. But the surroundings should be as pleasant as possible. All perhaps are aware of the effects produced by the presence of beauty and order. They elevate and refine the feelings. They open the mind to free enjoyment. The blood flows with increased vigor, because the heart is glad. The waste particles are removed more rapidly, and the deposits are made in greater numbers, and with greater certainty. A grove, from this cause, and since it abounds in the greatest variety of natural beauty, which renders it still more inviting, becomes the most appropriate place for a summer retreat. In a word, the place should be selected with express reference to moral and æsthetic as well as physical culture.

Art. 3—The Manner.—The manner in which these exercises should be conducted will next claim a brief attention. The reference will not be so much to the nature of the exercises as to a few cautions and general directions.

1. *Moderation* in the movements is one of the most important of these. The tendencies, especially after confinement to hard study, are to excess. Students in colleges, who perhaps have been accustomed to active life, are liable to err in this direction. They confine themselves closely to study, until they feel the imperative necessity of recreation or exercise, when, from an excess of vitality, they enter upon it so suddenly and so violently, that they often impair their health and endanger their lives. All exercises of this kind, and of every kind, in order to be profitable, must be approached gradually, and increased as the demand increases. At first they should be mild and of short duration, and, on each succeeding occasion, augmented slightly, both in quantity and quality, until the utmost power of endurance is reached, or until the object, whatever it may be, is accomplished.

2. Another caution seems necessary here, *i. e., suitable protection*. This condition or requisite is too much neglected, especially by girls. Their clothing, for instance, is often insufficient, both as to amount and style. *First*, it should be composed of strong but light material, but enough to protect the whole person from the chill that is apt to follow active exercise. If any portion of the clothing is removed for convenience, it should be replaced as soon as the exercise ceases. *Secondly*, it should be as equally distributed as possible, covering the entire arms and chest; and where there is danger from exposure to the damp ground, the feet

should be well protected. Numerous evils arise from the simple neglect of these two cautions. Colds, headache, rheumatism, chills, and sometimes severe attacks of dangerous diseases result. *Thirdly*, the style of dress should be such as to allow perfect freedom to all the parts, and especially to the arms and chest, since they suffer most from confinement to study. The present fashionable style is at war with this principle. It is with the utmost difficulty, that a young lady fashionably dressed, can lift her elbows as high as her head, without rending some portion of her clothing about the waist, especially if the motions are violent, as they should be in calisthenics. This is also true of the fashionable dress of boys and young men. No exercise can be profitable under these circumstances. The clothing, therefore, must be loose enough to allow freedom of motion and freedom of circulation. But enough has been said, the world over, upon the follies of fashion, and especially upon the evils of tight-lacing, to correct them long since.

3. *The mind must be free from care and anxiety.* It is of little service to engage in physical exercises for the sake of recreation, when the mind is brooding over some hidden grief, harrassed by care; or when it is absorbed in study. There must be a relaxation. All these things must be abandoned for the time being; and there should be a delightful play of cheerfulness and animal spirits. The reason for this will be apparent upon a moment's reflection. The brain needs the rest, and the body and limbs need the exercise. The blood should be attracted from the former, and invigorated and vitalized by coming in contact with pure air, and being supplied with wholesome chyle. It then returns, laden with the prin-

ciples of life, and the wheels of thought again roll on with increased vigor.

4. *There should be an object in view.* Hence the superiority of the games of rivalry; of the pursuit of game in hunting; and of the excursions in pursuit of specimens in natural history, etc., as described in "physical culture." There is excitement enough in connection with these to keep up that healthy flow of animal spirit. In case of a walk or a ramble in the woods, it amounts to but little to stroll about without an object, or even with one, if that object is inspired by nothing higher than the mere desire to exercise. Something exciting is needed to make the mind forget its cares, and to revel in the pleasures of the game or chase.

5. Recreation, as a general thing, *should be taken in pleasant company.* "Iron sharpeneth iron; so a man sharpeneth the countenance of his friend." It is not easy to estimate the value of human sympathy, or the power of conversation. They may enter into and form a part of nearly all forms of recreation. They serve as a medium for the expulsion of gloomy thoughts, and for the introduction of pleasant ones. Many exercises will not permit a connected conversation; but even in these cases, the pleasanter the company the better. The glow of sympathy, the beaming countenance, the common object and mutual energy and aims:—all serve to dissipate care, to invite happiness, and to beget a healthy flow of the convivial spirit. In the calisthenic exercises, the music and song, with which they are usually interspersed, the graceful motions of the body, and all the enchantment of the various figures and movements, have a tendency to beguile care and sorrow, to bring into active

play all the powers that please and delight the senses and the soul.

When conversation can be carried on, the theme should not be too grave or too exciting, or else there will be no rest to the mental powers, save that which might be experienced from a change of thought. It should turn upon pleasant topics, and should be rather lively than otherwise, even to the merry jest and the hearty laugh: the laugh is particularly valuable. It shakes the cobwebs from the brain and inactivity from the lungs; it stirs the sleepy tide of the vital stream. It is a perfect tonic, and acts with a more desirable force upon the liver, than a dozen doses of "*blue mass.*"

Section 3—The Varieties.

The various kinds of physical exercises have been frequently referred to, in the progress of our investigations; so that at present, it only remains to present a classification of those that may be used most advantageously in the schools. In doing this, we shall not attempt an exhaustive list. We prefer to give the outline in connection with a description of some of the most appropriate and convenient exercises, and leave the subject for whatever suggestions and improvements may be made upon it.

Those that relate particularly to the school, are the following. 1. For out-door exercises, *innocent and active games of rivalry* stand perhaps among the first. What we mean by *innocent* is, free from any immoral tendencies, such as betting, or any in which the loss of property or character is concerned, or any in which the evil passions are necessarily aroused—those that are free from the contaminating influence of vice. What we mean by *active* games, are those combining the lively exercise of the physical powers, without impairing their strength or activity; not those trifling amusements,—such as "marbles," "pins" or "button," nor yet the silly nonsense of "ring around a rosy," or "oats, peas, beans and barley grow!" nor those on the other hand, requiring too severe action, such as violent running or jumping (except as practiced in the gymnasium), wrestling or boxing, or any thing that would have a tendency to injure or impair the physical powers, or soil, or otherwise damage the clothing.

The following are among some that may be safely practiced, provided they are properly cared for by the teacher: 1. *Ball*, in all the varieties in which it is commonly practiced. This is the great play of the school, and it is doubtful, whether any other of equal merit could supply its place. It is a healthy and dignified play, and may be practiced by nearly all classes, and in some varieties by girls as well as boys.

2. *Throwing the discus* or *pitching quoits, rolling* or *playing at ten pins*, are remarkably healthy exercises for the arms and chest, provided both arms are used; and we see no good reason why they could not. These exercises, however, are chiefly confined to the gymnasium, and are considered appropriate only for boys; but I see no good reason why girls might not participate in some of them, at least. How much better this than the perpetual idleness to which they are doomed, by the hypocritical notions of a fashionable world! How ennobling and dignifying when compared with that insipid nonsense, which constitutes too much of their exercises (?)! What health and development of their chests and arms it would give them! The blessings they would thus be enabled to

transmit to their posterity, would more than compensate for any odium that might be heaped upon them, by bigots and hypocrites.

3. *Skating and coasting* are forms of amusement which certainly possess many excellencies, though for the want of convenient localities they must be circumscribed, so far at least as relates to the school. The first is eminently adapted to the wants of both sexes and nearly all ages ; and, could it be free from the dangers too often connected with it, it might be practiced with the best of results.

4. *Pleasure and scientific excursions* may be practiced in connection with school duties, though not with the same regularity that others are. They should be a kind of holiday pleasure, to which the pupils may look with expectation and delight. See Chapter Second.

5. *Calisthenic Exercises.* The practical illustration of the above named exercises, as practiced in our best schools, will occupy the remainder of this chapter. It will be found that these exercises furnish a greater amount of rational recreation and amusement than all others; and at the same time can be practiced, for the most part, in the schoolroom.

For the following arrangement, and brief but accurate description of them, we are indebted to the enterprising teachers of the city of Toledo, Ohio, in whose schools the exercises here laid down, are carried to a high degree of perfection. This system has been gathered from a variety of authors, and possesses the advantage of being brief yet eminently practical. It contains about all that can be practiced with success in the common school and college, and we believe may be introduced, in some form, into every school in the country. As such we most cheerfully commend it to teachers and parents.

The most of the following exercises are arranged for a class of sixteen, though many of them may be varied for a larger or a smaller number. In forming for practice, the misses are always arranged in a circle, assuming:

STANDING POSITION.—Head erect, shoulders thrown back, chest forward, hands at the side, and feet at an angle of about 60 deg. The circle is divided into 4 sections; the 1st in each section being its leader. The leader in the 1st section is also the general leader in every exercise. The 1st and 3d leaders stand opposite each other; the 2d and 4th opposite. The 1st in the circle and every alternate one is called No. 1; the 2d and every alternate one, No. 2.

MARCHING IN CIRCLE.—Commence with right foot, keep uniform time, step lightly. (Here follows an exercise in the *March*, directed by the teacher.)

STEPS.—*Directions for practice.*—*School Step.*—Touch first the heel, then the toe of the right foot to the floor, at the same time springing on the toe of the left. Repeat with left foot springing on right. This step may also be taken advancing or retreating.

Spanish Step.—Bring left foot in front of the right, carrying it to that position in a curve, springing at the same time on the right toe; carry it in the same manner back to the standing position. Repeat, bringing the right in front of the left in same manner.

Triple Spring.—Extend the right foot in front, resting on the toe; carry it to the right side, then resume the standing position, springing on the left foot with each change of the right. Repeat the same with the left foot springing on the right.

Quadruple Spring.—Extend r. ft. to r. side, resting on toe; carry it to l. side beyond l. foot; return it to r. side, then resume standing position, springing on l. ft. at each change of right.

Side Step.—Carry r. ft. to r. side, resting weight on toe. Bring l. ft. behind the r., resting on toe. Again advance r. ft., etc.

Promenade Step.—Extend r. ft., resting on toe; bring l. foot forward nearly even with right, bearing the weight lightly upon the toe, while the r. is again extended. Repeat, extending l. foot first. An easy gliding motion is desirable.

Slight Courtesy.—Extend r. ft. to the side, place the left behind the right, sink and then rise. Repeat, extending left ft. placing r. ft. behind left.

Arm Exercises.—With marching step the class pass half round the circle; the 1st leader and her mate pass through the center to the head of the circle, followed by the others, and form columns, all the No. 1's coming up on the right hand side of the No. 2's.

The columns being formed, they separate, by each bowing to her partner, leaving a space of about three feet between the columns. Then with school step the columns advance, meeting in the middle of the space, then retreat with the same step. Then to give space for arm exercises let the alternate ones of each column advance with school step to center of space, thus:

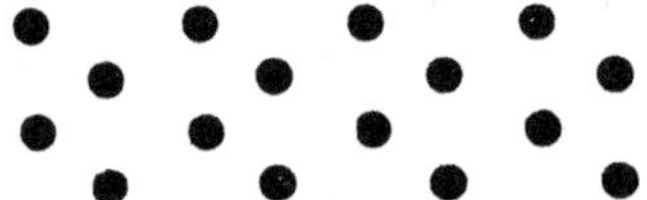

1st Ex.—Raise the hands to the top of the head, throwing them off with force to the side.

2d.—Place the backs of the hands under the arms,

throw the hands forcibly downward, closing them tightly.

3d.—Place the tips of the fingers upon the shoulders in front, throw the arms forward in a straight line, at a level with the shoulders.

4th.—Place ends of fingers upon the shoulders, throw the arms to the sides at a level with the shoulders.

5th.—Place the fingers as before; throw the hands upward.

6th.—Extend the arms in front, with the palms of the hands together. Throw them backward, meeting the backs of the hands. Each exercise to be repeated 8 or 12 times, with counting or singing.

Figures.—1st. *Winding Circle.*—The 1st leader passing just inside the circle, commences gradually winding up to the center, with side step, so that when she has reached that point, the form of the figure will resemble a watch spring. Turning, she unwinds, passing through the spaces of the previous winding, until a perfect circle is formed. Wind up again, the 3d leader passing inside the circle, winding and unwinding in the same manner.

Song: "Lightly Row."

2d. *Moving Columns.*—The 1st and 3d leaders march through the center of the circle, passing each other on the right. Each describes an oval figure. They pass each other three times, then form a large circle.

Song: "We roam through forest shades."

3d. *Single Columns.*—Form columns as for *arm exercises.* The columns being formed, the No. 1's pass to the right with promenade step, No. 2's to their left describing a circle. Meeting, the mates join hands, and, continuing the step, pass up to the place where the 1st couple stood in the columns. Separate, and pass around as before; all stop in the columns as at first. Pass singly to the left, forming a large circle.

Song: "Hail Columbia."

4th. *Intertwining Promenade Step.*—No. 2's step inside circle, facing right side, No. 1's facing left side. Mates join right hands as they stand; commence promenade step. Each No. 1 joins her left hand with the left hand of the next No. 2, so that they pass each other with the 1st step, reversing their places, No. 1's being inside the circle, No. 2's outside; No. 1's join hands with the next No. 2's, passing her with promenade step, and again exchanging places; continue this until mates meet the second time.

Song: "Harvest Hymn."

5th. *Trio.*—Pass about one-third round circle, the 1st leader stopping on the outside of the circle, forms with the next 2 a triangular figure; all except the last 4 form similar figure; the 4 stand in the center thus:

```
2   1               1
  2              2     1  1st leader.
          1    2
1   2     2    2       2
  1              1     2
```

Lead off into a large circle with side step; the 1st leader passing off 1st, while the other circles take the side step in their several separate circles, leading off in time to keep the line as unbroken as possible.

Song: "Up the hills on a bright sunny morn."

6th. *Double Columns.*—Pass half round circle, the 1st leader and mate stopping at the center. The last half form half a column in the same way, the 3d leader and mate coming up opposite the 1st leader and mate, thus:

1	2
1	2
1	2
1	2
2	1
2	1
2	1
2	1

Lead off with promenade step, the 1st and 3d leaders passing to their right, and their mates to the left. Having described half a circle, come up as before. Separate into two circles, the 1st half forming one, the second half the other. Take the quadruple spring, pass off with the promenade step, as before. Form the columns the 3d time, and pass into a large circle.

Song: "Bring Flowers."

7th. *Fronting Columns.*—Form single columns, separating as for arm exercises. No. 1's commencing at the head of the columns, join hands with their mates and pass down through the columns with promenade step, then separate, meeting after having passed half round circle; go through the center and separate as before. Again passing half round circle, the 1st leader and mate stop in the place they first occupied in the columns. The 2d couple go above the 1st, join hands, and pass down between them to their places. Each succeeding couple in like manner go above the 1st through the columns to their places. Then, 1st leader passing down through the columns with side step, each in order join hands, and with same step pass into a large circle.

Song: "Life on the Ocean Wave."

8th. *The Wreath.*—No. 2's step inside the circle, face their mates, and, joining hands, take the Spanish step; then all facing the center of the circle, the inner circle take the side step once around; the outside circle once around, both circles together once. The No. 1's and

No. 2's joining hands in their respective circles courtesy four times, the fourth time the No. 2's courtesying under the arched arms of No. 1's. Being thus twined, pass once around with side step; untwine by No. 2's courtesying from under the arched arms of No. 1's. The inner circle pass once around with side step; the outside circle once; both together once. No. 2's face their mates and courtesy half round the circle; the inner circle then pass once round with side step; the outside circle once; both together half round. Then form large circles, by the No. 2's falling back into the outside circle.

Song: For Spanish side step: " A rosy wreath we twine for thee." For courtesying: " What fairy-like music."

9th. *The Bower.*—Pass half round circle; the 1st leader and her mate stop facing each other, and with hands joined elevate them, while the 2d couple pass under their arched arms, stopping just above them, joining and raising hands in same manner; the 3d and 4th couples in same manner; the 3d leader with the remainder of the class pass under the arched arms, until reaching the head of the columns, then turns to the left, leading to the foot of the columns; then again under arched arms to the head of the columns; then turns to the right leading to the foot; then joining hands, they pass with side step to the head of the columns; the 1st leader and mate, with each of the couples above in order, joining hands and with side step pass into a large circle. Wreaths are desirable in forming arches, if convenient.

Song: " When the day with rosy light."

SYNOPSIS VI.

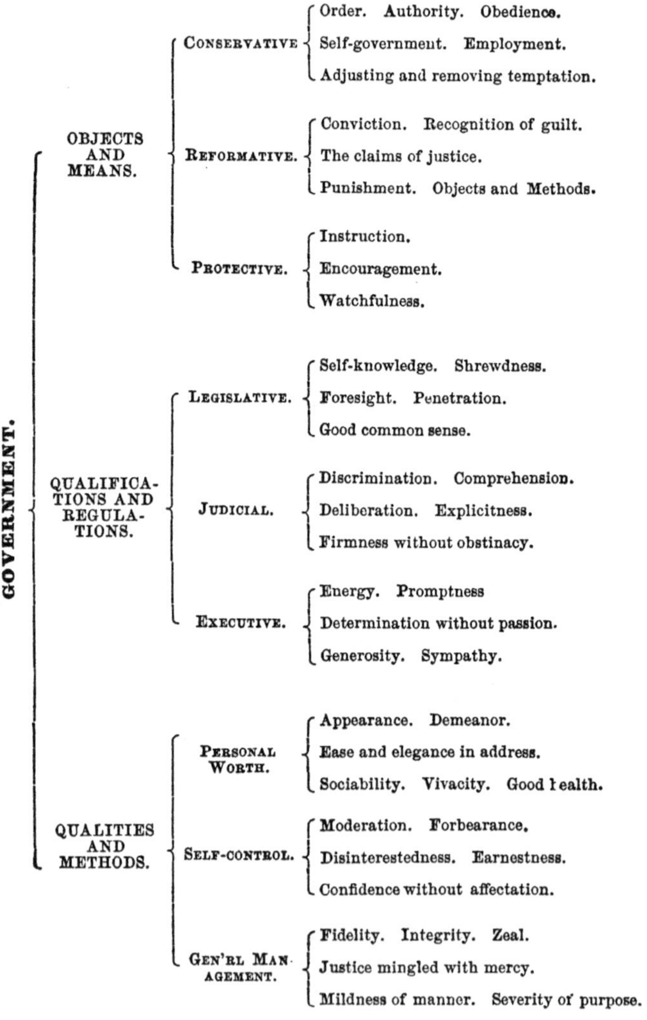

GOVERNMENT.

- **OBJECTS AND MEANS.**
  - **Conservative**
    - Order. Authority. Obedience.
    - Self-government. Employment.
    - Adjusting and removing temptation.
  - **Reformative.**
    - Conviction. Recognition of guilt.
    - The claims of justice.
    - Punishment. Objects and Methods.
  - **Protective.**
    - Instruction.
    - Encouragement.
    - Watchfulness.
- **QUALIFICATIONS AND REGULATIONS.**
  - **Legislative.**
    - Self-knowledge. Shrewdness.
    - Foresight. Penetration.
    - Good common sense.
  - **Judicial.**
    - Discrimination. Comprehension.
    - Deliberation. Explicitness.
    - Firmness without obstinacy.
  - **Executive.**
    - Energy. Promptness
    - Determination without passion.
    - Generosity. Sympathy.
- **QUALITIES AND METHODS.**
  - **Personal Worth.**
    - Appearance. Demeanor.
    - Ease and elegance in address.
    - Sociability. Vivacity. Good health.
  - **Self-control.**
    - Moderation. Forbearance.
    - Disinterestedness. Earnestness.
    - Confidence without affectation.
  - **Gen'rl Management.**
    - Fidelity. Integrity. Zeal.
    - Justice mingled with mercy.
    - Mildness of manner. Severity of purpose.

CHAPTER VI.

SCHOOL GOVERNMENT.

We now approach one of the most difficult yet most important subjects of the whole list of schoolroom duties, viz., Government, or the control and management of schools. Much, in a general way, has been said upon this subject. This seemed necessary, and indeed unavoidable, since the very nature and design of "schoolroom duties" are such as to involve the mode in which they should be conducted.

In the discussion of the subject of government, we shall avoid its general characteristics, except so far as they relate to the school, and shall endeavor to point out a system of government whose administration shall render the school self-governing, and fit its pupils for that task, after they become men and women.

All governments arise from about the same necessities, have nearly the same origin, and should have the same objects in view, viz., the good of the governed. The essential principles of government are the same every where, the distinctions arising more from the mode of administration than from any necessary difference in the principles themselves. Hence the different forms of government, such as the monarchy, aristocracy, democracy, etc., with their various restraints and modifications. All these forms, doubtless, had their origin in the family, social and commercial relations, and intercourse of the races.

Without stopping to discuss the relative merits of these several forms, we remark that the school is an association composed of the elements of families, representing the individual interests of each, and expanding and combining these, so as to meet the wants of the community and the State. It therefore represents all these departments, and should be so conducted as not to interfere with any of them; but on the other hand, it should prepare its subjects for a proper appreciation of, and participation in, the duties and responsibilities enjoined by these several relations. In other words, the school should be the model family, the model community, the model State. Therefore, whatever objects government has in view, in any relation in life, these find, at least a similitude in a well organized and well conducted school. It should have all the sympathies, all the restraints, all the encouragements, and all the high and noble purposes that animate, subdue, and elevate the human powers. It should be a place in which is warmed into life every principle of intelligence, and every generous impulse of the soul: in which every evil passion is subdued, and every unholy desire checked.

In form and administration, the school government should, perhaps, resemble, as much as any other, that particular kind of monarchy called the patriarchy; though it should certainly possess many, and perhaps all the restraints to the abuse of power, that are common to the best republics. And we might add here, that no teacher is prepared to wield this potent instrumentality, unless he has studied well its nature and design.

In presenting the claims of this subject, we shall endeavor to follow an order similar to that observed in the other topics; though such is the peculiar nature of this, that it will be more convenient to treat the *objects* and *means* of securing them in the same connection; and so, in the second place, the qualifications and requisites; and lastly, the directions to be observed in the administration of government.

Section 1—Objects and Means.

It is a matter of astonishment, as well as regret, that so few have a correct understanding, or an adequate appreciation of the real objects of government, or of the means to be employed to secure them. The motives to obedience have been so grossly perverted, the incentives to duty have been so essentially weakened, and the abuse of power has been so great, that not only many false theories have arisen, but the very existence of sound family and school government has been endangered. The mere matter of control or mastery on the one hand, without consulting the fitness of the means of securing it, or the uses to which it should be devoted when secured; and, on the other, the almost total abandonment of such control, would be about as true an exposition or outline of these two extremes as could be given; while the intermediate steps have been occupied with many errors and many excellencies. Some of these will be pointed out as we progress.

Article 1—Nature of the Objects.—The objects of government, as they relate particularly to the school, may, for convenience, be considered in three classes, distinguished from each other by their nature and office. 1. They are *conservative and self-perpetuating;* conservative, in that they maintain universally the same policy, and enforce the same claims and obligations; self-perpetuating, in that these claims, etc., are produced and reproduced by the necessary development of man's innate powers, and are co-extensive with his present relations: *i. e.*, the power that controls arises not only from man's necessary existence, but is self-sustaining, since it is itself controled through the agency of perpetual causes, acting and reacting, producing and reproducing both themselves and their necessities. This will be more apparent as the nature of these objects and duties are unfolded.

Among the first of these conservative objects, and one standing high as a means of securing the ultimate ends of all government—viz., the universal happiness of the governed—is good order. Without this, all the secondary objects would fail of accomplishment. It stands as a sentinel, truly conservative, and admits no fanaticism or discord to reign in the ranks of the governed. It is that to which all other objects tend. It pre-supposes, in the first place, rightly constituted authority; and, in the second, obedience to that authority. All other objects seem to conspire as much to produce this, and through this, the happiness of the governed, as any independent result. It becomes emphatically, therefore, both an object of government, and the chief medium through which its whole machinery is moved, in accomplishing all other results.

We remark, in the next place, that there must be a standard of order, and this must be backed by authority; for of what avail is law or regulations without the ability to enforce their claims, in case of any resistance or disobedience? It is this that adds the peculiar dignity to law, and commands that respect which renders it "a terror to evil doers; but the praise (and protection) of them that do well." This standard becomes a tribunal to which are referred cases of difficult adjudication; and before which all our ideas of right and wrong are summoned to testify in the struggle which justice and mercy, as advocates, wage, in the contest of truth with falsehood: not, however, that these advocates contend, the one for the right and the other for the wrong; but the one clamors for the blood of the guilty victim, while the other, admitting equally the guilt of the offender, and the claims of the law upon him, yet interposes its scepter, and points to the remedial agents, by which the victim may not only be saved but reformed, and yet the claims of justice be satisfied. Conscience is the great arbiter in this contest, and should be the ruling principle in the decisions of justice. The more of this ingredient there is mingled with the administration of government, the better. It is the conservator of order, and the safeguard of authority.

This standard also implies *obedience*, on the part of the subject, to the properly constituted authority: and the obligations become more or less binding, according as the standard approaches perfection. Obedience implies motives, which should be such as will secure the prompt, willing, and even cheerful compliance with the behests of authority, without impairing any essential principle of independence. This is the ultimate object of all obedience; while forcible measures should only be employed for the temporary purpose of removing the obstacles to voluntary submission. The different methods that may be resorted to in order to secure obedience, will be referred to again in the next section. They have also been discussed briefly in former chapters.

2. Another object in immediate connection with those already named, is that of *self-government*, or the power the individual subject acquires to control his own energies. In this will be seen the self-perpetuating nature of government. It should be the especial object of the family and school, so to develop the powers of the subject, that when the pressure of extraneous control (if indeed there is need of any) is removed, he shall go on, a self-acting and self-governing agent. This is *the* object which is sadly overlooked, and one to which we call special attention.

It is generally thought sufficient, at least in the school, that the child be *manageable*, or entirely submissive, while subject to the government, which is often so arbitrary and severe as to remove all necessity for the exercise of any other power than that of mere submission—if indeed, this can be called the exercise of any power at all. The labor and consequent advantages of such control are transferred from the subject that needs them, to the machinery that enforces them. Hence, it is not at all surprising that the former should languish for the want of them, while the latter should be impaired from excessive use.

It is a well known law of mind as well as of body, that the legitimate use of any power strengthens it; and that neglect weakens it. Now if these powers of self-government are not brought into active service in that stage of their growth when they are assuming form and character, they are neglected, and consequently weakened. This is the inevitable result of excessive governing, or of that form which takes all responsibility from the hands of the governed and forces submission "*nolens volens*." Hence, again, that form of government which places the greatest amount of responsibilty in the hands of the subject, and only holds him accountable for the proper use of it, is best adapted to the wants of rational and responsible beings. Self-government, therefore, is both an object of government and a means of securing and perpetuating its own blessings to those who are its subjects.

It will be seen that one of the most successful methods of cultivating the powers of self-government, is to afford the individual healthy employment for all his powers. Indeed, it is quite certain, that if the proper amount and kind of employment were furnished to all the members of society, not only vice and crime would diminish, but man would acquire the power to direct his energies to the full accomplishment of the purposes of life. We have had frequent occasion to remark, in the course of this work, that none of these powers were created in vain,—not for idleness, nor yet for mischief or for tormentors; that their chief delight, as well as means of growth and sources of power, consists in exercise, which they seek as naturally as the plant seeks the light and moisture; and that if left unemployed or uncontrolled, the great probability is that they will run into mischief or excess. For a description of the various kinds of labor and rest, recreation and devotion, the reader is referred to those sections where these topicts are treated more at length.

Another successful mode of cultivating the powers of self-control is, by *removing temptations*, such as are likely to prove too strong for resistance, and of adjusting others that must be met; so that their conquest by the pupil shall prove a source of power. This is one of the most successful means of culture that can be devised, and one that is most shamefully neglected. Indeed, in a great many instances a course is pursued which produces results exactly the opposite of those named in the above. The multiplication of commands beyond a reasonable extent, the great majority of which stand a better chance to be broken than obeyed, instead of removing temptation, and becoming, as perhaps they were intended, a means of restraint and a bulwark of defense, only add so much to the chances of disobedience. They serve as so many traps to ensnare the wayward feet of childhood into habits of disrespect and deceit. In the great majority of cases it were better not to give commands at all, if the prospects for disobedience are greater than those of obedience; since, in most cases, the sin of disobedience lies more in the simple act itself than in any results that might follow from the thing's being or not being performed. The habits of scolding, continual fault-finding and threatening are also fruitful sources of temptation both to stubbornness and to treachery. But these subjects have been treated elsewhere. Their appearance here, however, will readily be accounted for, when it is remembered that school government extends to every and all departments of the educational processes.

Again: the *associations* are a fruitful source of good or evil. Bad company is to be deprecated on all occasions, while the good should be sought. It is scarcely possible, under ordinary circumstances, to escape the contaminating influences of the one, or to counteract entirely the influences of the other; yet there are two extremes here worthy of special notice. The first is, the practice of exposing children to the influence of vice, without first fortifying their minds to repel it;

and the other is, the practice of depriving children of the associations of the world, for fear they may contract the evil habits of the world. The two extremes are about equally dangerous; and, what seems a little paradoxical, lead to precisely the same results. The influences and the results of the first course are sufficiently apparent. The second, however, is worthy of further notice.

It is a very common remark, and not without its significance and truth, that those children who have, for the greater part of their lives, been secluded from society for the purpose of shielding them from sin, when once exposed to temptation, fall most readily a prey to it. The reasons are quite obvious. Never having been exposed or tried, their powers of resistance are weak. Never having conquered, they know not the glory of the struggle or of conquest.

Since children, if they live at all, must live in the world, and be exposed sooner or later to the influences of vice; since they must, from necessity, meet and overcome temptation or be overcome by it; it were far better to bring them in contact with those influences, under circumstances where they can be assisted and defended in case the temptation should prove too strong, than to keep them in childish weakness all their days. By this we do not mean that they shall become wicked that they may learn what wickedness is, or that special temptations shall be invented in order to try their strength; but that they shall be strengthened and fortified against the encroachments of both.

There are constantly operating within us, and upon us from without, two distinct classes of influences, called by one writer the "Passive Impressions, and the Active Principles."* The first includes all the impressions that are made upon the mind, from influences of an objective character; the second, all those internal emotions and desires that arise from subjective causes. Now, the meeting of these two influences and their consequent agreement or disagreement will determine the character of the result.

Suppose, in the first place, that the influences or passive impressions are bad, such for example, as a temptation to evil; and that there is an acquiescence on the part of the individual, the active principles from within rising up and coalescing with the impression from without, the result, in this case, will be bad, since the deed itself will be evil, and the power to resist a like impression the second time, will be weakened. But suppose the active principle in man, which perhaps in this case is only another name for the will enlightened by reason and strengthened by conscience, rises up and opposes the temptation and overcomes it; the result will be a good one, since an evil deed has been avoided, a temptation overcome, and consequent strength has been developed to resist like encroachments in future; but, as in the first case, the power to resist grows weaker and weaker, at each successive temptation, until the poor soul loses all power to resist, and is led captive at the will of Satan, chained as it were, to the wheel of vice, and dragged, it may be an unwilling, yet powerless victim in the slavery of sin; in the other, at each successive conquest, the power to resist grows stronger and stronger; until by and by, the man stands up free, emancipated, as it were, from the thraldom into which temptation would force him.

---

* Joseph John Gurney.

Hence the injunction to "resist the Devil, and he will flee from you," etc.

But take another case: Suppose the outward impression is a good one, and the active principle rises up and meets it, as in the first case it did the bad one, the result will be good, since the deed itself is good, and it is obedience to a demand made by a legitimate desire. But suppose this good impression is resisted, as in the second case, the result then will be its opposite, since there are both disobedience to a legitimate demand, and resistance to good impressions. Under these circumstances the individual grows harder and harder to impressions, until what moved him once will scarcely make an impression now. This will account for the indifference and hardness often produced by repeated warnings. "He that being often reproved hardeneth his neck, shall suddenly be cut off, and that without remedy."

The same principle obtains in all the other cases. Take the first, for instance: the first time temptation to commit an act of injustice was presented, it created perhaps a horror. The first lie, or oath, or theft, or transgression of any kind pained the conscience, and perhaps brought tears to the eyes; the second, however, produced still less impression, and so on, until by-and-by there was little or no compunction of conscience. This class of transgressors is aptly described by the prophet when he says: "Wo unto them that draw iniquity with chords of vanity, and sin, as it were, with a cart-rope;" and again, by the poet, when he says:

> "Vice is a monster of such frightful mien
> As, to be hated, needs but to be seen;
> Yet seen too oft, familiar with her face,
> We first endure, then pity, then embrace."

We need only allude to drunkenness, cruelty, profanity, theft, and other kindred vices, of which these are but fair representatives, and the several steps by which they have been reached can readily be imagined.

But, take the third and fourth cases alluded to, in which the outward impressions are good, and are responded to, in the one case, by the active principle of good, but repulsed, in the other, by the active principle of evil, and what are the results? Suppose a man to meet, for the first time in his life, a most distressing object of charity, who, stretching out his emaciated hands, implores help. The individual thus addressed feels his compassion move toward the sufferer, and he obeys the impression from without, and the impulse from within. The suffering is relieved, and both the giver and the receiver rejoice together. Now, in this case the principle of benevolence has been exercised and strengthened; and, as a natural result, the next object of suffering is met in a still more welcome manner, and soon liberality becomes a fixed principle; the more a person gives, the more delight he experiences in giving, and his beneficence is only limited by his means. The same is true of good impressions from any other quarter.

But suppose, when the first appeal is made to the individual, that he closes his eyes to suffering and his hand against giving; that he shuts up his compassion and refuses to listen to the pleadings of mercy from without, or to respond to the call of conscience from within—what will be the result? In the first place, suffering will not be relieved; and in the second, his own heart will be hardened. The next case of suffering will be met with less emotion, and so on, until finally the needy will be repulsed with scorn or indifference; or the only effect will be to make the miser clutch his gold more tightly, and to steel his heart more effectually against all generous impulses; and thus it is with all good impressions, from whatever quarter. As paradoxical as it may seem, the same outward influences that have a tendency, when obeyed, to make a benevolent man, will, when repelled, have a tendency to make a miser. The same that develop the Christian graces, and establish a man's moral principles, if not received in a proper spirit will harden him against impressions of good, and confirm him in iniquity and crime.

Now these principles have a direct bearing in the government and education of children. There are four cases, which may be briefly recapitulated thus: first, the impression in itself may be evil and the result evil; second, the impression may be evil and the result good; third, the impression may be good and the result good; fourth, the impression good and the result bad; and all of the influences and results are, to a great extent, put within the reach of parents and teachers, or of the government. Therefore, let the temptations be so adjusted that the power that is within the child may resist them; and let the positive good from without be so presented as not to annoy or harden the subject, but "to produce the peaceable fruits of righteousness in them that are exercised thereby."

Article 2—Government, Reformative.—Thus far the objects and means of Government have been considered as they relate to society in nearly a normal condition: or, the conservative and self-perpetuating objects have been considered. But society is often deranged, and its members need reforming. There are offenses and offenders. It is safe to conclude this of all stages and forms of association composed of fallible beings. This of course will include the family and the school. "It must needs be that offenses come," and consequently there will be offenders, in this corrupt state of things; and perhaps this will always continue, so long as society is composed of the same or even similar elements.

Now, government holds *some* relation to these offenses and these offenders. It can not avoid them so long as they compose a part of the body politic; nor can it look with indifference upon this new state of things. Indeed, it regards offenders with a peculiar interest. The mutual claims of government, and of those under its control, when they depart from their integrity or violate their obligations, it shall be our present business to investigate in connection with the administration of that kind of control, calculated to produce the objects heretofore discussed.

And first, we remark, since government is compelled to deal with culprits, and since these, in many instances, are susceptible of reformation, therefore *it should be reformative.* It should reach down, but not in a vindictive spirit, to those of its subjects that have been unfortunate, and bring them up, if possible, and reinstate them, so that its claims upon them shall be the same as upon those who have not fallen. This function of government is manifestly neglected, both in public and in private associations. Those who have offended have too often been looked upon more as enemies of the commonwealth, lost to the claims of sympathy, and against whom the government hurls its bolts of vengeance, than as subjects entitled, if not to equal confidence, at least to its pity and extra attention. Punishment is dealt out with an unsparing hand, too often with no other object in view than merely to gratify a selfish motive, or at most, the demands of justice; when, in fact, the culprit as a member of society, and society itself, have as great demands upon justice as justice has upon its victim; and these entirely harmonize. Justice demands the satisfaction of a violated law, while society and the offender himself are not less urgent in their demands for the reformation of the latter at the hands of justice, as a matter of safety to the body politic.

The means by which offenders may be reformed will next claim attention. First, we remark, they must be convinced of wrong as an initiatory step. There can be no reformation from a point where there is no recognition of guilt. The culprit must first feel the weight, the nature, the tendency of the offense, before he can truly take a step toward reformation. The government and justice owe him this information. Hence the municipal law punishes no man unheard, or uninformed as to the nature of his offense. It labors even more earnestly to convict him than it does to punish him. In this it proves its sincerity for his reformation. In this it takes the most direct course to induce repentance—the first step of reformation.

Now this should be the course pursued in schools. No step should be taken, no policy adopted toward offenders, in which they may not recognize the benevolent intentions of government. For instance, a wrong has been committed; authority has been trampled upon; the integrity of the body politic has been wounded, and it suffers in consequence. The culprit himself, as a part of this body, is a principal sufferer. His reformation, therefore, is demanded by every claim of every claimant in that body. Now agencies must be employed for restoration; and it is clear, that if the offender be in the path of the agencies thus employed for healing the breach, or settling the claim, they will operate upon him, of course. And if these agencies, which have the double object, the satisfaction of the law and his reformation in view, demand his punishment as the safest and most direct means of securing both these objects, of course he must submit, not only as a matter of policy, which by the way is an urgent one, but of necessity, arising out of the claims of justice. This punishment, however, should have nothing but the most benevolent designs in view, and should be varied to suit the nature of the cases.

This brings us to the most peculiar and most difficult part of the subject, viz., the *kinds* of punishment, and the mode of administering it. Without attempting to discuss the merits of the several kinds, we might be allowed the general remark, that for ordinary cases, or where the powers have not been so impaired, or are so defective in their natural capacity, as to be beyond the reach of restoration from natural penalties, the reformation may be wrought, and the claims of justice equally satisfied by what are called purely moral means. For instance, if the child disobey, he should suffer the natural consequences of such disobedience, whatever they may be, so far at least as they would go to reform him. If he fail to get a lesson, which indeed would be, in common with almost all offenses, a species of disobedience, the natural penalty would be either the loss of it, or the additional labor and inconvenience consequent upon such a course. If he lose his book or property, *he*, of course, ought to suffer the loss; so, if he squander his time in idleness, or deface or destroy his desk or clothing, or do any thing of this nature, he should be made to feel the loss and suffer the consequent inconvenience until he can realize the immediate relations of cause and effect. Or, if he encroach upon the rights, person or property of another in any way, the inconvenience and punishment that his treatment would cause in others who are subjected to them, should, as far as possible, be visited upon himself.

In the great majority of these and kindred offenses, in addition to the natural penalties, the offender lays himself under an obligation to the authorities and "powers that be," similar, in many respects, to that which the debtor owes the creditor. The offender becomes amenable to the offended powers; and it is his business, when notified of the same, to render his account, and cancel its claims as soon as possible. If, however, after the lapse of a reasonable time, he fail to discharge this obligation, the debt will increase; and if he await a prosecution, he ought surely not to complain, if he have to pay the cost of such a process. A good plan, therefore, in case of short-comings of this character, is to notify the offender of his indebtedness and of his obligations to discharge such indebtedness; to give him an opportunity to seek a reconciliation, even to demand this at his hands. This will bring him in such a relation to the government that it can treat with him on more honorable terms. This will throw the responsibility where it belongs, and will relieve the teacher from the disagreeable task of hunting up offenses, or evidences against them. It will also be humiliating to the offender, and will constitute no small share of his punishment.

And superadded to all of these forms of punishment of a purely moral nature, which should be varied to suit the individual cases, is the loss, on the part of the offender, of the usual privileges of the school, until satisfaction is rendered, and a reconciliation effected. This course may be taken with a great many. It will both deepen their convictions, and hasten their return. It will become effective in proportion to the strength of the attachments, and the agreeableness of these privileges. But above all and more than all, the loss of the little attentions, the extra exercises, the smiles and approbation of the teacher or parent, which will be severe in proportion to his power and influence, may be a keener punishment than all the flogging that could, under ordinary circumstances, be administered; and certainly, in cases of this description, it is more in accordance with sound philosophy. Even some of the most aggravated offenses, can most readily be punished and corrected in this manner; for its severity on a sensitive mind, will almost always be in proportion to the enormity of the offense committed.

But if the courtesy of self-reporting on the part of the offender is withheld; and if these offenses, or any others are habitual; if the complaint is a deep-seated one; it *may* require some more severe remedy. All cases are not alike. In the first place the offenses themselves are diverse both in motive and in enormity; and in the second place the offenders are unlike as to age and susceptibility of reformation. But all offenses are evidences of disease, either chronic or acute, and all offenders are invalids varying in degrees of weakness and persistence, according to the nature, origin and standing of the disorder; and it is no more rational to conclude that the same kind of treatment or punishment will reform every case, than that the same kind of medicine will cure all diseases. It is not, however, beyond the memory of some of the present generation, when about the only remedy for the prevailing disorders of the body, was bleeding and purging. But this species of barbarism has been supplanted by a more enlightened policy in the practice of medicine. Would that a similar one in reference to the treatment of mental disorders had shared a similar fate!

The two cases alluded to are strikingly analogous. For one patient, it might be necessary to amputate a limb, or to resort to severe remedies, to reduce the system in order to arrest the disease; for others it would only be necessary to counteract the influences producing disorder, or to aid the powers to free themselves from the burden, and the recovery is equally certain. So in relation to the nature and office of punishment as a reformatory measure. For one it might be necessary to resort to severe remedies, to amputate and reduce; for others, the milder means and precautionary measures would be equally effective.

A great deal of late has been said about the kinds of punishment, and the mode of administering it; and indeed there is room for much to be said. Perhaps no practice in connection with school government has been subject to the same or to an equal amount of abuse. Corporeal punishment seems to be the feature attracting the greatest attention, and the form, against which, the chief objections are urged; and, as it is usually administered, it is certainly one of the most objectionable. But some, looking only upon the enormities practiced, have not been sparing in their denunciations against the whole system. Others scarcely less philosophical, have entirely mistaken the spirit and mode of administration in which its efficiency lies. Hence they have taken the abuse, to judge by it the legitimate use. This is manifestly unfair; for upon the same principle, scarcely a single practice in the whole process of education, would escape condemnation. Recitation itself would be condemned on the same ground; yet who would think of abandoning it, because forsooth some bungler had made a bad use of it? We believe therefore, that this kind of punishment has its legitimate use; and, as a strictly reformative measure, for certain cases, it has scarcely an equal, and surely no substitute. It can not be dispensed with in the present state of society, and in no state surely, so long as there are gross offenders to be reformed, any more than the use of medicine can be, so long as diseases of a violent nature exist.

In speaking of the modes of corporeal punishment, we select one, viz., punishment with the rod, as about the only kind not objectionable *per se;* and we shall endeavor to show that the objections arise entirely from its abuse. Indeed its use has been grossly perverted; and instead of its being a reformative measure, it is rather a vindictive one. For instance: an offense is committed, or a series of offenses, whereby the teacher's anger is aroused, or his patience exhausted. He falls upon the offender and beats him unmercifully, or until he thinks (if he think at all during the operation) that he has given about enough; or until his own feelings of revenge have pretty well subsided, when he sends him to his seat with something like the following taunts and threats: "There now! I told you if you did not behave yourself, you would *catch* it! Now you *have* got it! Go to your seat, you villain!

and if you ever do so again, I will give you ten times as much more!" And he does go to his seat; but is he reformed? No more than the tiger is, scourged within his prison bars. If that child be not a coward, or a Christian (not that these characters are the same), he goes cursing that teacher (?) for his meanness. And *it is mean! It is cowardly* to treat a boy so! for, if he wanted to fight, why did he not select one of his own size and strength, and not vent his spleen upon one unable to defend himself?

Now this is only a fair representation of what takes place in at least one-half of the cases of whipping, as it is commonly practiced. It is nothing more, so far as the principle is concerned, than a street fight, with this difference, perhaps, in favor of the latter, that the combatants in the last case are usually more equally matched. No wonder that whipping has received a bad name! No wonder that shortsighted philanthropists have condemned it, and sought to remove it altogether!

There are other modes of administering this kind of punishment, which ought to be noticed. Suppose an offense, as in the first case. Instead of consulting the circumstances and the nature of the offender, the punishment is administered, so many strokes for so much offense: and the culprit goes to his seat, relieved for the time being; for *he has bought an indulgence and paid for it.* He has paid all the penalties and has a clear balance in his favor, for the next half dozen offenses, at least, when another settlement may be expected. Now there is no reformation here either. It is only a bargain and sale affair, a hardening process. by which, I doubt not, many have been whipped into penitentiaries, or perhaps the last penalty has, or will be expiated upon the scaffold.

Again: Some children, when whipped, have the faculty of making a great noise, and loud professions of reformation; but it is soon forgotten: or it may be, the noise is only for effect, by which the teacher is deceived; and the pupil goes to his seat, congratulating himself upon his fortunate escape. Others, differently constituted, and perhaps having more honesty and principle, are in danger of excesses from an opposite direction; and others again, both guilty and innocent, are punished in less objectionable modes; and yet there is no recognition of guilt, no repentance, no reformation. The whole object seems to be too much either to give vent to angry feelings, to pay the penalty of the law, to maintain authority by force, or to seek the shortest way to enforce present obedience, without either consulting the nature of offenses and offenders, or the demands these have upon justice for reformation. But this objectionable use of punishment is only accidental; and no more necessary than war or murder is a necessity arising from the existence of firearms,—or than cruelty and oppression are necessary, from the existence of human power and skill.

The questions now arise, can punishment with the rod be free from these objections? Is there not something connected with it, necessarily calculated to arouse the evil passions? We answer most unhesitatingly, *No*, not necessarily; and will hereafter explain. But, does it not degrade both teacher and pupil? Does there not a great deal of evil grow out of it? And in view of this fact, ought it not to be abandoned altogether? To the last question, we reply as to the first; but to the two preceding it, we as unhesitatingly answer, *Yes*, when the punishment is accompanied by any of the evil passions; and here is the place where distinctions and discriminations should be made. When any anger exists in the teacher's heart, while administering punishment, it will most likely arouse anger in the pupil's heart; if revenge, revenge; if hatred, hatred, or some corresponding feelings; for like begets its like everywhere. But observe: *none of these passions should have any thing to do with teaching, much less with whipping*, one of the most difficult duties the teacher is ever called upon to perform. Those who oppose the use of the rod altogether, seem to overlook its legitimate use and predicate their objections entirely upon its abuse. Their arguments are therefore all admitted; but they do not tend to establish any objection against its proper use. They seem to think that before a person can whip, he must first have his feelings wrought up to what we may denominate the "whipping point;" and that angry passions must necessarily be aroused in the pupil. Now this last *may* be the result in many cases; but mark, these passions are to be subdued. It is similar in effect to the removal of a cancer or a tumor from the body. It may cause present pain, and all its angry humors may be goaded to madness; but the operation goes on nevertheless, until the offending portion is removed, when the parts may be healed. So with these passions. They may rage for a time like a tempest, but the opposite feelings accompanied by the proper use of means, will generally conquer them.

But it may be further asked, "How can the teacher

manifest these amiable feelings on all occasions, and especially upon this most trying one?" My friends, is there any occasion for the exercise of unamiable feelings, under any circumstances? If so, then it is barely possible that they may, with propriety, be manifested here. "But how can the teacher love those who are unlovely?" He may not love them with the love of approbation, or even of complacency; but with the love of pity and tender sympathy for their suffering. Again: how can he smite the object of his love and pity, or hold back his hand from vengeance, when provoked? Ah! that's the point! Here is where human nature is weak. Here is where passion and impulse get the better of judgment and reason; and no wonder that evil rather than good is the result. It is always so.

The question again recurs: Is it possible for the teacher to whip without first feeling these angry or revengeful passions, or arousing them by the operation? We answer by asking, Can he not strike a blow upon his desk without anger? Then why not upon the scholar, if he have a great and good object in view? Can he not smite with the same candor and earnest desire to do good that actuated him while reading the morning lesson from the Bible? Can he not inflict pain and still pray? Can he not punish and pity at the same time? Can he not love and lament the necessity that calls for suffering? If he can not, *then he ought not to teach, much less to punish.* He should never lay hands upon that fearful instrument, the rod of correction, until he can first lay hands upon his heart, and say, "O God, I do this to glorify thy name." "I do it to reform this pupil, and to bring him nearer to thee." Let him do this, and there will be little danger of excess. Let him do it, and half the punishment will accomplish the desired end.

This is asking no more of the teacher than we require of the surgeon. But suppose the latter should hesitate and say, "I can not perform this operation now, because I do not feel mad enough;" or stop in the middle of the operation, because, forsooth, the patient cries. We would call him fool or faintheart. Suppose, on the other hand, at every stroke he should grow more and more angry and vindictive, and should use threats and taunts, instead of words of comfort and encouragement; or suppose he should leave the patient bleeding and perishing from the wounds he had inflicted, we would call him a savage or a brute. And yet, teachers who object to the use of the rod, because some have abused it, must perceive that their arguments against corporeal punishment are subject to similar criticism; and that the same conclusions can be drawn from their objections to the rod, as would here be urged against surgery.

Again, it may be asked, how can physical punishment be made a reformative instrument? How can bodily suffering affect the mind and heart for good? We answer, Does it not? Is not bodily affliction one of the strongest instruments of correction and reformation, that is used by the Almighty himself? All philosophy and experience, as well as human and Divine law, recognize this, though an extreme, yet an effective agent in carrying out the ends of government.

There are at least three classes of appeals that may be made use of for correcting the irregularities of our nature, and reforming offenders: First, the purely moral; Second, the intellectual and moral; Third, these two combined and aided by physical force. The efficiency of these appeals is in direct ratio to the number of faculties addressed, and the potency of the means employed. The two classes acting in concert, are stronger than one; and all three, for extreme cases, than either the one or two. The first two have been described briefly. We propose now to speak of all three of these forces combined, as a governmental measure, keeping in view, all the time, the reformation of offenders, the prevention of crime by others, and the vindication of authority. In investigating this subject, however, it will not do to be guided by any preconceived opinions or practices. The principles, as they reveal themselves, will urge their own conclusions, which the student will not fail to recognize.

1. We should not *separate* these forces or appeals. In all such cases as may demand them, they should act as a unit. It may not be necessary, however, to employ all of them in the same case as has been intimated. They should be regulated according to the nature and persistence of the offenses. But the moment the higher forces or appeals cease to act, just so soon, and in the same ratio, is the effective force weakened. This is necessarily so. It is just like a human being endowed with all his powers in full play. His mind and moral force constitute his chief means of effective strength. Superadded to these he has physical force. There are some duties in life requiring little or no physical strength. Again, a person may be deprived of the power to act physically, and yet the mental force be unimpaired. But not so with the loss of mind. That gone, and all is gone. On extra occasions, therefore, and indeed, to a great extent, in the majority of instances in life, the mind calls to its

aid the physical man; and when all of these agents put forth their greatest strength, in harmony and in a good cause, it is then that man exhibits one of the sublimest spectacles in the moral universe. Just so in relation to these appeals, and their mode of application. The purely moral and intellectual, as they have been described, are the great motors and regulators, by which the wheels of government are to be moved. They will be adequate to the demand in the great majority of cases; but when a disorder arises that demands additional force, then these moral forces may call to their aid—mark, not as principal agents, but merely as auxiliary—the physical powers; and when the moral feelings of the offender can not be reached by the mere moral force, as implied in the above, then according to the same reasoning, these feelings can more easily be moved by the combined action of the two, or of the three. But there must be no separation. The moral and intellectual powers must lead. They should act even with additional energy, when they call to their assistance the other forces.

The chief reason why whipping in school and every where else, is productive of so much mischief, is because when the teacher or parent takes up the rod, he lays down common-sense, self-control, judgment and his moral powers. He is thus shorn of his chief strength; and what other results can we reasonably expect than those complained of? It is not an uncommon thing to hear teachers talk much about moral suasion as antagonistic to physical force, and as if it could not be used in connection with other means. The very strongest moral suasion can be exerted in connection with physical force and physical suffering. The two are by no means incompatible. If they were, then no moral effect could be produced by physical forces, or vice versa. They harmonize in every particular when properly used. There is therefore, as much moral suasion in a switch, judiciously applied, as in a sermon preached from the housetops; and for its specific purposes, it may be doubly effective.

Now, the whole matter is reduced simply to this: one human being may operate upon another for his good. The latter, of course, is susceptible to a greater or less degree. If his moral sensibility is easily affected, then the moral force may produce the result. In case the sensibilities have become somewhat blunted, or hard to operate upon, then the moral power may call to its aid the intellectual forces in the form of superior judgment and skill in management, which are from necessity variously employed throughout. But if these fail, as fail they must, if the resistance to be overcome is greater than the force employed to move it; if the avenues leading to the affections and will of the child are all closed, and no impressions can be made through them; these appeals must necessarily fail. But still there is one more resort left, the most powerful in all respects for the purposes in hand, the united force of man's moral, intellectual and physical powers, a concentration and harmonious action of all his energies to produce a given result, viz., the reformation of offenders and the vindication of the demands of justice. And on the part of the offender, the operation of these forces are equally philosophical. If, as in the case supposed, the moral and intellectual susceptibilities, the avenues to the heart and mind are closed to whatever forces the teacher has at command, there is yet one more chance, provided the nervous sensibility is complete. There is fortunately and designedly a close connection between the bodily sensibilities, and the mental and moral. The intellect, the sensibility and the will are all more or less affected by any suffering that may be inflicted upon the nervous sensibility; and if, when the suffering is inflicted, there is a clear apprehension on the part of the sufferer, as to its intent, and if it be administered in a proper spirit and in a proper quantity, it follows, from the conclusions heretofore reached, that unless the subject of such punishment is beyond the reach of reformation, these means may and will reclaim him.

This brings us to consider the particular mode of applying the punishment, and the extent. This is an important item, one which may decide the whole thing for good or ill. We desire, therefore, to be explicit upon this point, for it is a most dfficult one,—more so than either study or recitation; and, as in those duties there is both a science and an art, so in this. The first we have briefly sketched. The second involves the particular questions, where, or upon what part of the body? under what circumstances? with what? and how the strokes should be applied? We answer, in reference to the first, that upon the back, shoulders and lower extremities, since there is less danger of sustaining injury from the infliction of severe blows upon those parts; but never upon the hands, head or face, or any other place where it would injure the person, or offer any indignities. The clothing upon those parts should not be so abundant as to demand heavy blows, or injury might result from that quarter. Hence portions of it might be removed, under certain circumstances, and its thickness tested before the operation commences. This will also serve to convince the offender that you are really laboring for his benefit. The teacher should know and fully appreciate the nature of the duty in which he is about to engage; hence great caution should be exercised in the beginning.

To the second question, viz., "Under what circumstances, whether in public or in private," we answer, that when the vice is an individual or private one, and when a simple reformation from such vice is the main object, then a private punishment will be most effective; since the child will have less to contend with in this fearful struggle of passion with the moral powers: the opposing forces of an external character will be measurably removed, and he will more readily yield. But where the example is necessary, or where the offense has been mainly of a public character, or where the breach of the law is greater than the breach in the individual—both of which should be healed—or where the claims of justice are paramount to those of reformation, or where a greater good can be effected both with the individual and the body politic,—under such and similar circumstances, a public chastisement may be inflicted, keeping the same objects in view as heretofore described. I can also conceive of cases in which the parties alone concerned, *i. e.*, the injuring and injured, should be present; but these cases are rare.

With reference to the third, we answer, the instrument should be a switch. Not a pole, nor a club, nor a paddle, but a light switch: one with which you would not be likely to injure the muscle or bone. The chastisement should be confined to the surface. There perhaps is not a case within the reach of reformation so hardened as not to be reached without going below the surface. A ferule is a bad instrument of punishment, since there is great danger of bruising the hand or the parts where it is applied; and this is true of almost every other instrument except the rod, which is the simplest, cheapest, safest, most convenient, and the best every way.

The fourth question, "How?" would involve the frequency, severity, and number of blows. All these points should be understood by the teacher. He should study them just as carefully and accurately as he does his lessons and propositions. Indeed, a mistake here is more disastrous than any that might be committed in arithmetic or grammar. We remark, therefore, as to frequency, that the blows should not be repeated oftener than about once in a half minute; and for some purposes the intervals might even be prolonged beyond this time: first, because the child wants time for reflection between the strokes; secondly, he wants time to reap all the benefit of one before another is given. In this way, about one-tenth the number of strokes will suffice, since every one expends all its force before another is given; one is not lost or paralyzed in the pain of another; thirdly, because there is less danger of arousing the passions of either teacher or pupil. The former shows that he governs himself, and this of itself removes more than one-half of the indignity from the practice. Let him strike half-minute or minute strokes, and he will feel no anger, but rather pity and love; fourthly, because he then can witness and measure the extent of suffering, and mark its effects; fifthly, because it offers time for admonition and expostulation, which will frequently be necessary, and will do as much or more good than the bodily pain.

It will be mingling the moral and the physical forces together in due proportions.

There is a very remarkable incident recorded of an English horseman, which is to the point here. A certain nobleman came in possession of a remarkably fine horse; but unfortunately he possessed one bad habit that rendered him almost useless. He would stop while under the saddle, and no whipping or coaxing, or driving, would induce him to move. After every expedient seemed to be exhausted in efforts to conquer him, a celebrated horseman offered his services and was accepted. The animal was suitably caparisoned and brought out for trial. The cavalier approached him with an air of confidence and indifference, paying little or no attention to his eccentricities. He finally mounted him, when the horse started off a few paces, but soon stopped short, as was his custom. Without manifesting any unusual concern, the rider gave him the usual token to move forward. But no; he confidently affirmed (in his way) that he would not. The man, after giving him time to reflect a little upon his conduct, slowly, but deliberately and determinately descended from the saddle, and, stepping to his head, took a firm and decided hold upon the bridle; and after the necessary adjustment he gave him one severe blow with a weapon prepared for the occasion. He ceased. The horse was chafed and angered, no doubt; but, to his disappointment, the man did not repeat the blow. He expected a shower of them, mingled with curses, doubtless, or that he was about to be flogged as usual, and consequently had prepared himself to resist it. But the horseman leisurely resumed his seat in the saddle, and requested him to go, as before; but no, he would scarcely move. He again descended, and repeated the blow with additional force and coolness. The horse was astonished and confounded at such strange and philosophic treatment; and began to show evident signs of changing his policy. The man gave him ample time to determine upon his course, when he again placed himself in the saddle, and gave him the sign for going forward. There was evident hesitation and trepidation, which showed that the point was nearly won. He was evidently unprepared to resist such treatment, and his inclinations were balancing as it were between two points. This was the time to take advantage of the indecision and turn the scale—to give the finishing stroke. The horseman slowly descended the third time; and with an intrepidity and coolness that entirely outwitted the animal, he gave him such a stunning blow that it made every nerve tingle and every muscle start. The horse fairly leaped from the ground. His anger and stubbornness *were all gone;* and no sooner had he an opportunity, than he manifested the most entire obedience and willingness to go when and wherever his master desired him. He was thoroughly and completely conquered with those three philosophic blows; and it is related that he never returned to his old practices.*

Now what conquered him, the blows, or the good sense? Doubtless, both; but the blows never would have accomplished it without the good sense, nor the good sense without the blows. I suppose the horse had been whipped ten times more severely, and perhaps a hundred times as much, many times before;

* The above is related from memory, and may not correspond in all the minutiæ of the incident, as recorded in the account, but the main features are about the same.

but all to no purpose, simply because it had not been administered in a proper manner: and I venture to say, that nearly all the very hardest cases in our schools, if treated in as sensible a manner, might be reformed by one half the punishment endured by this horse. This is but a single case, it is true; but we have others on record, both of men and horses, equally remarkable; and I have no doubt that the secret of success attending the remarkable feats of subduing wild and unruly horses and other animals by the renowned RAREY, lies in the good sense and severe mildness (if we may be allowed that expression) of the treatment.

The *severity* of the blows must be regulated entirely by the temperament of the child, the deep-seatedness of the disease, and the objects to be accomplished; which last should be the entire reformation of the offender. In most cases where whipping becomes necessary, the blows should produce acute pain, for the moment. They should not be trifling nor trifled with, by any means; and they should rather increase than diminish in severity, until the turning point is reached.

The time of one operation should perhaps not be prolonged beyond ten or fifteen minutes (not all consumed, however, in administering blows), at one time, but may be resumed from day to day, until the reformation point is reached. It will be found, however, that three or four strokes, or a half-dozen at most, thus delivered, will usually produce the required results; simply because reason, judgment, good sense, sympathy, pity, love, suffering, justice, mercy, tears and prayers, instead of angry curses and vindictive rage, are all combined; and it must be a desperate case indeed that can resist all of these. Now let us compare the brutal beating, and trifling mismanagement, and retaliating process described in another place with this, and decide which is preferable, which will be most likely to produce the reformation? Or, should we prefer the coaxing and hiring process, and the covering-up of the corruptions of the heart, to good sound healthy punishment and reformation?

Now understand: if we can rule by love, we should do so by all means. But if that is not strong enough, we should strengthen it by other forces. We should bring to our aid every earthly device of an intellectual nature, not inconsistent with moral force; but if these all fail, we are inexcusable if we do not call to our aid whatever other forces God has placed within our reach. Remember, we have the destiny of immortal beings placed, to a great extent, in our hands. It is not for us therefore to consult our own ease or convenience, or to be influenced either by prejudice or preconceived notions with regard to punishment. We must do *right*, or God will judge us. Justice will meet us, and perhaps ruined souls that we might have saved, will haunt us, for not doing our duty. We should therefore examine the subject carefully, and not be led estray by false philosophy or shallow-brained philanthropy.

ARTICLE 3—GOVERNMENT, PROTECTIVE.—We will now suppose the offender conquered, subdued, reformed. His willfulness has yielded, and his wicked purposes are abandoned. His anger ceases, and he submits willingly, cheerfully, lovingly. What now is the duty of government toward him? Will it answer to turn him loose without protection, as one who has simply paid a penalty and is free from further obligation; or to say to him, "There, now take care of yourself; there is no further danger?" Will it accomplish the ends of government to abandon him thus and expose him to all the temptations that caused him to fall in the first place? I know our State governments do this in too many instances. Convicts are discharged from prison without a single safeguard; but they are rather weakened, disgraced, destitute, demoralized, and yet exposed to all the temptations of former crime. But what does the sequel show? How many recommitments! How few really reform, and how few of that number stay reformed under these circumstances! But this is but too sad a commentary upon the weakness of human law, but still more perhaps upon the inefficiency of our law-making powers.

In all rightly constituted governments, the offender, after suffering the penalty due to his crime, if he be not entirely cast off, and if he be not beyond the reach of reformation, is supposed to be convalescent. If he is not, justice has not done its whole duty. Now what is the true relation the government sustains toward him? He is supposed to be weak and powerless, or at least, entirely subject to the influences which have conquered him. This may have been the work of a day, a month, an hour, or a year. It may have been accomplished by moral, intellectual or physical means, or all combined: still these conditions and influences exist always in the same ratio. Instead, therefore, of casting him out to fall again, or of withholding its supporting influence from him, it takes him up in its arms of sympathy, and only exposes him as his powers are able to endure exposure. He now sustains a relation to government similar to that which a new subject experiences. He needs protection, instruction, education, encouragement, sympathy and watchfulness. This want should be the special care of the government, and solicitude of the teacher. If there is one object in all the school that deserves more special attention than any other, it is that poor unfortunate who has fallen, and now lies, as it were, bleeding at the feet of mercy, flung there by the hand of justice. Justice has had its demand; and, in executing its claims, it has wrought the necessary repentance, and brought the offender within the reach of mercy. Therefore let the government that smote him down, lift him up. Let it reinstate him in its favor and fellowship, and grant him all the immunities, claimed and enjoyed by other subjects.

Section 2—Qualifications and Requisites.

We have thus far considered government with reference to its conservative, reformative and protective characteristics, chiefly as they relate to the school. In doing this, it became necessary to make frequent allusions to the qualifications and requisites of the governing power, and also to the mode of administering it. This was contemplated in the beginning. It only becomes necessary now to revert briefly to those points for the purpose of showing their connection and completing a list of topics in a uniform order.

Article 1—Legislative Talent.—In order to carry forward the objects of government, legislative talent is necessary. Laws are to be enacted, and a general provision established for regulating and running the machinery. The teacher does not usually find these provisions at hand, any further than the general principles and common usage afford them. From these, and from his own judgment and knowledge of men and things, he must manufacture or frame a code to guide him in the management of his internal affairs. He therefore discharges the functions of a legislator to all intents and purposes. In this capacity, no knowledge will be more valuable to him than self-knowledge, or that which gives an insight into human nature and the motives and modes of human action. With these commodities, he is expected to operate. These forces he must provide for and control. The more familiar, therefore, he becomes with human nature in all its phases and aspects, the better.

He should possess *shrewdness*, *foresight*, *penetration*, that he may be able to anticipate and provide for the emergencies and difficulties which must necessarily arise in a perverted state of society. These are talents that characterize all good legislators. They might be embodied in that excellent quality spoken of by the wise man when he says: "A prudent man foreseeth the evil and hideth himself," etc. These qualities, joined with deliberation, are the opposites of precipitancy and rashness in the enactment or repeal of laws, the inauguration of a new policy, or a change in the general management. In all legislative proceedings, there is no quality more necessary, or that will add more weight to such proceedings, than a due exercise of caution and deliberation. There is constant danger of conflict from the various interests to be represented and consulted. Therefore, no law should be enacted or repealed, no change in the policy or general management be made, without first consulting all these interests, and weighing all the consequences.

Again: for the various emergencies that arise, both

in legislating in and administering the affairs of government, there is a constant and urgent demand for that kind of talent denominated by Mr. Locke, "good round-about common sense." It is possessed to a very limited extent by some of the most gifted. Indeed, notwithstanding it is "common sense," it is a rare accomplishment. Hence many possessing qualities that would render them successful in many departments of business, would fail, if submitted to the severe test of governing and teaching; since to do these things well, requires greater versatility of talent than almost any other employment. This last arises from the fact that almost all other employments are represented in right teaching. There is therefore a necessity here for a universal talent, or the faculty of adjusting the means to the ends to be accomplished, in a great variety of ways, and in a great many departments of business.

ARTICLE 2—JUDICIAL ABILITY.—Laws are to be published and expounded. All must be notified of their existence; their scope and meaning must be limited and explained by the teacher or the government. Hence arises another function of the teacher. He constitutes the judiciary, and to his tribunal must be referred all cases of difficult or doubtful interpretation. In addition to many other good qualities requisite here, we might name good judgment, or the ability to discriminate in difficult and complicated cases. It results, it is true, in a great degree, from a comprehensive knowledge of the various forces of human nature. Cases are continually arising for adjudication, that will tax to the utmost the teacher's discriminating powers. It is highly important that all his decisions be as nearly correct as possible, so that there be no necessity for revision or appeal. The teacher, therefore, needs time for deliberation. He should not be hasty in his decisions.

Again: all decisions should be rendered in as plain and explicit terms as possible. They should be so pointed that but one interpretation may be reduced from them, yet not binding or committing the teacher to any unpleasant alternative or unwise policy. Ambiguity often leads to misapprehension, and unintentional error, and leaves a given policy exposed where perhaps it was intended to guard it. There should therefore be a fair and distinct understanding in reference to the common duties of the school.

It also stands a teacher in hand to be *firm*. After a conclusion has been fairly reached, and the decision made known, it should not be changed for any ordinary cause. A case in which any change would be admissible, must be one in which a greater difficulty will result from adhering to it than from any modification. But there is a vast difference between firmness and obstinacy. The one never yields the truth: the other seldom yields to it.

ARTICLE 3—EXECUTIVE AUTHORITY.—Laws must be enforced as well as enacted and expounded. This gives rise to the third function of government, viz., the Executive. This department sometimes becomes the most difficult, owing chiefly to two causes: 1, the inadequacy or want of adaptation of the laws to be enforced; 2, the inefficiency of the executive power.

A good system of laws, with poor executive talent, would be about as inefficient, as poor laws would be with good executive talent. One of the leading characteristics in good executive officers, is *energy*, or internal force. It takes up the decisions as soon as rendered, and infuses life into them by putting them in progress of execution. Promptness to execute, is a rare gift; but it acquires additional strength and force when it is exercised in the affairs of the schoolroom. This quality has been noticed elsewhere in this book.

In executing the demands of government, so effectually does it call into exercise the powers of the mind, and so engaged do they sometimes become, that there is great danger of arousing the passions; hence what is needed here, is *determination without passion* or undue excitement. Again: the nature of the penalties is such that there will be a constant demand for *sympathy* and *generosity*. The very act of controlling or executing the laws, unless checked by a counter influence, is apt to degenerate into indifference or arrogance. The necessity for the exercise of these virtues will be seen from what has been said elsewhere.

Section 3—Qualifications and Methods.

The means to be employed and the methods of application may be briefly summed up thus:—

Article 1—Personal Worth. This may include a great many good qualities, but refers mainly to strength of mind and force of character. These constitute the most potent influences in the control of human beings. We instinctively yield a tribute of respect to talent, wherever found, but especially if found associated with high moral powers.

Personal worth may exhibit itself in various ways, among which are personal appearance and general demeanor. These are well calculated to make favorable impressions. No one can disguise the fact that a commanding appearance, neatness and cleanliness of person and habits, combined with a gentle and modest demeanor, will command respect everywhere; while their opposites, even if associated with the most brilliant talents, will fail to produce the good results desired.

The accomplishments, *ease and elegance in address*, highly cultivated social qualities, and the vivacity and cheerfulness arising from good health and physical culture, can not fail to constitute a ready passport to almost all hearts.

ARTICLE 2—SELF-CONTROL.— Again: the very faculty, whose cultivation is so strongly recommended under the head of "objects," viz., "Self-Control," is one of the strongest means of governing that exists. A man can never regulate and direct successfully the forces in others, until he first regulates and controls those within himself. In this, again, may be seen the self-perpetuating nature of government.

There will be frequent, and indeed almost a constant, demand for the exercise of *moderation and forbearance* in matters pertaining to the administration of the affairs of government; moderation in our views and expectations—for children are subject to temptations for which we are disposed to make too little allowance, and forbearance for their weaknesses and short-comings.

Favoritism in the schoolroom is sadly out of place, whatever may be its imaginary utility. In the administration of affairs pertaining to teaching, there must be an entire devotion to truth, and an equal distribution of favors and restraints, irrespective of any personal preferences or feelings. This will be a difficult task for many, and perhaps for all. So strong are the likes and dislikes of our nature, and so unconsciously and necessarily will certain qualities of mind and body win their way into our regard, that it will require more than an ordinary share of watchfulness in order to avoid biases in our judgment, and partiality in the administration of the affairs of the schoolroom. But *disinterestedness, and an earnest devotion to truth*, should mark all our intercourse with pupils.

In the administration of justice, there should be no hesitation or trepidation, or want of firmness or decision of character manifested by the teacher. The purposes should be well formed, and then executed with that confidence which the cause of truth, and the love of truth and the right alone can inspire. There should, however, be no affected confidence, nor overweening assurance. It should be tempered with becoming modesty and humility. This will inspire confidence in the hearts of the pupils for their teacher, and strengthen that bond of union so necessary between the governor and the governed.

ARTICLE 3—GENERAL MANAGEMENT.—We conclude with a few words in reference to general management, which will refer, in some measure to every department of schoolroom duties, but especially to the matters of governing.

In addition to other qualities and means already alluded to, *fidelity* and *integrity* should mark every transaction. It will not add either to the dignity or influence of the teacher, to make large promises or threats without a moral certainty, at least, of fulfilling them. Therefore let him avoid every thing, in his intercourse with pupils, that will have a tendency either to raise their expectations or excite their fears, beyond a healthy degree of interest: or that would, in case of unavoidable failure, or disappointment, destroy the confidence in his fidelity and integrity.

Let him manifest a *zeal* and *devotion* in the performance of every duty, and in the interest and welfare of his pupils, that will convince them that he is at once their best friend and benefactor, and abundantly able to reward the good and punish the bad. In all matters where punishment of any kind is to be inflicted, let him not forget its great objects, and that *justice mingled with mercy* is the divinest exhibition of the Infinite Mind we have on record; that the more closely he can imitate this superhuman pattern, the more nearly he fulfills the conditions of a perfect system of rewards and punishments; that no law should be enacted for the punishment of offenders, that does not look to their reformation as the one great central idea; and that no penalty, however trifling or severe, should be inflicted merely for the penalty's sake, much less to gratify revenge.

Lastly: let *mildness of manner*, coupled with *severity of purpose*, mark all his demeanor and intercourse with pupils; but more especially in those cases in which he is called upon to perform that most difficult and dangerous task, viz., the administration of punishment. And above all things, let him put his trust in Almighty God—the great and only disposer of events, —that he may be guided in the most arduous and responsible duty ever conferred upon mortals—THE EDUCATION OF HUMAN BEINGS.

BAYARD TAYLOR'S CYCLOPEDIA OF MODERN TRAVEL.

A Record of Adventure, Exploration and discovery for the past fifty years. Comprising Narratives of the most distinguished Travelers since the beginning of this Century. Prepared and arranged by Bayard Taylor. 1 vol. royal 8vo. 950 pages. Embellished with fine portraits on steel by Buttre, and illustrated by over forty wood engravings by Orr, and thirteen authentic Maps by Schonberg.

A magnificent octavo volume, which for general interest and value, is worthy of the distinguished compiler, and equally worthy of universal patronage. The volume really contains the value of a whole library, reliable as a book of reference, and as interesting as a book of romance.—*Springfield (Mass.) Republican.*

The popular lectures and writings of Bayard Taylor, have awakened in the United States a thirst for information respecting foreign countries and nations. A striking proof of this is given in the fact that a publishing house in Cincinnati, have issued under the auspices of Bayard Taylor, a volume of nearly one thousand pp., devoted exclusively to records of travel. These Reports are perfectly reliable; the matters ot fact of each explorer, often in his own language, are condensed into a consecutive narrative, by the most competent living author in the same department.—*N. Y. Independent.*

The reading public owes to Bayard Taylor many a debt for rare and valuable instruction, most agreeably conveyed; but we doubt if he ever performed a more useful service than in compiling this massive, varied and most valuable volume. The entire circle of books of which he has given the spirit and juice, would form a library; and many of them are now almost inaccessible. Mr. Taylor's part has been conscientiously done. It is not merely a work of selection and groupings; much of it is his own statement of the results more voluminously given, and written in a clear and elegant style. We can not but regard it as a very useful as well as entertaining work, well adapted to communicate accurate and comprehensive views of the world, and supplying for families an almost inexhaustible fund of pleasant reading.—*N. Y. Evangelist.*

No writer of the present age can be found so admirably qualified for such an undertaking.—*Louisville Journal.*

Such is the full title-page of a magnificent octavo volume of 956 pages, just issued. * * * We said "a magnificent octavo." It is so whether we consider its contents, or the superb style in which the publishers have gotten it up. It is just the book for the family library; all classes will be interested in its perusal.—*Ladies Repository.*

The conception of this work is admirable; and its execution is what might be expected from one of the most accomplished and intelligent travelers of the age. * * * It is remarkable for compactness, condensation and symmetry; and whoever will take the time to read it through, will possess himself of an amount of information, in respect to the physical, intellectual, and moral condition of almost every portion of the globe, which he can scarcely expect to find elsewhere. The work is illustrated with a large number of maps and engravings, which are executed with great skill and care, and add much to the interest of the narratives to which they are prefixed.—*Puritan Recorder.*

Mr. Bayard Taylor is the very Ulysses of modern tourists, and Emperor Adrian of living ramblers—and so is qualified to edit, or compile from the works of other travelers. * * * It is but the merest justice to say, that Mr. Taylor has done all that even an uneasily satisfied reader could expect, to produce a capital book.—*Boston Chronicle.*

Apart from the confidence inspired by the name of the writer, it needs but a brief explanation of its contents to show that it forms a highly important addition to the family library. Its pages are crowded with interesting information.—*N. Y. Tribune.*

From Professor C. C. Felton of Harvard University.

A scholar, traveler and writer, having a reputation so deservedly high in this threefold relation as Bayard Taylor, may be presumed to give his name only to works worthy of it. The present volume I have examined carefully, and have read a considerable part of it; and I have found it prepared and arranged with excellent judgment, and filled with matter of the highest interest and value. Both the plan and execution are in my judgment marked by ability, extensive knowledge, good taste, and good sense.

From Oliver Wendell Holmes, M. D., Author of "The Autocrat of the Breakfast Table," etc.

Mr. Bayard Taylor has done the reading public a great favor in bringing together the most essential and interesting portions of so many narratives within a very moderate compass, and in such a form as to be accessible to multitudes whose libraries must take little room and cost but moderate expenditure. It is safe to say that no man's selection would be accepted so unhesitatingly in America as those of our own favorite travel story-teller.

From Hon. Robert C. Winthrop, of Boston, formerly Speaker House of Representatives, U. S

I have examined it with great interest. It contains a large amount of entertaining and instructive matter, very conveniently and carefully arranged; and I shall value it as a work both for present reading and future reference.

www.ingramcontent.com/pod-product-compliance
Lightning Source LLC
LaVergne TN
LVHW020929110826
845150LV00004B/803

* 9 7 8 1 4 2 5 5 5 3 0 6 7 *